To Each Their Own
Camino

ONE WOMAN'S WALK ALONG SPAIN'S CAMINO DE SANTIAGO

ROXEY EDWARDS

◆ FriesenPress

Suite 300 - 990 Fort St
Victoria, BC, V8V 3K2
Canada

www.friesenpress.com

All of the events in this book actually took place, and have been described from my perspective. While all of the people truly existed, some names have been changed to allow each pilgrim their own Camino.

ISBN
978-1-5255-2449-3 (Hardcover)
978-1-5255-2450-9 (Paperback)
978-1-5255-2451-6 (eBook)

1. Travel, Essays & Travelogues

Distributed to the trade by The Ingram Book Company

While I undertook the Camino with the love and support of
all my family and friends, it was my husband,
Allan, who despite his own challenges, truly inspired me with
his courage and determination.

On the days the walk was hard and my spirits sank,
he was there, a voice across the miles,
to lift me up and encourage me on.

As I wrote, he patiently helped me work through phrases,
and often supplied just the right word . . .and supper!

Without his confidence in who I am, and what I am capable of,
the journey would never have been walked,
and the story never told.

Allan, I love you . . . more . . . ha!

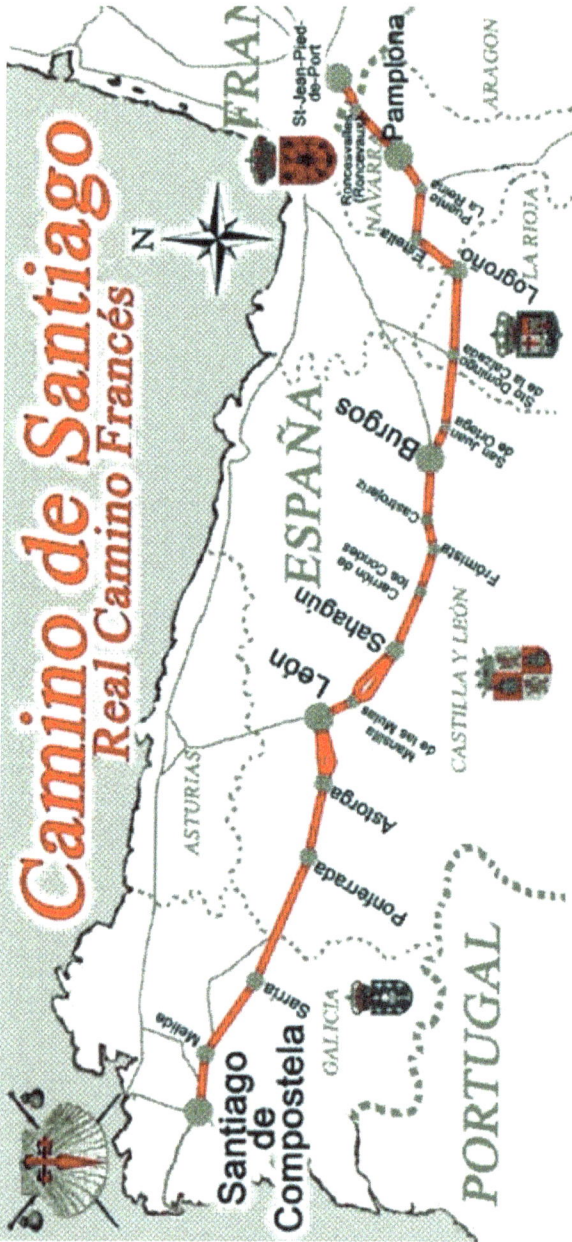

Camino de Santiago
Real Camino Francés

N

FRANCIA

St-Jean-Pied-de-Port

Pamplona

ARAGON

Roncesvalles (Roncevaux)

NAVARRA

Puente la Reina

La Rioja

Estella

Logroño

LA RIOJA

Sto Domingo de la Calzada

San Juan de Ortega

Burgos

ESPAÑA

Castrojeriz

Frómista

Carrión de los Condes

CASTILLA Y LEÓN

Sahagún

León

ASTURIAS

Hospital de Órbigo

Astorga

Ponferrada

PORTUGAL

Sarria

GALICIA

Melide

Santiago de Compostela

As I Walk in the Field of Stars

(Camino de Santiago de Compostela)
(The Walk of St. James in the Field of Stars)

The pilgrimage starts at home
Before I'm out there on my own
Before the planes and iron rails
Before my first step on the trail

I pack my bag and say goodbye
Torn by excitement and the urge to cry
I'll miss you all, each in your way
As I journey afar for many days

The time is now, this time for me
To set my wondering spirit free
To ask some questions, take time to hear
The thoughts revealed, the message clear

Quiet reflection upon my life
The wondrous joys and painful strife
There will be days I'll shed some tears
And take the chance to release some fears

God's gifts of love and strength to care
To seek right and kindness everywhere
Will guide each step, and fill my soul
As I journey toward my goal

While I travel the path with care
I'll hold your names each in my prayers
When meeting people in far off places
I'll be remembering all your faces

I'll keep my stories with you to share
When my journey ends and I am there
And when I travel home to you
I'll be ready to start life renewed

...... Roxey
(April 2016)

One stormy autumn night, my husband, Al, and I settled down to watch *The Way*. As the story progressed, I fell in love with the whole idea of travelling an unknown path, creating unforeseen relationships with an unlikely group of travellers. I was charmed by the idea that although none of the main characters had disclosed religious leanings, they all had very spiritual experiences by the end of the story. I was left wondering how such a journey would go for me. Nudge number one.

I have often doubted my religious commitment, wondering if I was just playing with God. I have a strong sense of ethics, a need to champion the underdog, and a drive to help out wherever I can. But my prayer habits are rather sporadic, and my life experiences have made me dangerously self-reliant. I've been through the fire many times in my life, and I've always struggled with the "faith thing".

I've often heard, "If you want to make God laugh, tell Him your plans!" I find the idea of not being in control of my destiny a challenge. I've been told I can make plans and worry as much as I like, but it is all just treading water if that isn't God's plan for me. What a relief it would be to turn it all over to someone else. Might not be such a bad thing, if I could just get there.

Visiting a friend's home, I was drawn to a stack of second-hand books. There I found *Incontinent on the Continent*, Jane Christmas' story of the trials of travelling in a foreign country with her disabled mother. My husband, living with MS, is reliant on a walker at best, and more often, a wheelchair. I understand the challenges of travel for disabled people.

Jane's story had me laughing and crying. I could identify with the scenarios she painted with her words, as they were so similar to my own life experiences. Loving her style, I ordered her books from our regional library without regard to their titles or subject. The first to arrive was *What the Psychic Told the Pilgrim*, the story of Jane's personal journey on the Camino de Santiago de Compostela, the same pilgrimage across Spain depicted in *The Way*. Nudge number two.

I really enjoyed Jane's book and appreciated that it was written by a Canadian woman around my age. It dawned on me that if she could do the trek, maybe I could too. Back to the library I went, ordering anything about the Camino. Obviously, the subject was popular, since the books were slow in coming. I eagerly awaited each arrival.

In February of 2015, I got very sick, very fast and was rushed to our urgent care centre. Apparently people get gall stones all the time, and a lot of people are walking around with their own personal rock collections. Me? I got one gall bladder stone, and it lodged itself in the neck of my gall bladder. Emergency surgery was required. Luckily, Al drives with hand controls, so he was able to take me to nearby Nanaimo for the surgery. A few hours later, he had me back home, sleeping off the general anaesthetic on the couch. Between naps, he advised me there was a book in at the library for me and asked if I wanted him to go get it. Looking up at him groggily, I told him to do whatever he wanted to do.

The next time I surfaced, he was there with another book about the Camino, *I'm Off Then*, by German celebrity, Hape Kerkeling. I cracked open the book and glanced over the first page and sat bolt upright. "You won't believe this," I said to Al and shoved the book into his startled hands. The very first page in this book I had ordered months ago spoke of the writer being deaf in one ear (as I am) and just having had his gall bladder removed; me too! I couldn't believe the similarities and the timing. Nudge number three.

"What would you think if I decided to do the Camino?" I asked Al. Now remember, he has MS and is reliant on me for much of his day-to-day operation. I knew that my biggest challenge to going would be his agreement, and even more so, my belief that he would be okay while I was gone.

"I was wondering when you were going to ask with all the books you've been reading."

"Yes, but how would you feel about me going? I'd have to be gone about a month or so. Do you think you could handle that?"

"Honey, if it's something you feel you need to do, one way or another we can make it work." Yes! That's one of the reasons I married the man! He never even raised a doubt as to my ability to backpack 800 kilometres across Spain. With Al's support, I started to seriously consider the journey. I pulled out the calendar and started planning my walk for the spring of 2016.

My eldest son Kenneth is a calm, take-it-as-it-comes sort of guy, married to the loving, but emotionally charged mother of our four-year old grandson. As they live within an hour's drive of our home, we see them frequently, so it worked out that they were the first we told. As I explained the plan, the distance, and the time involved, my son smiled and enclosed me in a warm hug of support.

"You're going alone! Are you going to take a gun?" were my daughter-in-law's first panicked words.

"Well, Amanda," I said calmly, "it's a pilgrimage. So, taking a gun would not really work with that." We all burst out laughing. I'd never even held a gun. Amidst a barrage of happy questions, we dragged out the atlas and looked at the map of Spain, trying to explain to my grandson, Matthew, what Gramma was planning. His confused expression said it was totally unreal to him and, to be honest, the reality hadn't sunk in for me yet either.

"Have you told Scott yet?" my gentle son asked. He knew, like we knew, that his brother was likely to react strongly to this idea. In fact, I was kind of dreading telling Scott, anticipating a landslide of opposition on his part. Both of my sons became very protective of their remaining family after their father died of cancer in their pre-teen years. This was only tempered slightly when I married Al, an old family friend the boys had known since childhood. Kenneth took that responsibility on stoically; Scott took it on aggressively.

By his late twenties, Scott had earned three degrees, including a masters in physiotherapy, and he was a young man of strong opinions. At the end of April, Al had an appointment two hours' drive down island, in Victoria, at the MS Clinic near Scott's office. We figured if we met him for lunch in the nearby restaurant, he'd be a little more restrained in public – cowards that we were!

"You're going where?" he asked, pausing over his pad Thai noodles. "And when is this? Okay," he said holding up his hand, "just a minute." He furiously keyed into his cellphone. "Jackie, look up Camino de Santiago. Yeah. Well, Mom says she's going to go there. Yes, really. Just a minute. Here." he handed the phone to me.

Scott's wife paused long enough to say happy birthday and to update me on the antics of our two-year-old granddaughter, Alayna, then Jackie excitedly launched into a million questions before ringing off to return to work.

"I was worried you'd lose your mind over this. I'm so surprised you're okay with it," I smiled with relief.

"Why would you think that?" Al and I looked at each other and smiled. "Okay," Scott admitted sheepishly, "I would be upset if you said you were going now, but we have a whole year to get you ready."

Of course I had already started getting ready. Armed with a Camino supply list from a reputable outdoor store, I'd decided to purchase one major piece of equipment a month so as not to break the bank. I had started training, walking to and from work, about seven kilometres each day. Through the spring, I added distance to my route until I'd doubled the kilometres.

I got a pair of walking poles, and excited to try them out, discovered they didn't work! I walked along and swung them, but they didn't seem to fall into place; something was wrong with them. They were definitely going back! Then I got the rhythm, and it dawned on me; how could they not work? They were just two sticks. It was up to me to make them work. I laughed at myself.

My coworkers and friends saw me walking all around town, poles in hand, and a weighted daypack on my back. Not knowing what I was doing, they collectively thought I had lost my mind. If I wasn't walking, I was in the gym working through a rigorous core and leg building program my evil (but wise) trainer, Dale, had devised. I came to hate the word "squat".

I had been part of an ongoing process in our church, working closely with Jeri, our resilient interim minister, who was helping our congregation make the shift from a long-term minister to a new, yet-to-be-hired minister of the future.

"You know," she said, "we're going to need to know who from this committee is willing to go forward to the selection committee." I knew I had to tell her I was not going to be available for that. "Well that explains all the walking now," she laughed. Relieved to have it in the open, I shared my doubts about going, specifically about leaving Al behind.

"Roxey, this is a calling," Jeri affirmed. "You may not know why right now, but you are meant to do this. You have to go."

I identified a walking mantra, one of my favourite scriptures from the bible, and one I try very hard to live by: "What does the Lord require of you? To seek justice, love kindness, and walk humbly with your God." I went to the local bead shop and using alphabet beads made myself an elasticized bracelet that read "Micah 6:8". I decided to make another bracelet, drawing on the first initials of the names of my family members. I would carry their names with me, ready to hold them close while I journeyed.

I have a good friend who's supposed to be retired, but who often fills in for me at work. Taking Kathy aside, I told her my plans. She hugged me and, her eyes sparkling with excitement, asked me to tell her all about it. Tucking her silky hair behind her ear, she agreed to keep it secret for now... but could she tell her husband?

One summer morning, Al and I joined Kathy and Don for breakfast at a favourite café. I brought them up to speed on my training, equipment, and travel plans. After our plates had been cleared away and we were lingering over cups of coffee, Don pushed an envelope across the table to me.

"You're going to need boots," he grinned. I opened the envelope and burst into tears. I told my two very special friends that this was the first tangible validation I had received of my plans. It was starting to feel like it was really going to happen.

"You'll want to read this." Al showed me an article in the local paper. Lynn, a pre-school owner in her early sixties, had just come back from the walk of her life. Excitedly, I tracked down her number and called, leaving a message that I was planning to do the Camino next spring. I said if she was willing, I'd love to talk to her about her trip. That evening the phone rang and I heard the words *"Buen Camino"* spoken to me for the first time.

I went over to visit and met her husband who (like Al would) served as home base during her Camino. Lynn pulled me into her den and showed me all the things she had packed across Spain. She argued one item against another's merits in the way of equipping myself as lightly, but as thoroughly as possible. Lynn talked about the training she did to prepare.

"You can't just go there and expect do this without preparing," she warned. "I'm so excited for you! Ask anything you want," she bubbled. I asked her if she had found it hard.

"Oh yeah. I was in tears so many times! I wrote a blog. Are you going to write a blog?" I told her I had thought about it, but I really wanted to remove all restrictions I could on my trip. Knowing myself, if I said I was going to blog, I would feel obligated to blog. My plan was to limit my communication home to Al and have him send out updates of my progress as I went. I wanted to make him feel involved.

"Okay, well anything you need to know, just send me an email or give me a call; don't hesitate!" she exclaimed, sending me out the door a bit overwhelmed. I knew this would not be the last time we talked.

I began walking where once I drove. Kirby, our little Welsh terrier enjoyed the extra walks. Then the walks got longer. In September, I asked my manager if he would mind giving me a ride to Nanoose on his way home.

"No problem," he said as we pulled out of the parking lot. I told him he could just drop me at the gas station at the foot of the hills.

"Well no. I can take you where you're going. It's no trouble." When I told him I was going home, he reminded me I lived in Parksville, fourteen kilometres behind us. I explained I was training.

"You're going to walk home along the highway, up those huge hills?" he asked incredulously. "Does Al know about this? Is he okay with this?" I assured him I had my husband's full support. Grudgingly, he left me by the side of the road.

The next day I met with my supervisors to tell them they would have to have someone cover for me in April. They waited, serious expressions on their faces, expecting bad news.

"I'm going to be walking an 800-kilometre pilgrimage across Spain called the Camino de Santiago de Compostela. I'll be gone for forty days." I rushed on, "And I've checked with Kathy, and she'll be available if you want. I'll be leaving in April and won't be back until mid-June."

"Whew!" There were great gusts of relief that I wasn't retiring early, and then the questions came. They were surprised to hear I planned to go alone, not with any sort of tour group, and that there was no "check-in" procedure. I told them that was a huge part of why I was doing this; to try and leave schedules behind and be responsible only to and for myself. I asked that they not share this news with anyone else at work for now.

Lynn and Bill came bearing gifts; things she used on her Camino. There were compression bags for organizing my pack, a cellphone charger for when I didn't have access to a plug, water-proof bags, and more. She even brought clips to attach my boots at the end of each day, so I didn't end up with a mismatched pair by mistake. Our husbands just ate cookies, drank coffee, and exchanged patient looks.

"Take what you need, and you can get what you don't need back to me when you return." I really appreciated that about Lynn; she was excited to share, but aware that this was my Camino. She made suggestions and offered information, but I was already learning each must walk their own Camino. Her excitement was catching, and I dubbed her my "Camino mentor".

In September, I got fitted for my pack, a purple 36-litre Osprey. The thing had more pockets and straps and buckles than I knew what to do with, and I was glad I was going to have a chance to get to know it before I left. No, I did not name it!

My training escalated with a wet, 400-metre-climb up Mount Wells, with Scott as my guide. My shorter legs struggled with the deep footholds his 6'5" frame took with ease. On the way down, my son carefully monitored my pole use as we traversed the wet rock faces, telling me not to put my pole where I wouldn't put my foot. His instructions would hold me in good stead on my journey.

I went online to the Camino Forum, a great place to ask questions and get advice about gear, routes, and places to stay on the Camino. The Forum is run by Ivar, who lives in Santiago, the endpoint of the trek. He offers a wide range of services, including acting as a holding place for pilgrims who find they have too much in their packs and want to send some things ahead for collection upon their arrival. Mailing things home can be costly and capricious.

Cautiously guarding my privacy, I introduced myself by first name only, saying I was from Vancouver Island and planning to do the Camino at the end of April 2016. Suddenly, a message popped up from a woman in Abbotsford (on the mainland, just outside of Vancouver, where I would be flying from) asking if I would contact her directly.

Cindy was very excited to find someone from her area travelling about the same time. She honoured my need to walk alone, but asked if I would at least like to travel as far as St. Jean Pied de Port with her and her friend, Joyce. I decided that if there was a seat available on her flight, I'd let that make my decision to leave two days earlier than originally planned. After turning our credit card points into flights to Paris and back, it looked like I'd be travelling with Cindy and Joyce.

Plane reservations made, I was fully committed and ready to share my news with the crew at work. Some were excited for me, some indifferent, and some doubtful, but all tried not to let me know they thought I'd lost my mind. I'm sure looking at their slightly overweight, gray-haired administrative assistant, pushing sixty in her heels and pencil skirt, they had difficulty imagining me trekking across Spain. The questions flew like rice at a wedding. "Across the Pyrenees? Walking? With a pack? By yourself?" and of course, "What about Al?"

I started receiving messages from Cindy daily, as she considered and reconsidered different *albergues* (hostels), flights, trains, and all things Camino. Cindy advised that in addition to her travelling partner, Joyce, she was actually part of a larger group that had met through the Camino Forum and asked if she could pass on my email address so I could be involved in the planning. With Jane Christmas' snowballing experience with group travel on the Camino in mind, I said I would prefer not to share my email address with the group. I reminded her that I wanted to travel independently, and she assured me that was okay.

Then Cindy emailed to say she had made reservations for her and Joyce at an *albergue* in St. Jean Pied de Port and gave them my name. The *albergue* would be contacting me by email for payment. Okay.

A couple days later, the phone rang and Cindy bubbled with news that other members of the group had alerted her to a flight from the Orly airport in Paris to Biarritz, which was a really good deal and, after an hour's shuttle, would get us to St. Jean by midday, but by the time she went online to book it for us, the seats were all gone. Breathe! But, she assured me, she found a train that left right from Charles de Gualle Airport that would take us all the way to St. Jean with a couple of stops. Did I want to be included when she made the reservations so we could all sit together? Well at least she'd asked this time! I popped a cheque in the mail to cover the costs, wondering what travelling with her was going to be like.

"Oh sure! You won't let me come with you," laughed my younger sister when I told her about Cindy, "but you'll let this cyber stalker girl go with you!" Given Joan's busy life and new love interest, I knew it was a protest made in jest.

I explored options for reservations for the second night of my Camino. Orisson was the first opportunity to stop after leaving St. Jean. Lynn had suggested that, having just having travelled for two days, I should go easy on the first day and stop there, allowing my body to adjust to the time and altitude. My online search identified only one option for an *albergue*, and I made my reservation.

That taken care of, I moved on to securing a place to stay once I arrived in Santiago. Positive thinking! I would arrive in Santiago. I checked the hotel Lynn suggested only to find it booked from May through September in 2016! Maybe I was reading this wrong. I emailed Ivar at the Camino Forum and asked him to check what I was seeing. As surprised as me, he confirmed it was fully booked and made other suggestions. I wanted something not too modern, not too expensive, and not too far from the cathedral. I chose the Hotel Avenida and booked my room. My return trip would take me by air from Santiago to Madrid, and then on to Paris. My last piece of work was reserving a hotel near the airport in Paris for my last night before my departure home.

Continuing with my training, I decided to take on a greater challenge: the Hump.

This is the affectionate title for the summit of the highway between our town and Port Alberni, where our eldest son's family lives. My goal was to start in McMillan Provincial Park, better known as Cathedral Grove; a protected coastal forest boasting majestic Douglas fir trees. Beginning with an easy slope, the highway reaches daunting grades that demand large trucks travel with hazard lights flashing and make mandatory brake checks on the downside.

Al dropped me off, gave me a half-hour start, then climbed the hill behind me. Not seeing me ahead of him, he started looking at the ditches, wondering if I'd bailed to avoid being struck by a vehicle. He continued to climb, pulling over when he finally spotted me through the rain, on the crest of the first hill.

"I can't believe how fast you took that!" he said. "I never thought you'd get this far this fast!" I told him that cars passing me had considerately pulled into the centre lane to avoid covering me with road spray, and that down-coming vehicles had flashed their lights at me and honked and waved. I wasn't sure if they thought I was a lunatic or if they were cheering me on. I chose cheering.

Al pulled out and waited at the summit, and again further down the hill, moving on as each time he'd confirmed my well-being. When I got in the car at the entrance to town, I was a hot ball of sweat, sucking back water, and grinning at successfully handling the significant challenge. In the back of my mind, however, I knew this 400-metre climb and the fifteen-kilometre distance would be a drop in the bucket compared to the first forty-eight hours of the Camino.

"Good job, Gramma!" Matthew flung his arms around my knees when we arrived at our children's home. It was the best award I could have received for my efforts. That, and a hot shower!

The following week we were down island for another visit to the MS Clinic. Scott met us for lunch, seeming a little more tense than usual. He poked at his food, reluctant to say what was on his mind. Finally, he told us that he and his wife were seeing a marriage counsellor. We were totally shocked. High-school sweethearts, they seemed to be a charmed "forever couple". It appeared they had been maintaining a happy front when they were with us.

We sent him back to work with supportive hugs and asked him to keep in touch so we'd know he was okay. We stopped by to see Jackie on our way out of town. Carrying our granddaughter down to visit with Grampa in the car, I climbed the stairs and held Jackie as she wept, totally at a loss in the face of this heart-breaking situation.

We returned home and waited for news, praying that their counsellor would help our son and his wife work this through. Time would reveal if our fractured family could be healed. All we could do was hold them in our hearts and carry on.

In November, we made another equipment purchase for my trip: a cellphone. Now I know everyone has one, but I am a bit of a dinosaur with regard to technology. I use computers all day long at work, switching between dedicated programs and two monitors with ease, updating multiple electronic schedules, spreadsheets, and calendars, as well as running the switchboard and the radio. But at home, I am a different animal, refusing (much to our children's disgust) to join social media and deferring to Al when it comes to running the remote control.

Al has always carried a cellphone to provide emergency contact while he's out and about on his mobility scooter. This would be a huge learning curve for me. We explored the options of this instrument that would become my everything; my camera, my clock, my calendar, my weather report, my flashlight, my music, my concierge, my communication with my fellow pilgrims, and most importantly, my source of grounding family photos when I needed a lift, and my essential link to Al and home.

Coming together as a family the week before Christmas was a strained affair, with everyone walking on eggshells. We tried to make it as normal a Christmas as possible, especially for the little ones, but we knew it would not likely ever be the same again. As our sons returned to their homes for Christmas celebrations with their wives' families, we prayed the New Year would bring a new peace in our family. I resigned myself to the probability that I wasn't the only one who would be walking a rocky path in the months to come.

The blustery dark days of winter filled our world with rain and our eyes with tears as Scott shared his decision to move out. What could we do but hold him and love him as his marriage dissolved.

In February, at her birthday party, our granddaughter bounced happily around the room with her cousins and playmates, running between her parents for reassuring hugs. The grown-ups in the room were aware of the impending separation and treated each other with careful politeness. The drawing of lines and the choosing of sides hung silently in the room full of the chatter of innocent children, excited by balloons and cake.

Watching the children's happy play, my inner sadness was not just for my son's pain, but for the potential loss of our relationship with a young woman we had known and loved for many years as a daughter.

After two hours of tears in the car driving home, I asked Al how I could possibly leave at a time like this.

"What would your staying solve?" he asked kindly. "As much as we want to help, this is between them. Them and their lawyers." Al had been divorced before, but this was my first experience with the process. "Until they get some things sorted out, we won't even know how to help them except to support them with our love and prayers."

"She can't come," the email from Cindy read. Joyce had suffered an injury. Her travel insurance would be void if she travelled against a doctor's recommendation. Her Camino was over before it began. Al watched helplessly as my shoulders shook with sobs (I seemed to be crying a lot these days), in grief for Joyce, a woman I had never even met. I felt her loss so deeply. I could only imagine how I would feel if someone told me I couldn't go at this stage of the game.

Our next trip down island was two-fold; to help our son settle into his new apartment and to get my "real" hiking boots. Knowing he loved to cook, we came bearing an early birthday gift (a microwave oven) and a care package full of kitchen basics. He delighted in each thing he drew from the box. Aside from the pain of separation from his daughter, Scott seemed happier than we had seen him lately. He seemed a calmer person. I took some comfort in that.

While he went with friends to pick up a second-hand table and chair set he'd bought, we worked in our granddaughter's room. I hung curtains I'd sewn and filled the bookcase with toys and books chosen from our supply at home. Al put together the tiny table and chairs and assembled a miniature kitchen centre. A playroom for now, Alayna's new bed would arrive in time for her first overnight stay. Bittersweet.

My training until now had been done in light training runners. I'd be trading those for a heavier boot, with solid structure, to protect my feet from the various trail surfaces that make up the Camino. It was suggested that I get a pair at least a half a size if not a full size too big in order to leave room for the swelling that occurs when feet are locked in leather, pounding pavement and treading treacherous terrain. The footwear specialist at the outdoor store shook his head, refusing to sell me boots too big.

"Your feet will slide back and forth causing hot spots that may blister. Your arch support will be in the wrong place, and your heel won't be properly cupped for stability." Good reasoning, I guessed. I was torn. Every book I'd read, each person I'd talked to had advised larger boots, but his words made sense.

That's the thing when gearing up for the Camino. You get inundated with information and alternatives. Fly or take the train? Paris or Madrid? Quick dry pants or leggings? Tape or Vaseline on your feet? Sandals or boots? Poncho or rain gear? You just have to sift through it all and make the best choices for yourself. Suffering from this level of information overload, I had stopped visiting the Camino Forum. I'd make a decision, then read some comments, and rethink my decision. It was agony! Finally, I turned it all off, made my decisions, and stuck to them.

With my boots, I decided to err on the side of caution in both regards, and talked him into finding me the best fit a half size too big and a pair of thick socks.

The gap between today and fly day was quickly closing. I arranged for a housekeeper to come in and someone to mow the lawns for Al. I'd registered with the Canadian consulate. I'd made copies of my travel documents and insurance to leave with Al.

At the beginning of April, Scott asked if I had started my tapering process on my training. What the heck was that?

"When athletes are training for a big event, they taper off for the last while before the event to save their bodies for the main push." I'm an athlete? Did I mention he had a bachelor's degree in kinesiology? I argued that I hadn't worked this hard to get my sloppy body ready just to let it all go at the last minute. "You need to slow down to almost nothing," he insisted. "You can take Kirby for short walks. You need to back down on everything else for at least the last ten days. That gives your body time to rest. Don't worry. When you need it, the muscle memory will kick right back in." Okay. It was good to have his expertise to keep me on track.

"To keep you visible and safe," my sister Joan insisted, thoughtfully contributing a neon yellow t-shirt, that completed my Camino wardrobe. My boots had reached the fine line of being broken in but not broken down. I packed my pack. I unpacked my pack. I packed my pack again. Just over twenty pounds; the magic goal. I unpacked my pack and removed some body wash, a pair of socks, and an extra roll of tape. I repacked my pack and rocked back on my heels and looked at it… there… sitting in the corner… waiting.

A week before, we'd had a family gathering to celebrate my upcoming birthday and departure date, which just happened to be one and the same. It was good to see our grandchildren playing together. Kenneth told his younger brother all about his new job, while Scott went over my first aid kit. Amanda fussed in the kitchen, organizing dinner. With a flourish, Al completed the meal with a cake topped with a chocolate slab that read "*Buen Camino*". By the time everyone left, I had up-to-the-minute photos of them all on my cellphone, and those photos would carry me through the harder moments of my journey. I hated to see them go, but there would be lots to occupy my mind over the last few days before I left.

I took the last day off work to handle all the final details. My talented hairdresser, Sherry, had shorn my hair and threaded beads forming my Micah mantra onto the tiny pigtail I had left uncut since my decision last year. My plan was to have Al cut this little talisman off, formally ending my physical journey when I returned. Carolyn, my physiotherapist, had my taped my weak knee and given me a crash course in taping to maintain support along the way.

Al and I took Kirby for an evening walk down to the ocean. I took it all in, saving the memory for my journey. I wondered if Kirby would forgive me my absence when I returned. We went out for supper at our favourite Vietnamese place, then home to watch movies until heads began to nod. Sleep still came hard for me. As I laid my head on Al's shoulder I soaked in the rhythm of his breathing and the warmth of his skin. It would be a long time before we were this close again. I would have to make do with holding him close in my heart for the next few weeks. I closed my eyes and slept.

Happy birthday! Al and I were at the airport coffee shop, sharing a celebratory breakfast. Suddenly, my cellphone lit up with a message from Air France warning of a pending air and rail strike in France. My heart skipped a beat and panic set in, but Al calmly reached across the table.

"Don't worry…just go. This is why we bought your flight insurance. Fly to Vancouver and leave for Paris. If you can't land, they'll divert you elsewhere, and you'll deal with it from there. Maybe they'll drop you at Madrid, and you can take a train or bus from there."

This was the part I worried about with this trip; the getting there.

"It's funny!" I had confided to my minister, "I'm not worried about walking 800 kilometres over the mountains, across the plains, through a country I don't know, or about not being familiar with the money or food and having only minimal Spanish to communicate with. I know God will have me in His hand through all of that. What I worry about is when I'm travelling to Spain, to the start of the Camino, when I'll be in the hands of people in airports and train stations." I saw Jeri's slow smile widen and the light bulb went on. "Oh right! Those people are in God's hands too, and I'm there with them."

The eight-seat Piper taxied towards the terminal, and I watched as they loaded my bulging purple backpack into the nose of the plane. Al and I hugged hard, telling each other to take care until we were together again. After a long kiss, holding back tears, I joined the other passengers as we folded ourselves into the tiny plane.

Despite Al's reassurances, my emotions were at war; excitement did battle with guilt at leaving him behind and sadness at not having him with me to share what was to come. We had never been apart like this before. I looked back as the plane lifted off the ground and saw him, in his wheelchair, pressed against the mesh fence, waving frantically. I knew he would not see me through the tiny window, so I had to trust that he knew a large part of my heart remained behind with him.

In the air, we quickly left Vancouver Island behind us, flying over Georgia Strait's collection of tiny islands. Touching down at the south terminal of Vancouver International Airport, I collected my pack and boarded the shuttle that sped me over to the main terminal. After checking in, I carried my pack, poles in hand, passing through security with ease.

I scanned the waiting room for the Cindy I knew from emailed photos. Instead I was noisily greeted by two other members of her group, Patti and Theresa. They saw my pack, assumed I was a fellow pilgrim, and came running over to find out who I was. We knew each other's names through Cindy's emails. Patti, petite and dark haired, provided a sharp contrast to the taller, more athletic looking Theresa. The young friends shared a boisterous, care-free spirit and asked if I'd like to join them for a beer. I told them I wanted to wait for Cindy, so off they went.

When Cindy arrived, I knew her. Her tiny, Filipino frame exploded in a riot of colour that could not be ignored; all pinks and purples. Eyes sparkling behind large, black-framed glasses, she pushed her long hair back behind her ears, revealing sparkly hoop earrings. Her backpack was purple, like mine, but decorated with a colourful assortment of patches and silk flowers. Her long nails glistened with fuchsia polish and even her hiking boots boasted neon pink laces. I had no doubt my travelling partner would be the most fashionable pilgrim in St. Jean. I felt like the dull sparrow next to this exotic bird of paradise.

She asked if I had met any of the others, and I told her Patti and Theresa were here and had gone for lunch. The public-address system announced boarding for our flight, and they came running back into the waiting room, giggling with nervous excitement. Hugs all around, we straightened up and got down to the serious business of presenting documents, boarding the plane, stowing our packs and poles in overhead compartments, and then collapsed into our seats, grinning like fools.

The nine-hour flight gave me a chance to get to know Cindy better, and I realized that although a little bit nervous about this adventure, she was very passionate about her journey. Eyes brimming with tears, she spoke of how she had meant to do the Camino with her father, but he passed away suddenly. She was doing it in his memory. Her Catholic faith was important to her, so the Camino held great significance for her. In face of her zealous declarations, again I questioned my own spiritual commitment. I told her, not being Catholic, my Camino wasn't so much church driven, as it was spirit driven.

Cindy droned on and on about her husband, her dog, her garden, her hiking group, the other ladies in her Camino email group, her training, and her equipment. I was lulled into peaceful slumber like a child hearing a bedtime story.

A couple of hours later, gently nudged awake, Cindy advised me she had been back to visit the girls and Theresa and Patti were doing just fine. She had only wakened me, she said, since our dinner was being served. The airline's crew had taken good care of us, and we landed in Paris fed, hydrated, and happy to begin the next leg of our journey.

Theresa and Patti sprinted by to catch a shuttle to Paris' other airport. They were flying from Orly to Biarritz, then taking a bus to St. Jean, where they would arrive mid-afternoon. Cindy and I, having missed the opportunity for that flight, scrambled down the hall following directions to the train station below the Charles de Gaulle airport. The timing was tight, and if we missed this train, we would have to wait another day.

We scurried downstairs to wait on the platform, seeing others bearing backpacks festooned with seashells, armed with trekking poles, and shod with durable hiking boots. These would be pilgrims, like us, waiting for the train that would carry us across France, thankful that the looming air and rail strike had not hit...yet.

Shortly after 10:00, we pulled out of the station, comfortably seated on the upper level of the quiet train. From comfy seats, it was amazing to watch the French countryside zoom by in silent speed. Watching as we passed fields of vivid yellows and greens, we chatted with other pilgrims, comparing equipment and sharing plans and route information. There were announcements that, with my grade twelve French, I deciphered to be about getting food and hot beverages on the train, but we made due with our bottles of water and the snacks we had in our packs. When we reached our first stop at Bordeaux St. Jean, we disembarked searching for food before our next train's departure. The only choice without leaving the station (and risking getting lost and missing the train) was McDonalds. We boarded the train carrying grease-stained paper bags and sweating, disposable cups.

After two hours, we arrived at Bayonne only to hear that the last train of our trip, the one taking us to St. Jean Pied, would not be running; the strike had finally caught up with us! The international assortment of pilgrims, crowding around in concerned confusion, were relieved to hear we would be bussed the last leg of our journey. While we waited to board the busses parked in the square,

I took in the historical buildings, the narrow cobblestone streets, the old men huddled in their overcoats and caps on the benches, and the small children, happily scattering flocks of pigeons as their mothers looked on.

We stowed our packs in the belly of the bus and smoothly pulled out of town, headed to St. Jean. I thought the trip would be longer, as the rails were likely a more direct route. But surprisingly, we rounded corners, climbed hills, and arrived at 7:00, ten minutes earlier than previously planned.

The tiny hamlet of St. Jean Pied de Port lay nestled in the valley at the foot of the French Pyrenees mountains. Shrouded in fog in the fading evening light, the tall, narrow, stone houses and cobblestone streets reminded me of the fairy-tale books of my childhood.

We walked through an arch, entering a narrow street lined with a variety of accommodations. Up the road we went, then down the road we went, finally finding our *albergue*. But the names, all in French, were so foreign that we mistook another for ours, and the *hospitalero* (host) there patiently directed us back down the street. A young, dark-haired woman welcomed us inside at "Ultreia". We had both prepaid twenty-two euros for our bed and breakfast, so our *hospitalero* registered our national passport information, stamped our pilgrim passports, and led us up six flights of narrow, highly polished wooden stairs, to a tiny three-bed attic room.

She gave us blankets and asked that we not put our packs on the beds, but rather place them in the plastic bins at the foot of each bed. She didn't say why, but we knew this was a safeguard against the *albergues* acquiring bedbugs from any traveller's pack. The *albergue* operators and pilgrims shared equal fear of this scourge. Infected *albergues* had to close, losing business while being fumigated and cleared. Travellers didn't want to add painful itching to the challenges of the trek.

Our *hospitalero* showed us the washroom, indicating we were responsible to supply our own soap and towels. She told Cindy the rest of her group was in the room across the hall, but that they had gone out for supper. Breakfast would be available in the dining room on the second floor at 6:30. The grand tour over, we dropped our packs, changed our boots for more comfortable sandals, and went in search of Cindy's group and a meal.

Although we hadn't eaten anything substantial through our travels that day, I didn't really want to have a heavy meal. I knew I'd already have difficulty sleeping. We saw restaurants proclaiming pilgrims' meals for anywhere between ten and fifteen euros, detailing at length the three courses that would have had me groaning. All I wanted was a bowl of hearty soup.

During our search, Cindy found her group just returning from dinner. Patti and Theresa had still not arrived; their flight out of Orly had gotten caught in the strike, and their postponed departure meant they were still awaiting transport from Biarritz. Everyone else had made it through, and they were just returning to their room to wait for the girls.

Introducing me, Cindy told them she would be there as soon as we found some supper, and they suggested the bar they had just left. Checking the posted menu outside, we saw they did serve soup, but only as part of the larger meal. Plodding back up the hill, we finally found a little coffee bar that boasted sandwiches and light meals. We asked if they had soup. The hearty, cream of vegetable soup was hot and flavourful, and along with the thick crusty bread, just what we needed.

Fortified, Cindy and I returned to the *albergue*. Pulling ourselves up the staircase, we entered our room to find the third bed filled by a sleeping Japanese girl. I grabbed my soap and towel and headed to the shower, checking with others first in case anyone needed the bathroom. They waved me off, and Cindy joined her group. She was still there when I tucked myself in and drifted off to sleep.

I was surprised how well I had slept the previous night, not being used to the bed, the pillow, or sharing my room with two other ladies. Iru, a young Japanese girl, was busily storing her sleeping bag in her backpack before stealing out of the room. Across from me, Cindy groaned, rolled out of bed, pulled on her socks, and padded across the hall to check in with her group.

By the time she returned, I was dressed in my new trekking pants, neon yellow quick-dry shirt, and soft wool socks. The clothes I'd worn yesterday were neatly folded, ready for donation. I had worn a soft, loose shirt I could travel and sleep in and a pair of gym tights that I could feel good about leaving behind. I would start my journey in clean hiking clothes, and the bonus was I was already lightening my load.

With everything tucked in my pack, I descended the steep staircase, leaving Cindy some privacy for dressing. In the days ahead, I would come to know that privacy for dressing is a luxury hard to come by on the Camino.

Four floors below, the breakfast room was abuzz with women chatting in a variety of languages. Iru and five others were enjoying their meal. The *hospitalero* directed me to the stack of cups and dishes, indicating one carafe was full of coffee, the other hot milk. I selected a hard-boiled egg, a couple slices of yellow cheese, and a wedge of thick-crusted bread. Along with a hot cup of coffee, I filled a small bowl with granola and topped it with some of the hot milk and a spoonful of honey. I thought this would be pretty standard breakfast fare on the trail since protein would help maintain energy for the day's work. I enjoyed the abundance in ignorant bliss.

Down in the foyer, I zipped tissues and lip balm into my front pack, and gloves into the pocket of my coat. I adjusted my poles, pulled on my white wool cap and hoisted on my pack. I wove past a collection of colourful packs, left waiting expectantly by the door. On the Camino, if you have an identified reservation, for a few euros you can have your backpack ported ahead to your destination, allowing you to trek unhindered by the extra bulk and weight. Cindy and her group had arranged to have their packs ported to our first stop, Orisson. Despite having a reservation, I had decided not to port my pack, thinking that if I couldn't handle it for 7.5 kilometres, how would I ever carry it for a full day.

I carried my twenty-pound pack out onto the steeply sloping cobblestone street, quiet in these soft, early morning hours, except for several pilgrims, just like me, excited to begin their journey. Cindy, looked like a fashion plate in her signature pinks and purples layered over stylish trekking pants. She was taking photos of arches and stonework as I joined her, and she enlisted a passer-by to take a "first day" photo of the two of us. Solidly built, at five feet, seven inches, I felt like a lumbering Amazon next to her tiny Asian frame.

Up the hill we walked, testing out our poling techniques, and in through the door of the pilgrim's office we strolled. On a rough wooden shelf by the window were a variety of brochures, a stand full of wooden walking poles, and a rack strung with scallop shells, emblazoned with the scarlet emblem of Saint James, in whose name the Camino is walked.

From their outside edge, the symbolic shells have lines radiating towards a single point, depicting the many different Camino routes to Santiago, the final resting place of the body of Saint James. Apparently, after Jesus' crucifixion, his apostle, James, travelled to Galicia in northern Spain and attempted to continue his ministry. When he returned to Jerusalem, Herod Agrippa had James beheaded and his martyred remains were transported in a stone boat by his disciples (or by angels, depending on the versions you read) back to the Iberian Peninsula. One story goes that after a storm, the boat washed ashore covered with scallops. Another popular version has a wedding taking place on shore. As the boat approached, the groom's horse got spooked and threw his rider into the sea. Miraculously, the young man, with the help of Saint James, emerged from the water alive, covered in seashells.

Now I'm not Catholic, and I'm not up on all the "saint stuff". For me, the shell signified the many faith paths we follow. As we waited our turn to register, Cindy examined the shells, wondering if she shouldn't get a new one to add to her pack. Her turn to register put an end to her quandary and after her, I quickly filled the next available chair in front of a volunteer.

Esther was a tiny, bespectacled, grey-haired lady with a sweet smile and a glowing face. She told me about herself as she took my information, carefully writing the details of my Canadian passport in her ledger. She was from the States and came to the Camino for two weeks each year to help others begin the pilgrimage she had completed years ago.

She asked if I knew my reason for making the trip. I told her I had felt called to make the walk. It was the culmination of many signals that this was something I was meant to do, although the "why" of it was still a mystery. Esther asked if she could bless me and, somewhat flustered by the offer, I accepted her gift. Standing just to my shoulder height, she held my hands, looked into my eyes, and asked for God's blessing and protection on my journey.

"Sometimes I know just who is going to make it and who will not. You will be just fine." I cleared my throat, choked with emotion, and blinked back unshed tears.

We followed the arrows down to the foot of the street, passing under an arch straddling the cobblestones between the rows of leaning, buildings. Crossing over a narrow bridge, we found "the group". Not being an actual member of "the group", I offered to take a photo, so they would all be in the picture. Then, as I was shouldering my pack and adjusting my straps, they started up the hill, unencumbered by packs, without me.

"Aren't we supposed to go down the path beside the bridge?" I called out. "I thought we were supposed to go down that way."

"Well I have done this before, and this is the way we are going," said an imposingly built, hard-faced woman I came to know as Shirley. "You go that way if you want to, but my group is going this way."

Okay then. I had been told. Thinking that was a pretty "unpilgrim-like" response, especially for someone who had done the walk before, I straggled up the hill behind the group as the road wound narrower and narrower around old buildings with heavy wooden doors and grill work on the windows. "Wonder who pissed in her cornflakes?" I muttered, immediately chastising myself for my own unpilgrim-like behaviour.

The sun shone down from a brilliant blue sky and already it was hot. Stopping to take my coat off put me a little more behind, but I found the separation from the others offered quiet solitude to enjoy the meadow to mountain vistas opening before me. Curly-horned, sheep grazed peacefully, looking totally unconcerned by the steady parade of pilgrims. Putting my legs into first gear, up and up I climbed. The sun glared down disapprovingly as I huffed and sweated my way up the road, my legs already burning and my pack gaining weight with each step. I had trained for this! Why was it so hard? Some of the group had stopped ahead by the side of the road for a rest and water, and it made me feel a little better to know I wasn't the only one feeling the challenge.

At the five-kilometre mark, I reached, Huntto, not actually a town, but rather a thatched mountain-side rest stop fronted by bright orange plastic chairs and tables. Dropping my pack, I used the washroom and grabbed a cold drink. Seriously, this was just five kilometres. How was I going to do a full twenty-five- kilometre day! Just as I buckled my pack's waist belt, others from the group arrived. I pressed on, seeing Patti and Theresa, probably the fittest and youngest of the group, kicked back, enjoying the sun on a grassy alcove at the side of the road. Their relaxed attitude and friendly bantering had me wondering just how they fit in the group driven by the abrasive Shirley. I wondered if Shirley was the intended leader, or had just made herself the leader.

Cindy, who had not stopped with the others at Huntto, pulled up beside me and for the first time that day we continued the climb together.

"I didn't know it was going to be this hard," she without a backpack panted. Even though we knew we were climbing 900 metres in the short distance between St. Jean and Orisson, it hadn't truly sunk in how steep the grade would have to be to accomplish that. To be fair, Cindy had suffered a bit of an injury to her back the week before we left, and she was working through that pain admirably.

"Watch your footing," I replied, motioning towards the loose rocks in the red dirt path that dropped off suddenly to the valley below. "We've only got 2.5 kilometres more to go. Thank goodness we didn't try for Roncesvalles." Not for the last time would I thank Lynn for her Camino insight. Many others would push themselves all the way to Roncesvalles this day.

We climbed higher in the mountains, the air growing cooler and clearer, and came to a plateau. Cautiously, we walked out towards the edge, feeling closer to the puffy white clouds than the miniature town in the valley below.

"Let's take a picture!" Cindy laughed, and we each assumed the "pilgrim reflectively perusing the view" stance and took photos in turn. The view was astounding! Mist-shrouded mountains folded in upon each other like eagles' wings reaching down towards lush green pastures dotted with tiny farmhouses. As I looked down at the village where I started my day, I couldn't believe I had come all that way. I was careful not to look up to see where I had yet to go.

As we continued up the incline, a truck drove by, and I have to admit to a small degree of jealousy as I sweated my load up the grade. I talked myself into getting to the next tree, and then I could have some water from one of the two dwindling bottles tucked in my front pack. And then the next tree. They really should have more trees…closer together…and a bench or two wouldn't hurt. Obviously, I was still getting in the pilgrim frame of mind.

I'd been on the road for just over three hours, and it felt like thirty years. Maybe I had bitten off more than I could chew. I really thought the months of distance walking, hill training, stair climbing, and weighted squats I had done would have prepared me for this, but now I felt like a limp rag. Doubts were quickly overwhelming enthusiasm. Oh look! Another tree!

Suddenly, after a stinky-hot, gruelling climb, there it was – Orisson! Like an oasis in the heat was a two-storey plaster and stone building on one side of the road, and, hanging off the side of the mountain on the other side, a deck, complete with umbrellas and cold mugs of beer on the tables. Deck or building? Deck or building? Fighting the dilemma, I entered the *albergue* with Cindy, congratulating myself on reaching the first goal of…thirty-seven more days like this?

There was only one line-up, and it was hard to tell if it was for rooms or beer, or both. We finally got to the head of the line, and my passport was registered confirming my prepaid bed. Cindy was told that since she booked two beds, she was being charged for both even though her travelling buddy had not made the trip. The *albergue* was full, so this was a little confusing as we were sure they could have sold that second bed. Knowing it would be a while before I could order a drink, I left Cindy to her negotiations with the *hospitalero*.

Dumping my pack against a wall inside, I went out to the deck, walking straight into a discussion with a woman who had planned to go to Roncesvalles, but was too tired to go on. Now, Leticia hoped to stop at Orisson, if she could just get a bed. *Problem solved*, I thought. I took Leticia into the *albergue*, up to the desk, and said she needed the second bed Cindy had reserved and that she would reimburse Cindy. Done deal! *Now, could I have a beer?*

I took my cold beer and a sandwich out to the deck, joining a happy and noisy bunch of pilgrims who felt they had slain the dragon and were enjoying basking in the sun. The chairs quickly filled with members of Cindy's group, chatting about their private room with its own washroom and arranging to port their bags on to Roncesvalles in the morning. I didn't see Leticia and guessed the bed she filled was in their private room. Either way, I figured if the meals were any good, the thirty-seven euros I'd prepaid was a reasonable price for my snug little bunk in the corner, supper, and breakfast. More importantly, I had survived the climb to enjoy it all.

Some people had already done laundry. The clothesline behind the *albergue* was a pageant of colour flapping in the wind. From my vantage point, across the road, at a wooden picnic table near the laundry area, I saw a slight, silver-haired woman obviously consoling a short redhead.

"I don't know why Angela needs to do that. She shouldn't use her energy on that woman. She is not her responsibility," Shirley spouted as she sucked on her beer. Not knowing the players or how everyone was connected, I sat back quietly and observed as Shirley continued to hold court. A self-professed "biker chick" from Ontario, Shirley was behaving very arrogantly, in a most un-Canadian fashion as she monopolized the conversation. She spoke of how solid her marriage was and what a great role model she was to her kids, both of whom were in relationships with long-time loves that would remain similarly solid. I asked how old her kids were; both in their early thirties, so obviously settled for life. *Oh really*, I thought; *and you're sure life's all set in stone? Good for you!* Then Shirley was onto health issues.

"They say cancer is in my family. It's just a matter of positive thinking. Someone in my family may have cancer, but it doesn't mean it's in my family; it's just in them." Okay, now she'd gone too far. A young widow, I had lost my thirty-six-year-old husband to non-Hodgkins lymphoma. His eldest brother died of leukemia at eighteen, and my father-in-law succumbed to colon cancer shortly after my husband. Add my sister-in-law being a survivor of breast cancer and four out of seven says it's in my family and that my sons need to be aware they are in direct line for all those genes.

Maybe not a good idea to make broad, sweeping statements out loud when you don't know your audience and who you might be offending. But then I didn't know Shirley either, and it wasn't my place to judge. I could put up, shut up, or go for a walk. Even after the day's haul up the mountain, the scenery and the sunshine was inviting, and I strolled a little further up the road to check out the view from a different perspective.

Having showered, changed, and put in my baguette lunch order for the next day, I joined my fellow-pilgrims on benches at long, trestle tables in the heavy-beamed room. My first pilgrim meal; how exciting! Pitchers of water and bottles of wine made their own pilgrimages up and down the tables, filling and refilling glasses, while baskets of bread accompanied by pasta and chicken legs were served family style. The conversation was happy, loud and very confusing to my distorted hearing.

After supper, our *hospitaleros* asked everyone to introduce themselves. Of the fifty pilgrims in the room, there were people from nine different countries. One of the British women was a bit of linguistic expert and was able to introduce her large group in four different languages. With much joking and laughter, each gave their name, country of origin, and a brief word about their journey.

As members of her group were introduced, Cindy mentioned meeting me online and that we were now best friends, leaving the room with the impression that we were travelling together. Leticia, the new owner of Cindy's second bed, stood up and shared that she was of Mexican descent (which explained her caramel colouring and compact size), but living in LA. She laughingly added that although she started alone, she had been adopted by "the group".

The last person to speak was Davina, the stout little red-head I had seen Angela consoling in the laundry area earlier that day. Pushing her thick, wire-framed glasses up her nose, the American woman stood up and introduced herself saying that she was making the journey as a tribute to her thirty-year-old son who had died four months ago. Voice wobbling with emotion, she said we should be thankful for our ability to do this trip and never take life for granted since we never knew what was ahead. Wow! Heavy words! True, but not quite what anyone was expecting. As she took her seat in the now silent room, strangers became friends, reaching over to give her shoulders comforting rubs.

Cold water on the party atmosphere, pilgrims pushed their chairs back and headed for their perspective beds. Among hushed conversations, I folded myself into my bunk, reflecting on the day, the people I had met, and wondering what tomorrow would bring.

My earplugs having abandoned me somewhere through the night, hushed whispers and quiet movements alerted me to the dawn. I had learned the hard way, not to choose a bed close to the bathroom. Many times through the night, the door slid open, light piercing my bunk before it was closed, and again when it was opened.

My socked feet hit the floor, and I realized that only women remained in the twenty-four-bed room. The men had all gallantly left us privacy to dress, an appreciated chivalry I would not see often on this journey. Dressing quickly and packing faster, I carried my pack outside, around the building, to the heavy front door, casting suspicious eyes at the gloomy skies. Inside, the early murmur of waking souls jostled with the jets of steam from the coffee machine. Given a choice of coffee or hot chocolate, I chose the milky hot chocolate, going for the extra milk protein. I took a thick wedge of crusty toast from a basket and spread it with butter and jam. I saw no cheese, nor eggs, nor cereal, so I chose another slice of toast, waving across the room at Cindy and her troupe who were just getting up to leave.

Having heard there were no facilities between here and Roncesvalles, I hit the ladies room one last time and walked out into a heavy mist. Leticia, hurriedly patting her dark curls in place, came running around the corner of the building and headed in for breakfast.

My pack, along with a colourful roll call of others, leaned against the rough wood wall, protected by the sloping overhang of the *albergue* roofline. Recognizing the wisdom in having my pack ported over the mountain but unable to sever myself completely from my load, I had transferred "essentials" into a daypack weighing about ten pounds. I'm such a control freak! If it were lost, I would have what I needed to survive until it was found; I would have what couldn't be replaced. At home, we operate on what we call the "umbrella principle". If you carry an umbrella, it will not rain. The more prepared you are for trouble, the less likely it will happen. So, in effect, by "protecting" myself, I was "protecting" the driver of the transport truck; it would not suddenly veer off the road, plummet down the side of the mountain, and burst into flames. Pretty good, hey? How powerful am I?

Cindy, Shirley, and a couple others from their group were adjusting poles and snaps, readying themselves for the climb ahead. Leticia burst out the door, dark eyes flashing angrily.

"They said I was too late for breakfast!" she muttered, angrily clutching her baguette sandwich for the day. "All I could get was coffee." Cindy reminded her the bags had to be at the front of the building in the next ten minutes for transport to Rocesvalles, or she would have to carry it, and Leticia ran off to grab her pack. From what I had seen of her in the last day, it seemed that things were going to be a bit more work for Leticia.

Once Leticia had dropped her pack by the wall, she joined our debate about suiting up for the rain. Cindy said being a west coast girl, she walked in this weather in the pants and jacket she was wearing all the time. I waffled between trying to suck it up as another "west coast girl" and caving in to using the bulky rain poncho weighing down my daypack. Cindy was still hurting from her back injury acquired in her last few days of training, and she said she was going to walk slowly. Shirley, dressed head to toe in upscale trekking gear said she would see us later, and strode off.

Within ten minutes of walking, the mist had worked itself into drizzle. To heck with this! I was not going to get soaked in the name of vanity. I may be a "west coast girl", but I also know when to come in out of the rain. Telling the others to go ahead, I shrugged off my daypack, pulled out my dreary poncho, and dragged it over my head, tugging the extended back over my pack. I looked a little like Quasimodo, but I would stay dry. I picked up my poles and walked on only to find the rest of the group, just around the bend, pulling out their ponchos. Smugly, I carried on, Leticia quickly falling into step beside me.

"Do you mind if I walk with you?" she asked. "It seems our pace is similar." I had the first unplanned partner of my journey.

We climbed the gravel track, winding our way around rocky hillsides, as the rain transformed into snow; how pretty! As we moved higher, the wind started to pick up, and the snow became hard needles of ice, driving itself into our eyes and any unprotected skin. Hmmm…ski goggles? Nope! I'm sure I didn't remember seeing them on the list of recommended equipment. Sunglasses would not work in this dismal lighting, so squinting against the snow and bending our heads against the wind, we pressed on. In white-out conditions, we barely made out pilgrim shadows below and above us; not so pretty now.

Suddenly, we rounded a curve to see a truck parked on the side of the track, its canvas awning flapping in the wind, but still providing shelter to the tables below. This Spanish farmer came up every day with his truck full of hard-boiled eggs, bananas, nuts, bread, cheese and, most importantly, hot chocolate. Leticia was all smiles, chatting with the man in Spanish, while I clutched the warmth of a cup of steaming hot chocolate. The wind threatened to rip the awning off the truck, but it held. More and more pilgrims arrived, crowding in for their turn under the shelter.

Just then, Cindy and Shirley walked in under the tarp. How did I end up ahead of Shirley? Cindy called out to me to wait, and she'd walk with me, but there was no room to wait under the tarp. They had reservations in Roncesvalles, but I did not, so I called out I needed to get going to make sure I got a bed. Leticia joined me after pocketing a wedge of cheese she had purchased from her new friend who assured her the cheese was made with his own hands, from his own cows…just this morning.

Upwards we climbed towards a rocky peak, the track narrowing to a path, barely discernable in the whirling snow. Buffeted by strong winds, when I raised my pole off the ground for the next step, it blew out sideways. I'm not a small woman, and I had extra weight in my pack, so I thought I could easily withstand a little wind, but this was pretty extreme. Crouching slightly to stay grounded in the loose rocks and gravel, I fought to stay my course, Leticia following in my footsteps.

I had read when choosing between this mountain route or the road route, pilgrims should heed the guidance of the locals who knew the tempestuous weather patterns of the Pyrenees. If there were concerns about the weather, they directed pilgrims to take the duller, but safer road route. While everyone hoped to cross the more picturesque mountain path, given what we were fighting through right now, I had to wonder at what point the locals would be concerned enough to divert pilgrims to the alternate route.

Up ahead, I saw a dark heap collapsed at the base of a fluorescent marker pole. As I approached, I discovered Davina, clinging to the pole for dear life. Like me, she had a small pack under her light poncho, which was flapping madly about her in the onslaught of the wind. I crouched down beside her, offering her my hand.

"No," she cried. "I can't do it! The wind is too strong, and I'm going to fall!" she screamed, eyeing the steep drops and forbidding crevices to either side.

"Let me help you. I am having trouble staying on course too. Let's do it together," I yelled over the howling wind. Seeing Leticia doggedly focused on her upward climb, I gently pried Davina's hands from the pole and helped her to stand, linking my arm through hers as we moved upwards. Adjusting my posture to accommodate her shorter height, we trudged our way up to the summit and over the ragged top. Miraculously, just as we started down the other side, the wind suddenly dropped off and the snow slowed to dancing swirls. We had been tested, and we had survived! Unlocking our arms, I stood back and helped Davina adjust her poncho.

"I'm okay now. Thanks," she smiled, recovering her composure. "I'm just going to rest a bit before I go on." I gave her a hug, told her to be safe, and fell in step with Leticia.

A short reprieve, the trail now wound along the edge of a valley, a rail on one side protecting us from the steep drop. We walked above the treetops, climbing steadily through heavy rain towards the highest summit, Col de Lepoeder (at 1450m). We found a small stone house stuffed with pilgrims taking a few minutes of refuge to rest and eat. I went around back to relive my complaining bladder, but the piles of waste left by previous pilgrims sent me scurrying back to the shelter. There was no room to sit, so everyone chomped their sandwiches as we stood. It was hard to drink in face of the cold, the wet, and my bulging bladder, but I knew it was important to rehydrate. As more pilgrims arrived, we left to make room, climbing up and up, knowing that when we reached the top, a steep, 500-metre drop lay ahead.

We came to a stone cross that I remember Esther mentioning back in St. Jean. She was very emphatic about staying to the right of the cross. A sign emblazoned with a huge exclamation mark put me in mind of the slopes my sons dragged me down on the ski hills back home. Strong, brave (or reckless) skiers, they couldn't understand why my face blanched at the sight of the terrain they wanted me to hurl my novice bones down.

I peered over the edge of the path indicated by a yellow arrow, and, glancing over at the gravel road that wound downwards from the cross, on the left, I walked over to join the discussion at the trail's head. We did not know where that road went; it might lead in a totally different direction, some argued. We started carefully down the steep gravel trail, using the encroaching bushes for extra support as we descended.

Coming around a sharp bend I saw Davina, collapsed in a sobbing puddle at the side of the trail. She must have walked past us when we stopped at the stone house. This was the first of many powerful spots on the Camino; a place where grieving parents would bury a memento of their child, asking blessings on their memory. Given the freshness of Davina's loss, this would already be an emotional marker on her journey. Her breakdown was amplified by her discovering a token left by a previous grieving pilgrim when she went to bury her own. She shared their pain without even knowing them. The connection of past to present was very profound and palpable.

Leticia asked what we should do. Having suffered extreme losses in my past, I recognized that grief needed a place to happen.

"The rain has stopped, it's only mid-day, and many more come behind us. Let's leave her to her grief. She is in a safe place, and she needs to do this." Leticia followed my lead uncertainly as we continued carefully down the rocky trail.

We came out through the bush onto…the nice, smooth road we had spurned above! This would not be the last time the maps and directions would fail me. We travelled, poles tapping, down the gentle slopes, finally coming out into a clearing in which an imposing stone monastery stood; Roncesvalles, the first major stop for Camino pilgrims for hundreds of years.

Leticia and I used the muck scraper to clear the mud from the bottom of our boots before entering a huge, arched hallway where we lined up with others in the reception area. A sign on the chest-high counter said "Please Remain Calm" in several different languages. The *hospitaleros* knew their clientele, tired, cold, wet, and anxious. The patient staff gently guided us through the process of purchasing a bed, selecting sittings for supper that night and breakfast the next morning, and collecting ported backpacks. The monastery and adjacent *albergue*/restaurant were equipped to accommodate 300 pilgrims. Having arrived fairly early in the day, we secured beds on the second floor and were directed to open-fronted cubicles of four. I was greeted by my bunk-mates, three of the cheerful British people I had already met in Orisson. Pushing my pack into the remaining locker against the end wall, I claimed the final top bunk and went in search of a shower.

Clean, warm, and dry, I reached the bottom of the wide, tiled stairs to see the line still winding its way around the reception counter. The air was thick with multi-national conversation, steaming damp clothes, and excitement at a big hurdle overcome.

While I waited for Leticia, I talked with one of the *hospitaleros*, a three-time volunteer from Sweden. Once having walked the Camino, many people return from all over the world for two-week periods, volunteering to assist new pilgrims. He told me their room and board were covered, but they were responsible for the costs of getting there and home.

"I am addicted to the excitement of the pilgrims," he said. "There is so much hope, but at this stage, there is a lot of doubt and confusion too. Anything we can do to encourage those on their journey helps. Sometimes it just takes a smile or hearing your own language."

There is no limit on how many people are on the Camino. It is a self-guided religious pilgrimage and people start almost every day of the year, even in the winter. I asked about all those still registering and what would they do if too many came. He said they had gotten to the point they had brought in truck containers and filled them with bunks. Everyone would find a bed tonight he confirmed with confidence. Then I saw Davina, bunk ticket in hand, coming out of the reception area.

"You made it!" I congratulated her with a gentle hug. She nodded, smiled happily, and dragged her tired little body up the stairs.

"I found someone to do my laundry!" Leticia crowed as she rounded the corner. Hair done, in full makeup and fresh clothes, she looked like a tourist at an alpine resort rather than in a centuries-old *albergue* full of exhausted pilgrims. "Yes, a woman told me you just take your laundry downstairs and the volunteers will wash and dry it for six euros. All my laundry will be clean!" Okay, let's remember we are only on day two of this journey. Obviously different things are important to different people, and different people have different comfort zones.

We strolled through the ancient high-ceilinged stone hallways, finding a common room where people were seated at industrial-styled tables, bent over guidebooks and sharing refreshments pulled from glossy vending machines. This was our second night without Wi-Fi (pronounced weefee by Europeans), so I was sure some people were going into withdrawals.

I hoped that at home, Al was not worried by our loss of contact. We had discussed the probability of not being able to connect in some of the more isolated locations. I was pretty sure I would be able to reach him in Zubiri tomorrow. Luckily there was still cell reception, and Leticia was able to use her Spain-enabled phone to make a reservation for us at an *albergue* in Zubiri. We could enjoy the rest of the evening knowing that modern technology had served us well within these historic walls.

We lined up at the dining room for our supper, hoping we would be done in time for mass. When the doors finally opened, we were seated based on our preference for fish, chicken, or vegetarian meals. Leticia and I ended up sitting with a couple from Holland. After a creamed vegetable soup, we were presented with a huge bowl of pasta served family style. I thought I'd said chicken, but obviously they had us at a vegetarian table. The server told us to keep our plates and silverware and returned with chicken and chips. So the pasta wasn't the main meal? I was confused. The Dutch woman was also confused. She said she had asked to be at a vegetarian table so now she was faced with no main course. I suggested she take the remaining pasta for herself. Leticia was also confused.

"We have to use the same dishes for different food?" She was appalled. Her North American roots were showing. Dessert was our choice of fruit, flan, or ice cream. Those who selected flan got a wobbly custard, those choosing ice cream got a Drumstick, and those choosing fruit got a banana.

The delay in the start of dinner meant we missed the start of mass, so we returned to the monastery in search of Leticia's fresh laundry. When the volunteers presented her with the folded pile she hugged the clothes happily. Up the stairs we trudged, saying goodnight at the corner that took us different ways, knowing we would meet again at breakfast.

Tucked into my bed, my bunkmates already snoring softly, I scrolled through my photos of home, remembering each person signified on my bracelet in prayer. I tucked into my sleeping bag, pulled the covers up to my chin, and said goodnight to the Camino.

In the middle of the night, I woke to the sound of snoring. It sounded like the woman below me was the culprit, but with my messed-up hearing, I was often confused as to the source of sounds. I eased myself down the side of the bunk and quietly crept down the softly lit hall to the washroom, hearing the even breathing of sleep, punctuated frequently by a snoring sleeper. Returning to bed, I noticed the patter of raindrops on the cold, dark windows along the corridor and, climbing back up into my bed, tucked in for a couple hours more sleep, hoping that the rain would stop by morning.

Complete chaos occurs when hundreds of people wake to the dawn with bathroom, breakfast, and departure in mind. The shouted whispers, as pilgrims tried to communicate with others without disturbing anyone left asleep, seemed louder than if they had just spoken. The rustling, snapping, zipping, clearing of throats, and scrunching of departing boots formed a morning symphony. In my bunk, I stuffed my sleeping liner into its bag, pulled off my leggings and wriggled into silk long underwear bottoms and then my pants. I changed my sleep shirt for this day's walking shirt, and, ever hopeful, covered my face with moisturizing sunscreen. I massaged Vaseline in between my toes and around my heel and carefully peeled my seamless socks over my feet. This process would quickly become my new morning routine on the Camino.

Around me, the Brits, a fiftyish married couple and their female friend, chatted brightly, each jokingly accusing the other of snoring. They passed items back and forth as they distributed the weight of their belongings between their packs. It was close quarters, and we danced around each other as we gathered equipment and pulled on outer wear. They cheerfully waved as they went to find the rest of their group.

Pack over one shoulder, poles in hand, I descended the wide stairs to find Leticia, hair done and make-up on, tying her boots. We had first seating for breakfast and walked through the morning drizzle to the picturesque restaurant. There, we joined the crowd of pilgrims waiting impatiently for the doors to open. Our first lesson in "Spanish time": 7:00 does not necessarily mean 7:00.

The wait gave me time to look around and appreciate the small, stone chapel across the way. I regretted I hadn't made it to evening mass and determined to make a better effort in the future. Mountains looming in the background, the walkway back to the monastery where I'd slept was lined with knobby, leafless trees looking like rows of sentries standing guard.

When the restaurant doors opened, we surged inside, backpacks colliding, more in a rush to get going than in a rush to eat. We were told to line up and one by one we were given the hot drink of our choice (coffee, tea, or hot chocolate packets) which we carried past the crowded waiting line, to trestle tables in an adjoining room. There, plates of lightly toasted bread and commercial packets of jam waited us as our breakfast. I looked around for eggs or cheese, but there were none to be found. This was disappointing given that we had a twenty-two-kilometre walk including a steep descent ahead. Some grumbled at the time it took to get a cup of coffee, an inefficient process that could have been streamlined by carafes on the tables next to the pitchers of water and juice. Maybe this was part of our Camino education to slow down, be patient, and leave the rush of our home lives behind.

Knowing that our being seated late meant the second round of pilgrims were waiting for their breakfast, we ate quickly, gulped down our coffee, and headed out. Under leaden skies, Leticia and I posed for a photo at a sign proclaiming Santiago was 790 kilometres away. Our smiles belied how daunting that felt, or perhaps spoke more of ignorant bliss. In her trendy plaid jacket, sunglasses, and gloves, Leticia resembled an alpine skier who'd lost her skis.

Leticia, having ported her backpack to Zubiri, took the lead as we walked down a mushy, tree-lined lane. We came to a small, neat town where each doorway had a stone slab drawbridge under which the street's storm water ran. Some pilgrims, either better informed or luckier than us, stopped to have a hot breakfast, paying much the same price we had for cold toast; lesson learned.

We walked out of the town, down a muddy trail beside pastures where half a dozen large brown horses with creamy manes grazed. Ahead on the path, an elderly man was accosting the pilgrims, smiling and cheering them on their way. When we got to him, he grabbed my hand and planted a kiss, intended for my lips, but with a quick turn of my head, landing on my cheek. He babbled on excitedly in Spanish and laughing, I gently pulled my hand away. Leticia felt pretty smug that she had dodged this ancient Casanova. I just smiled and fell in behind her again, feeling foolish and touched in equal parts.

Coming to a bubbling stream, we carefully crossed on blocks set in the water as a contrived bridge. I looked down at my boots on a block and saw them totally surrounded by rushing water. On through the quiet countryside we walked, taking in the gentle foothills rising up into imposing heights. White dots in the distance were identified as sheep, and I admired their ability to graze peacefully on the steep slopes.

After passing through two Sunday-silent towns devoid of people, we found a walled cemetery. Leticia stopped to take a photo telling me that she was in the funeral business herself. She said that she met with wealthy families to arrange plots and services, so it was very important to be and look very professional. This explained her concern for clothes, hair, and make-up.

"I was starting to have trouble at work so they decided, since my previous work was so valuable, that they would send me on a paid leave to recover myself, so here I am. I have been to Spain before and loved it, and I thought I could just do this walk and then spend a few days in Barcelona before going back to work. Maybe I will meet someone along the way." Surprisingly considerate employers, I thought.

On we walked, me leaning forward to counterbalance the weight of my pack as we started to climb a steep grade of corrugated cement. The man-made path turned into a forest trail, winding up and around the mountains.

It was warm, despite the clouds, and Leticia and I decided to stop for a picnic. She had been complaining about her feet and her back hurting, and this seemed like a good chance for recovery time. Plunking herself down on the grass beside the path, she removed her boots and socks and wriggled her toes in the cool air. As good as that looked, I decided that since my feet would have swollen with the work, taking my boots off for a rest might lead to difficulty getting them back on. We pooled our food, enjoying bread, nuts, and cheese. I was anxious to get going, but she stubbornly maintained that she needed at least a half an hour to rest.

Leaning back on my pack I resigned myself to wait, and I chatted with pilgrims as they passed. Suddenly, a small German shepherd bearing two saddlebags appeared. Surie's parents, a young Spanish couple, told us she was just a year old and that she was packing her own bowls, food, and water. Having a dog along on the trail was a challenge sometimes as most *albergues* did not accommodate pets, and they often had to seek private accommodation. The tall, young man patted the huge pack on his back and joked that if all else failed, they had a tent and would sleep outside with their dog. A few pats and wags of her tail and they were off. I wondered how Kirby would feel about an 800-kilometre walk.

Biting into the creamy cheese she passed me, Leticia shared the story of the loss of her husband just over a year ago. He had been a little older than her, and she was his princess. She brushed away a threatening tear as she explained how she was making a new life for herself in their home in California, declining her family's invitation to return to their fold in Mexico. She did not want to be alone for the rest of her life and was open to a new relationship. I assured her that fifty-three was not too late to start again and told her of the loss of my first husband and my remarriage, with teenaged boys in the picture, in my early forties. I said I hadn't gone looking. Love, in the shape of an old friend, had just found me. I considered myself blessed to have had the love of two good men.

Finally, Leticia consented to put her boots back on, and we were back on the path. Since she was a few years younger than me and wasn't carrying her pack, I was concerned about the constant whining (*let's call it what it was*) about her feet and her back. I wasn't sure how much further she could go and how much further I could stand going with her! I started to wonder if she really couldn't go on, here in the middle of nowhere, what I would do. Oh! There it is! I had taken on the responsibility for the well-being and safety of another person, just like I always did in life. I reminded myself this trip was supposed to free me from that habit.

Crossing another roadway, we came to a truck serving refreshments. Patti and Theresa were already there and commented on the good time we were making. We were pretty much keeping up with them. Was that a dig about our age? I decided to take it as a compliment.

As Leticia purchased her bottle of orange juice, I shared my concerns about her. Just then a van pulled up, and the driver was talking to another couple about a ride down to Zubiri.

"Oh," said Patti, "you'd better keep Leticia away from him or you'll be walking alone!" she joked. Finishing my lemonade and banana, I crossed over to Leticia who was reading a sign over a box of underwear. "If you leave a piece of your underwear here, you will find your true love by the end of the Camino." I smiled at Leticia. She just smirked back at me.

Then we came to the steep descent indicated in our guidebook with a bright red exclamation point. The going was tough, and there was a bit of a conga line as people slowed to get down safely. Leticia, moving cautiously ahead of me had started a conversation with a tall British man from the group we met in Orisson. As he chatted her along, she was all smiles and moving well. I smiled to know he was basically talking her down, distracting her totally from all her bodily complaints. Fine with me; whatever it takes!

Behind me, Davina had appeared. With her shorter legs, she struggled to make the long strides needed to get from one solid footing to another. The terrain put me in mind of a dried-up creek bed; all loose rock and gravel. The larger rocks' smooth surfaces were slick with a greasy mud courtesy of the previous night's rain. I just finished telling Davina to take it slow, not rush, and be careful when down I went! I landed hard on my right knee but was able, with the help of my poles, to stop a complete fall. I assured my fellow pilgrims I was okay. My layers of long underwear, hiking pants and the bonus of the taping my physiotherapist did just before I left had cushioned my fall and saved my knee, but not my pride. I gathered myself up and continued the downward trek, meeting up with Leticia at the bottom.

There, the trail opened out on to a country road leading past a pasture of big-eyed cows, into the town of Zubiri. We crossed the bridge and made our way to our *albergue*. Arriving just before the 3:00 deadline (when they can give away reserved beds), we were quickly registered, had our pilgrim's passports stamped, deposited our boots and poles in the racks, and climbed to the second floor. With our electronic pass card (seeming incongruent in this ancient hostel), we accessed the first door, passed through a bunkroom of twenty beds, and into our room of ten more. Gone was her effervescence of the descent with our charming British *compadre*. Leticia collapsed on a bottom bunk with a groan, and I slid my pack up onto the bunk above her.

Leaving her to recover, I delighted in the hot, forceful shower that washed sweat and fatigue from my body. With no one else waiting, I took the opportunity to wash my underwear and shirt, wringing them out in my quick dry towel. Downstairs I found a door off the great room that led to a breezy lawn where clothes hung on racks, drying in the sun.

"You can put your things here," a sandy-haired man offered as he adjusted his glasses and pushed a pair of grey wool socks further down the rack. "There is still room on this rack. I'm Ian, by the way," he continued with a friendly British accent. Ian looked to be about fifty, slim in build and average in height. "I'm used to hiking, but that was some descent," he added. "Hard to keep your footing on all that loose shale."

After introducing myself, I confessed my fall and quickly assured Ian I hadn't been hurt; just embarrassed. As I added my things to the rack, he asked if I was walking alone. I told him about Leticia and that she was finding the going a challenge and was upstairs resting.

"Well I'll see you out there," he smiled, and I went back inside.

Back upstairs, the first bunkroom was fragrant with the smell of analgesic cream. One of the British ladies was vigorously rubbing it into the calves of her friend who purred with ecstasy.

"She's a nurse you know," she groaned, jerking her thumb at her masseuse. Thinking this type might be better than the one I carried, I asked to see what type of cream she was using and took a photo of it for future reference, leaving them to their friendly therapy.

I passed through to the second bunkroom and found Leticia still in bed. I asked her how she was doing.

"You know," she said, "I don't think I can do this. My feet and legs hurt so bad. I'm thinking about taking a bus." Again, I wondered why she was feeling so badly. She hadn't even carried a pack. The terrain, while challenging, hadn't been as bad as the previous day's. Maybe it was all catching up with her. I told her to give me her feet, and as she poked them out from under her sleeping bag, I took each one in turn, applied a little analgesic cream from my pack, and gently massaged it into her sore tootsies. She sighed with pleasure and then piped up.

"You know, what I'm going to do is set my phone to ring every two hours and then, no matter what, I'm going to stop, take my boots off and rest for a half an hour." I paused in my ministrations. Not exactly what I had in mind. My goal was to do this trek as spontaneously as possible. Go until I got tired, stop when I'd had enough. While my naive approach would succumb to reality later in the journey, I would not allow my Camino to be programmed by technology. For now, I would walk with Leticia, but I vowed that if I felt my walk was being controlled by her needs, I would continue alone.

"We can eat here so you don't have to walk anywhere for dinner. We just have to make a reservation and pay for it now. The menu looks good; a little pricy at thirteen euros, but okay." We were already paying fifteen euros for our beds (including breakfast), and I was getting very close to my thirty euro per day budget limit. "If you want, I can go take care of it, and you can rest until supper."

I was torn between frustration (*why am I babying her…she should be stronger than this, she's younger than me*) and concern (*I hope she's able to continue*) and guilt (*am I only concerned about her because her Spanish is helpful*). I took our money down, made arrangements for supper, and went outside into the sunshine to keep company with the laundry drying in the breeze.

I had Wi-Fi connection finally, so, my hard-working toes toasting in the sun, I quickly sent off some messages to Al, bringing him up to speed on my journey. I tried to find the balance between letting him know the reality of the challenge so far and not alarming him. It would be so good to hear his voice, but I knew I had limited minutes for that, so I decided to wait until I really needed to talk to him. I settled for typed words and looking at his photo. Swallowing powerful emotions, I took my warm, folded laundry upstairs, to roust Leticia out of bed.

"I feel so much better now," she sighed, towelling her unruly curls. Pulling a small mirror from her bag, she sat on her bottom bunk as I perched on the small table between the bunks. I watched as she applied moisturizer and dusted her eyelids with shadow. Thick lashes made mascara unnecessary, so with a smear of lip gloss and a quick brush of her hair, she was ready to face the world.

"I was thinking while I was in the shower. If I continue tomorrow, I may not be able to go the rest of the way, so this is what we're going to do." *Oh, so now she's ready to take charge.* "We will look for an *albergue* in Pamplona and book it tonight. Then, tomorrow I will take the bus there. You can come with me or walk as you choose. I will be there holding our space either way. I will decide there what I will do next. Maybe with rest, I will be fine. This is the only way I think I can go on."

It was a workable plan. She could do the Camino her way, I could do the Camino my way, and we could still explore Pamplona together in the evening. Reservation made, we went down the stairs for dinner.

In the dining room, I waved to Ian across the room as I was directed to a chair between two tall men at the back trestle table. Leticia was seated across from me between a young Asian girl and a tall, skinny, black-haired boy. Josh and Pete, sitting on either side of me, were healthy specimens of American early retirement.

They were neighbours back in California, combining their love of walking with their love of wine as they left their wives behind and toured northern Spain via the Camino. They teased Lisa, to the left of Leticia, about how hard it was to keep up with her pace, and Benjamin, to the right, smiled sheepishly admitting to the challenge. Lisa chatted happily with no trace of an accent and shared that she had been going to school in the US for the past four years.

We were served traditional appetizers, followed by creamed vegetable soup before a main course of tasty pork ribs and potato slices. This would be the last potato that didn't look like a French fry that I would have for the next three weeks. The generous abundance of *vino tinto* (red wine) led to lots of laughter, some singing, and boisterous toasting in a myriad of languages. Leticia became quite the life of the party as she joined Spanish salutes and her lively eyes sparkled with the playful conversations. Josh and Pete smiled at her obvious enjoyment and glances were exchanged between them. Oh, I thought, two more conquests to add to her belt. Well she was looking for love, and they were grown up men, so not my place to judge.

Finishing a wonderful tiramisu, we were just leaving the dining room when I ran into Patti and Theresa. "The group is all over the place," they mourned. "Some people couldn't get a room here and were told they could sleep on the floor in the school gymnasium. Others took a taxi and went on to Larrasoana to try to find beds there. Cindy and Shirley still haven't come in as far as anyone knows. We're staying at another *albergue* but heard the food was really good here." I assured them it was well worth the price and thanked the fates that brought us here early enough to get beds.

As everyone filed away, I saw Pete in the corner, working on a small laptop. Not quite ready to haul myself up onto my top bunk, I accepted his invitation to join him. Turns out he was an "IT" guy back in the States and had all sorts of information about electronic gadgets. I asked him a couple of questions about my cellphone, embarrassedly explaining I had only had it a couple of months. Pete seemed to enjoy introducing me to aspects of my phone I hadn't realized, and we spent a friendly half hour exploring options before the lights dimmed, signalling lights-out time approached.

Walking through the first bunkroom, still fragrant with medicinal rub, I whispered good night to one of my English friends who was reading by flashlight.

In my darkened bunkroom, Leticia, earplugs in, eye mask on, was breathing softly, already fast asleep. I moved the towel she had hung to dry away from the ladder and climbed the narrow rungs to my second-storey sleeping place. I remembered the heavy black beam I had seen earlier in the day and took care as it was directly above my bed. Tucked safely in my sleeping bag without concussion, I fell quickly and deeply into sleep.

Sometime through the night, tossing and turning I heard a "plop" and realized my pillow had just dropped off the end of the bunk. Now what? It was dark, and everyone was sleeping. Tapping my cellphone for a quick burst of light, I negotiated the beam and carefully climbed down the ladder. Crawling to the head of Leticia's sleeping form, I gingerly reached between the head of her bed and the wall and retrieved my runaway pillow. I crept back up on my bed, refusing my body's request for the bathroom. My pillow firmly under my arm, I drifted off to sleep until a variety of electronic alarms and groans signalled the end of slumber for this day.

My pillow behaved itself for the rest of the night, and I climbed off my bunk well rested. Leticia was still snuggled down in her covers while the rest of the room came alive with dressing, packing, and leaving.

Down in the breakfast room, I joined a table and enjoyed a quick breakfast of coffee, toast, and jam. Leticia, padded into the room, the only one not dressed for the road, and despite my friendly smile, took a seat with a different group of pilgrims. Draining my cup, I waved goodbye, grabbed my poles, and started off for Pamplona on my own.

Crossing the bridge out of the town, I came across the Brits I'd met the first day in Orisson. We'd shared rooms for three nights. Most of them were only travelling as far as Logrono this time and would return with their pilgrim passports next spring to complete another segment of the Camino. One couple hoped to make it as far as Burgos this year, and another were hoping to go the whole way. With limited holidays and the proximity of Spain, many Europeans choose to walk the Camino a bit at a time, a method that may be easier on bodies as well as bank accounts.

Climbing up through the outskirts of Zubiri, buildings became fewer and then non-existent as I followed a narrow track between a thick forest and wide, green pastures punctuated with nodding sheep and colourful blooms. A babbling brook kept me company as I walked. From time to time, I stepped to the side while faster pilgrims passed by, cheerfully calling out "*Buen Camino*" as they went.

An hour later, I came upon the picturesque town of Larrasoana and couldn't resist the pull of the water. I plunked my pack down on a grassy shoulder overlooking the sparkling river that cascaded over man-made terraces, as it poured out from beneath the arched stone bridge. Mindless of the pedestrian traffic passing behind me, I laid back against my pack, enjoying the warmth of the sun and the sound of the rushing water as I munched on some bread and swigged water from my bottle. A big, shaggy, black and white dog sauntered over to greet me until a whistle from his owner called him back.

I watched the town go about its business on the other bank of the river. A young woman hung freshly laundered sheets from her balcony. Laughing children playfully threw stones in the water as they ran. A man in a slope cap and with rolled-up shirt sleeves was delivering bread from a huge basket to waiting housewives. A store proprietor in a bibbed apron rearranged his display of fruit and vegetables. Two old men sat on a bench in the sun, leaning on their canes and smoking their pipes, a dog resting peacefully at their feet. It was an idyllic scene that invited me to stay, but Pamplona called.

In my languorous stupor I had lost track of the route. Maybe I needed to go back to the stone bridge and cross over into the town, but this way sure didn't look right. Summoning courage to try out some of my survival Spanish, I stopped two passing pre-teen girls in school uniforms.

"*Disculpe, donde esta el Camino por favor?*" With giggles (I'd like to think they were just happy, not laughing at my efforts), they erupted into a rapid set of instructions that included much waving of hands in the direction of the green, metal foot bridge ahead. Back to the smile and nod process I defaulted.

"*Gracias,*" and over the bridge I went. Once in town, I had my choice of following signs to Pamplona (a bit risky since they are meant for motorists) or following backpacks ahead, with the hope they knew where they were going. I chose the backpacks and was quickly through the town and off again into the lush, green countryside.

As I walked, I spotted a lone female pilgrim sunbathing by the side of a river in the picnic area near Zabalkika. It looked very inviting, but I followed the yellow arrows across the bridge, up the hill, and along a narrow trail paralleling the park below. I noticed a paved road fronting the picnic tables and looked longingly at the outhouses interspersed among the trees. The side of the hill was thick with bushes and very steep, so I decided not to risk a fall for the sake of a toilet.

Funny thing is I thought toilets would be a big issue, but it seemed as much as I had to drink, with the heat and the work, I didn't feel the need to go as often as I did at home. It was frustrating seeing smooth, flat road below while plodding along the loose gravel track, dodging scratches from the encroaching growth. Then, the trail led downhill to that same road!

A little ways down the road, the insistent yellow arrows directed me back up the hill. But miracle of miracles, there in the middle of nowhere, was a concrete building with a flush toilet inside, and toilet paper, and a sink, and paper towels! I wasn't going to pass this up.

Out in the sunshine, I was alone back on the trail, taking in all the vivid greens of the fields and the trees and the crops waving gently in the breeze. The quiet surrounded me and uplifted me so that my steps fell softly despite the weight on my back. It was an easy place to remember my family and friends at home in prayer.

Entering Burlada, I was only about three kilometres from Pamplona, but the distance proved to be busy and confusing. With a lack of signage or backpacks to follow, I searched through squares of dining Spaniards and streets of noisy traffic, looking for some direction on where to go. Finally, I stopped a pair of matronly women with string shopping bags over their arms and heavy shoes on their feet.

"*Disculpe, estoy perdido.*" I shared my predicament. I didn't even have to ask about the Camino. Perhaps the pack on my back gave me away? They pointed down the road holding up two fingers and then gesturing that I should turn left. I thanked them, and following their directions, was relieved to see the familiar yellow arrow. And then there, just up the road, more backpacks!

I crossed a bridge and winded my way along a path around the outer wall of Pamplona's old quarter. Before me, an ancient drawbridge led into the city. I was impressed with the orderliness of the cobblestone streets. Everything was neat and tidy and well kept. Grill-covered storefronts displayed a variety of hiking equipment and souvenirs. Wrought iron signs hung above colourful doors offered massages and foot specialists.

The *hospitaleros* welcomed me at the *Albergue Plaza Catedral*, and advised me that Leticia had already paid the fifteen euros to guarantee my bed. After stamping my passport, they showed me where to drop my boots and led me upstairs to a bright, modern corridor of bunks in sets of four. An unknown Asian girl was snoring softly in one top bunk, and Leticia was sound asleep below her.

My bunk was the lower one across from hers, and I was pleased to see it came equipped with a private reading light and my own plug for recharging my cellphone. This would be the second of three private *albergues* that Leticia had booked for us (her Spanish coming in very handy), and while it was good to know I had a bed waiting and they were well equipped, the higher-priced *albergues* were wreaking havoc on my budget. After tomorrow's stay in Puenta de la Reina, I would have to take my chances and insist on staying in the more affordable municipal *albergues*.

When I returned renewed from my shower, Leticia was awake, all smiles, talking to a tall, young man who was hobbling painfully on bandaged feet.

"The doctor says he must stay two days to rest," she translated for the young

Argentinean. "He has torn a ligament and needs to heal. He will stay here an extra day and then bus to Estella to stay on track." With *albergues*, you could only stay one night unless you were injured and a medical person recommended you rest.

Down in the lobby I said I found it surprising; this was the second young, athletic person I had met with serious injuries. The *hospitalero* advised it was not unusual that the young fall.

"They think they are invincible, and they run where they should walk. Those with older bones take more care."

Being in a city with a population cresting 200,000, and plenty of shopping opportunities, Pamplona challenged my budget. Knowing if I bought it, I had to pack it, I held back. I was determined, however, to get t-shirts for my grandchildren in Pamplona.

The main tourist attraction here is the running of the bulls, an event that happens in mid-July. The fiestas were originally celebrated in honour of San Fermin, the patron saint of Navarra, but the religious aspect has somewhat lost ground to partying and fun. From the corral in Calle Santo Domingo, men race, in mixed parts of bravery and foolishness, before the charging bulls, through the barricaded streets to the bullring. This event is celebrated in a myriad of souvenirs, and Leticia helped me select tiny, bull emblazoned t-shirts for each of my grandchildren. Then we selected postcards and headed off looking for the post office to mail them home.

Despite Pamplona's size, being in the old town was very relaxing. We sauntered along sunlit stone-arched breezeways, crossing squares surrounded by tall, narrow, ice cream coloured buildings with wrought iron balconies and trailing flower boxes. Pearl-coloured pigeons fluttered to the ground and, just as suddenly, took flight again. Small, well-dressed children scampered happily along, miniatures of their cosmopolitan parents. Heels, pencil skirts and bangles, cardigans, tasselled loafers and sleek hairstyles; they seemed from another world. Where were the jeans and hoodies and sneakers of young families I knew back home? Monks, real sandal-shod monks, in homespun robes with ropes for belts, strode the wide plazas, hands tucked across their chests up opposing sleeves. Elderly couples tottered along with lacquered canes, the men in slope caps and suit coats, their ladies in twin sets and sensible shoes. This was a people-watching paradise.

We finally found the post office, a huge, imposing edifice with heavy doors at the top of wide, stone stairs. Inside it was all business; flashing signals and intercom announcements.

"Please take a number and wait your turn. Please proceed to station number..." What a difference from the Renaissance world outside the door. On one side of the high-ceilinged room, there was a station just for boxing items pilgrims had purchased or found too much to carry from their packs. If by now, you realized you were carrying too much weight, Pamplona was the first opportunity to send it home, or on to Santiago to wait your arrival. Postcards stamped and gone, we escaped back out into the sunshine.

The options for supper were overwhelming as street after street offered restaurants, bars, ice cream and chocolate shops, bakeries, and specialty grocery stores. We finally chose a tapas bar. For ten euros, we each had a large glass of robust red wine and shared a selection of four tapas; large concoctions of bread, cheese, prosciutto, seafood, and grilled vegetables. Sufficiently fed, we traced our way back, stopping at a *mercado* (market) to get provisions for tomorrow's walk.

Back at the *albergue*, Leticia loaned me one of her shawls to cover my bare arms, and we walked over to the cathedral for evening mass. Inside the dark, cavernous cathedral, we found places on polished benches. I reminded Leticia that I wasn't Catholic and didn't understand much Spanish so I was relying on her for cues for when to stand and when to sit. She smiled and directed my attention to a procession of parishioners following a chanting priest, responding to his chants with songs of their own.

"They are singing the rosary," she advised. It was very calming, very beautiful, and even though I didn't understand the words or the theology, I was moved to tears. Once everyone reached the front and was seated, the priest moved to the altar and gave a blessing. Then everyone got up to go. That was it? Even Leticia seemed confused. Maybe we missed the beginning. Maybe the time was different on weeknights. Still, I was happy to have had the chance to experience this new type of service, and we shuffled out into the fading evening sunshine.

Back at our bunks we found the Asian girl still asleep. In hushed tones, I thanked Leticia for coming ahead and giving me the security of knowing my bed was waiting. I was able to take my time and fully appreciate the day. I shared with her how peaceful it was and how at ease I felt even when I got lost. I told her I was glad that choosing the bus today meant she was ready to walk again in the morning. As we packed, she advised that since we had reservations at our next stop, she was sending her pack ahead, taking only the small messenger bag she had purchased that day in Pamplona.

Tomorrow there would be a significant climb and an equally challenging descent, so sleep was in order. We hugged goodnight and snuggled into our bunks behind the privacy of our towels hung to dry from the bunks above. I drifted off to sleep to the sound of repetitive pings of a cellphone in the next bunk set. It reminded me to make sure my sound was off when I went to bed.

After a breakfast of yogurt and granola in the common kitchen, Leticia and I were out the door. It was a little confusing finding the markers in the maze of the old quarter, and we lost a little time with a false start in the wrong direction. We left the old city behind us, quickly transitioning into a modern world. High rises and traffic signals, directional signs and billboards, we could have been in any North American city.

"You don't have to wait for me you know." Leticia was in tourist mode, stopping to look in store windows.

"Okay," I replied. "I just want to get over that big climb before it gets too hot. We have to go up about 350 metres and that just puts us at the halfway point for our day."

"That is today?" she asked wide-eyed with surprise. Now she realized my motivation, and she fell quickly in step beside me. Following pewter shells embedded in the wide sidewalks, we crossed a four-lane road and walked along the edge of the university gardens. The shells gave way to yellow arrows as we walked through the suburbs of the city.

The temperature climbing rapidly, I stopped to take off my coat and tuck it in my backpack. Leticia, unencumbered by a pack, was not feeling the heat the way I was, and she continued on without me. As I replaced my water bottle in its pouch, I watched her plaid jacket and bright gold "Pamplona" pack pulling ahead up the road. At first, I was confused and a little hurt by her not waiting, but then I reminded myself that I had intended to walk alone, and how much I had enjoyed doing so yesterday. I relaxed into the cadence of my walk, poles swinging rhythmically before me in the warm Spanish sun.

Leaving Pamplona behind, I joined a file of pilgrims wending our way through waist-high fields. I met an older couple from France who, like me, had stopped to admire the ruins of an old building surrounded by a field of bright yellow. Not sure of the crop, the colour itself was uplifting. I trekked on up the hill, catching glimpses of Leticia's similarly gold daypack. I stopped to take pictures wondering if it was even possible to capture these colours, or if it was my heart that was creating their intensity. On the hills above, I saw tiny white windmills that would become giant as I reached the top of the mountain.

Climbing the gentle slope out of the valley, I reached a sidewalk café at Cizur Menor. I saw Leticia in animated conversation with two men, gave her a wave, and went inside to get coffee. From behind, a slim, pleasant-faced bespectacled man tapped my shoulder. It was Ian, the man from England I had met while doing laundry in Zubiri. He suggested I try a *café cortoda* instead of the regular *café con leche*.

"It's a short coffee; less milk and very intense if you like strong coffee. I think the fellas behind the bar get tired of making the same drinks over and over, and it seems they do a really good job of something different." I needed that caffeine boost, but I didn't want a lot of liquid (the bathroom shortage issue in mind) so I agreed to try it, and he called out an order for two to the smiling barista.

While we waited, Ian told me he had started his walk the day after me. He had gone all the way from St. Jean to Roncesvalles in one day. His goal was to get to Santiago by the end of the month. Impressive! Accepting the tiny cup of coffee, I pulled out my wallet, but Ian had already handed over the money.

"My treat. See you later," he smiled as he took his coffee over to a shady table by the wall. I joined Leticia in the sun.

Leticia, her shades perched on her head, introduced me to her new friends from Italy who were just pulling on their packs. "*Buen Caminos*" all around, and they were on their way.

"Beautiful country!" I said. "What a great walk through all those fields. I met a really nice couple from France, and we stopped to take photos among all the canola blooms. Someone else thought it might be mustard, but we weren't sure. This is a great little coffee," I commented as I watched her apply her lip gloss. Not much into conversation, or maybe wanting to catch up with the Italians, she pulled on her daypack and tapped off. *Okay, so was she mad, or what was happening here? I didn't do this trip to get all caught up in somebody else's drama,* I silently stated to her retreating back.

As I finished my coffee, Cindy and another woman with blunt red hair, collapsed on chairs at an adjacent table, wiping sweat from their faces.

"Hey, how are you doing? I asked. "I haven't seen you since Roncesvalles." Cindy told me that her back injury had really been giving her trouble, and that she'd slowly, but surely been separated from the rest of her group except for Anne-Marie. I hadn't remembered meeting the French-Canadian nurse before. Cindy went on to say she and Shirley had arrived quite late and spent the night on the cold concrete gym floor in Zubiri. Feeling really sore the next morning, they opted to take the bus to Pamplona and spent the day exploring the city. Shirley had decided to stay an extra day, so Cindy and Anne-Marie started out this morning without her.

Cindy continued, saying Patti and Theresa were staying in hotels all the way, and she had no idea where they were right now. She'd also lost track of Angela. There were a lot of conversations and questions flying between all the group's cellphones, and it seemed to me a chaotic way to do what was meant to be a reflective journey. I wished them luck and shouldered my pack, eyes focused on the windmills atop the hill before me.

As I climbed, I stopped to take a video for Al of the soft, rustling grasses, rippling like ocean waves in the wind. I wished he could see all this beauty for himself and was determined to bring Spain home to him. I overtook Leticia, tapping her way along, now in the company of Ian. Not wanting to interrupt their conversation, I tucked my chin against the building wind, pulled down my cap against the glowing sun, and worked my way up the hill, a solitary soul in a string of pilgrims.

Reaching the 790-metre summit of Alto Del Perdon, I was greeted by a procession of wrought-iron medieval pilgrims, their heads, like mine, bent against the strong wind. The sculpture's inscription, translated as *"where the way of the wind crosses the way of the stars"*, seemed very appropriate as I struggled to hold onto my hat while taking Leticia's photo. We were atop a long mountain ridge with mammoth white, wind turbines, like candles on a birthday cake, stretching out in both directions. Enjoying a water break, below in the valley we had come from, I saw the sprawling city of Pamplona as well as the little hamlets we had passed along the way. Vast fields of green were interspersed with others of brilliant yellow, providing a patchwork feast of colour for our eyes.

Leticia introduced me to Ian, and I told her we'd already met, and thanked him again for the coffee.

"You enjoyed it then?" he asked. I nodded as the three of us fell into step and began the steep descent to the valley on the other side of the ridge. Although we had shared the company of a number of pilgrims at the rest stop, we seemed pretty much on our own as we gingerly picked our way down the loose gravel trail. That is how it happens on the Camino; you're with a group, you go around a corner, and you're alone. All it takes is stopping to take a photo or retie a boot and you might not see a walking partner for days.

Leticia was telling us how when she arrived from Mexico she had learned English by watching television. We talked of favourite shows, specifically British comedies. I asked Ian if he was familiar with the *Vicar of Dibley*, and we launched into laughing descriptions of our favourite episodes. Leticia, who didn't know the series, brought up the rear.

The light bantering helped us down the hillside in the oppressive heat and the discussion turned to our favourite drinks. Then lo and behold! There was a bar! The shady patio beckoned, and Ian said he was going to stop for a beer, inviting us to join him. I'd noted a bit of a connection developing between my younger walking partners and I didn't think they needed an "old married lady" along. I checked the guidebook and said we still had a good hour's walk to go, so I suggested they stay and I'd go ahead and check us in at the *albergue* so we didn't lose our beds. Without much convincing, they sauntered off down the path, and I struck out for Puente La Reina alone.

Entering the bustling town of Puente La Reina along a tree-shaded roadway, I saw no sign of the bridge after which Puente La Reina (Bridge of the Queen) is named. It was constructed in the eleventh century at the request of a prominent lady, however as with many things in Spain, there are differing stories as to exactly who she was. The six-arched bridge was built to facilitate pilgrims on their journey to Santiago. It used to have three defensive towers, with the central one housing the Renaissance image of the Virgin del Puy, also known as the *Txori* (little bird in Basque). A charming local legend tells of a little bird who visited the image, using its wings to dust away cobwebs and washing its face with water collected from the River Arga.

I walked through the maze of roads, dodging traffic and searching for the *Albergue Puente*. Finally, as the 3:00 deadline approached, I desperately confronted one of its 3,500 inhabitants, and the smiling Spaniard set me on the right path. In through the door to the tinkle of the chimes, I was greeted by a friendly young woman. I happily handed over my passport and explained that my roommate was still coming, walking behind me. Leticia had paid in Pamplona, so I paid for both beds and made my way up to the third floor to the luxurious bliss of a semi-private room with two real beds.

After a quick shower and changing into sandals and shorts, I locked our door and went to explore the *albergue*. On a lovely, rooftop oasis, pilgrims lounged on cushioned chaise lounges ingeniously built of wooden shipping pallets. White shade canvas, strung from the roofline to garden rafters, rippled like sails in the warm breeze. Peeking over the rail, I saw the tree-lined boulevard fronted by all sorts of storefronts, *albergues*, and sidewalk eateries, preparing to serve the needs of their pilgrim customers.

When I ducked back inside to check out the laundry, I was suddenly accosted by a petite woman wearing a plaid cotton shirt and a short black hiking skirt over black leggings, her pink painted toes peeking out of trekking sandals. It was as if I should know her. She certainly seemed to know me, or was she just this comfortable with everyone?

"Do you want to share laundry?" she asked without preamble, tucking her long, straight, greying hair behind her tiny, elfin ears. "I'm doing laundry. I don't have too much, but I just want to wash some things. There's room for more if you want. If you don't, that's alright." Her words, spoken in a slow, soft drawl flowed effortlessly in a steady stream, and I wondered what part of the southern States she was from. I struggled to remember her name.

"It's Patricia, Patricia from Tucson. Tucson, Arizona," she clarified, her silver-grey eyes shining with uncanny perception of my confusion. I told her I was sorry I hadn't remembered her name. "It's alright," she said, "we meet so many people, it's hard to keep track; it's Patricia. We met back in Orisson. I was part of the group. So, do you want to share laundry? I don't have much and there's room if you do."

I got the feeling that I really didn't have to enter this conversation for it to continue. Patricia was well able to carry the whole thing herself, her words rolling in circles back upon themselves.

"I think we need tokens. It costs three euros. I have one euro, but I don't have any other change. Do you have any change? If you don't that's alright, I can go get change. We have to get tokens anyways." I showed her I had enough change for what we needed.

"So, I'll owe you a little. I can pay you the next time I get change. I can go get the tokens if you want to get your laundry." And with that, she was gone, and I guess I was sharing laundry. As we pulled our clean clothes from the washing machine, the debate as to using the dryer was on.

"Most of my things are quick dry so I think I'll just hang them. The socks take a long time to dry; they're thick, and they take a long time. I don't want my stuff to shrink. Sometimes the heat can make them shrink. I'm not sure about my socks. I'll just hang my things." Her soft voice and meandering phrases sounded more like those of a young girl, belying the tiny lines etched upon her face by sun and time.

"My Buff dries fast too. I love my Buff. I use it for everything. I wear it around my neck to keep warm and at night, I pull it up over my ears to hold my earplugs in. It covers my eyes too if someone puts the light on. I love my Buff." She shook her head incredulously upon learning that while I did have a Buff, I hadn't yet used it. I had packed one, hearing they were essential equipment, but I found the colourful tube scarf a little confining around my neck.

Laundry done, next on the agenda was supper. Leticia had arrived with stars in her eyes, giddily telling me that she and Ian were going out for supper. While I watched her putting on makeup, I asked where they were going. She said she wasn't sure. Ian's *albergue* was just down the road from ours, and the avenue was littered with sidewalk cafes. Without her asking, I got the feeling she wanted me to steer clear and, not wanting to be anyone's fifth wheel, I was happy to do so.

Since Leticia was busily preparing for her "date", I drifted out to the patio at loose ends. Should I shop and make something in the communal kitchen, or should I eat by myself in one of the many bars in the square. Suddenly there was Patricia.

"Do you have plans for supper Pat?"

"Oh, I had something to eat when I first got into town. I was so hungry. I had to eat. When I stop walking, I feel so hungry. And it's Patricia. Not Pat. Not Patty. Just Patricia."

Corrected, I extended my invitation. "Well I'm going to go find a pharmacy and get some rub and then get something to eat. Would you like to join me?"

"I could come for the walk. I'm not really hungry. Maybe I could have some dessert. Maybe they have something chocolate. I love chocolate. I should find a banana and some chocolate for tomorrow."

We walked down the cobblestone sidewalk, under the arch into the main square of the town. Stopping by the pharmacy, I showed the chemist the photo of the rub the Brits had used in Zubiri. As she presented me with the tube, a stout townswoman in a pencil skirt, knitted twin sweater set, and sturdy shoes, stepped into the store and started talking with the chemist.

The exchange, which was loud and sounded fairly serious, turned out to be about me. I hadn't noticed the red rash on the backs of my calves, just above where my sock line would be. I assured the two women I was not in pain and hadn't even noticed the red bands. The chemist advised it was quite normal for pilgrims. She said it was not dangerous unless the area continued to grow, otherwise it should go away in a couple of days. Okay, so I have this mysterious red rash that pilgrims often get, it wouldn't kill me and it would go away. Good to know.

The shadow of the church steeple fell across the café tables where pilgrims rested, chatting and draining glasses of *vino tinto*. I love to eat outside on warm evenings and cast longing looks at the bistros, but Patricia pulled me across the lane towards a row of bars.

"I had soup here when I got to town. It was really good. The price for the pilgrim's meal is good. It's only nine euros."

All of a sudden, we heard our names called out across the square and Cindy and Anne-Marie strolled over. Cindy looked just as exotic as ever, a fresh little bird of paradise in her hot pinks and purples. Anne-Marie looked a little more like she had walked that day.

"We were just going to find something to eat. Would you like to join us?"

"Yes," said Cindy, "But where is Leticia? I thought you were walking with Leticia?" Was that a question, a statement, or an accusation?

"I have been, but she's got other plans tonight. She and a man we met are having supper together at one of the little places on the street near our *albergue*. I told her I would find my own place and not cramp their style."

"Ohhhh! I see," Cindy drawled. Nudge, nudge, wink, wink. What? Were we in high school?

"Well, there's nothing wrong with that." I felt the need to defend Leticia. "They're both single, and if they want to have supper together, what's the harm?"

"Oh, nothing. Did she know him before?"

"No. He's from England. I met him in Zubiri, then lost track of him. Today we met up with him again at morning coffee, and they've been walking together most of the day. Seems like they've really hit it off so that's great. Now where would you like to eat?"

Decision made, we entered the bar and were escorted past noisy tables crowded with locals more focused on the television screens than their plates. In the dining room at the back, we were the only diners, and although it felt a little odd, it was quiet and peaceful. We hadn't realized we had come in just at the start of dinner time, and the tables quickly filled around us.

Suddenly, there was Leticia and Ian being seated at the table across from ours. Leticia caught my eye, raised her eyebrows, and I just nodded, and turned back to my tablemates. Anne-Marie, Cindy, and Patricia all looked at me, and I shrugged.

"So, what's everybody going to have?"

"I had something to eat earlier, so I'm not really hungry," Patricia affirmed. "I wonder what they have that's chocolate. I hope it doesn't take too long for the food to come. Our *albergue* locks the door at 10:30, so we have to be in by then. Maybe I'll order water instead of wine. Then I can take the leftover bottle for tomorrow. Maybe we should tell the waiter we need to order now."

While munching though my lovely salad, slicing up the white asparagus (a regional specialty) I glanced across at Leticia and Ian. I was glad to see them deep in a conversation of discovery, and as I watched their wine glasses being refilled, I wondered what time Leticia was going to make it back to our *albergue*, or taking in her shining eyes, if she was going to make it in at all.

By the time Patricia and I walked back to our *albergue*, it was approaching 10:00, but the locals seemed in no hurry to return to their homes. I guessed the siesta thing takes a big chunk out of their day, and they make up for it by taking back the time from the night.

"I'm just going to go get my laundry. I hope it's all dry," Patricia said. I made a quick stop at my room, and then popped down to find her, quietly folding clothes.

"You'll get more use out of this than me," I said, handing her my purple and pink-striped Buff.

"Oh really! You're giving this to me?" she squealed. "I love it!" I knew she would.

Enjoying her delight, I wished her goodnight. "Maybe I'll see you on the way tomorrow."

"I walk pretty fast. Everyone has to walk their own pace. Maybe we could walk together. But I walk pretty fast. Have a good sleep. Thank you for the Buff. I really love it."

It had been a long day, and the wine and filling dinner had left me drowsy, so after checking my laundry (which I had hung from my trekking poles jammed in an empty closet as impromptu drying racks), I tucked into bed. I knew Leticia had a key and I wasn't going to wait up for her. I mean I'm only a few years older than her...not her mom. Ohhhh...a real bed, real sheets and blankets...and sleep.

"Oh, I had such a great time. Wait until I tell you everything about it! Were you sleeping? I didn't mean to wake you."

I was instantly propelled back to talks with my younger sister, Joan, following her distressing divorce. Her ex-husband had shattered her self-confidence, leaving her with doubts as to her ability to find real love. Her search led to one "great guy" after another. There was always this excitement of discovery, usually short-lived, before the bubble burst. I would smile as she went on and on about the current love of her life, glad that she was finding some happiness after all the heartache her ex had put her through, but I worried she'd get hurt again. It seemed Leticia was, in the wake of losing her husband, in this same desperate search mode. I hoped things would work out for her as well as they finally had for Joan.

"I have so much to tell you," she said. "Ian is so great. He really likes me. He has a nice smile and pretty eyes. I think he is very special," she gushed, stretching languorously on the bed beside me. "But it will never work. He lives in England and I live in California. We talked about everything. He is fifty-six years old. He is a computer programmer, and he has never been married or in a long-term relationship. I asked him if he was gay. No, really, it was okay. We can talk like that. It is all honesty. He is not gay. I don't think it can work with the distances. Just let me go to the bathroom and wash my makeup off. I'll be right back and tell you everything!"

What more was there to know? I groaned, rolled over, and drifted back to sleep not even knowing when she came back.

The next morning, I looked across at Leticia. She had a pink satin mask covering her eyes and was sleeping soundly. Giving her a chance for a few extra winks, I dressed quietly and went in search of coffee. In the kitchen, I raided the fridge for some yogurt and took it out to the sunny breakfast room where I found coffee, hot milk, and granola. In quiet companionship, fellow pilgrims were bent over maps, quietly discussing the day's walk. I consulted my guidebook and took heart that it would be mostly rolling countryside today. Knowing it was also going to be a hot day, I decided to tie my boots to my pack and try wearing my trekking sandals.

"Good morning. I'm just about ready to go," I said to Leticia, awake, but still lounging in bed. "It's supposed to be a hot day, and I want to get as much as I can behind me before the sun hits." She stretched like a little cat, and rolled on her side, cradling her curls on her arm.

"I won't be ready to go for a while. You can leave if you want to. I'll catch up later." I hesitated in my packing and looked at her. I wondered if she was just having trouble getting going or if she was going to meet up with Ian and walk with him. "Everyone has their own Camino," she continued, checking her nails vacantly. "I will see you later." I had been dismissed.

"Okay, we'll see you in Estella. Take care out there." Through shadowy, narrow streets, I wound my way, finally discovering the famous, graceful bridge that would start me towards Estella. I crossed the peaceful waters, looking back at the sleepy little town behind me with mixed emotions. I felt badly about leaving Leticia behind, but part of me was excited for another day of independent walking. After recalling each of my family members, I added Leticia to my walking prayers.

I looked around at the undulating green hills, dotted here and there with stone farmhouses whose smoking chimneys spoke of breakfast done and farmers in the fields already. I saw a woman in a long skirt and apron hanging laundry on a line and was transported back to simpler times. A sturdy farmer on a horse-drawn cart was trundling down the road with a load of canvas sacks; seed for planting, I guessed in these early spring days. He tipped his hat as he passed. Already, big white cows, bells clanging gently as they moved, sought the shade beneath spreading trees.

My hiking boots hanging off the bottom of my pack were kicking me in the butt, so I stopped and retied them securely across the top of my pack. The landscape became more arid, and the lush greenery became tufts of scrub grass. I began to dry out too as the sun climbed higher and hotter in the blue sky.

I stopped at a crowded bar in the hamlet of Lorca. Most of the tables were full, so I asked a woman sitting by herself if I could share her table to eat my cheesy tortilla (something like a cross between a quiche and scalloped potatoes). Moira, a sturdily-built woman from Atlantic Canada, was enjoying a salad (probably a better choice but I opted for protein) and welcomed me to join her.

Being about the same age, and both coming from Canada (albeit the two opposite coasts), we were comfortable with each other. We discussed the challenges of the walk and the quest for beds. We agreed that the problem might be that everyone was following the same guides, with the same thirty-three-day plans for where and when to stop. It seemed that seeking shelter one town before or one after the designated stops might make it easier to find a bed for the night. Ruffling through the pages of our guides, we discovered that there was a private *albergue* called *Casa Magica* one town before Estella, the next designated stop, and another, called the La *Perla Negra*, in Azqueta, a town just past Estella. Working towards an average of twenty-five kilometres per day, I didn't want to stop earlier than Estella and planned to go through to Azqueta. Moira agreed that it was a good plan, and as I shouldered my pack, she pulled on her Tilly hat and headed for the washroom, waving me off as she went.

Out into the heat I went, sunglasses on, hat pulled low, and a new sense of purpose in mind. That sense of purpose seemed to evaporate as quickly as my water supply. I was burning up and dripping with sweat in no time. The brutal sun beat down without mercy and the sparse trees and bushes offered no respite. Fellow pilgrims plodded by with little interaction or enthusiasm, murmuring "Buen Camino" and walking on. The heat was taking its toll on everyone it seemed.

I came up behind the small Korean girl, probably about ten-years-old, I had met in Roncesvalles. It appeared from her red skin and tear-stained face, she was not enjoying her Camino. I touched her shoulder, offering a stick of gum, but she spoke no English and shook her sad face. Her mother, looking back, seeing me with her daughter, stopped, waiting for us to catch up. Smiling, she encouraged her daughter along. I hadn't realized that there were a lot of Catholics in Korea. It was likely this was more of a pilgrimage than a holiday, but I wasn't sure if a child's body was ready for the physical hardships of this journey, no matter how character building it may be.

Passing through a collection of dusty buildings, I rounded the corner on the edge of a wide valley. Across the way, I saw something on the sloping hill. When I focused my heat-hazed sight on it, I realized someone had planted shrubs that formed the outline of a huge map of the world. In spite of the heat, I smiled. Someone knew we were coming and had planted this welcome to encourage pilgrims from all over the world. It was amazing!

"Will you look at that," said the large, beefy man in a grey bucket hat who had huffed up behind me. He removed his hat, wiping sweat from his brow. "That's fookin' brilliant!" And so, I met John, from Ireland.

I introduced myself and we walked a ways together, coming to some very deep stairs cut in the hard ground. I had to sit down and swing my legs over on a couple of them, their depth too much for me to take like regular stairs. On the way up, bracing my hands on the stair above, I had to haul myself up, dragging my poles as I went. Breathing hard, John chugged along behind me, stopping to light a cigarette. As I looked back at his portly build and sweat-soaked golf shirt, it seemed unlikely he would go the distance. Chances were, I would not see him again.

Entering the tiny village of Villateurta, the fluttering flags of *Casa Magica* beckoned to me. I saw the low-slung building wrapped with a shady veranda, sprinkled with pilgrims resting on wicker chairs. Through a haze of heat, I remembered hearing of beds, not bunks and massages; maybe I should stop.

But no, I had decided I was going to walk onto Estella and find a way to call forward to Azqueta to see if there was a bed available. I knew my chances of finding a bed at Estella's municipal *albergue* were slim to none. I hoped if I could offset the designated stops in the book from this point, I'd have better luck in the race for beds as I travelled the rest of the way.

On I trudged. My knees ached, my feet were on fire, and every rock felt like it pierced right through my trekking sandals. I would wear my boots from now on, I vowed. I struggled to reach my third and last bottle of water tucked in the back pocket of my backpack. A tall, lean pilgrim couple were just passing by, and the young man, seeing my flailing hand, reached over, pulled out the bottle, and passed it to me, asking if I was okay.

"Yes, just hot and tired."

"We are almost there. Just take it easy. It will be okay." Are all angels tall and blonde?

As I neared Estella, I rounded the corner where the view opened up on a river, bordered by lush, willowy trees, their branches trailing in the water. In the middle of the flow, a man-made diversion ridge had been built following the curve of the river, causing the water to gently fall off to one side like a very low dam wall. What was designed for flood protection, to my hot, tired eyes became a water feature! The water, aquamarine, and so clear that the rocks on the bottom were visible, looked cool and inviting. In my state of heated fatigue, I envied the ducks floating placidly on the surface. Savouring the coolness of the scene, I extravagantly drained my last bottle of water.

There was a building with a sign that said something about pilgrims' information centre, so I plodded up the ramp. Following on my heels, unseen since the café until now, Moira materialized and followed me through the door. A man greeted me and I asked if he could help me contact the *Perla Negra*. He smiled and nodded and repeated my words. I instantly knew English was a challenge for him. Leading me down the hall, Moira in tow, he called over a woman. She smiled and asked me how they could help. I explained I wanted to contact the Black Pearl and see if there was a bed. She said she could not call them. I asked if she could call a taxi for me so I could go there to see if they had a bed. At this point, Moira looking a little embarrassed by my request for a taxi, turned around and scurried out of the building. She was probably torn by the ethics of needing to walk every pilgrim mile. I felt the same, but at this point, I wasn't proud, *I was done! Let Moira think what she liked about me.*

With a look of tolerant patience falling just short of compassion, the Spanish woman said no, she couldn't call a taxi and that I should just go to the municipal *albergue*; it wasn't far. Gathering the remaining shreds of my dignity, out the door I went, frustrated, limping, and sweaty.

I came around the corner and saw a beautiful old stone church and thought, "Oh, just another church." At day six! Just another church at day six! Now I knew the heat had gotten to me.

Actually, what I was really focussed on at that moment was the beautiful stone drinking water fountain in front of the church. Suddenly, a group of schoolchildren swarmed across the road, rushing to get drinks and fill their water bottles, joking and pushing and spraying water at their classmates. I paused. *Was I really going to go in like a linebacker, tossing small boys aside to get to the water. Maybe!* As I drew near, however, the children parted silently, and motioned me forward to fill my bottle. I almost cried.

Straggling down the road, I found the municipal *albergue*, went inside and joined the line for beds. Although it was close to 3:00, if there was a line, there were beds. Surprise and relief washed over me. I would have a place to sleep tonight. I was too exhausted to remove my pack. I knew I'd just have to pick it up again. And I was too tired to stash my poles. I needed them to hold me up. When I reached the head of the line, the *hospitalero* smiled, stamped my passport, handed me the standard disposable sheet to put on my bunk, and sent me off to room two.

I hauled myself up two flights of smooth, tiled stairs and walked into room two, which contained twenty-four of the *albergue's* ninety-six iron-framed bunk beds. Bedrolls and backpacks reserved some bunks, while others already contained sleeping pilgrims. People clustered about, changing out of walking shoes and gathering shower supplies and clean clothes. There was one bunk left; a top bunk, right in the main corridor. My feet were so sore! I looked at the narrow rungs that constituted a ladder with dismay.

Maybe there's a bottom bunk in another room. Up another flight, I checked out rooms three and four. No open bottom bunks. Back down to room two. Having a minor melt down, sure that I just couldn't do this anymore, I was standing there, pack on back, poles in hand, looking at the offending top bunk.

"Are you okay?" a friendly voice asked. I must have looked as bad as I felt. I said I was good, just looking for a bottom bunk. He asked if I was hurt and I told him my feet were so sore I wasn't sure about the ladder. "No problem!" he smiled. "I have a bottom bunk; take mine." Again, I almost cried. So not all angels are tall and blonde.

He quickly started to transport his things from a bottom bunk by the window, rearranging them deftly on the remaining top bunk. My champion seemed to have so much energy in his compact body. I put it down to his being younger (*fortyish I guessed*) and having already had a shower.

"My name is Jose. I am Brazilian, but I live in Toronto. I see you are from

Canada too." He indicated the maple leaf patch on my pack. We shared a smile and I introduced myself. Thanking, him I told him how beat down I felt and that I had been so worried about getting a bed. Jose smiled and put a hand on my shoulder. "It is my second Camino. Everyone goes through something like this somewhere along the way. Good for you it happened early and now you can carry on. Don't worry about beds; just walk. It is a rule on the Camino; no pilgrim will sleep outside. You will be okay."

Reassured, I struggled out of my pack, pried off my boots, and leaned my poles by the wall. Tucking my passports, cellphone, and valuables into my dry bag, I gathered clean clothes, and with my towel and soap in hand, went in search of a revitalizing shower.

Restored to some semblance of normalcy, I crossed the shady street to a bar and discovered my Zubiri dinner companions, Josh and Pete, seated on the riverside patio at a table laden with mugs of beer. "Roxey, come join us," Josh called. "Are you alone? Where is Leticia? Did she take a bus again?"

"Oh, I'm not sure. When I left Puenta la Reina she was still in bed." The two men exchanged looks. "I think she's just having a little trouble with her feet."

"I think she is just a little high maintenance!" piped up Pete. *What could I say?*

I called the waiter over but was advised that the kitchen had just closed and wouldn't open for three hours. I checked out the tapas still available on the counter and chose a small plate of cheese, drizzled with olive oil and sprinkled with herbs. I lamented that it would have been great to have a nice salad too, and the man taking my money smiled.

Back at the table, a tall glass of beer in hand, I asked if the others had seen the map of the world. They said they had not. I shared my cellphone photo, astounded that anyone could have missed it. A crisp salad surprisingly arrived at my elbow, and I munched happily. Josh and Pete were talking about their upcoming wine tour. They were going as far as Logrono and then taking a sidebar to sample some of the local wine before resuming their Camino. I asked if their wives had not wanted to come along or if they were unable to get time off work.

"They don't like to walk," said Josh, "except to the mall!" he winked.

"Have you heard what's happening back in Canada?" asked Pete. He had all the latest electronic gizmos and never lost touch with "the real world". When I shook my head, he continued, "There's a big fire in Alberta, Fort McMurray, to be exact. They're evacuating the whole area." I knew the big oil-production area and wondered how that would affect fire-fighting efforts.

BC had suffered an extremely dry summer last year, and the whole province had been on wildfire alert. Our own town's skies had darkened with debris from fires burning in every direction on the island. Although the nearest serious fire was about eighty kilometres away, our car was dusted with ash by the time I left for work each morning. Given that Vancouver Island is on a fault, we always have an earthquake "go bag" ready, but with tall stands of forest on two sides of our property, Al and I had moved non-replaceable items to the car and had formulated our own fire evacuation plan. I felt for the people whose homes were being threatened, who lived with the fear of impending and actual disaster, and I prayed the fires would be contained and brought under control quickly.

I returned to my room to charge my cellphone and met Armin, a tall, bone-thin man from Belgium. His round wire-framed spectacles, white hair, and tuft of a beard made me think of an overgrown elf. As he bent to plug his cellphone in the wall plug, his knobby knees, exposed by walking shorts, wobbled shakily. I reached over and plugged it in for him.

"*Merci*," he thanked me.

"You're welcome," I replied, and he quickly switched to English to introduce himself. Armin's command of English was impressive and again I mourned the fact that we North Americans seemed far behind in linguistics. Most Europeans I met could speak at least two languages fluently and enough English to communicate sufficiently at least. We were such slackers!

Armin asked if I knew where I was going next, and I said Los Arcos seemed the most likely, if I could get a bed. He said there was an *albergue* there run by a Flemish confraternity and that maybe they would have room for us. I advised him it was a municipal *albergue* so they wouldn't take reservations. Not deterred, he suggested we go downstairs, find a phone, and try.

The *hospitalero* showed us how to work the pay phone on the wall, changed our paper euros into coins, and gave us a list of *albergues* to try. Amid the noisy chatter of the lobby, I held the receiver, and dialled the numbers my elderly companion read from the list. Then Armin quickly popped the coins in the top. All of them tumbled out the bottom to the floor like a winning slot machine.

"No, no!" called the *hospitalero* from his desk, as I bent to retrieve the coins.

"You have to wait for the connection before you put in the coins." Obviously, this was a finely-tuned system. Giggling like school kids, we geared ourselves up for a second attempt. I told Armin it was ringing, and he quickly popped in the coins. With my minimal Spanish, I was able to convey that we were looking for *dos camas* (two beds) for tomorrow night and was advised there was no room. Click. Looking vacantly at the silent receiver, and then up at Armin, we prepared to try again. Second *albergue*, same response; no beds. Third one; no answer at all.

"Let me try the Flemish place," Armin suggested, so we switched places, and I held the coins ready. Connection made, I dropped the coins and he launched into a friendly conversation. I watched his eyes sparkle and his face light up at conversing in his own language. "It is done," he reported proudly. "They are full, but they always save a couple beds in case a fellow countryman comes. There are not so many of us." Later in my journey I would meet another Belgian who would become very important to me, but I happily hugged the one in front of me, knowing against all odds we had beds for the next night.

Back upstairs, I reorganized my pack and watched with a degree of apprehension as Armin popped a series of pills out of blister packs. I knew he had a heart condition. He told me he was sixty-five, but I was thinking that might have been a language barrier thing, since he really looked more like seventy-five to me. For the second time on this journey, I wondered about emergency evacuation procedures. I was a little worried about the twenty-two kilometres we would walk tomorrow and wondered what I would do if something happened to Armin along the way. It was going to be another hot day, and we had some significant hills to handle. It appeared that, against my vow not to do so, I was again making myself responsible for another person. Maybe caretaking was my purpose in life. I took solace in the fact that while I very well might be God's earthly tool, Armin's safety wasn't totally up to me, and I went to bed adding him to my night time prayers.

As usual, I started the day by massaging Vaseline onto my feet, taking care to go between each toe. Then, I carefully pulled my wool sock over the salve, making sure I didn't strip off the protective barrier I had just created. Some people taped their feet each morning, but I had chosen this approach to protect my feet, and so far, it was working. Even with yesterday's walk in sandals, not one blister did I have. Today, I laced on my sturdy boots, reserving my sandals for end of day walking only. I watched my elderly Belgian friend as he tucked his drug blister packs in his backpack and went in search of water to fill his bottles.

"I'll see you downstairs," I called. He waved vacantly in agreement.

My pack on one shoulder and my poles in my hand, I descended the wide tiled staircase to find a place to wait in the communal kitchen. The plan was to stop for breakfast at a café along the way, but I enviously watched the Korean contingent festively sharing plates of glistening fruit, tangy pickles, and dishes of fragrant, hot noodles and broth. One man, noting my interest, pushed the plate of apple segments towards me. I held up my hand to refuse and he pushed it closer, his gestures insisting I partake. Nodding my thanks, I chose a couple segments and sat on the end of the long bench, munching the crisp fruit while I waited for Armin.

Next to me, a woman with sun-stained skin and fine, grey-streaked curls, was enjoying a cup of coffee. It smelled so good! Kirsty, as she introduced herself, was from Denmark. Her clear blue eyes smiled as she asked if I'd like a coffee. I looked warily at the line in front of the vending machine.

"No, not there," she said, "I have packets," and she passed me a bright orange envelope of coffee crystals. "I have plenty. Take one for later too," she insisted.

Not knowing if I would have time to boil water and drink my coffee before Armin arrived, I walked past the noisy breakfasters to the stove at the end of the room. There, a tall man had just finished pouring boiling water into a cup. He held out an empty cup to me and poured in the remaining hot water, transforming my dry crystals into fragrant java. I smiled my thanks. Rejoining Kirsty in companionable silence, I savoured my coffee, enjoying how things were falling into place for me this morning.

Armin waved to me from the foyer and I ran over to rinse my cup, thanking Kirsty again before wishing her, "*Buen Camino.*"

"Perhaps we will see each other again on the way," the petite, slim woman called with a wave and a smile. Out through the door, shadows of the night lifted to a waking Estella.

A man, all in blue except for his grey bucket hat, stood with his back to me, cigarette smoke curling up over his shoulder as Armin and I stopped to adjust our packs and poles.

"Good mornin', missus," he said as he turned around. Noting my confusion, he said, "It's me. John. John from Ireland. We met yesterday by the map of the world." I would never have recognized him. Yesterday he looked like a sweaty, hot mess, a product nearing its expiry date. This morning, his shining black hair and neatly-trimmed moustache framed his swarthy face and his blue eyes twinkled merrily. "I clean up okay," he joked.

I introduced Armin and said we were walking together today. "Oh, now you know she walks like a dervish, don't you?" he warned Armin. "One minute she was beside me and the next I couldn't see hide nor hair of the girl."

"I don't walk that fast," I protested. "You must have lost sight of me when I went behind a bush or around a curve. That's all it takes you know." I asked to take their pictures, admitting to myself that my motivation was mostly so I didn't forget who they were. This was a problem even back home for me. If I saw someone in a different place than I usually saw them, I might be embarrassed by not recognizing them. Given the drastic change in John's appearance from yesterday to today, I knew the risk was real.

When I saw John yesterday he seemed much heavier, and I doubted he would make it even to the next town. Today, he seemed robustly healthy, and I was glad to know he would be walking along with me and the fragile Armin. The road started to climb gently as we left the wakening town, and despite his long legs, Armin was moving very slowly. Perhaps he's just warming up, I thought.

A short way down the road, we came to the *Fuente del Vino*, a fountain that dispenses wine, provided for the pilgrims by the local bodegas. Okay, wine at 8:00 in the morning? All the laughing pilgrims posing for photos as they filled receptacles with wine seemed to have no problem with that. Common practice had pilgrims using their scallop shells to taste the wine. Having been warned that the silky strings often break, I had used a plastic tie wrap to bind my shell tightly to my pack, so that wasn't going to work for me. I carried two little water bottles in pockets on either side of my front pack and decided to dump one out to try the wine. No! I wasn't going to fill the whole bottle and then try to walk in the sun all day! When my turn came, Armin took my photo as I poured from the spigot marked "*vino*". I'm glad he hadn't taken the picture as I tasted the wine since I'm sure my sour expression would have reflected the harshness of the brew. I tactfully poured the wine out into a gravel bed and approached the second tap to fill my bottle with cool, clear water. Apparently, the wine was a blessing for the journey, so even John, who advised us he didn't drink (an Irishman who didn't drink?) took a mouthful to ensure the way.

Passing the nearby *Monestario de Irache*, we came to a decision point. One path would take us a shorter distance but had a steeper climb in addition to another significant challenge above Azqueta. The other path was longer, but the climb was much gentler, at least until we got to the Azqueta peak. Decision made, we veered off to the right, following dusty trails past budding vineyards. The sun climbed higher in the deep blue sky as we climbed higher among fields of yellow and green. Several times Armin stopped, enjoying the view or resting; I wasn't sure. John stopped too, but for a cigarette.

"Filthy habit you know," he muttered as he repocketed his pouch.

The lush crops dropped off as the hills sprouted dusty collections of scrubby plants. The hot sun beat down upon us. I bowed my head against the glare as I dug in to plod up the dirt track. Behind me, Armin and John were trudging along, and I slowed my pace remembering my promise to walk with Armin. Any pretence of freshness was gone as I gradually wilted in my sweat-soaked clothes. Tiny dirt devils kicked off the ground with each step of my dusty boots. My water supply was disappearing fast, and I scolded myself that I would run out before Azqueta if I didn't slow down my consumption.

In the distance, graceful cypress trees moulded themselves around the walls of an ancient stone church, their crooked trunks beckoning us forward to the shade. On one side of the path, we discovered a square building fronted by two elegant arches, and tiled stairs leading from the dusty road down to a man-made pool of brackish water.

"It is the *Fuente de Los Moros*," a slight British woman resting on the top step advised us. She was a professor of archaeology in London and shared her knowledge generously. "It was built by the Moors in the thirteenth century, and used for bathing." Well despite the heat, no one was going to be swimming in it now, and I felt its sadness, a once beautiful edifice abandoned to the rigors of time.

We carried on into Azqueta and stopped at a quiet bar for lunch, or was it breakfast? Well water and a toilet for sure! Armin was rubbing his aching calves and John stepped away to "have a smoke". I shared the nuts and raisins I had in my pack, and Armin pulled out some dried apricots. We dawdled over our cups of coffee, putting the climb ahead off as long as possible.

"We have to go," I stated firmly. "It's only going to get hotter. I know they're holding beds for us, Armin, but they usually let them go if we're not there by 3:00."

"They will hold them for us," he assured me. John wondered aloud if he would find a bed, and Armin said he would say he was part of our group so they would give him one.

"Brilliant!" John said. "Let's get going then before the missus leaves us in the dust!" I wanted to assure them I would slow down, but I didn't want Armin to feel badly. I'd made a commitment to him, and he'd found a bed for me; we were in it together, whatever came. I slowed my pace and stopped and "admired the scenery" with him more often as we climbed up and up.

When the going got hard, I chanted my walking mantra over and over to pull my tiring legs up the hill. Behind me, I was again leaving the men behind. Armin was stopping frequently, but when he arrived where I waited, he gasped he was fine between laborious breaths. John and I exchanged concerned looks. It was actually harder for me to do the hill slowly than it was to go faster, but my main concern was Armin's safety. I worried if he worked too hard to keep up, we might have a bigger problem on our hands than not having a bed.

"You're terribly fit, missus," John stated, pulling out a cigarette to stretch the break. "Here I am fifty and there's no fookin way I'm keeping up with you. Isn't she fit, Armin?" Armin nodded sagely. I had worked hard to prepare for this trip, but after a lifetime of fighting flab, I didn't consider myself overly fit. I blushed at the compliment.

I consciously slowed my pace, asking the men to stop for pictures frequently. John smiled at me; he knew what I was doing. I encouraged Armin to tell us about his wife back in Belgium and about his home there. His hobby was wildlife photography, which explained the close-up shots he was taking of any bloom along the way.

John told us about Jeri, his partner back in Ireland, and his lovely twenty-something daughter, the light of his life. By the time I had told them all about Al, my sons, my daughters-in law, and my grandchildren, we found we were already over the top and heading down the hill.

Pilgrim traffic was light at this point, and we enjoyed the solitary silence but for our plodding footfalls. John became the toddler in the back seat with "are we there yet" and "how much further?" Armin laughed every time I said we'd probably see something just around this corner, and then there was nothing. I found myself leaning forward to look around the curve prepared to announce a town, but nothing. I also found myself looking for a bush bigger than my backpack behind which I could relieve the pressure on my bladder. The guys were lucky; they just stopped where they liked, but I had to be careful when I turned around, that they might not be stopped to take a picture!

We came to a big field where we saw the trail run down the side and across the bottom. Seasons of passers-by had carved an impromptu short cut through the field, and we eyed it with interest. Then we saw a rope across it and a hand printed sign that, in Spanish, probably threatened all sorts of abuse to those who crossed it. We erred on the side of caution, trudging down the side and starting across the bottom only to see some less ethical (or braver) pilgrims strutting down the short cut.

"Bastards!" muttered John. I was becoming used to his working Irish use of colloquialisms and decided it was just part of his charm.

"Okay," I said, "that's it! I'm going to have to go down in that ditch and pee. I just can't wait any more!"

"No, you're not, missus!" John's big hand clamped down on my shoulder. "You don't know what's fookin' down there. There may be snakes, or you might fall in a hole and break your leg!" John exclaimed. "We, Armin and me, we will be your wall and guard your modesty."

My modesty? The two men linked arms, faced the road, and I scuttled behind them and dropped my pants. Do you have any idea how hard it is to pee with two men standing right beside you? Job done, pants rearranged, I thanked them for their chivalry as we started off down the road again. Chest puffed out, John seemed inordinately pleased with himself

"We did it, Armin. Just like in the movie wasn't it?" Obviously, he had seen *The Way* as well. Armin, with his old-world manners just smiled quietly.

It was already 3:30, so I resigned myself to accepting that the beds were either going to be there or not and gave into enjoying the men's bantering and the rolling landscape. Suddenly, ahead at the side of the road, in the middle of nowhere, there was a coffee stand, complete with plastic tables and chairs and umbrellas. "Edwardos" mobile snack trailer was a welcome respite in the unforgiving heat, and I treated myself to an ice-cream bar. John took his coffee over to a separate table to enjoy a smoke.

"These little cakes," he said holding up the complimentary cellophane-wrapped pastry tucked on the side of his plate, "they're brilliant!"

"It's just around this corner. It must be!" I called out. But no. On we trudged in what seemed to be the longest day of my life. The gravel path shimmered in the heat.

"Do you see anything?" called John from behind. I told the men there were signs up ahead so hopefully we were getting close. I swear Spanish kilometres are longer! We turned around another sloping curve, and a clutch of low buildings came into view. As we approached, we passed pens of chickens and goats, and I stopped to snap photos for my grandchildren. The men laughed, but I silenced their ridicule saying toddlers weren't interested in pictures of churches and fields.

As we walked in through the town, searching the narrow streets for signs of our *albergue*, John and Armin were plotting how we were now going to get three beds instead of the promised two. Armin seemed confident, which was good since pilgrims we passed called out that it was full everywhere. It was 5:00 and the next town was seven kilometres away.

Finally, finding the Flemish *albergue*, Armin introduced himself to the barrel of a man at the door. Broad smiles and back slapping and we were led down the hall to the office. Guided to a pair of beaten-up wooden chairs against the wall, John and I sat quietly, like kids called to the principal's office, exchanging nervous glances and watching the discussion we couldn't understand. We worried when we saw two fingers become three, followed by shaking of heads and escalating volume. But the next thing we knew, Armin was asking for our passports. We were in! Armin had a bed in the room with the Flemish *hospitalero*, and John and I were directed to the iron bunks upstairs. It didn't matter. We had a bed and this day's journey was over.

Having agreed to meet out front in the courtyard for supper, I rushed through my shower, rinsing my underwear and shirt. Towelling my hair as I walked back into our bunkroom, I found John freshly showered.

"Done and dusted," he bragged, indicating he was going out for a smoke. I quickly rearranged my things, hanging my damp towel and shirt, more to establish some privacy from the men in adjacent beds than for drying purposes. Downstairs in the yard, pilgrims were milling about in the warm evening air, some taking advantage of an old washer ringer to get their clothes as dry as possible before hanging them on the clotheslines. Across the way I saw Jose, my Brazilian angel.

"Roxey," he called out, "You made it! How are things going with you?" I told him about John and Armin and our nine-hour trek, sharing my concerns about Armin's health.

"I'm not sure he can make it. We had to stop a lot today, and it was still very hard for him."

"You know," Jose said carefully, "there are some who come on the Camino to die. For them there is no better place. When you die on the Camino, they erect a memorial and everyone who passes remembers you. Perhaps he does not mean to make it," he finished gently. Panicked at the idea I was accompanying someone with a death wish, I shook my head no. I assured Jose that wasn't Armin.

"Why would he bother taking drugs and taping his feet if he planned to die? He has too much joy in life, taking photos of flowers and noting nightingale calls and talking about his wife. No, I'm sure he is not planning death. He's just not really well and needs to take more time." Jose touched my shoulder gently and with a sad smile, told me to take care of myself and perhaps we would meet again.

Just then, the subject of our conversation strode out the door, showered and shaved, looking like a new man. The Flemish *hospitalero*, Gerard, accompanied Armin, collecting John as they walked towards me. Gerard was taking us to see where John could get more smokes and where we could get "the best supper in town". We walked through the square, past sidewalk cafes (where he pointed out the best place for breakfast in the morning) and the impressive *Iglesia de Santa Maria*, to a small hotel with an upstairs dining room. Here he shook our hands and returned to the *albergue*.

At a table set with linen and fine dishes, a waitress served us the pilgrims' meal: crispy salad, topped with canned tuna and a grilled chicken breast (steak for the men) accompanied by…French fries.

"No one told me it was going to be this hard to get a bed," John exclaimed after we had toasted our thanks to Armin for securing us places to sleep. "Even on my first night, there on the mountain, they didn't have a bed for me, and I slept in a truck box." He had been one of the unlucky ones in Roncesvalles, and he showed us photos of a row of dismal container boxes with pallet stoops, looking like something out of an internment camp. Inside each were four sets of unpainted, metal bunks and while the containers were insulated and lit, there was no additional heating. Their showers and toilets were in adjacent portable trailers, a chilly run on a dark, wet night. "Is it always like this? Why are they not better prepared?" he asked. "It takes from the journey to have to race for a bed."

"When I first started planning this trip, I was careful to avoid a "holy year" because there are hordes of people on the Camino in those years. Usually that's only when St. James' birthday, July 25, falls on a Sunday. That doesn't happen this year, so I thought I was safe. Then, I was talking to some people in Zubiri, and they say this is one of the busiest years they've ever seen this early in spring. Apparently, in reaction to the recent terrorist attacks in Paris, the Pope declared this year a special holy year for peace. That's probably why the numbers are higher. I hadn't known about that, not seeing it on the news, nor on the Camino Forum. But then, not being Catholic, I probably just hadn't tuned into it, and by the time the decree was made, my plane tickets were bought, so I would have come anyway, I guess," I shared.

"Yes, it is very busy," Armin earnestly agreed. "It is very important for us Catholics to do the Camino in a holy year. To achieve a Compostela earns a plenary indulgence, a reduction of penance for sins, and the temporal punishment after death in purgatory. To complete the Camino in a holy year widens the scope of the indulgence," he advised seriously. I looked at this gentle man and wondered quietly what sins he could have committed that drove his failing body over the mountains, through the chilling rain and oppressive heat, looking for a reprieve from eternal retribution. I was glad that my vision of a loving and forgiving God had me doing pilgrimage for spiritual growth and wasn't dictated by fear.

While we waited for our dessert, I showed John and Armin the poem I had written before coming on the Camino. It spoke of what I was leaving behind, and what I was hoping to find. When Armin finished reading it, he passed my phone to John while he dried away his tears.

"That's fookin' brilliant!" John declared. He pulled out his cellphone and took a photo of my screen. "I'm going to hang that on the wall right next to my certificate and don't you be coming after me for royalties, missus!" Two very different reactions from two very different men.

"Do you write a lot then, girl?" John asked. I told them I had always written, even when I was a little girl. Journaling and writing poetry had gotten me through some of the toughest times in my life and helped me to hang on to some of the greatest joys. "Are you going to write a book about this then?" John questioned, cocking his head. I said I wasn't sure. I would probably write it out for myself, but whether it would become a book, time would tell. "Well if she writes a book about us…we're plainly fooked!" he grinned over at Armin who sheepishly returned the smile.

Well fed and happy, we strolled back to the *albergue*, exploring the town as we went. In the main square we ran into some people I had last met in Puenta La Reina. They told me Leticia was here, staying at a private *albergue*; had I seen her? I said no; we'd gotten in quite late and had just come back from dinner. I was glad Leticia had made it this far, but whether she had walked or had continued to bus, I could not know. Chances were, she was already on her way to bed… unless she was out on a date!

Among lengthening shadows, we sauntered back to our *albergue*. In the failing light of the courtyard, John finished his last smoke of the day. After today's lengthy walk in the hot sun, I planned to stop at Viana rather than going the additional nine kilometres to reach Logrono. John and Armin agreed that nineteen kilometres would be enough for them too. To beat the heat, I suggested we meet for breakfast and try to be on the road by 7:00. The men agreed, and I left them in quiet companionship.

Upstairs, most of the twenty beds around me were occupied by the time I skimmed off my shorts and replaced them with leggings. I was getting pretty good at dressing under the covers. I put my Vaseline, sunblock, and lip balm beside my socks, ready for a quick getaway in the morning. Pulling out my phone, I plugged in my portable charger and was just saying goodnight to my family's pictures as John stuck his head in under my hanging towel.

"Good night, missus. Sleep well," he whispered, and he was gone.

The bunks started emptying at 5:30, pilgrims stealthily rustling into their clothing and packing their bags. Half hour later I joined the exodus, coming out into the pre-dawn darkness. Across the courtyard, I saw the glow of a cigarette and walked over to ask John if he'd seen Armin yet. Just then, Armin and Gerard appeared in the doorway, shaking hands, enjoying these last moments with a fellow Belgian before Gerard returned inside to begin his day as an *albergue hospitalero*.

Together, the three of us walked through the silent square and into the dimly-lit café, fragrant with freshly brewed coffee and warm bread. Our first rest stop was seven kilometres away, so we savoured our hot coffee before going out the door into the cool morning.

"Girl," John opened, "I've been meaning to ask you about the beads in your hair," he said reaching over to touch the beads trailing down my neck. "What are they about if you don't mind my asking?"

"They are my walking mantra, from the bible, Micah 6:8. It talks about seeking justice, loving kindness, and walking humbly with God," I explained. "It's how I try to live my life," I elaborated. "When I'm digging in to climb a hill, or I need a spiritual focus to get me through something, I just repeat those words." I showed him that I had the same beads on a bracelet around one wrist, and a multi-coloured bracelet composed of the initials of my family members on the other. "I start each day, touching each bead, and remembering them in prayer."

"Now that's just lovely. Something like a rosary, init Armin?" he asked. "Wonder why I never thought of doing something like that. 'Tis a special gift you have, missus," he smiled, placing his empty cup on the table.

Armin was moving slowly this morning, but he was moving, and he told us how much he had enjoyed his "private" room. John teased him that he'd missed the usual snoring symphony, going into great details about the heavy German man below him who belched and farted all night. In high spirits we strode through the countryside, taking in the rolling green hills, stopping from time to time for Armin to take a photo and give an impromptu lecture on the flora of the moment. I broke off a bloom and pressed it between the pages of my guidebook.

Before we knew it, we were coming into Sansol, and if we blinked in this tiny hamlet, we'd be through it just as fast. The only sign of life, a busy little market, invited us in with the gushing of an espresso machine and we joined the lineup for coffee. The tiny store was packed with all things imaginable, both for daily town life and pilgrim passage. Shelves were stacked floor to ceiling, and more items hung from hooks from the low, heavy wooden beams. It was a good thing everyone had left their packs outside; one unguarded turn with a backpack and inventory would have tumbled. It was almost hard to find the cheerful man behind the till, so crowded in by goods was he.

Armin, out the door already, was waving a bag of cookies to share. While John had a smoke, I watched a young Asian peel off his thick socks to reveal red and blistered feet. He painfully replaced the failing tape covering his wounded toes, and I gave thanks, not for the first time, for my healthy feet. The daily applications of Vaseline seemed to be working. I was thinking about getting more soon as the little travel tube I was able to get through airport security was already getting low.

Back on the road, we crossed a stone bridge over a small river and entered Torres del Rio. Seriously, it was a whole different town, just across the bridge. You could stand in one town and read the nameplate of the other without any effort. This was the last opportunity for food, water, or a washroom until Viana, but since we had taken care of that at the last town…you know…on the other side of the bridge, we decided to keep going.

We followed a gentle climb, surrounded by rolling hills of dirt rows, planted with twisted, woody vine roots, tentatively bearing tender green leaves, pushing their way up to the dull sky. An upwardly climbing roller coaster, one hill building on the next, we continued to climb. Anticipating the equally challenging drop after the summit, we broke through the scrubby woods to find the shoulders of the path peopled by small inuksuks. Here, along with other pilgrims, was Davina, kneeling on the ground, writing a message on a paper to sandwich it between layers of rock. I saw no tears upon her face, a promising sign that she was beginning to heal as she worked through the layers of her grief.

Obviously, this was a field of prayers. I walked respectfully along the tiny statues, shaking my head in wonder at the hundreds of people who had stopped to leave their prayerful messages here. My fingers went to my family bracelet, and I touched each beaded initial, remembering my family members, giving thanks that while their lives were not without challenge right now, they were whole and healthy and safe.

Climbing again, I heard a familiar voice behind me, and there was Leticia, walking and chatting with an unfamiliar middle-aged man. As she approached,

I called out her name cheerfully. She looked right through me and kept on going. I guess my face must have registered my shock and my hurt. John asked me what that was all about. I told him, as we walked, about Leticia and how we had travelled as friends for a few days and then I had to leave her behind.

"And she didna' even speak to you?" he asked incredulously. "Well, girl, don't you be worrying yourself about her. There's some that's worth it, and some that's not. We've got you now," he said, Armin nodding in agreement as he patted my shoulder.

Coming down the hill, we crossed a modern highway only to climb higher yet on the other side. Here comes that steep drop I had mentioned. A red sign warning of the 10% grade descent alerted pilgrims to take care with each step. Loose gravel and fine dust made for slippery footing despite the arid ground. A rolled ankle could result in serious injury, or send me tumbling, especially with the weight of a backpack. I used the skiers' approach, creating switchbacks to slow my descent, and Armin followed suit behind me. Purple thistle and yellow broom brought bright contrast to the gloomy skies and gathering clouds.

At the bottom of the red dirt hill, I kicked into mantra mode, repeating the words over and over, pushing myself up another hill. I dug in and pushed hard with each step, willing myself to the top. Wiping the sweat from my face, I turned and saw Armin and John still at the bottom of the hill, assessing their approach, delaying the inevitable climb. I sat and had a drink, waiting their arrival, taking their photo as they crested the hill.

"Roxey, you were using your beads on that hill, yes?" puffed Armin. With a smile I told him, yes, I had, and I had asked for extra help for him up the hill as well.

We were now entering the Rioja wine region, and vineyards were everywhere. Small blue bachelor buttons grew beside bright red poppies, and I selected a bloom to press in my book to remember this leg of the journey.

"You have a lovely way about you," John smiled. "You have your beads and your prayers, and you notice the small things along the way. You have a gentle touch with an old man, and you are a good friend. But you walk too fookin fast!" Oh well! It was a tender moment for a while.

We crossed a busy highway, dodging transport trucks, and walked up a roadside path into the town of Viana. As always, the road into town was uphill; a defence strategy of old I assumed. Higher yet above the ancient walls of brick and stone, the tower of the church stood alone, declaring its presence by an iron cross mounted on its red-tile clad turret. Past arched wooden doors and wrought-iron window boxes overflowing with vibrant blooms, we trudged up the roadway, looking for the *albergue* Gerard had booked for us.

As we pressed inside the doorway, we were welcomed not only by the *hospitalero*, but by Patricia, who had arrived just ahead of us. We were quickly assigned the last three bunks in her room of twelve, and we dragged our packs up two flights of stairs to claim our beds, leaving Patricia below in discussion with our *hospitalero*. She had left a favourite fleece sweater behind at the last *albergue* where she stayed and was looking to see if it could be located.

When I returned to the bunkroom after my shower, Patricia was there, eyes shining with happiness. "They found my sweater. They're sending it forward with the ported backpacks. It's going to cost me five euros, but it was an expensive fleece, so it's worth it. It was my warm layer. I really love it and it keeps me warm. It should be here later today. Do you want to share laundry?" So here I was sharing laundry with Patricia again. We might not walk together in the daytime, but our underwear seemed to share close confines on a regular basis! I asked John if he needed laundry done, and he said he was going to do the whole lot so it would be a load in itself. Armin said he would wait until tomorrow in Logrono.

Following yesterday's long, hot haul, the ups and downs of the day had taken their toll on Armin despite the coolness of the weather. We'd actually made good time, with less stops, but it was obvious he was hurting. Armin had decided that he would take the bus to Logrono in the morning, and then arrange there to hop ahead to Burgos. He would decide there whether to walk some more or bus some more.

"It is much flatter after Burgos," he explained. "Maybe I can walk some days and then go ahead by bus again to Sarria and walk the last hundred kilometres from there." He was at war with himself in making these plans, but his practical Belgian nature won out. "I will still see so much of Spain, and I will still get my certificate. I will also go home sooner to my wife. That will make her happy," he smiled. I knew I was going to miss this gentle stork of a man, but I was happier knowing he would reach his destination safely with this new itinerary.

Counting through my remaining euros, it was time to find a bank machine. No one dealt with credit cards or interact here; everything was done on a cash-only basis. I couldn't run the risk of ending up without cash in a town too small to have a bank machine.

"They're doing our laundry, and it's too early to eat. I already had some chocolate, so I can walk over with you, if you like. Maybe we should take a coat. I'm so glad they're bringing my sweater. I'm really glad I'm getting it back. It's safer to not to go to a bank machine by yourself. Do you want to walk over to the bank now?" Patricia asked.

Confession time: Here I am fifty-eight years old, and I have never travelled outside of my home province by myself. Every hurdle I conquer strengthens my confidence on this journey, but it was with trepidation that I approached a foreign bank machine for the first time. My Camino mentor had wisely counselled that I get a second interact card so that if a Spanish bank machine ate mine, I wouldn't be lost.

With Patricia on guard and providing moral support, I inserted my card, held my breath as I struggled through the Spanish prompts, input my PIN number and…nothing. The bank itself was locked for siesta, so no help there. Maybe I got the numbers mixed up. With bated breath, I reinserted the card, translated the prompts, and plunked in the PIN numbers slowly. Voila! The machine started spitting out euros.

"I don't get out much!" I apologized to an embarrassed Patricia as I finished my celebration. Pulling our hoods up against a sudden cloud break, we scurried back to the shelter of our *albergue* to check on our laundry and await the arrival of Patricia's sweater.

Finding a quiet corner in the great room and quickly doing the time conversion, I took the opportunity to give Al a call. As soon as I heard his voice, I struggled not to cry. I was doing okay now, but I was missing him a lot. I asked about how his days were going after our first week apart, and he said besides missing me, he was doing fine.

"Kirby is really missing you too," he said. "She keeps watching the door, and every time anyone comes, she just goes nuts. Then she calms down and starts watching the door again." I wondered if she'd be glad to see me or give me the cold shoulder when I returned.

All of the systems we had put in place were working out except for the visitors' roster. His sister, Sylvia, who planned to come stay with him for a week, had suffered a fall resulting in a concussion, so she was in no shape to travel. The boys, busy with work and their own lives were still planning to visit, but Al said he was doing just fine with trips for pool therapy, to church, and conversations with the neighbours.

"Everyone asks me where you are and I tell them I don't know; she went out for a walk a week ago, and I haven't seen her since!" Then he would explain, and the questions would double and triple. He brought me up to speed on the happenings in our sons' lives and the fire in Alberta. "It's totally out of control," he said. "They're evacuating whole towns, and the fire has spread into Saskatchewan."

"Those poor people!" I sighed. I couldn't imagine what it would be like. Remembering last summer's fires, I knew if those fires had gotten out of control, the whole island would be in trouble and evacuation would be bedlam. I gave prayers of thanks that we had dodged that bullet and added prayers for the people in Alberta and now Saskatchewan.

I had a top bunk again and there were no chairs in the room, so I just pulled the thick blanket down off my bunk and made myself a little nest on the floor. Rubbing analgesic cream into the muscles that ached, I listened to the conversation in the room while I stretched my legs and my back.

"You're really quite flexible aren't you now, missus," smiled John. "I'm going out for a smoke and then to get my laundry. It should be done by then."

"It says in the book that the road into Burgos is very busy and dangerous. Also, you're just walking in through the industrial area of the city. My Camino won't be enriched by that," Elsa expounded in her thick Australian accent. Elsa was a sturdy, middle-aged woman whose opinions were as blunt as her dark hair. She gave the impression that she was used to being in charge and that she would brook no resistance. I bowed lower towards my right foot. "You can take a bus or a taxi from the last town before Burgos, and it takes you right into the city," she continued. The Dutch representative in the room, Kevin, agreed, saying he had heard someone was killed on that road just last week.

"They're still fookin' wet!" John exploded through the door, his blue eyes flashing in anger. They don't know what the fook they're doing down there. One person puts things in the dryer, another takes things out, and they're still wet. I paid good money to have my laundry done, and now I have a bag of wet socks with not a one dry to wear tomorrow!" His Irish accent got much thicker when he was angry.

Putting my hand on his shoulder to calm him, I suggested, "What about taking them back down and asking them to put them back in the dryer?"

"No! I won't. There's not a one of them down there that knows what the fook they're doing, missus! They've got pans of wet laundry stacked all around, and there's no such plan as to what goes in and what comes out. I'm just going to hang them up here and hope at least one pair is dry for the morning."

Things didn't bode well for our laundry since Patricia had taken it down after John took his. I said I'd go down and check things out. I saw our clothes, still wet, sitting in a washtub on the floor. The girl running the machines quickly assured me they were going in right after she finished folding the ones she was taking out. I hung around checking out brochures until I saw her push our clothes into the dryer. Reassured I went back upstairs to broach the idea of exploring the town on our way to supper.

Although it only boasts a population of about 4,000, unlike the other deserted towns we had passed through that day, Viana was a bustling community. Now that siesta was over, music erupted from the stores and bars, and the streets were alive with people, meeting, greeting, and eating at the sidewalk cafes. Men were huddled around tables, drinking wine and discussing the latest football match. Whole families were touring about, the children running and playing under the watchful eyes of their parents and grandparents. Teenagers sat staggered on the steps of the cathedral, the girls eagerly sharing the displays on their cellphones while the boys casually tossed a hacky sack back and forth, trying not to appear interested.

With so many options to choose from, we finally settled on a subtly lit bar that served a full pilgrim's menu for ten euros. The table was a league of nations: June the tiny Japanese doll; Kevin from Holland; his older friend Tom from Germany; a tall, slim, young black woman from New Zealand; Elsa from Australia; and Armin, Patricia, John, and I. Nine nationalities at one table. It was more like a family reunion than a meal between virtual strangers. At one point, the Spaniards by the bar simply joined our table and while not everyone understood everything, we all had a good time. My damaged hearing, confused by the language buffet, left me just sitting back, enjoying the hum of the banter while savouring the robust wine one of our new Spanish friends had poured in my glass.

Outside in the cool evening air, the church bells began ringing, and we stopped to enjoy the unexpected symphony. The bells pealed for about ten minutes, making conversations – even as simple as good nights – a challenge, so we just waited them out. Hugs all around, we trekked back to our respective *albergues*. Patricia jubilantly picked up her ported sweater, hugging it like a long-lost friend. On my way up the stairs, I collected our pile of dry and neatly folded clothes, sorting them out with Patricia as we packed them away for the next leg of our journey.

Climbing into bed in the near darkness, I had to smile as John came up from his last smoke of the day and checked his socks.

"Still fookin wet!" he muttered as he crawled into his sleeping bag. Perhaps they would be dry by morning.

Peeking past the window shade, rain-slicked streets greeted the morning. A poncho day for sure. I climbed down the ladder, nudging John awake on my way to the bathroom. When I returned, Armin was dressed and carefully rolling his things into his backpack. I sensed a resigned sadness as he prepared to take the bus alone rather than to walk with us. I sat on his bunk beside him, and he enclosed me in a long-armed, fatherly hug as we assured each other we would stay in touch.

"Listen to your body, Armin, and take care of yourself. Ride if you need to ride. Rest if you need to rest." He wiped tears from bristled cheeks as a slow, sad smile grew. "I know this isn't how you wanted to do the Camino," I consoled him, "but it's not so important how you get there, as it is that you get there. I want to hear all about your arrival in Santiago, and again when you get home to your wife in Belgium. I will be waiting for your messages. Don't forget me now!" He nodded silently, emotions seeming to have stolen his English words from him. John came over to say his good-byes, and I gathered my pack and my poles. One more hug and, without our senior companion, we quietly descended the staircase.

Patricia was just coming out of the common room as we reached the front door, and ponchos pulled over our packs, we walked out into the rain. Following the shells, we circled the cathedral through narrow, silent streets. From glass-fronted niches built in the stone arches straddling our way, statues of saints gazed down at our passage. Patricia had chosen the rainwear as opposed to a poncho, and she deftly wielded a bright blue trekking umbrella, bringing cheer to the dreary morning. As we left the town of Viana behind, her slim, petite figure pulled ahead and the blue spot gradually disappeared from view.

John and I were well matched in our pace as we trekked along towards Logrono. We talked little, having exhausted our concerns for Armin's safe travels, and settled into companionable silence, each with our own thoughts. I noted, avoiding gathering puddles on the path, a number of large, sage-green snails oozing across the path and thought they should find a safer place to travel than under the thundering boots of oncoming pilgrims. The drizzle became full-out rain as we reached a highway with a wooden pedestrian bridge to take us safely across. I was impressed to see the builders had taken cycling pilgrims into consideration by including a narrow flat track on one side of the stairs to enable cyclists to push their wheels alongside their more pedestrian Camino companions.

Under dismal skies, the rural foothills gave way to the industrial outskirts of the capital of the La Rioja province, a substantial city with a population crowning 200,000. Shaking rain off our ponchos, we stopped at the Logrono tourist information office and had our pilgrim passports stamped before starting off across the seven-arched bridge spanning the Ebro River. Ahead of us, two elegant storks reviewed the parade of pilgrims from their nest high atop a hydro pole. John was, as usual, on a mission to find smokes. I was on a mission to find breakfast. A friendly Spaniard directed us up the hill, narrow streets fronted by balconied buildings, leading the way to a bright, open square with stores, restaurants, and bars lining every side of the plaza.

Locating a tobacconist, we moved on to a café where John ordered coffee and a tortilla, and I indulged in my first Spanish hot chocolate. The rich, dark chocolate was so thick, it was more like hot chocolate pudding. You pretty much had to eat it with a spoon, or, as the Spaniards do, ladle it out with sweet, sugary churro sticks. Totally decadent and totally delicious, this is not an everyday treat, but I had to have it at least once.

Outside in the square, a street market was coming to life. Vendors covered their tables with an assortment of fruits, vegetables, cheeses, baking and, of course, wine. We strolled past the booths, fighting the urge to buy what we then would have to carry. Taking our lead from a bronze statue of modern-day pilgrims, striding purposefully along on their journey, we headed down past the heavily ornamented cathedral and centuries-old buildings, moving out into the more modern section of the city. It took a long time to walk out of this thriving metropolis as we followed shells and arrows through busy streets, around roundabouts, and past old stone buildings snuggled up next to new chrome and glass constructions.

John was moving ahead at a good pace as I stopped to take photos of fountains and floral displays in the beautiful *Parque de la Grajera*. Beneath a canopy of leafy trees, on a wide brick promenade, I watched a young couple playing with their dog and missed Al and Kirby all over again.

The long, treed walkway, shared equally by pedestrians and cyclists, came out to a wall fronting a small lake that turned out to be a water reservoir. The path continued around it, leading into a lightly forested picnic area where noisy, happy families laid out blankets and unpacked baskets of food. I crossed a foot- bridge and coming to a coffee shop, took the opportunity to use the washrooms. I saw John, kicked back in a chair, enjoying a cigarette and coffee.

"There you are, missus," he said. "Did you want a coffee or something?" I assured him I was good and was going to keep on walking. "Alright then. I'll soon be coming as well," his heavy-lidded eyes slid back to the tranquil scene before him.

Leaving the peaceful park behind, the trail gently climbed upwards, curving along a gravel road, the area's famous vineyards stretching in every direction. Budding, tidy green rows cut their way across tracts of crumbly red dirt. Remembering advice to look back from time to time, I saw the park, the reservoir, and the city stretching below me and wished I'd had more time to explore Logrono. I knew there was still more to see ahead on my journey though, and I continued my solitary way along the gravel track.

Soon the trail narrowed and ran along a bluff above a busy highway with cars and transport trucks below noisily speeding to their own destinations. A chain link fence provided protection from the traffic below, and I noticed crosses woven into the links. The few became many until they filled the fencing from bottom to top. Twigs, strips of bark, and brittle grasses formed these emblems of prayerful hopes and thanks. Some were very simple; others quite complex, a dried blossom added here, a strand of wool or ribbon there. Like yesterday's inuksuk forest, some bore notes rolled and tucked between the woven arms, holding private prayers, left respectfully undisturbed by years of passing pilgrims.

My head was filled with thoughts of my family, wondering how everything was going in their worlds right now. Remembering that I was working on this "faith" thing, I stepped back just at the point of worry and touched my beads, remembering them each in prayer instead. I added Armin to my prayers and then expansively all the other pilgrims I had met along the way, including John behind me and Patricia ahead. My horizons were broadening with each new face, each new town, each new step.

The *senda* (path) was climbing a hill towards a stone-walled town. Surprised that I had already covered the thirteen kilometres since Logrono, I climbed tiredly towards Navarrete. The cobblestone streets were set with brass plates depicting the shell and cross symbols of St. James. I followed the markers up the hill, carefully descending a steep staircase to reach the *albergue* we had reserved.

Welcomed warmly by the *hospitalero* couple, I was led up the tiled stairs to a sunny blue room full of sets of glowing wooden bunks, each offering a thick, wool blanket. As I was placing my things on a bottom bunk tucked away in a quiet corner, Patricia entered the room.

"This place is so nice. It's pretty and clean and the *hospitaleros* are so nice. You can put your backpack in the wooden locker next to your bed. Mine is next to yours. There isn't anyone else here yet, so you have lots of time to shower. The shower is huge! It's not like a little shower, it's a whole room! You should go have yours before anyone else arrives." Not needing to be told twice (or had I been told twice?) I grabbed my shower kit and towel and enjoyed a long, hot shower. Having the space and the time, I took the opportunity to wash my shirt and underwear while I was at it. I towelled my hair and fluffed it up, admiring my pigtail mantra beads in a gilt-framed mirror. Done deal; I loved short hair!

As I exited the steamy bathroom, I saw our *hospitalero* leading John up the stairs. The heat of the walk since Logrono had left him tired, dusty, and sweaty. Clutching my soggy laundry to my chest, I indicated I was going to find a place to hang it, and he waved his hand towards the shower. In the short time we had known each other, we were already communicating without the need for words.

Outside, I pinned my clothes to the lines strung on a rack fixed to the balcony. I looked down over the tiled roofs of the town below me. A sharp bark directed my gaze to a silky black and white dog in the courtyard below. He looked up, barking an invitation to play. I called down to him, and he wagged his tail. If I didn't pay more attention to hanging my laundry I'd be joining him, at least long enough to recover the fallen item!

"Done and dusted," John was right behind me, wet socks in hand. "I'm just going to have a bit of a smoke and then let's go get some food okay, missus?" I left him to his puffing on the balcony and went to find Patricia who, munching on piece of chocolate, was on board with the thought of finding a meal.

"Someone was smoking outside the room and now the room is full of smoke. It smells really bad!" she complained, just loud enough for "someone" to hear.

It was still siesta time, and the stores were locked and shuttered, but we found an eatery on one of the lower roads. I hadn't eaten much in the day and was really hungry, but it was that funny time; too late for lunch and too early for supper. I was excited to see a picture of bacon and eggs on the wall and decided on that, thinking I'd make it my main meal and just have some fruit and nuts later.

John chose a steak, and Patricia assembled a plate of mixed tapas. Tall, cool glasses of beer (and a coke for John) in hand, we settled at a table to await our food.

"This place is really strange," Patricia whispered. We looked around and saw we were surrounded by elderly men, some in wheelchairs, most of whom were focussed on the football match on the television in the corner. "Do you think this is an old folks home or what?" she hissed.

"Well we came in and no one stopped us. They had a bar and a menu and took our orders, just like at a regular restaurant," I reminded her. "Maybe it's just where they all come to watch TV during siesta."

"I don't care either way!" John exclaimed. "As long as I get some fookin' food, I'm not mindin' where we eat." I looked at Patricia and saw no concern with his cursing. I knew John's curses intended no offence; they were just part of his normal day-to-day language, as inherent as the Canadian "ehs" sprinkled though my own conversations. He dove into the plate of steak and chips put before him, and I savoured my first plate of bacon and eggs since home. The bacon was actually more like prosciutto; very lean with a smoky, salty taste. And beer with breakfast…what a concept!

Back out in the sunshine, we strolled the streets, admiring the sculptures in the tidy square and the family crests and shields secured above the broad plank doors of the homes. The church was open, so we quietly walked inside, John and Patricia crossing themselves as they reached the centre aisle. Although this was a tiny town, the ornate gold decoration and porcelain sculptures were breathtaking. The huge arches drew the eye up to enjoy panes of biblical personages, brought to life in coloured glass. I especially liked one statue of an enthroned Madonna and child, and another of Mary rising from a cloud of creamy lilies. Affixing the stamp of the cathedral to our pilgrim passports, we pushed coins into the donation box and silently exited out the heavily draped door.

We found the local market, open now that siesta was over, and purchased some cheese, bread, and fruit for the next day's walk. In the Spanish equivalent of a dollar store, I also bought a package of emery boards so I could sand the ragged edges of fingernails broken and torn by all the abuse they had taken. I figured I'd keep one and leave the other behind on the bedside locker in case someone else needed one. That was the Camino way, I was learning; if you didn't need something, you left it behind for someone who might.

"Isn't it funny," John began, "we walk all day, then we get to a town, and we walk some more!" He was right. Thing is, it was hard to sit still once you'd been moving all day. We continued our lazy stroll, greeting the locals as we passed through their streets and shared the warm, friendly ambience as families enjoyed their evening promenades. While some answered the bells' call to evening mass, others settled in chairs at sidewalk cafes, and we sauntered back to our *albergue* to check emails and laundry.

Out on the balcony, I was taking in the last warm rays of the setting sun, munching on almonds and raisins and continuing my earlier conversation with the dog down below. John came out, a coke in his hand, and asked if I minded if he smoked while I was there.

"Filthy habit, I know, missus," he apologized, carefully blowing the smoke away from the bunkroom windows. Folding my laundry, I leaned against the railing. "I tried to quit you know," he continued, "but it's hard. I quit drinking. That was easier." I mentioned with a grin, that he was probably the first Irishman I had ever met that didn't drink.

"Well, I'll tell you why that is, missus. I used to drink. I used to hang out in the pub with my mates every night, you know. Then I went overseas to work for a few years, built up my skills, and saved some money to buy a little house. I came back to my town and went down to the pub and weren't they all there, my mates, just the same as they ever were. They hadn't done any fookin' thing different in all the time I was away. I thought, this isn't what I want, and if this is what drinking does, then I don't want that either. I wanted better for my family, and I quit. Just like that." I admired his courage in breaking the mould.

"I'm happy to know you, John," I told him, noticing I was picking up a bit of an Irish lilt. "'Tis a pleasure to be sharing this journey with you whether we walk together for an hour or a day. You're a good man and a good friend."

"Oh now, missus, 'tis you that is a good woman. Your husband is a lucky man. But you set a wicked pace don't you now? Hope you didn't mind me dropping behind today. You were alright on your own?" I assured him I was fine and that I hadn't taken his absence amiss.

"I needed to work things out. I'm a bit worried I'm not going to have enough time to get this done. I have to be back at work the first of the month you see. So,

I must be leaving Santiago by the 31st," he mused, blowing a final puff of smoke into the night before squashing his butt out in a ceramic bowl on the window ledge. "I really wanted to do this whole thing and go in through the Port of Glory."

"Maybe you need to think about jumping ahead a day or two by bus, so you save some time and can focus on the remainder of your journey without worry," I suggested.

"You may be right, missus, but I don't want to leave you behind," he admitted. I told him I would be sad to see him go, but that he had to do what he had to do to make his Camino work. I agreed it was hard for those of us who's Caminos, due to jobs or other such obligations, were time-limited this way.

"Well I may go ahead, or maybe just stop and come back another time and finish. I'll have to decide soon. Either way, I'll not be forgetting you, missus." Done with the day, we gathered up our things and went inside to prepare for bed.

"I hope there's no fookin' snoring tonight, I'm that tired!" he said looking wonderingly at the unoccupied bunks below and beside him. "Probably out drinking. Better not wake us all up when they come in!" he exclaimed. Patricia and I exchanged conspiratorial glances as we pulled our covers up, and I smothered a giggle knowing that it was John's snoring we had heard the night before.

"Goodnight John," we called in unison.

I awoke to the angry muttering about "fookin' snoring" from our sleep-deprived Irishman. Patricia and I smothered giggles and shared secret smiles as we packed our bags. We were both well aware there had been some significant snoring through the night, but from our perspective, John certainly had a leading part in the nocturnal symphony and not just, as he swore, the man below his bunk. Earplugs are simply a necessity for sleeping along the Camino. Of course I have the added bonus (which I use at home as well…sorry Al, but I do) of being more or less deaf in one ear, so I simply roll onto my good ear to decrease the decibels and sleep much better for it.

The most immediate solution to sleep deprivation is coffee, so packs on our back, Patricia, John, and I headed down the road to the coffee shop by the town square. The tiny shop was bursting at the seams with pilgrims, this being the only place open on a Sunday morning. I pushed my way inside to find only one man behind the bar. This was going to take a while! Without their morning coffee, pilgrims can be ruthless, and there was no polite waiting your turn. The crowd pushed forward every time an order came up, sure that this was theirs, and frustrated when it was not. From outside on the street, Patricia hollered in through the door.

"We can't get in! Just order three coffees, and we'll get something else later."

Nowhere along the Camino had I found a "coffee to go"; no disposable cups in sight. I'm not sure if this is to ensure pilgrims stop and rest at least long enough to drink a cup of coffee, or if it's a strategy to limit litter along the trail. Juggling three saucers and cups, I squeezed back out the door, handing hot java to my grateful friends.

"That took a bit, thanks!" said Patricia. "I can't believe there's only one place for coffee and breakfast open for all these people." I reminded her there probably wasn't anything open for the medieval pilgrims of the past, so we were doing okay.

A late start with a long day ahead, we struck off down the road, leaving Navarrete rubbing sleep from its eyes. Clusters of pilgrims travelled the rolling path before us as we wound our way among the fields.

"I've been thinkin' I may have to leave you girls," John announced. "I've been counting the distance against the days, and there's no way I'm making it to Santiago by the 31st at this pace. I know we're making good time, but I'd have to walk a couple hours more a day to get there in time." Patricia and I each had a few days more than John, and given our conversation the night before, I knew what he was up against. Seeing our disappointment, and perhaps enjoying it just a little, he continued.

"Then maybe I'll just continue on and get as far as I can and come back another year and finish. 'Tis only that it's a holy year, and I'm wantin' to go through the Porta Santa. It's only open during holy years." I knew, from our conversations, that going through the door of pardon (as it's commonly known) was important to John. "I'm only five days short. What do you think then, missus?" he asked me.

"Like I said, John, if you have to, you can always hop a bus to make up some time. Why not walk with us as far as Burgos, then see about a bus from Burgos to Leon to make up the days you need."

"I'm not feeling good about leaving you behind," he said, looking down at his shoes scuffing in the dirt. "You're like family to me now. And I wanted to walk the whole thing don't you know. I thought I'd have time, but I'd have to put in close to thirty-five kilometres a day to have a chance."

"John, the simple thing is you have less time than we do, so you've got to do what you've got to do to get there in time. There's no shame in that. You'll still be walking that last hundred from Sarria." Patricia nodded in agreement, placing her hand on his shoulder. "You have time to make that decision. Let's just enjoy the walk today," I said patting his back. "And if you're feeling badly about abandoning us, you can buy us breakfast at the next stop." He threw back his head and laughed.

Above us the skies were overcast, a storm looming as we approached Najera. We escaped into the first café we came to, dropping our packs at the door, leaning our poles against the wall. John approached the bar to buy some smokes. When he paid for the cigarettes, the barista pushed a button behind the bar that unlocked the cigarette machine. This was the Spanish way of ensuring that minors were not able to buy cigarettes from their machines.

Patricia and I were more interested in lunch, which was really breakfast. We opted for selections from the tapas bar. A crusty piece of bread, topped by a slice of tomato, cheese, and an egg, as flavourful sandwich, accompanied my coffee.

John stepped out for a smoke just as our Japanese friend, June, exited the bathroom. Patricia walked out with her as I savoured my coffee. Walking out of the town, I saw John just up ahead, leaning on the wall of a bridge, gazing into the water below. I looked past him to see the dark openings of caves dug into the red clay hills above the town. Consulting my guidebook, I discovered that as far back as times of the Roman Empire, during turbulent periods of skirmishes for control, people of the community would seek refuge in these caves. During more recent wars, soldiers, caught behind enemy lines, sought haven in these rough sanctuaries as did members of the resistance. It was haunting to see these abandoned remnants of ancient worlds and violent history silently watching over the relatively peaceful new world below. When I looked down again, John was gone.

Under overcast skies, I left the town in my dust, trudging up the serpentine gravel road, coming out on a plateau of rolling fields cut through red clay hills. The rise and fall of the green, the brown, and the red put me in mind of a patch-work quilt. I stopped and inhaled the greenness of the iridescent emerald grasses, a colour so vibrant it seemed unreal. In the distance, dark cloud-shrouded mountains loomed mystically. The silence, but for the whispering grass, was overwhelming. In my solitude, my thoughts turned back to my conversation with Al last night.

Our youngest son was still struggling to find his feet in his new situation. Al advised meetings with lawyers were scheduled, property and custody issues on the table. I knew any separation from his three-year-old daughter would be heartbreaking for Scott; he was a very "hands-on" daddy. It was probably a good thing I wasn't there to agonize over the details. I felt such a coward. I trusted Al to give him good counsel, if he asked.

Our older son, Kenneth, had just started a new job at a fish packing plant in Tofino. It was labouring work, with a two-hour crew bus ride each way. Port Alberni used to be a bustling mill town, but downturns in the forestry industry have made it difficult for men to find jobs. I wondered if the town would ever pick up again, or if it would suffer the same fate as the ghost towns I had walked through these past days. His wife, Amanda, made a decent salary working as a visiting care aid, but like most young families these days, they needed that second income to make it. I was worried about my son's long days, but I knew Kenneth would do anything to support his family. He had even talked about going to work in the camps at Fort McMurray.

I thought then of Fort McMurray, of the many people I knew who had gone there, away from their families for weeks on end, but returning with payoffs that sustained them in BC towns where good-paying jobs were scarce. Al told me the camps had been evacuated, workers returning home to wait until the fires were under control. I thought of those who had lost their homes and their jobs, dispossessed of everything. I envisioned the panic and confusion as they chose what to take, if time allowed, gathering their families and fleeing for safety.

Remembering Vancouver Island, with the looming threat of an earthquake, my heart did a flip-flop as I imagined hearing news of a serious earthquake back home. What if, while I was out here, wandering around in the Spanish countryside, a devastating earthquake struck our island? What if my loved ones were hurt, struggling, or in danger? Unfounded panic grew. What if I lost everyone important to me? How could I go home? Would I go home? What would I have to go back for? Why would I go? How could I stay? Where would I stay? Okay, calm down, I lectured myself. That hasn't happened, and it may never happen.

I felt so alone. But no. I was not alone, was I? Part of this faith journey was to trust in God. I'd travelled safely so far, and everyone I loved was safe, so far. I had to put my faith in God to hold us all and keep us safe. I had to trust in Him to keep Al well and see our sons and their families through life's ordeals. I'd been told by some well-meaning person when I lost my first husband that God doesn't give you anything you can't handle. That statement is not true to me. I think life gives you things you may not be able to handle; God gives you strength to handle them. No earthquake. It's just the isolation talking. Carry on.

Azorfra is a little community of time-worn cream and mustard stucco houses that exists almost exclusively due to the Camino pilgrims. With the municipal *albergue's* sixty beds, pilgrims equal about a quarter of the resident population. Approaching the town, I had a gunshot view down both streets, all the way to the exiting road. Quiet now during this siesta time, I walked past a market and a couple of bars displaying welcoming menus for pilgrim meals. Turning the one and only corner, I sauntered down to the *albergue*, seeing John on the path just ahead of me. The two-storey yellow brick and wood building boasted rows of tall, narrow windows and looked suspiciously utilitarian.

Through the front door just as the rain began, it was a different world —a big, bright, high-ceilinged common room with the registration tucked in the corner.

As I waited my turn to sign in, I looked across at pilgrims seated on benches at long white tables, writing in journals, recharging phones, playing cards, and sharing drinks and food. At the far end, I saw a well-equipped laundry room and communal kitchen, another hive of activity.

John elbowed in behind me, having finished his smoke outside, and asked the *hospitalero* if we could stay together. She looked at me and asked if I wanted to be in the same room with him. Puzzled by the question, given that we'd already shared rooms on several occasions, I said okay, and she stamped my pilgrim passport and handed me a paper with a bed number.

John followed me up the tiled stairs to the second floor where we found the door to our room, with only two beds inside, each covered with a bright, plaid blanket. I now understood now the *hospitalero's* concern. A moment of hesitation and I shrugged my shoulders. The particle-board doors of our two-bed cubical opened onto the long, window-fronted hallway along with about ten others. The walls didn't even go right to the ceiling so privacy was minimal. John had shown himself to be a proper gentleman, concerned for my welfare on many occasions, so no worries.

I took myself off to the shower, gave my sweaty clothes a quick wash, and warmly dressed, went back to our cubicle. We had a narrow window that had a bit of a lip, safe from the rain, between the glass and the outside shutter, so I put my boots out to air. Adjusting my poles, I jammed them in the window opening to create a hanging rod for laundry. John came strolling in the door in his flip-flops just then.

"Done and dusted," he quipped. "Isn't that brilliant!" he said admiring my innovative clothes rack before adding his wet socks. "This is a bit all right now isn't it, missus? Real beds, with real blankets and no fookin snoring." I rolled my eyes and smiled. He went out for a smoke.

Out in the hallway, I heard Patricia's voice and discovered she and June had the next room. I asked Patricia if this was too weird, sharing a semi-private room with a man.

"Oh, it's just John!" she smiled and I laughed, agreeing that he was much like a protective younger brother. She ran down the hall to grab a shower, as I sat in the hallway, charging my phone.

With the rain backed off again, we explored the tiny town, stopping at the local *mercado* for fruit, nuts, and sundry items for our next day. I loved the oranges in Spain, so juicy and sweet, but considering their extra weight to my pack, I bought them only when I could eat them right away. Patricia, as usual, was famished, so she and June stepped into a bar to eat while I returned to the *albergue*.

When I called Al, it was so good to hear his voice and to hear that although he missed me (good!), he was doing fine (even better!). I asked after the kids, the dog, and the tomato plants, anything to keep him with me for a while.

"Your photos are amazing!" he said, referring to the ones I had sent him so far. "The country is so beautiful, and the colours are so vivid! You're doing good, right on schedule. You sound much better too. Guess you got past that rough spot."

Now would not be the time to share my day's panic attack! Instead, I shared stories of the people I'd met, the food I'd eaten, and the places I'd stayed, trying to bring my journey alive for him.

"When will you call again?" I told him that we'd been warned there might not be Wi-Fi in the next two places we were stopping, and that if he didn't hear from me, not to worry. "Love you's" exchanged, we rang off, and with a sigh, I went to look for John to go for supper.

As we walked towards our table, I stopped to watch a cluster of elderly man, engaged in a serious dominos battle. In their sloped hats and cardigans, they mulled over their next move, rapping the table loudly before laying their tiles. We play dominos at home, and as I looked at the tiles, I could forecast their next moves. I would have loved to join in, but I was pretty sure this was an "all boys club", and they wouldn't have welcomed my female interference.

John and I joined a table and met Gwendolyn from Texas and Robert from Holland. Four for four, all different nationalities at the table again. I asked the server if it was possible I could have two "firsts" instead of a "first and a second".

"Is possible," he smiled, as I ordered salad and pasta from the "firsts" section of the menu. John poured the wine, and we shared that and stories of our journeys so far.

Running through the sprinkling rain, reaching the *albergue* doors just before the real storm hit, John said he was just going to stand in the back courtyard for a smoke. I realized he was really giving me privacy to change and get in bed before he came in. Guys were lucky, they more or less just pulled off their pants and slept in their shorts.

"Are you decent, missus?" he asked and I told him I was already in bed. I heard him sit on the bed and drop his shoes, one by one, onto the floor and that's the last I knew until morning. If John snored, I didn't hear it.

Bright shafts of sunlight streaming in between the blinds, I grabbed my clothes and trundled down to the washroom to dress for the morning's walk. Patricia was there, shaking off sleep, pulling her hair into a ponytail through the loop of her ball cap.

"Did John snore again? I didn't hear any snoring. I was pretty tired though. We should walk together today," she suggested. "My pace is a little faster but that's alright. I might go a little faster later, but we can start together. Do you want to walk together?" I said I'd meet her out front.

Back in our room, John was up and dressed. As he hand-combed his thick black hair into place, he told me what a great sleep he'd had. So, it seems we all slept better last night; probably because we were split into small rooms. With a big stretch, his large frame filled the tiny room, and I ducked under his arm to fill my pack. John was going down to shave and trim his moustache, so he'd catch up with me later.

In the courtyard, Patricia was waiting, and we fell into step with each other as dawn lit up our path out of town. The land around us was pretty much flat farmlands with fledgling plantings pushing through the red dirt, promises of a healthy crop to come. I started my morning walking prayer ritual, only to be interrupted.

"It looks like this is going to be a really nice day. I didn't even put my rain layer on today. I have my sweater on. It's my warm layer, and I need to keep warm. Probably I'll take it off later. It looks like it's going to get warmer today." Down to my t-shirt already, I agreed with her. I found that as I walked, even my light coat became too warm. Despite overcast skies, the temperatures were warmer than back home, and I had been teased for walking bare-armed in light rain. I'd rather be a bit cool than hot and sweaty. Back to my morning prayers.

"Oh, look there, see those purple flowers? That's called ice plant. We have those back home in Tucson. They grow everywhere in the desert around our home. We have a nice place. It has no fence, so the wild critters get the plants, so we just let natural flowers grow." Patricia had retired from her engineering job a year ago. In recent years, with the drop in the economy, there had been extreme downsizing. She had felt, being one of the newer staff members, that it was only a matter of time before she was laid off too, so she took matters into her own hands.

"My husband and I had prepared well, and I was turning sixty, so I decided to go before they told me to go. At first I missed my job, but now I can travel to see my grandkids, so it's alright."

The landscape remained changeless, no trees or large bushes in sight. Refocusing, I touched my prayer beads.

"I really gotta go pee," Patricia interrupted again. "We didn't even have coffee yet, but I have to go bad. There's nowhere to hide. I don't know what to do. Maybe I can wait." We continued along, her level of anxiety growing, eyes darting here and there, looking for a likely hiding place.

"Patricia, just go there in the ditch. There's no one around except for that farmer on the tractor, and he's too busy to notice what you're doing. We're getting close to the road, so your opportunities are going to be less. By my figuring we have at least another hour's walk before we reach Ciruena." In desperation, she ran over and crouched in the ditch while I remained on lookout as instructed. Deed done, she returned, rearranging her plaid shirt over her slim hips. She said she felt much better now and I smiled. "You were starting to remind me of my dog Kirby when we're walking, and she's scouting for a place to pee." Patricia laughed and thanked me for making her stop. I decided I'd say my prayers later.

We reached the highway, and our path rose and fell in gentle waves paralleling the pavement. On we walked, up a hill, down a hill, through fields of greens and golds, Patricia gradually pulling ahead while I maintained my steady pace.

In the distance, I saw a small collection of white buildings and knew we were coming to Santo Domingo de la Calzada. Entering through the industrial section, I lost track of Patricia, but found June. I had to laugh when I saw her, clothes arrayed about her like a hooped skirt. She had taken a plastic circular clothes racks and moulded it around her pack, pinning her wet laundry to dry as she walked.

The perky young Japanese woman was doing her Camino with support through a blog. Over lunch, she told me she had left Japan after her father had died, not being able to reconcile herself with her step-mother. Living in Sweden with her Swedish boyfriend, her visa was running out. June had degrees in communications but had been unable to get permission to work and might have to return to Japan to support herself. Before she had to leave Europe, she wanted to achieve her goal of walking the Camino, so she had created the blog asking for support to do so. Apparently, it was a hit, and she faithfully reported her journey at the end of each day. I was torn in two directions; admiration that she had creatively utilized modern technology to achieve her goals, and frustration that while I (and most people I'd met) had worked hard and sacrificed to do this pilgrimage, she was getting a free ride. Then I reminded myself June's approach had no effect on my Camino, except that it enabled me to enjoy her company. She stayed to work on her blog, and I walked out into the bustling streets of Santo Domingo de la Calzada.

The cathedral in this town houses a pair of live chickens as symbols of an old Camino legend. In the early days of the pilgrimage, a couple was travelling with their young son. An innkeeper's daughter took a fancy to the young man, and when he spurned her affections, she arranged his arrest for theft by hiding a goblet in his pack. At that time, the punishment for the crime was hanging. When the mourning parents went to collect their son's body, he was still alive. They went to the leader of the town and said their son was alive and could they cut him free. The man ridiculed them, saying the boy was no more alive than the chicken on his plate, whereupon the chicken came to life and took flight. Apparently, the pardoned boy had been held up on the ghostly shoulders of St. James. Although I had planned to stop and check out the chickens, the price they "suggested" for admittance put me off. John had just caught up, and I saw him putting his euros in the box as he stepped inside.

Not being Catholic, the great religious cathedrals didn't have the same pull for me as for many of my fellow pilgrims. For them it was a matter of religion. For me it was the pull of history. I preferred to visit the smaller, less opulent houses of worship, although even in small towns, the churches were often impressive. Always a fan of the underdog, I was attracted to the soft, crumbling stones, the aged cracks, the weathered doors, and the fading frescos that spoke of the passage of time. As I meandered on my way, I had no idea it was in one such church I would sleep that night.

In solitude, I walked contemplating the vibrant colours of the Spanish countryside. As trucks trundled by on the adjacent motorway, I cast my gaze out across the fields to the purple foothills in the distance. In the quiet, I finally found time for my walking prayers. I called each of my loved ones by name and felt the presence of their love and support as I walked.

My late husband, Terry, came to mind, and I wondered what he would have thought of this journey. He was a good and simple man. Proud of his Ukrainian heritage and his family, he was not excessively religious, but one of the most Christian men I had known. High-school sweethearts, I felt so blessed to have known him and to have been loved by Terry. I gave thanks that after losing him, the empty space in my life was filled again by another good man.

Al had re-entered our lives, having never been a parent, just as my boys entered their teens. A turbulent time at worst, an interesting time in the best moments. Al and Terry had been friends and co-workers, sharing a love for hockey, baseball, and fishing. My sons had known Al all of their lives, and when we married, he said he was proud to finish the parenting work his friend had started. He kept their father alive for the boys, and while they didn't call him father, they introduced him as their dad.

Who was I to be so blessed not once, but twice? I knew other women who were, even at my age, still searching for their first good fit. I battled with the irony of having had to lose my first love to find my second, paralyzed to decide how I could give up one to have the other, given the choice. My greatest joys and my greatest sorrows intrinsically entwined, impossible to separate. Realizing my face was wet with tears, I resigned myself to the fact that these loves had been put in my life, each in their own time, for reasons yet unknown. Again, the power of solitude had opened my heart.

Ahead in the distance, at the top of a hill, I spied a small town. *Had I really travelled the seven kilometres to Granon already?* It's amazing what your body can accomplish on auto-pilot while your mind wanders off on its own. I recognized Patricia's plaid shirt ahead of me and saw that she was walking with a hefty, white-haired man.

Patricia introduced me to Michel, a man from Atlantic Canada she had met previously. Michel had a shock of silver white hair, translucent eyelashes, and the fairest skin I had ever seen. It turns out he was a year younger than me, although, despite his stocky build, he appeared older. This was Michel's second visit to Granon, and he led us around the back of the cathedral, through a weathered wooden door, down a low, winding cave-like passage, to a stone staircase. As we passed an alcove with signage requesting the deposit of boots and poles there, I recognized it was good to have someone with Camino experience along. I would never have found the way otherwise.

Inside we were welcomed with hugs by two petite, dark-haired women who bade us sit and rest while we waited our turn to register. Instead of the standard rubber stamp, our hostess drew a tiny angel in my pilgrim's passport; a special touch. Michel and John, who had also arrived, had been assigned beds one floor below. Patricia and I were led past the tiny kitchen, through the great room (equipped with a welcome wood-burning stove) and up a wooden staircase to the loft. We chose pallets (similar to gym mats) on the planked floor, staking our claim by rolling out our sleeping bags and stashing our backpacks on the rock ledge of the stone wall which would be our common headboard. I watched a young man stretching on his mat and realized he was the boy with the badly damaged feet I had seen back in Sansol. It seemed his feet were healing, and I was happy to see he had made it this far.

With only one shower, there was a wait for my turn, so I went in the kitchen to scare up a cup of coffee. Out in the great room, I saw Michel walk over and pick up a guitar left leaning in the corner, a feeling of familiarity that it had just been there, waiting for him to arrive. Strumming soft chords, he warmed up his thick fingers and then broke into Simon and Garfunkel's *Sounds of Silence*. A small crowd quickly gathered, pulling up softly cushioned chairs and worn wooden benches as they sat in quiet appreciation of the minstrel's skill. Quick segues from one folk song to another, many found their voice in familiar lyrics. Patricia touched my elbow, and I tore myself away to take my turn beneath the hot water.

Joining John on the street, we explored the town. The streets were quiet, and when the skies darkened and raindrops fell, even the curious pilgrims retreated indoors. We collected ourselves for the evening mass, mingling with locals who materialized with the ringing of the church bells. The haunting echoes of song and prayer filled the cavernous church, endowing us with a peaceful sense of belonging as we joined first in communion and then for a special pilgrim's blessing. As the smiling townspeople nodded encouragingly, the pilgrims were called to the front and, as a group, held in prayer for a safe and meaningful journey on to Santiago.

Shaking hands and receiving hearty embraces from our Spanish hosts, we walked back around the church, and up the stairs to join in the preparation of a family-style supper. Some men were put to work cutting loaves of bread, while

John and others were assigned the task of rearranging tables and unfolding chairs, transforming the great room into a dining room for fifty. A little Korean lady, who'd found a place inside the cramped kitchen, handed me a bowlful of peeled carrots and an ancient flat grater and, through motions, indicated I should shred them all for the salads. I saw her hand Patricia pitchers of water and Michel glasses to place on the tables. Each had their task as, like at any large family event, the room and the meal was prepared.

Seated knee-to-knee between John and Patricia at the wall-to-wall tables, we joined in a sung grace, toasted our *hospitaleros* with glasses of red wine, and waited hungrily as bread, salad, and pasta made its way up and down the tables. At one point, a late-coming pilgrim chose to miss dinner, wanting only to get to her bed in the loft. Unable to find a way past the tables, we watched in frozen silence as she simply stepped up on a chair, walked across the table, and stepped down on the other side to make her way up the staircase to the loft. The jovial chatter resumed, and glasses and plates were refilled until everything was gone.

Our *hospitalero* then announced that there would be meditation in the gathering room on the floor below and that anyone not wanting to participate could help with the dishes. She further advised that breakfast would be served at 7:00 am and that no one was to get up before then. Everyone rose to help clear the dishes and restore the sitting room. Having already been to church, I opted to help with the dishes, drawing comfort from this familiar task. Modern North American standards would be shocked! No sterilizing dishwasher here! We four who remained, took the dishes from sink, to towel, to rack.

My job done, I took advantage of the empty bathroom, then climbed to the loft. I snuggled into my sleeping bag, resting my head on the travel pillow I was using for the first (and last) time. Next to me, the Korean kitchen coordinator and her husband were snoring softy, each with their covers drawn over their heads like silky cocoons. Patricia tucked in beside me and, as I laid in the musty darkness, I listened to the soft pitter-pat of raindrops on the dormer windows and drifted deeply into sleep.

Disregarding the rules, when I woke at 6:00, some pilgrims were already packing, and others were already gone. Patricia rolled over, groaning that her hip was aching. Returning from the bathroom, I overheard our frustrated *hospitaleros* muttering about "not following the rules" and "it is too early" as they raced to put coffee, cut fruit, and cookies out on the counter for the impatient travellers. Seeing John in the corner chugging down a cup of coffee, I told him we'd be right down.

"I'll meet you out front, missus," he said, waving his package of smokes as explanation.

Patricia and I shouldered our packs, treading carefully down the stairs, stuffing a banana and a short stack of cookies in my pockets as we gave our thanks and said our goodbyes. A cool, misty world greeted us with silence. Not seeing John, we assumed he'd walked up to the head of the road, ready to start the day's trek. When we got there; no John.

"You stay here, and I'll go back down and see if he went across the street to get smokes." Patricia nodded her agreement, stamping her feet to keep warm. I checked the cafe on the square; no John. When I rejoined Patricia, I suggested we head out. "Maybe he wanted to walk alone to think about his plans."

As we dropped down into the valley, we saw the silvery sunlight breaking over the hills behind us. A roll of mist hung like cotton batting amongst the unfenced fields. Small, dark clusters of clouds warned that the rain may not yet be done with us.

After about an hour, we entered the hamlet of Redecilla del Camino, a place I remembered reading was not known for hospitality to pilgrims. Ever being one to form my own opinions, we stopped in at the town information office and asked to use the washroom. The solemn, dark-haired woman in a navy blazer and crisp white shirt behind the desk said it was "not possible". Okay, so maybe the reputation was well-earned.

"So much for improving tourist relations," I muttered to Patricia.

At a nearby hotel, we dropped our packs, and after using the facilities, carried coffees out to the roadside tables. We shared cookies from my pack and waved through cycling pilgrims, watching always for John. Draining our cups, with still no sign of him, we hit the road.

We came upon a fish vending truck as we were leaving town. Too small to support a market, the town relied on mobile shopping opportunities for fresh fruit and veggies, meat and fish, and bread. A stout woman, in a plaid housedress pulled over pants, waited watchfully as the vendor heaved a slab of silvery fish onto the scale. A lively negotiation broke out between the two, and I hoped she was getting a fair deal, not just settling because she had no other choice. They were both smiling as he slammed the doors on the cargo hold though, so I guessed everyone was happy.

A lightly clouded sky made for cool, comfortable walking, the gentle rises and dips adding interest to the trail. Up ahead Patricia spotted a familiar shirt.

"I think that's Michel. He wears a green shirt like that, and I think that's his hat too." We picked up our pace and caught up with Michel who was humming as he strode along. His Acadian roots showing, Michel was all about music. As we walked, he expounded on the different influences on his music and on his teaching of music over the years. He was recently retired, burning off the remainder of banked holiday time, and looked forward to the uncertainty of his future. He and Patricia stopped for a break at Castildelgado. Ready for a little quiet time, I walked on.

About four hours later, I reached Belorado. The narrow streets were lined with buildings, a labyrinth of stone, brick, and red tiles. Not yet siesta time, the locals were out and about, delivery trucks squeezing down tight passageways, shoppers with loaves protruding from bags slung over arms or secured on pedal bikes. Along the roadway, tiles were embedded with handprints and footprints. The Belorado walk of fame, I wondered?

I rounded the corner to the inviting fragrance of coffee, only to meet John coming out of the café. He gave me a hug. I told him I was sorry we had missed each other this morning, and he admitted he just wanted to walk alone for a while.

"'Tis nothing against you, girl," he quickly added, touching my shoulder. "I just needed some time on my own to think. I'll catch up with you at our next place, and we'll have a coffee. Good?" I assured him I understood and entered the cafe.

Ordering tapas, I settled down with my coffee, watching a young woman in the corner playing with her baby girl. When you're on the Camino, you hunger for children. Most of the towns I've walked through resembled ghost towns, few children, and not always a friendly welcome from the remaining adults.

I guessed the pilgrims were somewhat a necessary evil, like the summer tourists in my own town. When they flocked to our ocean-side city to enjoy the sandy beaches, the traffic got heavy, lineups at the stores got long, and the beach got so busy that locals pretty much avoided it until September. For northern Spain, the pilgrims definitely supported the economy, keeping otherwise dying communities alive, but I could only imagine the frustration of dealing with the never-ending stream of foreigners pounding down the paths and roadways, looking for directions, for beds, for food, and asking questions in a thousand languages.

The barista crossed to hug the young woman, obviously the mother of his child. In walked the grandparents and it was a spontaneous family reunion. Noting my interest, the proud grandmother came over and introduced her granddaughter, who I understood to be about a year old. In broken Spanish, I said I had a three-year-old granddaughter at home and we were instantly bonded in grandmother-hood. I hauled out my cellphone and shared pictures of my grandchildren, illogically believing a complete stranger would be interested, and happily finding she was. She told me they were beautiful, and I expressed how much I missed them. I was very touched when she unhesitatingly tried to pass me the baby, but I indicated my less than pristine condition and thanking her, sat down to enjoy my meal.

Just as I was finishing, the barista came over with a little cake I hadn't ordered. I looked over at the Spanish grandmother and she beamed, nodding, encouraging me to enjoy. A long, silky-haired dog stood with its nose poked in the door. I wasn't sure if it was begging or if its master was within. Children and dogs…I was missing home. Time to get going.

I heard Patricia call my name. Apparently, Michel had met some other friends and was visiting with them for a while. We left the stork-topped church of Belorado behind and struck off between fields of deep greens and bright yellows. The terrain became more hilly, and the *senda* ran parallel to a roadway. Across the road we saw what looked to be a church embedded in the side of the clay hills, the bell tower constructed on the surface with cave-like openings leading into the darkness. This would be Tosantos, where some 800 years ago, a woman known as *La Ermita* (the hermit) lived in the caves above the hamlet, ministering to passing Camino pilgrims. In her honour, the church fronting the caves was built, and it's still the site of annual celebrations.

A half-hour's walk further, we came to Villambistia. There, we found John waiting outside an *albergue*.

"They have beds here, fifteen euros each," he informed us. The building looked relatively new, surrounded by a gravel yard in which tufts of grass struggled to take hold.

"This isn't the place in the book," Patricia argued. "It must be new. Did you see the rooms? Are they alright? Can we do laundry?"

"I dunno. I was waiting for you girls to come."

I asked the man behind the counter if he could show us rooms, and he asked if we would just wait a few minutes. Those few minutes became longer, he and his wife having disappeared up the staircase.

"Should we go look at the other place, the one in the book?" Patricia questioned. I suggested she and John go look for the other place and I'd watch their things.

"Don't leave my bag will you now, missus?" asked John. "It's got my passport and all in it." With a smile, I assured him I would take good care of it and off they went. Mr. and Mrs. *Albergue* finally came down the stairs ready to show me the room. Carrying John's pack as well as my own, I struggled up the steps to find a bright bedroom with four single beds. They showed me a large bathroom with a compact shower stall in the corner. I advised I had to wait for my friends to return to decide. John came back, saying they'd found the place; it was great and would I come and see for myself.

Apologizing to Mr. and Mrs. Albergue, I followed him out the door and down the hill. Entering through a tiny café/bar, I was propelled up the stairs to a large room with seven sets of wooden bunks dressed in lime green coverlets. It was clean, bright and, so far, empty except for the three of us and the belongings of one more. The bathroom was large and airy, three toilets and three roomy showers. I was sold. I made sure to get a bottom bunk in the corner, away from the door.

When I came out of the shower, having rinsed and wrung my laundry, Patricia led me out to a sunny rooftop patio where I added mine to the lines of laundry dancing in the breeze. Seated in the corner, writing in her journal, was Kirsty from Denmark.

"Remember Elsa, the Aussie we met in Viana? She has just arrived downstairs and has two Romanian boys with her," Patricia updated me. So that was seven already. Not bad, considering I'd slept in rooms of twenty-four already this trip.

Down in the small café, we joined John over coffees as two young Spanish men lounged against the bar behind us, laughing with the barista, who was also the cook and owner of the *albergue*. In through the door came a compact, dark-eyed, dark-haired man who greeted her warmly. This, it turned out, was our *hospitalero*, who helpfully spoke better English. He completed our registration and told us supper was included with our beds, advising that we would take it in the private room adjoining the café. Tomas, as he was called, then went into the kitchen to act as sous chef in the preparation of our dinner.

When he came out, bearing baskets of slices of thickly crusted bread, Tomas observed us bent over our cellphones and guidebooks, planning out our next few days. On his return trip, empty-handed now, he stopped and sat down.

"You should not spend too much time planning. I have walked the Camino three times. You need to relax and let it unfold for you. There is no telling what you may experience in the next few days. You need to leave yourself open to it." We agreed, in principle, but shared our concern about our difficulty finding places to stay. "There will always be a bed for you," he assured us. "I never had to sleep outside, and some of the best places I stayed were the most unlikely. Now I must go help Alica. Your meal will soon be ready, and you will enjoy it, I guarantee."

Seated in the dining room, the seven of us bypassed language barriers getting to know each other. Where one's language was limited, others stepped in as translators, often meeting in a different, but common language. The Romanian boys, on holiday, leaving their office jobs and young wives behind, were enjoying the more physical, outdoor journey of the Camino.

Tomas came through the door, bearing platters of crispy salad, followed soon after by chicken simmered in a creamy, fragrant sauce. This we ladled over thick fresh pasta as we enjoyed glasses of robust red wine. Alica presented her dessert – hot chocolate cakes, drizzled with chocolate sauce and topped with fresh whipped cream and berries. Cheeks reddening at our applause, the young woman bowed slightly and retired to leave us to our dessert and conversation.

Clearing away the last of the dishes, Tomas, who lived in Madrid and volunteered as a *hospitalero* every year, advised us that the door to the café would be locked, but that breakfast would be waiting at the foot of the stairs for us in the morning. With that, he wished us a good night, *Buen Camino*, and departed for the night.

Well satisfied with the flavourful meal, some went for a stroll while others brought in their laundry. As I tucked my clothes into my backpack, I saw that all the top bunks in the room were still empty, so it would just be the seven of us this night. The price of the two *albergue* options being the same, but a wonderful dinner included here, I was glad we landed in this place. Everyone was tucking in for the night at the same time, and it was a family-type "good-night" session as salutes in several languages floated around the room. As I drifted off to sleep on the crisp pillowcase, I counted this as one of my nicest Camino *albergues* so far.

The sunrise illuminated the lime green curtains. My feet on the floor, it was not long until I was fully dressed and packed and, along with Patricia, was set to go. John was not far behind, as we snuck down the staircase to find hot coffee, fruit, and baskets of muffins and cakes, anonymously waiting our arrival. One muffin for breakfast and one for the road and we were out the door. Nothing else was moving in this tired little town; not even a dog to cheer us on our way.

Clouds were gathering, but that meant a welcome respite from yesterday's heat. As long as it remained dry, I was happy with cool. Our different strides separated us quickly, and soon I was walking alone. I knew I'd see the others somewhere along the way, at least when I got to the day's destination, Atapuerca.

I welcomed the solitude, reciting my morning prayers as I walked. Somehow it was just easier to do this alone, while I was walking. My mind was free of clutter and confusion and prayer came as easy as breathing. I gave thanks for my continued good health, my safety, and for those who had helped make this journey a reality for me. Looking about, I saw no one in sight. *Yo camino solo con mi Dios* (I walk alone with God). So…*not alone.*

Gradually climbing, my walk took me through rolling farmland, sometimes very close to a busy highway. After an hour, I arrived at the truck stop at the edge of Villafranca Montes de Oca. I remembered that this tiny hamlet had a history of welcoming pilgrims as early as the ninth century, but this would just be a quick stop for me today; bathroom and a coffee and I was off again

Climbing the hillside, I left the town below and came out on a gravel road, noticing shy clumps of pale yellow primroses growing randomly at the bases of bare-branched trees. On one side of the road, the land dropped sharply to the valley floor and the view was breathtaking. Tender green fiddle heads appeared as ferns awakened for the spring. More clouds gathered as the road climbed in a gentle curve around the hillside, thick with large heather bushes, all vivid pinks and purples.

I reached the Monumento de los Caidos, a symbol of remembrance dating back to the Spanish civil war. The wrought iron fence surrounding the monument was tied with ribbons and prayers as it stood hauntingly alone midst the dark forests. It appeared the storm was not going to hold much longer.

"Hey there Canada!" a voice called out. I turned to see a tall, robust man striding after me. "I see by your backpack you're Canadian. I'm Doug," he smiled, pushing his fine, white hair back from his deeply tanned face. "I'm from Pennsylvania originally, but now I've retired to Florida."

I introduced myself as I struggled to free my banana from my pack, and we continued side-by-side, him telling me all about his journey. Doug was travelling with a group of Dutch men, but they'd left early this morning, so he was in catch-up mode. There was a refreshment stand at the summit, and Doug joined other pilgrims clustered about to see what they offered. I waved and walked on, anxious to get to Atapuerca in time to get a bed.

Suddenly, the clouds shattered and rain plummeted to the ground. Glad that I had at least covered my pack with the shell, I sheltered under the trees edging the road, pulled out my poncho, dragged it over my head, and headed off down the road.

Suddenly, I heard my name. I stopped and saw only Doug's legs. The rest of his body and head were swallowed by an attacking sheet of plastic. He struggled, fighting the wind, hunting for armholes, pulling a dollar-store poncho around him.

"Roxey, can you give me a hand?" he called out. I sighed. I always seem to get stuck with needy people, and one of my Camino goals was to fight my instinct to fix everything and help everyone. But it wouldn't be very "pilgrim" of me to walk away and leave someone begging for simple assistance, now would it? So back I went to help Doug find his armholes and tame the flapping poncho.

"Got this just in case. I was really hoping I wouldn't need it. Where are you staying tonight? The guys I was walking with are stopping in Ages if they can get beds." I told him, between gusts of wind driving rain at my face, that I was aiming for Atapuerca, a couple of kilometres further, and was meeting friends there. After he did the kilometre to miles translation, he suggested he could go that far today. I didn't remember asking him to join me.

The chapel at San Juan de Ortega was locked, but the café beside it was doing a steady trade. Inside, out of the rain, I saw Patricia and Kirsty at one table, and John just paying for his meal. How and when did they get so far ahead of me? John cocked his head looking at Doug standing expectantly at my elbow. I tried to convey to John that this guy had kind of attached himself to me and I was looking for rescue, but it was kind of hard to do with Doug standing beside me! My friends said they'd see me at Atapuerca. I had hoped Doug would walk on to find his friends at Ages.

When I came out of the washroom, there he was, waiting for me. He'd ordered a *bocadillo* (a meat and cheese foot-long sandwich) and asked if I'd like to share. Then, wanting to thank me for my assistance, he insisted on buying my coffee as well. I was at a loss of what to do. My Canadian instincts just wouldn't allow me to be rude and tell him to shove off. My practical instincts said I'd really only wanted half a sandwich to begin with. I didn't feel I had much choice, so I sat down on the chair he'd pulled out. Oh well. It was only a few more kilometres, and then he'd go his way.

Under clearing skies, we found Doug's friends, sipping beer outside the *albergue* at Ages. They called out that there was a bed left for him, but he cheerfully announced he was going on to Atapuerca with his new friend. I looked around and saw only me. On we walked, him telling me all about his wife, his kids, his grandkids, and his dog. In full sunshine, we arrived at Atapuerca to find everyone there, backpacks still attached; not a good sign.

"There's no fookin beds!" John declared. "We have to go on to the next town. It's another five and a half kilometres." He glanced over at my new walking partner, giving me a questioning look. My responding look said "whatever" when my voice couldn't tactfully do so.

Patricia, Kirsty, and John took the lead as Doug and I brought up the rear. Leaving the gravel roadway, we wound our way along a narrow trail up the side of a steep hill. I'd already stowed my poncho and taken off my coat, yet in the oppressive heat, I started to falter. Doug continued to talk, and I focused on the drone of his words to pull me up the hill. The others were pulling ahead as we cautiously dodged sheep droppings and loose rocks.

"If there isn't a bed at the next place, I'm calling a taxi and going to the next town and getting a hotel room!" I stated. "I just can't walk anymore hills in this heat!" He was with me on that idea and said maybe we could share. I was hoping he was just suggesting the taxi and not the hotel room.

We continued to climb as our companions disappeared over the ridge. Doug's chatter had slowed to the occasional query as to how I was doing. I had to appreciate his concern and found that annoying in itself, in view of my earlier thoughts about him being the needy one. At the top of the hill, stood a tall, white cross. With no information marker, I wondered if it was a special place of prayer, or if someone else just hadn't made it over the hill.

Below us, the group reached the dirt road, a promising collection of buildings just ahead in the distance. Reaching the road ourselves, I spied a large barn, rolls of hay bursting out the dilapidated front door.

"We could always just sleep in the barn. It was good enough for Mary and Joseph!" I was getting giddy by this point. My water was gone, it was hot, I was tired, and I felt abandoned by my friends.

Finally, we reached Cardenuela Riopico, and we dragged ourselves to the door of an *albergue*, gaily announcing itself with waving flags. I had no energy to wave back.

My friends hadn't abandoned me! They had told the *hospitaleros* we were coming and the last two beds were ours! Euros paid, passports stamped, I dragged my pack over to the separate bunkhouse, feeling every one of the thirty kilometres I'd walked. Twenty bunks lined the two sides of the long, narrow room, many already occupied by exhausted pilgrims. Dropping my pack at the end of the bunk next to Patricia's, I grabbed the last blanket by the door and put it on the remaining bed for Doug as my thanks for his steadfast company and encouragement over the sheep trail. Doug collapsed on his bunk, and I went in search of a shower.

Back in the main building, John, Patricia, and I sat in deep, cushy couches, consulting our guidebooks, debating our earlier plans for Burgos. The book recommended bypassing the dangerous stretch of highway by taking a taxi or bus the last seven kilometres into the heart of the large city. We had planned to stay in Atapuerca, walk thirteen kilometres to Castanares, and then taxi in. With the lack of beds forcing us to move, we were already that same distance from Burgos itself. Should we taxi? Should we walk and then taxi? Should we just walk? We fought the goal to walk every step, against the safety concerns of walking along the highway. We decided to wait until the morning when we were more rested and we knew what the weather was doing before making a final decision.

Our *hospitaleros* were setting the table for our family-style supper. I ran over to the bunkhouse and shook Doug awake, telling him to come for supper. When I returned to the dining hall, John and Patricia had saved a seat between them at the end of the table. I looked around realizing there was no nearby seat for Doug. Patricia tugged my arm almost angrily.

"Just sit! He can find his own place." Torn between guilt and relief, I had been reclaimed by my pack.

When Doug came in, the meal already in progress, he looked for me and saw no empty seat nearby. I shrugged apologetically. The *hospitalero* directed him to a table in the corner.

The chicken in front of me floated grease, and the limp fries made the salad and bread the best part of the meal. I was so tired, so beat up, and so worn out, I ate mechanically. And then, a magical thing happened! Our *hospitalero* placed a frosty glass bowl of fresh strawberries before me. Strawberries! Cold, clean, and sweet. How perfect! More refreshing than my shower, the vibrant fruits renewed my spirit. I savoured each slice of berry, catching an errant dribble of juice with a flick of my tongue.

As Patricia and I lay head to head in our bottom metal bunks in the dimly-lit room, we quietly discussed plans for Burgos. This was the first major city we were coming to. Initially I had planned to stop two days there for a rest day.

"If we're going to taxi in, we'll get there early, so we'll have lots of time to explore the city. I don't really want to stop two nights though. I think, for me, the best way to rest would be to do shorter days, but still keep moving. I think I'd really like to stay in a hotel instead of an *albergue* though. I'd love a real bath and a real bed for a change."

"Oh, and some clean laundry!" Patricia oozed.

John walked over and crouched by our beds. "Don't be talking about a taxi too loudly, girls. There's them that would frown on that idea," he whispered, tossing his head at the full beds around us.

"If you want, we could share a room," whispered Patricia. "I'd like a private bed for a night too." I nodded my agreement as I nodded off to sleep, visions of bubbles foaming over the side of a porcelain tub of steaming, hot water dancing in my dreams.

We awoke to rain beating against the windows of the bunkhouse. Amidst heavy sighs, some pilgrims resignedly packed and geared up for a wet day. Others pulled their covers over their heads in denial.

Running through the rain to the main building, Patricia, John, and I huddled at a corner of the breakfast table, hot cups of coffee clutched in our hands, considering our options for the day. Castanares was seven kilometres away, about an hour and a half's walk and plenty of time to get soaked in this weather before jumping the recommended bus for the last bit to Burgos. We weighed the ethics of walking against the sanity of arriving dry and decided in favour of the last.

"We'll just have our breakfast and let some of these others clear out, and then we'll call the taxi," John cautioned. I really didn't know what all the subterfuge was about. By this point, most people had taken a taxi or a bus at least a short distance for one reason or another. Even the guidebook suggested that this was an area worth bussing for the safety of avoiding the busy highway into the city.

Just then, the door blew open, and Doug strutted into the room, collapsing in a sodden heap in the empty chair across from us.

"So," he said, "what are we doing?" We exchanged guilty glances, wondering how to tactfully disengage ourselves from this older man who continued to insinuate himself into our little group. Coming up with nothing, I told him that we were taking a taxi into the city.

"Patricia and I are going to share a room if we can find a place that isn't too expensive," I advised.

"So, there should be room for four in the taxi, which will lower the cost for everyone," Doug reasoned. "And you," he said, looking at John, "we could share a room like the girls if that's okay with you." I saw John do silent battle, not wanting to share with Doug, against the reality of his dwindling funds. The lure of a semi-private room forced his decision, and he agreed to share with Doug for one night. Doug wasn't doing anything wrong, but there was still an aura of resentment of his sense of entitlement to tie his Camino in with ours.

It took twenty minutes to ride what we would have walked for almost three hours in the pouring rain. The six euros we each paid was definitely worth it as the taxi dropped us off right downtown. The tourist information office wouldn't open for another hour, so we sheltered in a nearby coffee shop, indulging in creamy coffees and pastries. In a grand gesture, Doug insisted on buying "the round", but we asserted our independence, each determined to pay our own way. The rain continued to fall from leaden skies, striking the cobblestones of the square as pedestrians rushed by, hats, umbrellas, or newspapers held over their heads as they ran. Across the street, we had our pilgrim passports stamped and received maps of the city indicating nearby hotels. Patricia quickly made a call, reserving two twin rooms in a nearby hotel. All we had to do now was find the place.

The rain had backed off as we walked out into the renaissance city. Two and three-storey buildings, pristinely maintained, stood shoulder to shoulder along the narrow streets. The storefronts of the old city displayed fashion for young and old. The men had to tear us away, as Patricia and I oohed and ahhhed over European, hand-made outfits for toddlers and glowing leather shoes for us.

"If you buy it, you'll have to pack it," John reminded us playfully, tugging on our packs to get us moving.

Following the map, we crossed under an archway and out to a modern inter-section, busy with automobiles of every type. Crossing the road paralleling the river, we continued down the wide, intricately patterned sidewalk, searching for the Hotel Rice. Patricia and I carefully noted the location of the "All Things Chocolate" shop for future reference.

As we entered the high-ceilinged, opulent lobby, we wondered if we'd made a mistake. Conscious of our boots and backpacks, we felt like intruders in this soft world of glass, chrome, and deep, plush carpets. The young woman behind the desk smiled up at us and Patricia advised her of our reservations.

"Oh yes, I have you here," the girl stated in beautifully accented English. "Your rooms are not ready yet," she advised as we filled in registration forms. "May I invite you into our dining room to enjoy a complementary coffee while you wait. Walking across the lobby, we looked at the lovely tables, set with linen, crystal, and silver, fine upholstered chairs sinking their feet into the carpet. Mid-day, the room was empty, but we still looked at each other and at our feet doubtfully.

"Or you could just rest here at this table, and I will have coffee brought to you," she suggested, sensing our discomfort. A less formal table was tucked into a corner just inside the door. A young waitress arrived with porcelain cups of scalding black coffee, a pitcher of warm cream, sugar, and a plateful of pastries. Now this was the way to wait!

Advised that "the ladies' room" was ready, Patricia and I were whisked to the third floor in a smooth elevator. A short way down the hall, the door opened to our waiting room. Two real beds, a television (which we agreed not to turn on), and best of all, a deep, white bathtub; we were in heaven.

"There's toilet paper…and a seat! And real towels!" Patricia exclaimed. How quickly these little things had become important. The butter yellow walls were decorated with creamy crown moulding, and heavy drapes hung to the floor framing a large bay window that looked out onto the street and river below. Giddy as school girls, we decided on quick showers for now, with plans for long tub soaks before bed.

While Patricia showered, I took the opportunity to call Al and bring him up to date on my progress. I told him about the "no room at the inn" walk from hell, the rain, the heat, and the hills. I shared my frustration with Doug's presumptuous attitude. When Al asked if John was still with me, I said yes, but he was probably going to bus out in the morning, so it would be just Patricia and me.

"I'm glad you decided on taking the taxi. I'd much rather you arrived by car dry and safe than you did trying to walk that nasty stretch in the rain." Validated by the man I loved, I switched places with Patricia, seeing her pick up her cellphone as I closed the bathroom door behind me. Dressing in our cleanest clothes, and careless of the cost, we sent everything we weren't wearing to the laundry and were advised by a smiling housekeeper that it would be returned to our room by late afternoon.

"Our room just came ready," John said when we joined him in the lobby. "Doug's taking a nap. I just changed and brought my laundry down. I'll shower later. The sun's come out. Let's go explore."

Out into the day we went, lighter without our packs, retracing our steps under the arch. We followed shell symbols from the square by the information office, up the narrow winding road. Fluffy, white clouds had replaced the gloom of this morning's sky, and slashes of sunlight invaded the dark medieval passage ways.

We strolled on, dodging sandwich boards advertising meals and lodging, still looking for the famous cathedral. And then suddenly, the street opened up into a brilliantly sunny square featuring a massive meringue concoction of spires, statues, buttresses, turrets, and impressive stained-glass windows. Construction of the Cathedral de Santa Maria began in the early 1200's. Like so many of the significant cathedrals in Europe, its final construction was the product of many different architectural styles, the hands of master builders adding their embellishments over many generations. Its sheer size and dazzling edifice left us speechless. Necks craning to see the top, we circled the cathedral wondering which of the many heavy, arched doors was the entrance. Down a wide, stone staircase on one side of the building, we came out to the huge lower square where an old woman, begging at the foot of another massive staircase, directed us up to the ornately carved portal above.

Coins in a cup, once inside, finely sculpted arches towered above the glossy tiled floors, filtered sunlight pouring in through the leaded windows of the central tower. Sculpted stone pillars drew our eyes up to masterpieces of stained-glass windows, exploding in colourful religious scenes. Denied entrance by the locked wrought-iron gate, we strained to see the main altar. Doorways led off to side chapels, promising more beauty and inviting exploration. If only the gate were open.

In the square, deserted but for a few lingering pilgrims in these siesta hours, we took photos of each other seated beside the bronze pilgrim's statue. With a haggard expression and body torn and abused by his own journey, the pilgrim sat resting, as if trying to convince himself to take up his staff and carry on. I looked at his mangled bare feet and gave thanks again for my own healthy feet. The square was encircled by old stone and plaster buildings; homes of great medieval families, now divided into multiple apartments. Above their tiled rooftops, I saw dark clouds, heavy with unspent rain, ominously gathering again. Glancing up, John suggested we head back down the street for a late lunch at a little café we had spotted earlier.

"Oh good!" Patricia exclaimed, "I'm starving." She was always starving, this tiny slip of a woman. Where did she put it all!

"Tis really making the most sense as you said, missus, to go ahead by bus," John said, broaching his travel options. "I don't want to leave you girls, but I don't think I have a choice." Despite my reluctance to see him go, I assured him we would be alright, and that he had to do what he had to do to get there in time. We consulted our map and found the bus station was nearby.

"Let's go check it out," I said, trying to put his indecision to rest. "We can find out the times and the costs, and you can plan tomorrow around that." It was like coming through a time travelling tunnel to find ourselves back in the more modern section of the city, where we found our way to the cavernous bus depot. At the wicket, I employed my minimal Spanish to help John get the information he needed. Unhappily resigned to his new plan, his ticket for Leon in hand, we headed along the busy streets, back to our hotel.

In the lobby, Doug stood, freshly showered, hands in pockets, feet jammed in flip-flops, waiting our return.

"Hey guys! What's say we go get something to eat," he called out, all chipper after his afternoon's snooze. Exchanging frustrated glances, John told him we'd been out walking all afternoon and suggested an hour's break so he could shower before we walked out again. "Well I'm going to have a drink in the bar then. Come get me when you're ready," a disgruntled Doug stated as he stomped off.

Upstairs in our room, Patricia and I delighted over the beribboned cellophane packages of neatly folded laundry waiting on our beds. They were almost too pretty to open, and it seemed a shame to stuff all those carefully folded items back in our packs. In the bathroom, the bottles of shampoo and bath gel had mysteriously multiplied during our absence. Passing time, we hung out the window and watched the scene come alive as siesta ended; doors were pushed open and Burgos took to the street in noisy, vivacious activity.

"Done and dusted," a more cheerful John met us in the lobby, Doug sauntering out of the bar behind him.

"I feel like a nice, big, juicy steak," Doug declared. "But I don't want to walk too far." We advised him from our earlier recon, that the best opportunities really were back in the old city.

Patricia and I, determined to stop at "All Things Chocolate" dragged the men in through the door where a buffet of chocolate desserts greeted us. Wide-eyed, like kids in a proverbial candy shop, we finally made our selections, and the young woman behind the counter tied up shiny gold boxes for each of us.

Swinging our treasures by their ribbons, we entered the old city to discover an Australian couple we'd met in our early days. Chatting happily, we asked about others we hadn't seen in a while and learned that several had dropped off as early as Logrono, and even more here in Burgos. Hugs all around and *Buen Camino's* said, we led Doug to an eatery we had spotted earlier in the day.

Our lunch having filled us more than we'd expected, we just ordered salads, bread, and drinks while Doug ordered up a three-course pilgrim's meal including steak. When Doug's dessert arrived, Patricia and I joined him, opening up our decadent chocolate packages while John went outside for a smoke.

As evening fell, walking through the darkening streets back to our hotel, we brought Doug up to speed on John's plans to bus out in the morning.

"I don't go until 10:00," John said, "so I can sleep in a bit and have a decent breakfast before I walk down to the bus station."

"Okay then, girls," Doug said, "what time do you want to meet to walk out in the morning?" Torn between not wanting to hurt feelings, but also wanting to wrest back control of my own Camino, I dug in, refusing to let Doug buttonhole us into his schedule.

"We're not sure what time we're leaving. We may explore a little more in the morning and then just walk a shorter distance for the day. We really just want to let our journey unfold for us," I said, Patricia nodding in agreement. Obviously, this type of vague, unstructured approach was not comfortable for Doug. He shook his head, wished us well, and walked off to the bar saying he's see John back in the room later.

Stifling giggles, Patricia walked over to the hotel desk to settle her bill while I sat out on the stoop with John, enjoying a few quiet moments together. He said he'd probably not see us in the morning. He didn't like goodbyes. I replied that would probably be a good thing since I didn't cry pretty.

"If you need me, you have my number. You just give me a call, and I'll come back for you, missus," he insisted softly.

"Aw now, and how are you goin' to be doin' that when you're in Santiago?" I teased back, affecting an Irish lilt. "I'll be fine, John. I'll miss you…but I'll be fine. I'm not sure if this will fit," I said, rolling my Micah bracelet off my wrist, "but I want you to have this to remember me by."

"Oh, now you're going to have me bawlin, girl!" He took the bracelet and stretched it over his large, tanned hand. "I'll wear it for now, but I know my daughter is going to claim it when she sees it when I get home. It's been a pleasure walkin' with you, missus," he said folding me in a hard hug. We walked into the lobby and rode the elevator up with Patricia, who wished John well in the hallway before we turned to our room.

"My hip is so sore. I guess I've been walking too fast. It' really hurts," Patricia muttered.

"I have a tennis ball in my pack," I suggested, "you can use it to roll on a sore muscle, sort of like a massage."

"What a great idea!" I dug in my pack and handed her the ball, watching with interest as she lay on the floor, and placing it under her hip, rolled back and forward. "Ohhhh. This really hurts! But it hurts really good," she groaned.

"Glad it's helping. I've been carrying it all this time and never used it yet. Why don't you carry it and use it. If I need it, I'll get it back from you."

"Really? That would be great! It really is making my hip feel better. I'm so glad you got rid of Doug!" Patricia giggled, changing the subject. "He is way too needy."

I protested, I didn't "get rid" of him.

"Oh, you're so Canadian!" she laughed.

I left Patricia to her "massage" and ran a bath, liberally dumping miniature bottles of lemon bath gel into the gleaming white tub. By the time I dragged myself out of the steaming scented waters, Patricia was fast asleep. Goodnight Burgos.

In a shroud of mist, burdened with our packs, we left the warm luxury of our hotel, heading back into the old city for a hot breakfast before heading out. Watching the city waken, we quietly sipped our hot coffee, each wrapped in our own thoughts, but likely both missing John. We had not seen him, nor Doug, as we left the hotel. Likely Doug followed through on his plans to strike out early, and John on his plans to sleep late.

We tapped our way up the drizzly street, passing the silent cathedral, following shells out of the old city. When the signals disappeared, we asked a woman who told us to just follow the river, and we would be fine. The promenade paralleled the rushing water, huge trees trailing branches into the river. Following bobbing backpacks ahead, we crossed a footbridge to the other side and there, Kirsty materialized, joining our exodus. Leaving the city limits, we came out to ragged grasslands, and eventually a crossroads, where we met a couple of pilgrims puzzling over directions. The bright yellow arrows that dictated our passage had us stumped; two different arrows pointed in two totally opposite directions. The rain began in earnest, so I used the pause as an opportunity to pull on my poncho.

"Maybe one arrow is for pilgrims coming into Burgos, and the other is for those leaving," Kirsty mused. We agreed on what we thought was the more logical choice and stepped out in faith that we were going in the right direction.

I was happy to leave Kirsty and Patricia chatting, seeking the quiet for my morning prayers to which I added John (and somewhat reluctantly, Doug). I was surprised at how saddened I was by not having John's cheerful Irish banter along. As well as proclaiming himself one of the few Irishmen who didn't drink, John was one of the few people I knew who didn't have an email address.

"My daughter is always on me about setting up email," he'd laughed, "but I can't be bothered you know. I don't have time for plunking away at a computer, and these don't make it easy," he joked, waggling his thick working hands. Before we parted, I'd given him my address. I told him he could get in touch with me by email through his daughter if he wanted, at least until he joined the rest of the world with email! I wondered if I'd ever hear from him again.

I guess I was not really one to talk. Much to our children's disgust, Al and I refused to join the network media frenzy they used so easily. We told them if they wanted us to know something to send us a message or give us a call. If they wanted us to have photos of their lives, they'd have to send them to us and not expect us to fish them off the internet. We would always "like" them, and they'd always be our "friends"; we didn't need technology for that.

About three hours later, we reached the tidy hamlet of Tardajos.

"I need chocolate!" Patricia stated as she and Kirsty, poles and packs colliding, pushed through the narrow doorway of the local market. I asked them to grab me a banana, and lowered my pack to wait. A young woman was helping a stoop-backed, elderly man to sit on a bench over by the town fountain. *Was she his daughter, or his granddaughter?* I wondered, unable to discern her age. Maybe she was a caregiver, not related at all. My hometown had a predominately senior population, and over the years, I'd learned not to make assumptions as ages and roles blurred and became less easily defined. My own husband, grey haired, debilitated by MS, and in a wheelchair by his late fifties, probably appears older than he is, and I'm sure people who don't know us wonder at our connection.

Al, always worried that my life was held back by his condition, was concerned I would begin to resent him for the limiting confines of our lives. I thought that was probably part of why he was so supportive of me doing this pilgrimage; a time for me, not impeded by his MS. While a lesser person might have succumbed to depression and bitterness, Al pushes on, accepting that it is what it is, and making the best of every situation. We have a plaque in our home that states "Carrying on Regardless", and that's us.

Actually, I don't resent Al, but I do resent MS. It has stolen so much from him as a man and from us as a couple. It is hard to see couples, twenty years our senior, walking hand-in-hand on the beach, playing in the water, as I walk along beside his wheelchair, confined to the sidewalk, not even able to hold hands because he has to steer and work the controls. I thought how much he would have loved this trip, discovering new places, new foods, and new friends. He is a people person and I could imagine his smiling blue eyes as he charmed the locals and fellow pilgrims alike. I missed him deeply and wished he could be here, sharing this journey with me. As the ladies returned, I dashed tears from my cheeks, selling them as raindrops from the brim of my cap.

Under leaden skies we walked on, Kirsty dropping back to find her quiet place, and Patricia falling into step with me, full of chocolate and chatter.

"These are amazing chocolate bars! Look how big they are!" she beamed, pulling out a mammoth slab of chocolate. "They only cost three euros. This would be about ten dollars at home. I just love chocolate!" Really? I would never have known! As she passed me a chunk of chocolate, we continued along the gravel *senda*, flowing over rolling hills of green. In the distance, I saw one lone spreading tree, no other bushes or trees in sight. Its solitary nature enhanced its beauty, and we stopped to appreciate this one-tree wonder, admiring its persistence to survive.

At the foot of the hill, we saw a village and knew our arrival at Hornillos del Camino was imminent. As we descended the slope into the town, Kirsty said twenty kilometres was enough for her, and she was stopping here for the day. Mindful of the previous days' difficulty of getting a bed, Patricia and I had decided to push past this popular stop indicated in the guide book and travel on to the next town, San Bol. We said our farewells and, walking past a donkey laden with bags patiently waiting its pilgrim owner's return, we struck out on the road again.

"Kirsty is really nice, isn't she nice?" Patricia asked. "She's so calm and peaceful." I agreed, saying that it was a real gift to be able to find that level of peace in the midst of everything going on in our lives. "It's pretty quiet out here, isn't it?" she continued, looking around at the emptiness around us. On the *meseta* now, in every direction all we saw were gently rolling fields; no hills, no trees, no buildings, and no other pilgrims. The red dirt road before and after us was devoid of life except ours. "Do you think we're going the right way?" Did I mention no markers? "Are we going the right way?" she repeated.

"This was the only path when we left Hornillos as far as I could see," I replied. It's supposed to be six kilometres to San Bol," I said as we took a gradual incline around a corner. We walked on in silence for another half hour when the crunch of feet warned of a lone pilgrim behind us.

"Where did he come from? That's just spooky! He came out of nowhere," Patricia worried. "Do you think he's stalking us?" It did seem strange for someone to be behind us suddenly, but then it only takes a small hill or a corner to separate people from sight. Perhaps he had been behind us all the way, just far enough that the minor hillocks prevented us from knowing he was there.

"Well, there's two of us," I smiled. "And we both have poles, so I think we'll be okay. It can't be too much further." But still, we saw no sign of buildings or towns. Suddenly, a pair of cycling pilgrims overtook us, wishing us *Buen Camino* as they passed, clods of red dirt churning up from their tires as they climbed the slope ahead and disappeared from sight. Well at least we knew we were on the right track.

Looking across the fields, I saw a couple of old buildings to the left. I remembered in the guide that it said San Bol was a bit "off route", so maybe that was where we needed to go. As we reached the bottom of the dip, we looked more closely at the buildings. One was obviously a ruin, but the other was in a bit better repair.

"Let's check it out," I suggested and we trekked down the road towards the solitary building. As we approached, there it was, a big sign on the side of the stone wall "San Bol Municipal Albergue". Excuse me? How can you have a municipal *albergue* without a municipality! The building was charming; old stones, red-tiled roof, and a bee-hive shaped turret at one end. A sparkling brook ran through a grove of poplar trees adding to the peaceful tranquility of the *albergue*.

"What if we're the only ones here?" whispered Patricia. "This is kind of strange." Or unique. I preferred unique. We pushed open the heavy door and stepped inside the warm foyer to be greeted by a voluptuous young woman with chestnut curls falling to her shoulders. We quickly determined that yes, this was the *albergue* and no, she spoke no English. Through motions and fragmented Spanish our smiling *hospitalero*, Camilla, checked us in and showed us to the bunkroom wherein we found a young Asian woman and a tall, dark-haired man stretched out in yoga poses on mats on the floor.

"Roxey, it is me, Iru," exclaimed the Asian yoga instructor. "I have not seen you since we left St. Jean," she said as I smiled with recognition. "This is Jean. He is from France. We walked together from Burgos today. I was teaching him how to stretch." It was amazing how you could go for days without seeing anyone you knew and then all of a sudden, there they were.

"This is the first time I've used my bedroll since I started," quipped Jean. "So, I did need it after all."

There were two beds in the loft, but given our choice, we selected two lower bunks in the main room. The room was very warm, which was nice after the chill of the day. There was only one bathroom, and it included the solitary shower. When I came back from my shower, rinsed laundry in hand, Patricia showed me she had laid hers on the floor under the bed to dry. Jean guessed there must be hot water pipes running under the tile floor which made the room so warm. There were actually spots so hot you couldn't stand in bare feet. Spreading out my wet t-shirt on the hot tiles, it wasn't long before I saw steam rising from the cloth. Toasted clothes; what a concept.

Outside we explored the property and found the pond. A local myth had it that if you soak your feet in the blessed waters for three minutes, you would not have a blister on the Camino. Well so far so good, but not one to leave things to chance, balancing shakily on the rock wall, I kicked off my boots, and peeled off my socks. The icy water dripped from my numb feet as I pulled them from the pond, having kept them in as long as I could stand.

"Not sure that was three minutes," joked Patricia who gamely pulled off her own footwear. Bravely she plunged her tootsies in the water and almost as quickly pulled them out. "Damn! Shit that's cold!"

"Not sure that was three minutes," I teased. When I first started walking with Patricia, I wasn't sure I could travel with her without getting a cavity, so sweet did she seem. Her slow, southern draw sucked you right in, smooth as molasses, but as I came to know her, I realized my first impression was deceiving. This feisty little lady could curse with the best of them, and she didn't hesitate to call a spade a spade.

Back in the *albergue*, four more men had arrived and we wondered if any were the "stalker pilgrim" we had seen behind us. Not much to do but read our guidebooks, compare travel notes, and flip laundry, so we wandered out to help set the table for dinner. Finding one of the late arrivals in conversation with Camilla, we asked if he could find out why the police had been here. We'd seen them getting back in their truck on our way back from the pond. We were informed that they came by from time to time to check passports registered, especially if they were trying to locate a pilgrim whose family was trying to reach them. So, nothing to do with the "stalker pilgrim". Good to know.

Having quickly secured chairs next to the wood stove in the bee-hive dining room, we held our glasses as a young Swiss man filled them with red wine from unmarked bottles. A large tray of salad lay near my spot, and I suggested people pass me their plates and I'd serve it out.

"Okay, Mom," laughed Jean as he passed his plate. Oil, vinegar, and salt made the rounds, followed by a basket of thick slices of heavy bread. Camilla entered, proudly placing a huge round pan of paella on the circular table. Colourful and fragrant, the rice and chicken dish was heavy with tomatoes and peppers, a robust meal for this chilly weather.

"Will you serve again, Mom?" asked Jean. "They say if you want to ensure good weather for the next day, you must eat everything." An interesting ploy to ensure not having leftovers, I thought, spooning paella on plates until the pan was empty. When the plates were removed and the wine glasses refilled, Camilla came in with ice-cream cups for dessert and presented me with a key and a note written in English.

"It seems," I started, "that Camilla does not stay here at night. She will do the dishes and then leave for the night. We will be on our own overnight. The note says that the last pilgrim to leave in the morning is to take this key and give it to the barista at the first bar in the next town." Despite the confused looks exchanged around the table, Camilla's beaming face reassured us this is just how it was done, and there was nothing to worry about. We applauded her supper and thanked her as she smiled and gathered up the last of the dishes.

After as much wine and conversation as I could manage, I excused myself to retrieve my dry, warm laundry from under the bed. Folding clothes into my compression bags, I stuffed my backpack using my system of one bag for underwear and socks, one for long, warm clothes, and one for shorts and t-shirts. When you're used to having a place for everything, living out of a backpack for weeks can test you; finding a way to organize the contents saved my sanity. On my last trip to the washroom, I walked past the dining room door, saying *buenos noches* to those lingering over another glass of wine.

As I climbed into bed and pushed in my earplugs, I wondered who would be taking the black iron key on the table to the next town in the morning.

Morning spilled in through the narrow, curtainless windows. The German man in the next bed continued to snore, as he had through most of the night. Having gone to bed early, I got at least a couple hours of solid sleep before his slumber-sapping symphony began. It was going to be a long day, I thought as I prepared my feet for the day's trek. Not much sleep last night, twenty-five kilometres to go, and no coffee until Hontanas, five kilometres away.

Pulling cautionary rain shells over our packs, Patricia and I walked out into an anvil-grey morning, dodging puddles in the gravel road as the San Bol track merged with the main Camino *senda*. Green fields, stretched in all directions, glistening with the night's rainfall as a soft breeze shook drops from blade tips. The road, however, was not as pretty. As mud sucked at our boots, we struggled to keep our footing and, fighting the additional twenty pounds on our backs, our balance.

"Just think of this as resistance training," I laughed. Patricia was a good companion in the challenging work, laughing when others might have complained or whined.

"Can you just imagine what John would be saying about this!" she giggled, switching her Arizona twang for an attempted Irish lilt as she imitated our absent friend. "'Tis nottin but fookin' mud all around!"

We probably added distance to our walk, meandering back and forth trying to find the least muddy part of the trail. At some points the track was so bad, we resorted to climbing the shoulder and walking through the crops. I apologized silently to the farmer for any damage we might have done. A couple of cyclist pilgrims approached, wrestling their wheels through the greasy mud. As they passed, we stifled giggles at the stripes of mud being painted up their backs by the thick spray from their tires. Of course our boots were not faring much better, having probably gained another ten pounds of mud caked into their treads. As carefully as we stepped, mud was spattered up our pants as high as our knees, and we agreed that laundry would be in order when we arrived at Itero de la Vega.

When we arrived at Hontanas, we scraped as much of the mud as we could from our boots. Some of the mud had dried to clay, determined to become permanent parts of my soles. In the nearby coffee shop, a young man smiled out at us from behind the bar. Efficiently preparing our extra-large, creamy coffees and selecting glossy chocolate croissants for our breakfast, he asked where we had stayed last night. We told him we had been at San Bol. He told us he was waiting for the key to arrive. I thought it was likely, since he was still in bed when we left, the last man out would be the German fellow. I hoped he remembered his job to lock up and bring the key.

As he continued to fill orders for incoming pilgrims, I asked Sebastian if he lived in Hontanas. He told me he lived in Burgos and drove each day to work in the coffee shop. Seeing that it had taken us about a day and a half to get here from Burgos, that seemed like an extreme commute. He assured me by highway, it was only a fifteen-minute drive each way. I looked down at my mud splattered pants and my mud-caked boots and realized he hadn't even had to drive on that muddy road let alone walk it.

I discovered, as I continued to walk the Camino, that the towns were much closer than they appeared, and by car, the routes were very direct. By foot, the path wound its way over hill, over dale, making sure no small town, nor tiny church, nor significant marker was missed. This was the timeless focus of the pilgrimage.

Sebastian travelled in the real world; a world built on clocks, schedules, and paved roads, but even then, he did it with a relaxed nature. He went on to tell me that his parents owned the bar, but they too lived in Burgos.

"This town is too small. Not even a hundred people live here. There is nothing here for us but the pilgrim trade. We take turns coming. Five days my mother and me; two days my sister and my father," he continued in his melodic English. "Most of our days are done by noon. The *albergues* here provide evening meals, so we close for the day at siesta. I drive home and spend the afternoon and evening with my wife and my baby son. I come back here again for the pilgrims each morning. I like meeting the people from all over the world. Many of my friends work in Burgos, but this is what I like," he said, with a smile. Paying for my breakfast I asked him to include a banana for the road. Passing the fruit across the bar, he had included a napkin-wrapped pastry.

"Just to keep you going. It is a long way to your next stop. *Buen Camino!*" he winked.

The clouds were thinning, the sun working hard to break through, so off came the raingear, and soon we were down to t-shirts again. We left the undulating dirt track, finding drier footing on the edge of a country road. Sporadic roadside clusters of trees, barely just leafing out, provided respite to the flat terrain. In the distance, soft foothills were topped with windmills.

Coming around a corner, the weathered ruins of Convento de San Anton straddled the roadway. The sign at the foot of a remaining stone wall said the convent was founded in 1146 and the order was dedicated to the care of pilgrims and the cure of those who suffered from the "Fire of San Anton", a disease prevalent in the middle ages. Here, pilgrims were conferred with the Cross of Tau as a sign of protection against evil on the way. The order disappeared in the 1700's, and in 1835, the convent passed into private hands. Portions of the building's remains were preserved and restored, still a sanctuary for pilgrims today. Passing under the arch I could feel the centuries rush back and envisioned the thousands of feet, human and perhaps animals, which had passed through this entranceway under which now modern-day vehicles travelled.

In the distance, a hill, topped by the ruins of a ninth-century castle, rose abruptly from the low-lying mist. At the base of the hill we discovered the town of Castrojeriz, and Patricia suggested we stop for a break. The cafe was built against the wall of the church, the patio and gardens overshadowed by its looming stone walls. Quickly draining glasses of freshly squeezed orange juice, we shouldered our packs and walked out through the quiet, clean streets of this small community. I knew this was another struggling town, yet everything in it was pristine; no crumbling walls here. There also didn't seem to be any open *mercados*, which was unfortunate since we hadn't had an opportunity to replenish our walking provisions before we left Burgos. As we resumed the *senda*, a large herd of silky, gold sheep was being driven out on the road before us. As they found their pasture, we found our trail.

Sometimes we could see exactly where we were to go, tiny bumps on the path alerting us to the trail ahead. As we looked up this mountain in the middle of nowhere, one that dwarfed the hill with the castle behind us, we hoped we were wrong. But no, there, snaking up the side of the mountain, pilgrims climbed towards the sun. A warning sign at the foot of the path alerted us to a very steep climb, advising it was a 12% grade. My heart sort of sunk, and I knew it was going to be a long, hot haul up that hill.

"This is the *meseta* for goodness sakes! This is supposed to be a plain. Where do they get that there should be a mountain in the middle of the plain? Isn't there some sort of path around it? I'll bet there's an alternate route for the cycling pilgrims," I muttered. As I looked around me, to my surprise, I found I was already about a third of the way up and not even breathing hard. I dug in and continued up, seeing Patricia's backpack disappearing above me.

"Well, this isn't so bad after all. I thought it would be way worse. Maybe I'm just getting good at this." Logic should have told me that after over two weeks of a variety of hiking challenges, my body had to be adapting and growing stronger, yet still I was surprised.

Pulling over the top, sweaty, but still in control of my breathing and my heartbeat, I rejoiced with Patricia at the top. I couldn't believe how easy (well comparatively easy) that had been. From the top, I saw the rolling fields, stretching in an endless pallet of greens. I could see tiny pilgrims, like ants, ascending towards me. I saw Castrojeriz and the hilltop castle behind it. Two hills on a plain; I had the irreverent vision of a woman, floating on her back in a sea of green, two boobs raised to the sun, and I laughed.

Slugging back water and sharing a granola bar, Patricia and I started our descent, an 18% grade down the side of the mountain. On this side, however, someone had constructed a corrugated cement path. Utilizing switchback skiing techniques to deal with the grade, we wound our way down without much trouble at all. Below us, the path stretched across the fertile green valley like a long ivory ribbon, following the shallow dips and rises of the plain, until it disappeared from sight far, far, far in the distance. Under the lightly clouded skies, it would likely be a comfortable walk with easy grades.

It's funny how when you're not challenged by the terrain, you're often challenged mentally and spiritually. You don't have to focus on the footwork, so the mind takes over. Leaving me alone for once, the *meseta* muses visited Patricia, and her words came pouring out unchecked.

"My husband didn't want me to come, you know. He told me he might not be there when I got back," she confided, tucking a hank of hair behind her tiny elfin ear. Excuse me? Hadn't she said her husband was really great?

"He likes me to be at home when he gets back from his business trips, and he didn't really want me to go. I'm sure he'll be there," she continued shakily. "I'm paying for the whole thing myself, so it's not the money. He just doesn't really understand this." She told me he was going to go spend some time with one of their daughters, and then later with his sister in another part of the States. Her grey-blue eyes searched the future.

"I'm sure he'll be there," she mused thoughtfully. Who was she trying to convince; me or herself? It was hard to imagine, since Al was being so supportive, cheering me on every time I called him, encouraging messages texted in between calls.

"I never could have done this if I hadn't thought Al was one-hundred percent behind me. If I thought there was any doubt he would be okay, I couldn't have left him. He may be disabled, but he's got a great attitude, and we've got systems in place so he's pretty independent. I still worry a bit, but I'm trusting in God to keep care of him there while He keeps care of me here. That's the best I can do. Maybe your husband was just feeling left out."

"Well, you might be right. I'm sure he's going to be there!" she affirmed. "We hike sometimes together in the desert, but we can't do that a lot because he's still working. He was just in a bad mood when he said that. He's really a great guy. He's the best. It will be alright. I'm sure he will be there."

"It's easy to over think things out here," I suggested. "There's so much time and space, and thoughts you'd never have otherwise just pop into your head. Before you know it, you've built a mountain out of a molehill. It's just the *meseta* talking. We all say stupid things sometimes, maybe in a moment of fear or anger, but they don't really mean anything in the scheme of things," I assured her. "From everything you've told me about your hubby, it sounds like you have a pretty good relationship. Maybe we'll have Wi-Fi when we get in today, and you'll have a chance to touch base with him again." She smiled, nodding happy agreement.

And our arrival wouldn't be too long away, which was good. My stomach rumbled, and I realized we hadn't had any lunch. Mid-afternoon, we strolled into the Itero de la Vega, searching for the *albergue* we had picked out of our guidebook. We passed one *albergue* with a bustling bar, chairs filled with pilgrims in high spirits, but we had our heart set on this particular *albergue* with real beds.

"It says to go to the *mercado* and ask for Carlos," Patricia read. Funny, an *albergue* at a market? Maybe it was rooms above the store? Finally, we found the market and inside the stocky, dark-haired proprietor, Carlos. With a loud welcome, he tugged off his apron, and led us out the door, flipping the "closed" sign as he closed (but didn't lock) the door behind him. In through the door of the adjoining building he introduced us to his wife who confirmed yes, they did have one room left.

Thankful that most of the mud had broken off our boots through the day's walk, up the stairs we trudged after her ample behind. Maria opened the door to a bright little room, two beds dressed in floral linens before us. We were so happy to find such a great room after the long, hot walk, we hugged her. Beaming, she showed us the big bathroom equipped with a large shower. A pilgrim, towels and toiletries in hand, waited patiently for the tour to end so he could shower. Hungry, we opted just to change into clean shorts and shower and do laundry later.

Out on the dusty street, we looked for direction as to which way to go. Finding none, we struck off towards the left, past a brick building, and wound our way through a maze of streets only to find ourselves back at the same brick building. We looked at each other and laughed.

"Well that didn't work!" I stated the obvious. We struck out again, going one more street before turning the corner and had better luck as a series of *albergues* and bars were revealed. Although *completo* signs advised all beds were taken, the attached bars welcomed us in despite our arrival during siesta. A casually dressed teenager, thick, black curls tied back with a bandana, quickly laid plates of eggs, prosciutto, and thick slices of golden bread before us. I loved the eggs in Spain. The yolks were so orange and rich with flavour. I knew I was going to be disappointed by the anaemic eggs back home. Hot mugs of *café con leche* completed our meal, and we sat back relaxing, watching as the *albergue* staff enjoyed animated conversation while they prepared for the evening rush.

Returning to our room, Patricia and I took turns showering off the grime of the day, savouring the large, private shower and indulging in the seemingly endless supply of hot water. In clean clothes, we turned to laundry, hand washing the mud from our pants and rinsing the rest of what we had been wearing. A drying rack fixed outside a window held a colourful assortment of pilgrim apparel. It accommodated our bigger items, but there wasn't room for everything. Back in our room, I looked up and solved the problem. I cranked open the stubborn window to let in a gentle breeze and, as we left the room, our "dainties", hung drying above our waiting beds, waved farewell from the chandelier.

Next door at the *mercado*, we chose provisions for the next day. We had learned our lesson not to strike out without a banana and some cheese and nuts, and of course, as Patricia reminded, chocolate. I looked wistfully at the yogurt, really missing my dairy. I hadn't had a glass of milk since home! Usually yogurt was only sold in four-packs, and with no way to keep it cool, I had to take a pass. Carlos, seeing my interest reached over and broke the cluster apart, triumphantly handing me a single.

"Put in fridge for breakfast!" I smiled my thanks and added a large, fragrant orange to my order.

While Carlos was putting our things in a bag, Michel walked in through the door, removing his sunglasses and waiting while his watery eyes struggled to adjust to the dim lighting. Recognizing us with big hugs, he shared he was staying at the *albergue* just down the road.

"Some of the ladies from there are meeting me for supper at the bar, just over there," he said waving his hand in the general direction. "Why don't you join us?"

I smiled, finding it interesting that Michel seemed always surrounded by women. Perhaps his quiet, unassuming manner and apparent vision issues made this gentle, white-haired giant seem an unthreatening male companion. Either that or they just enjoyed his singing. We waited while he made his purchases and walked out into the square.

Pushing through the glass door, we were hailed by a small group of women, and we pulled heavy, red vinyl covered chairs up to their table. They were already well into the wine, and Michel called the waiter over to order a meat and pasta dish. Having eaten a late lunch, Patricia and I settled for a light salad, topped with the ever-present canned tuna and accompanied by wine and bread. As strange as the tuna thing seemed at first, I was actually acquiring a taste for salad finished this way.

The bell at the door jangled and in walked the Australian couple I had met first in Viana and more lately, in Burgos. Accepting our invitation, they pulled chairs up to our table.

"Where is your husband?" she asked.

I was confused. "My husband is back home in Canada."

Now they looked confused. "No, the man you were travelling with. The big man with the moustache and the Irish accent," they clarified.

"Oh, John!" Patricia started laughing. "That's not her husband. That's just John."

I explained that John and I had met back on the way to Estella and just fell in as walking companions along the road. It was interesting how travelling together breeds a sense of familiarity that translates into family connections along the way. I waved away their apologies and told the couple that John had tighter time constraints that forced him to jump ahead by bus.

"He is, by now, somewhere between Leon and Santiago, hurrying home to his wife Geraldine in Ireland." I went on to tell them about my real husband, Al, and how his disability prevented him from joining me. I shared one of my favourite photos of him and Kirby out for a "walk and roll" on Al's scooter.

"So you're alone," they mused. I assured them I was only as alone as I wanted to be and right now, I was travelling with my Camino sister, Patricia, who grinned back at me.

In our room, we tucked into our "real" beds, pulled up the quilts, and sighed. I caught sight of our lingerie chandelier, closed my eyes, and was gone.

Down in the kitchen, I whipped up breakfast; instant coffee, yogurt, orange slices, and bread. Along with my ongoing bathroom facilities survey, I was intrigued by the different plumbing configurations along my journey. But here I was stumped! For the life of me, I couldn't figure out how to make the water come on at the kitchen sink. There were no taps. I looked for motion detectors, knobs on the front, on the backsplash; nothing! Then a German pilgrim paused in pulling on his second boot and pointed at the floor. There, just under the cupboard, was a pedal. I stepped on it, and voila! Water! Pretty cool…and hygienic too!

Today was going to be an easy one, only fourteen kilometres to walk, and pretty flat terrain to boot. As Patricia and I trudged along, she told me about her daughters, both of whom were dancers, and her pride shone in her words. One of them lived in Seattle, and I told her we had spent some time there on our honeymoon when Al and I were married in 1998. With Seattle so close to Vancouver, we discussed the possibility of meeting up there sometime in the future. But I knew this was Camino talk. While I hoped we would stay in touch after the pilgrimage, I'd heard too many stories about "friends for life" promised on the trail than to expect that every friendship I made would last.

We strolled along the Canal de Castilla, originally built to facilitate trade, now an out-dated victim of modern transport, though still useful as an irrigation system for the surrounding lands. The serene waterway flowed soundlessly through fields, the reeds and grasses along the banks home to a bounty of birds and small creatures, unseen but not unknown since the constant birdcall and croaking filled the air. In this idyllic setting, the warm sunshine, the buzz of lazy bees and the gentle breeze lulled me into a deep sense of calm. No rush; no worry. This was a rest day, still moving forward, but without hurry. Even Patricia seemed to embrace the quiet, natural calm as she walked in companionable silence, our shadows sharing footsteps.

"I think I'm getting a cold or something," sniffed Patricia. "My throat is a little sore, and my sinuses are getting clogged. Maybe we can find a drugstore or a clinic, and I can get something to nip it in the bud. If I let it get away on me, it can get really bad."

"I have some allergy tablets in my first-aid pack if you think that might help," I suggested. She thanked me for the offer, and said she'd take me up on it if things got worse.

A short distance from Fromista, we found decommissioned canal locks, their stone walls stained by water and the passage of time, lying empty and expectant, lonely for the busy barge traffic of bygone eras. Crossing over a little stone bridge, we followed the roadway into Fromista and easily located the municipal *albergue*.

The gates still latched, I placed my backpack next to the gate to hold my place. Others followed my lead, and a conga line of packs grew quickly. The gates finally opened, and inside the *albergue* we had our pilgrim passports stamped and our national passports registered. Upstairs, we found large bunk rooms, broken into groups of sixteen beds. I chose a lower bunk next to the window and looked down at the line of pilgrims still snaking in through the door. Patricia, worried about finding as quiet a place as possible, chose a bunk in the far corner across from mine.

Showers and changing done, we walked out into the sunny courtyard and there was Michel.

"Michel!" Patricia called, "Hey, Michel. We're going to look for a drug store. Did you register yet? Where is your bed? Did you want to come with us? You could come with us if you're ready." Her cheerful chirping seemed determined to make up for her quiet of the morning as we walked through the square.

With a population of less than 1,000, this friendly little town boasted a variety of bars and restaurants, mostly situated in the square adjacent to the impressive eleventh century *Iglesia de San Martin*. The Romanesque church was known for its exquisite proportions and intricate stone carvings inside and out. All I got to see were the outside embellishments, however, as it was locked up tighter than a drum. Despite its beauty, it felt austere and unfriendly to me; a stone church, dropped in a pristine tiled square, no trees or signs of nature to bring it to life, and locked against those who would worship.

What the town didn't have was a pharmacy where Patricia could find some help for her increasing discomfort. We found a clinic, but the sign in the window indicated that it was part of a travelling practice, that was only open on Tuesdays and Thursdays. Wandering back down the road, we found a small *mercado*, and the best they could offer was a selection of cough drops.

Returning to the *albergue*, the beds were pretty much filled up. I grabbed my cellphone and looked around for a place to charge it. Crossing to the receptacle by Patricia's bunk, I found her sulking in dismay.

"That door," she motioned to the door beside her bed, "leads to another bunk room. There's a steady stream of people coming in and out the door all the time. I got hit in the butt while I was digging in my pack!" she continued indignantly. "So now, it's going to be swinging all night!" It looked like her plan to find a quiet spot hadn't worked out quite the way she hoped.

"Let's go outside and enjoy the sunshine as long as we have it," I said, distracting her. Down in the gravel courtyard, pilgrims were kicked back on plastic patio chairs, chatting amiably, sharing drinks and snacks. Some were reading, some were checking cellphones for messages, others were consulting their guidebooks for the next day's walk.

"Kirsty!" Patricia exclaimed, as our Danish friend walked in the gate. "Are you staying here?"

"Yes, I've got a bed on the bottom floor. It's a pretty big room; maybe thirty beds, so probably not much chance for sleep tonight," she smiled. "I was just going to go for a walk to find dinner tonight. Would you like to join me?"

We fell in step with her and, as we exited the courtyard gates, we saw Michel sitting on a bench in the square, peering at his guidebook through a magnifying glass. We introduced Kirsty to Michel, who stood up, stowed his book, and said he'd join us for the walk. Beside me, Patricia was sniffling and eating the cough drops like they were candies. Kirsty and Michel trailed behind us, deep in conversation.

Very few locals were out and about despite the sultry evening glow. At outdoor tables, waiters repositioned cutlery, moved around folded napkins, and placed and replaced menus in efforts to look busy and attract customers. A herd of skateboarding youths trundled by, their lively banter the same as between teenagers anywhere. Good buddies, with a healthy dose of friendly competition and jockeying for pack position thrown in.

Consulting posted menus, we settled into the patio chairs outside a small, but busy (always a good sign) restaurant. Patricia and Michel chose seats sheltered from the sun by a green canvas umbrella, while Kirsty and I sought the sunny seats. A waiter hurried over, menus tucked beneath his arm, and welcomed us to our table. He advised all meals included the choice of beer or wine. Selections made, we sat back enjoying the friendly ambience provided by pilgrims clustered around the food-laden tables.

Cool glass of beer in my hand, I let the chatter drift off as I focused on the Gothic *Iglesia de San Pedro* across the street. I watched a stork couple feeding their young in a huge nest atop the church tower while, attending evening mass, locals in their Sunday best disappeared through the massive wooden doors below.

Less than a week since my last mass in Granon, and less than a week until a mass in Leon, I felt safe that God would find me along the trail each day. My daily walking prayers and spiritual reflection, as well as my sincere appreciation of the beauty of God's creation in this amazing country would be my church for a while.

As the sun sunk below the horizon, the evening became cooler. I wrapped my jacket around me. We pushed back our chairs and strolled the short distance to the *albergue*. We were planning an early start the next day, so face washed, teeth brushed, and things organized for the morning, I crawled into bed, my silk sleeping bag liner once again providing me sufficient warmth and cover. Over in the corner, I saw Patricia fussing with her things, and I could hear her muttering softly as the door by her bed opened and closed behind a returning pilgrim. I opened my cellphone and scrolled through my photos of home, tucking in each family member until I, in turn, tucked in and closed my eyes to the day.

Leaving with the breaking dawn, shadowy pilgrims tapped along before us. In quiet companionship, Patricia and I walked, me silently moving through my morning prayers, she lost in whatever thoughts were hers. A half an hour out, we reached Poblacion de Campos and breakfast. Greeting fellow pilgrims as we carried coffees and pastries to the planked tables, Patricia searched for Michel.

"I wonder where Michel is? He was right behind us when we left. Do you think he's going straight on?" Just then Michel pushed through the door, holding it ajar as Kirsty joined him inside the warm café. "Oh, there you are!" Patricia exclaimed. "I was wondering what happened to you."

"I was just taking my time," he assured her, pushing a shock of white hair back from his brow. "Kirsty and I match our pace, so we just walked and talked," he explained. Settled at our table with coffees and croissants, we discussed places to stay at Carrion de los Condes. "The last time I was here I stayed with the nuns at Santa Maria. They took very good care of me there, so I will go there again. Maybe I will see you there," he finished as we dragged our packs off the floor, swung them onto our shoulders, and walked out the door calling out "*Buen Camino*" behind us.

Leaving town, we had two options: head down the *senda* along the side of highway for a shorter trail, or veer off to the right, taking the longer scenic route along the river. Hmmm, hot unsheltered gravel path along the sun-baked roadway inhaling vehicular fumes, or a gentle, sun-dappled trail by a peaceful river? The sun was already beginning to climb and that made the decision easy. The trees and bushes along the river were alive with birds, their calls and songs filling the morning air. Fat frogs croaked as they basked on sunny rocks while the current eddied around them. Dragon flies, butterflies, and bees floated on warm air currents as they celebrated the tranquil morning.

"Oh!" muttered Patricia from behind me. I looked back to find her consulting her phone which she wore in a small shoulder holster for easy access. "There's news from the girls," referring to the group she had started out with back in St. Jean. Although they were no longer walking as a group, they kept in touch, updating each other on their trials and their progress. "Cindy is still walking with Anne-Marie. They are a day behind us. I told her I was walking with you, and she got all bent. She said why is Roxey walking with you? I asked her to walk with me and she wouldn't. She said she wanted to walk alone. I guess she just doesn't like Asians!" My step faltered as I turned back to Patricia.

"Really? She said that? That I don't like Asians, and that's why I wasn't walking with her? Maybe she needs to think about the possibility that I'm not walking with her because we're moving at different paces and have different goals with this journey. Maybe she needs to consider it has nothing to do with her being Asian, and everything to do with her being Cindy. I mean really! Are we back in high school? Don't like Asians…" I muttered as I impatiently brushed a bug from my neck and self-righteously stomped off. If nothing else, my indignation was going to make this a quicker day.

"I told her it has nothing to do with her being Asian," Patricia assured me as she caught up. "I told her it was a matter of pace and yours and mine worked well together." I felt a little bit like a bone being tugged between dogs, which was a bit of a change for me. I had always had close friends, but not a lot of friends, and certainly no one ever fought over spending time with me. I didn't know if I should be flattered or exasperated.

"I told her I was done with the drama, and that she shouldn't text me if she doesn't have anything nice to say," she snapped angrily. Obviously, I had been missing out on some other tidbits, and perhaps ignorance was bliss. I paused and took a few deep breaths, concentrating on my peaceful surroundings. A couple of pilgrims tapped by, calling out "Buen Camino" as they went. Refocused, I told Patricia that perhaps she would enjoy the walk more if she disconnected and gave texting a bit of a break, at least until we landed for the day. "Yeah, probably a good idea," she said.

The sun continued to climb in the deep blue sky, and as the path wound along the river, we enjoyed the shady reprieve. Across the flat fields we saw the alternate route, a parade of pilgrims walking in the full heat of the sun, sucking fumes along the highway.

"I'm glad we didn't go that way," Patricia commented. "I wonder if Michel went by the road or by the river. It's so much nicer here by the river." Our steady footfalls beat a muffled tattoo on the dirt track, and we fell into a companionable rhythm. Off in the distance we saw rambling farm houses, and at one point came upon a large hermitage. I started to giggle when we read the sign, and Patricia gave me a questioning look.

"Well if it's a hermitage, why would it have to be so big. Don't hermits live by themselves? If a bunch of hermits live together, are they really hermits?" She rolled her eyes and muttered something about the heat getting to me.

The river path ended, and we walked along the side of a country road, knowing our steps were taking us towards the main highway and the final five kilometres along that unforgiving route. We decided to stop for a break at Villacazar de Sirga. At a small, air-conditioned café, we treated ourselves to a chocolate pie strata and coffee. Slipping a forkful of creamy chocolate between my lips I knew ecstasy!

"Good...right?" Patricia said, eyes shining. We were in a happy zone all our own.

We turned right onto the *senda* shouldering the highway. Cars and trucks roared by on my left, which was lucky since that is my bad ear. To the right, endless green fields stretched up the gentle slope, natural beauty defying the track of progress to the other side. Cycling pilgrims thankfully rode the side of the pavement, leaving the gravel shoulder to pedestrian pilgrims.

We saw our destination at the bottom of the long, gradual hill. Being so flat that we could see a town that far away put me in mind of the joke about watching your dog run away for three days on the Canadian prairies. I told the joke to Patricia, and she laughed so hard it seemed phoney and forced. It was a good joke, but really not that funny. Maybe the heat was getting to her.

Crossing the busy pavement, we entered the city of Carrion de los Condes. The local legend regarding the name of the city is that back in the day, the lord of the manor had invited three counts to come to marry his three daughters. For some reason, when they arrived, they refused to marry the daughters and the angry father had them killed and their bodies laid out for scavenger birds. Cheery story.

Although we had been walking for six hours, it was only noon, so we were confident of getting a bed. Hot and tired, we were confused, trying to remember what Michel had said about where to stay.

"It was Santa Anna or something. And there were nuns," supplied Patricia.

"There!" I pointed to a high brick wall with a plaque reading "Santa Clara". "That must be it." Then a nun in full habit walked out the gate, and that sealed the deal. Through the gates, across the courtyard, we found the office and registered for a semi-private room with three single beds. Neither of us could really afford a private room, but maybe no one else would come and we'd have the room to ourselves, or maybe Michel would want the bed, and that would be okay too.

The *hospitalero* escorted us across the sunny courtyard, soft paving stones framed with moss under our boots. One tree blessed the grounds; at its base was a unique, almost abstract metal sculpture, rusting with age. The figures, meant to represent Mary, Joseph, and baby Jesus in a cradle, rested in the dappled shade, their blank faces silent witnesses to our passing. A nun carrying a basket of laundry smiled down at us from the walkway above.

"That is the nuns place," we were solemnly advised. Through a wide-planked arched door our tour guide led us, providing a running commentary as we went. "Here is the kitchen where you can cook. There are some things to share in the shelves."

A soft-smiling nun had just placed a large basket of fresh tomatoes on the counter. With a deferential nod, he silently stepped aside to let her pass and continued. "The nuns have provided you tomatoes from their garden. You are welcome to have many. Down here, is the laundry. The machines are there, and soap, and here is to hang your clothes." Numerous lines, many already hung with a colourful collection of laundry, were strung in a small sunny patio area. This would be our next stop after showers.

"Up these stairs," he continued, leading us up a narrow, winding staircase. "Here is your room with three beds. You can take any you like until someone more comes. The toilet and to wash is just there," he motioned down the hall. "The gate is open all night so you can come and go. There are many nice places to eat here. Maybe the bar with the black awning is best. There are stores and a *mercado*, if you need. Also, there is mass at the cathedral at 7:00. The nuns will sing. I go back to my office now. More pilgrims will come. *Buen Camino.*" And with that, he was gone.

Patricia chose the narrow bed by the furthest wall, and I took the one in the middle, just under the small window through which a gentle breeze played. The clean linens smelled of soap and sunshine, and I looked forward to laying my head on the pillow that night. The coarse blanket would not provide much heat, but not much was needed in these warm spring nights.

We were just unpacking our bags when the door opened and a heavily-moustached man in a leather, wide-brimmed hat poked his head in. Louis was from

Atlantic Canada, and we asked him if he'd met Michel who was from the same area. He hadn't, but we assured him Michel would probably show up later. We looked at each other and silently agreed that we wished he had shown up before Louis, but what can you do? Without more conversation, Louis unceremoniously dropped his pack in the corner by the door and said he was going out and would see us later. We looked at the closing door, then at each other, and laughed. We went downstairs, ran our clothes through the washer, and after hanging them to dry in the sunshine, went out to explore.

My pilgrim's passport was starting to fill up, and I knew I'd need more space, especially once we got to Sarria, so I was looking for another. We strolled up the streets, buffeted by fragrant aromas wafting out of bars and cafes. Many of the stores were closed due to siesta, so we walked on. At the crest of the hill, the streets opened up into a sunny central plaza, framed by impressive official buildings. A wide street beckoned us down the hill and led to broad, stone stairs leading down to a peaceful park by the river. Beneath shady trees, formal rose gardens encircled lawns and benches, inviting us to linger to enjoy their fragrance and the gentle burble of the water. As we wandered up and down the pathways, we watched a silver-haired, well-dressed man fishing on the opposite bank and a young mother playing with her toddler in the playground.

You would think that with all the walking we did between stops we would be done, but not taking the opportunity to explore where we landed would have wasted much of what the Camino was about. I paused to wonder the real distance I had walked since starting this journey. Not the markers. The real distance; between the towns, and then in and around the towns. I wondered if it would be hard to stop walking when I got home and life's realities imposed themselves once more.

Climbing back up the staircase to the plaza, we found stores opening and while Patricia meandered between shelves lined with all things pilgrim, I purchased my second passport from the friendly Spanish proprietor. On our way back down to the *albergue*, we were again assaulted by the fragrance of food.

"You know what I miss?" I said. "I'd love a plain old grilled cheese sandwich. Why don't we go to the *mercado* and get some bread and cheese and go back and cook up a grilled cheese sandwich?"

Patricia grinned in agreement. "That sounds really good. I saw some oil in the kitchen. We could get a lemon and make a tomato salad with the tomatoes the nuns left." Plan in hand, we entered the store, one much like a small supermarket at home, language aside. We bought a package of white cheese and a crusty loaf of bread, as well as bananas for tomorrow's walk. Patricia supplemented her chocolate supply. Now those who know me at home will wonder 'cause they know I love chocolate, but there was no way I could keep up with my elfin friend's consumption. I continued to wonder where she put it all.

Back in the kitchen, we found onions as well as tomatoes and, as I sliced bread and set up the sandwiches, Patricia created the salad. Curious onlookers seemed mystified by the grilled cheese sandwich, so I cut the first one into fingers and offered them around. Food has an amazing way of breaking through language barriers, and it wasn't long before I was slicing up the rest of the loaf and producing as many sandwiches as our supplies could generate.

"I thought you were making something for your breakfast tomorrow," one Norwegian woman commented. I explained that grilled cheese was a North American standard for lunch and that we had been missing this reminder of home.

Back out on the street, we walked past a bar on the edge of the cathedral square when Kirsty and Michel called out.

"There you are. I wasn't sure you had made it. I asked about you at the *albergue*, but they said you were not there," Michel said, inviting us to join them.

"But we were here hours ago," I claimed. "We have a room for three and hoped you would join us, but we ended up with some other guy. Oh! He's Louis, and he's also from Atlantic Canada. We told him about you, but he said he hadn't met you yet. Seemed a little stand-offish actually," I continued as we pulled up chairs and sat down.

"Really," he insisted, "I asked for you. Where is your room?" I started to explain how to get to our room to him, and he shook his head. "You are not in the same place. I think you are in Santa Clara, not Santa Maria. Kirsty and I are in Santa Maria. It is lovely there. The nuns take good care of us there."

"Well we have nuns too!" blustered Patricia, "and real beds with sheets! And they left us tomatoes for lunch!" So were we seriously in a Camino competition for the best nuns? We all laughed as a waiter delivered tall glasses of cool beer to our table. The two *albergues* were only a block apart, and we were all happy where we were, so now it was time to relax and enjoy each other's company, comparing notes of our day's journey. We told Michel about the park by the river, and he advised that was the way we would leave in the morning.

The evening was so warm that it felt a shame to go inside for mass even though, as with most of the buildings built of stone, the cathedral would likely be nice and cool inside. An itch brought my hand to the base of my neck, just below my beads. A minor irritation on this balmy night, I remembered the bug I had brushed from my neck yesterday. A small price to pay for the peacefulness of the walk by the river.

As 7:00 approached, locals began drifting towards the cathedral, and still we lingered. Then we saw the huge double doors on three sides of the cathedral pushed open wide. Prayers and music poured out softly into the night. Pilgrims gradually gathered on the outside benches and sank onto the low garden walls as we all took part in the mass el fresco. The natural, outside setting brought its own beauty and magic to the service, and I carried a feeling of community and contentment as we sauntered back down to our *albergues*.

After saying goodnight to Michel and Kirsty and making plans to meet for breakfast in the morning, we slipped in through the convent gate, located the key, collected our dry laundry, and made our way up the stairs to our room. Louis had not yet returned, so we quickly changed and snuggled into our beds, ready to enjoy a good night's sleep. We thought.

Just drifting off to sleep, the door suddenly flung open, light spilling in from the hallway. In the half light, we saw Louis sorting around in his pack before disappearing to the bathroom. Through the walls we could hear him hacking and coughing. Patricia propped herself up on an elbow, worried that he was sick. I took the opportunity to reverse my pillow, choosing to sleep toes to nose so if he was, I wouldn't contract something across the narrow gap between his bed and mine.

The door opened again, and he settled himself on his bed only to begin coughing again. I could sense Patricia pulling into herself, willing a protective force field around her bed, and hopefully mine. All through the night, I'd just start to drop off and the coughing would begin again. When it got too bad, he'd return to the bathroom.

"Sounds like he's coughing up a lung!" my sleepy friend muttered. "I hope whatever he has isn't contagious!" And so the night went, and so the morning came too early and with too little sleep.

As we dressed under the covers, my gentle companion became a spitfire, a terrier in full fight.

"Louis!" she barked. "What's wrong with you?" she accused his back. "Is what you have communicable? If you were sick, why didn't you get a private room!" she spat. "You shouldn't be spreading your germs everywhere and coughing all night, keeping us awake!"

By now my Canadian politeness was cringing under her attack. Maybe he had cancer or something. Maybe he was really sick, but not with something we could catch.

"We have a really long walk today, and now we have to do it without sleep!" She pounded her things into her pack. "What were you thinking? If you are sick you should not share a room." He stared at her with narrowed eyes as he pulled his shirt over his head, not saying a word.

Furtively stuffing my pack, I kept my head low, not wanting to become another target for her anger. I felt a bit the coward, feeling bad for Louis, yet not telling her to take it easy. However, everything she was saying was true. One of the biggest fears, behind injury, is getting sick on the Camino. With no home to call our own, illness can land us looking for a place to heal, losing valuable time we might not be able to recover. It's kind of an unspoken rule for pilgrims to work together to maintain the health of all, doing our best to isolate ourselves if sick, and get well before continuing the journey.

We did have a long walk ahead today, and it was going to be another hot one. A good night's sleep should have been easy in a room of three and would have been helpful for the day ahead. Angrily slinging her pack over her shoulder, Patricia stomped out of the room and down the hall. Following in her wake, I tried to pour oil over the waters.

"She's not a morning person, and doesn't do well without enough sleep," I apologized pathetically. "Be better soon." I hustled down the stairs, catching up to her as she blew through the doors of the café.

A whistling Michel cheerfully pushed through the door, casually dropping his pack by the wall as he pulled up a chair at the table.

"So, how was your night?" he asked, having missed my subtle warning look.

"Shitty! Really shitty!" Patricia suddenly spat. Furiously stirring a hole through the bottom of her coffee cup, she launched into an angry description of how much sleep we didn't get and just whose fault it was. By way of an apology for this bitter start to his morning, I carried over a coffee, thick with milk and sugar, the way Michel like it, but he waved away my offer of a croissant. By now the stirring was slowing, and Patricia was running out of steam. I hoped we wouldn't meet Louis later in the day

The guidebook warned that this would be a long, steady walk, with no toilets or opportunities for refreshments along the way. Equipped with bottles of water, bananas, and tomatoes purloined from the nuns' basket, we strode out into the morning, allowing Patricia's anger to set the pace. Making our way out of the city, we were joined by more pilgrims, shaking off the night's sleep and bracing themselves for a long, hot walk. By the time we crossed the bridge into the countryside, it was obvious there would be serious competition for beds today.

While there were two towns with *albergues* before Terradillos de los Templarios, it was likely most pilgrims travelling with us this morning would be following the guidebook and trying to go the full twenty-seven kilometres. It didn't take a rocket scientist to realize that coming from the much larger city of Carrion de los Condes behind us, the 102 beds available between the two *albergues* at our destination would be in high demand.

As promised, the *senda* was flat, hot, and without interruption. The trail was actually a rural road, a ribbon of grey bordered by fields stretched wide, their varied hues of green dotted with sprays of yellows and whites, liberally sprinkled with plumes of deep purple, and accented with sporadic bursts of red. It was a feast for the eyes. On the horizon, large spreading trees had the appearance of grazing buffalo; big mounds without definition.

Michel and I poled along behind of Patricia, her pace still fuelled by anger, but slowing a bit. I figured another couple kilometres and we'd have our usually sunny Patricia back. Suddenly a sparkly chime rung out and the call "bikes" was passed up the line. Scattering to either side, the pedestrian pilgrims waved the cycling pilgrims through.

"Well at least they warned us," pouted Patricia. See? She was in a better mood already! I watched after the departing wheels with a small degree of jealousy, knowing they would reach a cool drink and shady rest long before we did.

Our morning coffee and all that water was starting to play havoc with our bladders. Men had that double bonus; larger bladders and an easier way to relieve themselves. They could basically just turn their back to the road, take in the scenery, and do what they needed to do. Patricia and I searched in vain for a likely bush for a pit stop. Of course, the more you think about it, the more pressing the issue becomes. When the challenge became too great, I suggested we employ Patricia's little travel umbrella to establish the necessary privacy.

"I can't pee when somebody is watching me," she stated.

"Well, I'm not going to be watching you," I protested. "I'm going to hold the umbrella for you, and then you can do the same for me." Realizing we really didn't have another option, Patricia finally conceded and we moved down a furrow in the field. Of course, everyone knew what we were doing, and that added to the "somebody watching me" issue, so it took a little time to get the job done. Finally, adjusting our clothing, we returned to the road to find…oh no!…Louis talking with Michel.

Louis had caught up and, finding another Acadian man to talk to, had fallen into step with Michel. I looked at Patricia nervously. She stood, hands on hips, one foot thrust out and her lips pursed, spoiling for a fight. Quickly, I scrambled through my front pack and pulled out a bar of chocolate.

"Here," I handed her a piece. "Let's just enjoy this before we go on. We can catch up with Michel a little further down the road." Patricia sulkily accepted the chocolate and soon we were back on the road, happy little endorphins released all around. Louis walked a bit slow, so in unified silence, Patricia and I poled past the men, our synchronized steps setting a faster pace.

"I'm really not sure if I want to go on to Finisterre," Patricia mused, not for the first time. She had a way of verbally exhausting every thought. She'd talk it out, from every angle, and usually end up right back at the start, only to raise the issue again somewhere down the road. I found myself getting a little tired of the verbal tennis matches, wanting to tell her "just make a decision already!"

"What day do you fly out?" she asked. "Right, June 10th; I fly the 8th. What day do you plan to get to Santiago? Oh, right. The 6th. So, I can slow things down a little and walk with you, and I'd still have two days in Santiago. Or I can go with my original plan and get there a couple days ahead of time so I have time to walk out to Finisterre. I think it would be great to see Finisterre. But maybe next year I'll do this again with my daughter, and maybe from Portugal. So, I could go to Finisterre next time and stay with you for now. We could stay together in

Santiago. At least until I fly out, then you'd have your room to yourself. That would work. Do you think that would work?"

I wasn't sure I wanted to make it work, regretting a little the loss of peace I had meant for this trip.

"When I made my reservation, it said the room would have a private bathroom with a bathtub, but it may have a double bed or may have twin beds. I guess we could call when we get closer, but if we get there, and there's only one bed, you'd have to get your own room."

"Right, but if we…oh, hi Michel!" she stopped suddenly, acknowledging our third companion who had caught up with us. "What did Louis have to say about me. I'm sure he told you what a bitch I was."

"Actually," Michel advised smoothly, "he didn't mention you at all. We were talking about Canada and our jobs and things like that. He has a bit of a heart issue and has been trying to stop smoking, so that is part of this journey for him. He is a good guy, and I'm sure he did not mean to cause you any problems last night," he continued generously. Patricia looked contritely at the ground. Then, with a wide smile, Michel broke into song and stepped into the lead.

"You will be our pace car now Michel," I called out. Questioning the term, I explained how with car races, they often send out pace cars to form the others up into a group moving at the same pace. "Usually it's when there's been a bit of an incident, and they need to get everyone back in order so they can restart the race." Not missing my underlying message, he smiled and agreed to be our pace car. We followed behind, sweating through the dusty kilometres, one boot in front of the other, by now more concerned with getting somewhere than checking out the scenery around us.

Finally, after a hot and sticky seventeen kilometres, we, and a mass of other hot bodies, straggled into Calzadilla del la Cueza. While we ladies lined up for the washroom, Michel staked out sun-bleached plastic chairs around sun-bleached plastic tables and ordered coffee from the bar. Carrying my coffee and a croissant out to the yard I saw, in the glassless window of the bar, a large turtle catching rays in his shallow tank. I thought how nice of them to have a pet that allowed me some feeling of linguistic accomplishment as I translated "*Tortuga en la ventana*". Okay, so my time spent trying to learn some Spanish wasn't totally wasted and who knew I would find an opportunity to string those unlikely words together!

Sipping my drink, I looked around the yard and, in addition to myself and Michel, I identified seven other Canadians I had met over the past couple of weeks. That's the way it goes on the Camino; you meet someone, lose track of them, and then they pop up again somewhere along the trail. I drew some comfort in knowing that some of my countrymen were along for the journey.

Resuming our journey, we clung to the shady side of the street knowing we would soon be out in the relentless sun. Just reaching the end of the street Patricia called out.

"Oh-no! I left my sticks behind!" After a heavy sigh accepting frequent Patricia's forgetfulness, Michel and I patiently waited in the shade, while she skittered up the street to retrieve her forgotten poles. We walked along the roadway beside a row of sapling trees meant to provide sun, but they would only be able to do their job when the sun swung over to the western sky and we received no respite from their whispering leaves.

God, it is hot here! That sun just won't quit! Maybe I should have worn shorts today, but that decision carries its own arguments. To wear shorts means using a lot of my quickly disappearing sunscreen. There's also the risk of suffering the fashion statement disaster of "white socks". When you remove your boots and socks, your feet are milky white from the ankle down while the rest of your legs are tanned golden. Also, I wouldn't have clean dry, sweat-free shorts to wear when I landed. Three strikes and that idea was out, so I sweated along in my hiking pants, sucking back the water, pulling down the bill of my cap and adjusting my...

"Oh no! I left my sunglasses behind! Well we've come too far to go back. They weren't expensive. I'll just pick up another pair along the way," I sheepishly mumbled. I walked the gentle rises and falls of the path, choking down chunks of humble pie at my earlier comment about Patricia's forgetfulness.

The gravel *senda* now followed a roadway where clusters of cycling pilgrims rolled smoothly by on the pavement. Sporadic trees and shrubs provided minimal relief from the broiling sun and again, I envied the cyclists. It's easy to forget the gruelling hills that would be such a challenge for bikes when you see them sailing by in the heat, their happy little bells jingling annoyingly. Focused on the backs of Michel's boots, I dragged on through the heat.

Within the hour, we came to Ledigos, the last stop before Terradillos de los Templarios. Here pilgrims sought reprieve under umbrellas scattered around the bar. Those without packs had obviously decided to stay, but with only about another hour's walk, Patricia, Michel, and I pressed on.

The irritated patch on my neck had been aggravated by the heat. My searching fingers found, to my shock, a hard, grape-sized lump bulging beneath the skin. I was suddenly transported back to the day my late husband's cancer was identified.

For eight weeks, Terry had seen several doctors and had undergone a battery of tests in three different hospitals with no diagnosis of his severe stomach cramps in sight. While waiting for his bed to be changed in the crowded Victoria hospital room, he rested on a chair in the hallway, his head laid tiredly against my chest. As I stood behind him, I tenderly ran my fingers through his thick hair, coming to pause on a large lump at on the back of his neck. Not wanting to cause alarm, I silently scanned over to the other side of his neck, looking for a corresponding knob. I thought, perhaps it was normal structure that hadn't been noticeable before his sudden loss of weight. But no. No matching lump. I called a nurse over and showed her what I'd found. Six months later, at the age of thirty-three, I was a widow, fighting to hold our world together for my two young sons.

Panic grew in my chest. *Is this the reason for my Camino? Was I brought here to discover I was going to die? Did God intend this journey to help me come to terms with one final disaster in my life? Could life really be that cruel? Calm down! Don't jump to conclusions. It's just a bug bite reaction!* I slowed my breathing and concentrated on my steps. My panic subsided and my heartbeat calmed. Amazing the scenarios that came to mind when you had so much empty time to think. Resorting to my long-learned practice of stuffing down my feelings and presenting a strong front, I buried my fears in a deep compartment in my mind. I resolved to keep a watch on the lump and deal with what came when, and if it did. I would tell no one . . . unless it became an issue.

By now I had entered that zone, a place where all I could think about was getting out of the heat and finding a bed and a cold drink. Suddenly I realized I was now in front.

"Roxey's our pace car now, and it appears she is in high gear!" Michel called out as we followed a roadside trail up a gentle hill. A steady procession of pilgrims plodded behind, and I was driven with the thought of not letting anyone pass us. If there were limited beds left at Terradillos, they would be ours!

We came first to the lush lawns of the *Albergue* Los Templarios, only to find the *completo* sign posted prominently at the head of their path. Digging into my last reserves, I pounded on up the hill, around the corner, and down into the tiny town. Rounding the corner of the *Albergue* Jacques de Molay, I surged through the gates, past pilgrims lounging on the patio, and up to the registration desk.

"We need three beds. Do you have three beds?" I panted, dropping my pack to the floor.

"Yes, yes…we have beds. Just wait a moment, please." The *hospitalero* was doing double duty as a waitress in the bar. I looked at the thermometer on the garden wall by the desk; thirty-six degrees! No wonder I was cooking! When she returned, Patricia and Michel pushed past a couple other pilgrims to join me in line. I felt a bit badly about that, but the next *albergue* was over three kilometres away, which in this heat would feel like six, and there would be no guarantee of a bed there.

Pilgrims' passports stamped, we were led across the lawn, past the one and only shady tree, and into the bunk area. Some pilgrims were already enjoying a siesta snooze and from the snoring going on, I wasn't too sure we'd get any more sleep this night than we did the previous night. I also wasn't sure I could handle another cranky Patricia day. Laying claim to a back-corner bottom bunk, I grabbed my kit and went for a cooling shower. Rinsing and soaping the dirt of the day off my outer layer, I stripped my shirt and pants off to drain on the floor, while I turned my attention to myself. Lathered and rinsed I felt like a new woman.

While hanging my laundry in the sun, Patricia surfaced, also looking like a new woman, and suggested a tour around the town. When we had walked in, it didn't seem like there was much of a town here, so I knew it wouldn't take long before I could seek the shade again, so I followed her out the gate. After doing the two-block circuit, we found ourselves back at the *albergue*'s gate. We had talked to a townsman along the way, asking if there was a *mercado*. He had motioned back towards the *albergue*, so we guessed either he didn't understand us, or there wasn't one. We would have another long, hot day tomorrow, and I wanted to make sure I had some fruit and nuts along for the day.

"Let's go ask at the bar," I suggested. "Is there a *mercado*?" I asked the slight young woman wiping down tables.

"One moment please," she smiled. She went behind the bar to talk to the matronly woman polishing glasses. With a sigh, the steel-haired woman put down her cloth and motioned towards us.

"You come." We followed her out the door of the bar, towards another door halfway down the walk towards the bunk room. Pulling a ring of keys from her smock pocket, she opened the door and motioned us inside. Voila! We were in the middle of a tiny store, the shelves busy with tissues, sunblock, sun glasses, lip balm, headache pills, Band-Aids, gum, chocolate, nuts and all things pilgrim. Quickly the space behind us filled in as pilgrims poured into this previously unknown treasure. I guessed with only eighty residents in town, this *albergue* did it all.

I was really glad we were at the head of the line and ecstatic to walk out with a tube of almonds, an orange, and a banana. Interesting how big small things become on a journey like this.

"You didn't get sunglasses. You lost your sunglasses. Remember?" Patricia asked, unwrapping a bar of chocolate.

"Theirs were pretty pricey," I responded. "I find I do okay if I just pull the bill of my hat down a bit further. I'll look for new sunglasses when we get to a bigger town. Let's go get some supper." Back into the bar we went, only to find Michel sitting in a chair, savouring a glass of cold beer. As we joined him, the waitress slapped laminated menus down in front of us, before rushing away to clear used dishes from another table. The bright yellow walls of the bar were hung with a colourful assortment of historic farm implements and pilgrim memorabilia. At one end, the bar was crowded with locals enjoying drinks and loud, happy conversation in equal measure. Pilgrims scattered about the blue-check covered tables were sharing food and toasts for a day well walked.

Patricia and I had just put in our order for sandwiches and salad when Michel's burger arrived. It was enormous! Watching Michel trying to get his mouth around it, I was glad I had ordered something smaller. But when our sandwiches arrived, bulging with salami and cheese, Patricia and I both broke out laughing. Well they certainly did not take advantage of the pilgrims. They may be the only game in town, but they were a pretty good game! Munching down crisp salad dressed with oil and vinegar, we cut our sandwiches in half, wrapping one part in napkins to save for breakfast.

We drifted back out to the courtyard, settling on the lawn under the tree, joining in conversation with new friends and old, discussing our plans for the next day. Many were planning to stop in Sahagun, but for us the goal was Bercianos, a small town, ten kilometres further.

I stepped away to try to talk to Al through WhatsApp, but the signal kept getting dropped. It was bittersweet to hear his voice. I was happy to know he was doing okay, but I missed him terribly. It felt very strange to be doing something that felt this important to my life without him by my side, but realistically, I couldn't begin to imagine the trip with a wheelchair involved. I texted that I'd try to talk to him again at the next stop and sought comfort in the company of the others in the courtyard.

As the sultry evening slipped away, we collected our dry laundry and headed indoors to bed. Given today's heat and the length of tomorrow's journey, we had decided to get up at 5:30. We figured we would just dress and go, getting morning coffee at Moratinos or San Nicolas, an hour down the road. It was quiet in the bunkroom, most of the others still lounging on the patio.

Preparing for bed, I realized the lump on my neck had finally broken. It was a reassuring sign that it was just a bug bite; I wasn't going to die! Cleaning the area, I applied Polysporin and covered the wound with a band-aid to prevent infection. I snuggled in, knowing I would sleep much better this night

Up before the sun, Patricia, Michel, and I snuck out of the *albergue*, leaving most of our roommates still snoring softly. Without our morning coffee, we walked out of Terradilos de los Templarios in near darkness, determined to travel the twenty-three kilometres to Bercianos before the main heat of the day hit.

The plan was good except for one small thing; we couldn't see where we were going. I had brought along a camping headlight, but Patricia already had her cellphone out lighting up the path. This worked fine until we came to a crossroads. Not being able to see any markers, we didn't know which way to go. Directional logic had us turning left, and we were relieved to see a couple shadows moving up the road in the distance. We met the shadows only to find they too were perplexed as to which way to go. Great! We had been following them, and now it seemed a case of the blind leading the blind.

I hauled out my book reading directions to turn right off the road onto a path after solar panels. Really? We could barely see the road let alone some solar panels that were God knows where in relation to the road. So much for the great plan of starting early.

Out of the darkness, a couple more pilgrims came up behind us, and we shared our confusion with them. Modern technology came to the rescue. One of the men had a GPS and moments later, we all trekked off to the right, bypassing a collection of large solar panels just becoming visible with the dawn.

Forty minutes into the walk, under full daylight now, our little troupe wandered into Moratinos. Breakfast was a steaming cup of *café con leche* with a slice of rich, cheesy tortilla. Patricia joined Michel and I, a chocolate-filled croissant in one hand, a glass of freshly-squeezed orange juice in the other.

"I am so hungry. I'm glad we got an early start, but I sure miss having morning coffee before we walk." A puzzling statement from someone not actually having coffee. We smiled.

Back out on the road, the sun continued to climb, blazing its way up into the clear, blue sky. The *senda* led us along rural roads without much to look at besides the occasional tree. After about an hour's walk, we began to follow a paved roadway, lightly trafficked by trucks of all sizes and the occasional sedan. Gradually climbing, the gravel track took us to the top of gentle hill.

Below us lay the city of Sahagun, sizzling in the valley bowl, surrounded by planted fields, turned almost white by the glare of the mid-morning Spanish sun.

I remembered hearing how artists flock to Spain specifically for the light. I had already seen that my photos reflected that very special lighting with impossibly vivid greens, yellows, and blues in a land where even the browns and reds of dirt seem amazing. It was going to take some work to convince people back home that the colours weren't somehow enhanced.

Just outside the city, we passed between two stone sculptures, three times my height, one of a priest and one of a knight. These imposing sentinels guided our way into a sprawling city, the size of which belied its moderate population of less than 5,000 occupants. It wasn't always wise to stop at the first bar we came to for breaks since they were often crowded, and here, the number of packs outside the door testified to that. We walked on, knowing that there would likely be other opportunities for refreshment. Strangely, though, the almost silent streets seemed devoid of eateries.

Getting our bearings, we stopped to take a photo of the beautiful Arch of San Benito which straddled the roadway. This arch used to be the doorway to the Royal Monastery of San Benito, most of which was destroyed in 1835. Now instead of monks and penitents, minivans and trucks pass through this portal of gentle, golden curves.

Crossing the cool, lazy river Cea by way of an ancient Roman bridge hung with draping ivy, we came to the outskirts of Sahagun, still not having found a place to use a washroom or get a bite to eat. What was with this? Don't they know there are pilgrims melting out here? Even the sports complex and the campground we walked past were closed. It was Wednesday, before noon. We'd come to expect closures on Sundays and Mondays and had adjusted to the rhythm of siesta shutdowns during mid-afternoon, but this didn't make sense. On we walked, sweating the abuse of the searing sun. We still had another ten kilometres to go before reaching our destination.

At Calzada del Coto, we were offered the option of an alternate route, but more importantly, a bar providing a much-needed bathroom break and a cool drink. We didn't stop long, driven on by the need to beat the sun and win a bed at the municipal *albergue* at Bercianos. We dug in and focused on the dry gravel and dust below our boots, poling along in grim determination as sweat dripped from our brows.

The welcome sight of a noisy, pilgrim-infested bar greeted us as we approached

Bercianos, and we were further cheered when, after passing a few crumbling buildings, we came to a second bar, a little quieter than the first and boasting a cool garden patio. Stowing that location for future use, we plodded on to find the sun-baked municipal *albergue*, a squat, brick, retired schoolhouse. Outside, on bleached wooden benches, pilgrims baked in the sun, waiting for the 1:30 opening of the massive doors.

Having learned the process in Fromista, I loudly announced that I was leaving my pack to save my place and was going over to the shade-sheltered playground side of the building. Leaving my pack, I walked away. Behind me, I heard an urgent discussion in foreign languages, then, with a scramble of dumping packs, I was quickly joined by a relieved posse who pulled out water, cookies, cheese, and nuts and an impromptu celebratory lunch was on.

A white van suddenly pulled up across the street, its horn blaring. Oh yes. Grocery time again. This being one of the struggling hamlets in northern Spain, the *mercado* probably had very limited supplies. Delivery trucks pulled into towns, blaring their horns to notify residents of the arrival of perishable foods; bread, meat, fish, dairy, and fruit and vegetables. Once stopped, the trucks waited a few minutes and if there were no takers, they'd drive on, stopping elsewhere in the town and repeating the process. It was only as this truck pulled away that we realized, through it's open back door, they were carrying fruit and vegetables, but it was really just too hot to run after them. It was only a half hour until we would be allowed into the coolness of the brick refuge.

As we waited, a large couple struggled up the road towards the *albergue*, he bearing both packs, and she, swinging a leg encumbered by a heavy black brace from mid-thigh to ankle. "Bogie" as he liked to be called, was a mountain of a man, his weathered face accented by a trim moustache and beard, grey hair streaming from his navy sweatband, into a long pony-tail trailing down his back. His lady, "Bacall", fair hair pulled back from her smooth, moon face, lowered her substantial size down onto the wooden bench with a relieved sigh and loosened the straps on her brace. When they spoke, their Tennessee accents were as strong as syrup, to the point I almost thought it was put on, but I realized their words were as fresh and honest as their faces.

They told me they had been retired for a while now, and spent their time walking together. Big walks. All over the world. The sturdy build of these two, strapping people put me in mind of mountain people of years gone by, simple living and hard work being their making. These were "salt of the earth" people, robust, true, and full of life. They spoke of their children and grandchildren waiting their return and of family gatherings out on the porch of their mountain farm. They knew their priorities, their God, and each other. While the big man tenderly fussed around his wife, she shooed his ministrations off with a smile, embarrassed and, at the same time, loving his attention.

"We'll just keep walkin' 'til we can't," she beamed. I knew I would be seeing them along the way.

When our *hospitalero*, a stout Spaniard with a wide smile and benevolent face approached, we held back the urge to rush the door. With part acquired pilgrim patience and part fatigue born of the heat, we waited, in order of our packs (which by now trailed from the front door, around the corner of the building like a colourful caterpillar), and were welcomed by Ramon, one of the two brothers that ran the *albergue*. I quickly understood that he spoke very little English, and the registration process was completed with a lot of smiles, nodding, and pointing.

The sun spilled through the wide doorway, illuminating the most amazing floor I had ever seen. It was a wall-to-wall mosaic, a variety of coloured and differently sized natural stones to forming complex swirls and patterns. It felt borderline sacrilegious to walk on such a work of art. The beauty of the floor was reflected in soft frescos painted on the plasterwork and the intricately carved wooden staircase. I thought of the love and dedication of the craftsmen who built this place of beauty in which the youth of the town, their own children, could grow and learn. I grieved for them that there were no longer enough children here to enjoy it as a school.

After several sleep-interrupted nights, our room was almost filled with women, and we wanted to keep it that way. Now I'm not saying that women don't snore; we do. But men, they snore the loudest and the deepest, and we were determined to have as snore-free a night as we could manage. By the time the twenty-bed room was filled, it was all women. Well except for Michel. But Patricia and I had shared rooms with him before, and we vouched for him.

After quick showers in a large, sunlit co-ed bathroom, we rushed downstairs to do our laundry. The sun was shining, and the wind was blowing briskly in the schoolyard; prime time for laundry. Along the building wall, there were three stone sinks, with paint-tray-like bottoms, we could use for scrubbing out days of dirt, grime, and sweat. It was a fight not to lose our clothes to the grasping winds, and we hung tight until, using rough wooden pins, we had secured them to the lines strung along the back fence. We went off to explore the town, knowing the laundry would be dry upon our return.

We walked among the thirty or so buildings that made up this tenacious little town, working our way back to the peaceful bar we had seen earlier. Small tables surrounded by lacy, wrought iron chairs were scattered on a shady terrace between the side of the building and an ivy-draped wall. Gentle breezes ruffled the leaves and tiny birds darted about, searching for crumbs in the gravel below the chairs. Behind the bar, a tall, young Spaniard in rolled-up shirt sleeves was polishing already clean glasses. Upon his suggestion, I ordered a glass of the local *vino blanco*, preferring in the heat, a cool white instead of a tepid red wine. With great flourish, he brought glasses of wine to our courtyard table along with small bowls of snack crackers.

"We have six children here," he replied to my question about the town. "Two of them are my own. They all go to school at the church. Next year," he continued, "they will be closing the classroom here and our children will have to bus ten kilometres to Sahagun for school, but this is our home, so we will stay."

Just then, his young wife walked in bearing a freshly baked tortilla. She pushed a scarf back off her jet-black curls and gently touched his shoulder. I felt sad for this young couple struggling to make a life in a dying town and did what I could do to help. I ordered another glass of wine and slice of tortilla and Michel and Patricia followed suit.

Having accessed the bar's Wi-Fi, we all checked in with loved ones at home, sending messages and photos, letting them know where we were and how we were doing. Retrieving our warm, wind-whipped laundry from the schoolhouse courtyard, we carried it up the curving staircase to pack for the next day.

More pilgrims had arrived while we were away, and there was a hungry crowd in the dining room when the doors opened for dinner. Every inch of the benches along polished wood trestle tables was full. Ramon smilingly introduced his brother, Edwardo, the cook of the evening's meal. With their limited English they quickly appointed a young man who spoke Spanish and English as their official translator. Our dread-locked translator advised us that first we would sing for our supper, pointing to the posted Spanish words for a song about the pilgrimage, set to the tune of "*My Sharona*". Among much laughter, we struggled to do the song justice.

Then the brothers brought out two huge pans of paella and drafted two young Italian men to pass platefuls down the waiting tables of hungry pilgrims. I looked across the table and saw Doug, his red, sunburned face shining like it had been waxed. He looked pretty done in by his day's march in the heat. Hands passed baskets of hearty bread, poured cool pitchers of water, and filled glasses with robust red wine. The brothers, ever watchful of their charges, called for emptied plates, insisting on refilling them until the paella ran out.

Stomachs satisfied, it was time to sing again! The brothers, through their young interpreter, communicated that we would break into groups by nationality, and sing a song representing our country. I frantically looked around the room. Remember all those Canadians I spoke of earlier? Three; that's all that were left in this group of sixty! There were only three Canadians including Michel and myself. Lindsey, a nineteen-year-old girl from Manitoba reluctantly joined us. Michel and I had decided not to follow the Americans singing something as unoriginal as their national anthem, and chose "This Land is Your Land, This Land is My Land". Problem was, Lindsey was too young to know the words. While the Italians robustly sang "*Volare*", Michel and I hurriedly taught her the basic refrain.

At the front we made a comedy of getting ourselves in the right order so that when we sang "from Buena Vista to Vancouver Island", Michel from Atlantic Canada was first, Lindsey was in the middle for Manitoba, and I was last for Vancouver Island. A tall, lean, dark-haired beauty between two older grey-haired bookends, we banked on the attention being focused on Lindsey and not our woeful singing.

Through the designated translator, our brotherly *hospitaleros* communicated the morning rules. No one was to get out of bed before 6:30. Applause from those tired of the early risers determining everyone else's start time. Breakfast would be served as part of the price of the bed. More applause.

"And now...what?!" the young man exclaimed, knocking his own cap off his head. We all asked what they had said, and he was reluctant to tell us. We demanded to know. "They say the men have to do the dishes, and the ladies are to go to bed." Well at least half of the people in the room were happy, and actually, the men took on the task in good humour.

Up in the washroom, the ladies took advantage of having a male-free environment to prepare for bed. Instead of the frantic hurry to strip off clothes and scramble under the privacy of covers, there was languid laughter and conversation as the transformation from clothes to nightwear took place. Hair brushing, face washing, and teeth brushing; all were accompanied by a happy babble of female chatter.

Crawling into my bottom bunk, after the day's long walk and incessant heat, I think I was asleep before Michel made it up from the kitchen.

We had been told not to get up before 6:30, and I was going to suck up every one of those restful moments! I swam to the surface of wakefulness to find Michel and Patricia hovering above me in whispered conversation.

"Do you think she's okay?" whispered Michel.

"I think so. I haven't seen her sleep like this before though," responded a concerned Patricia. I wondered what all the worry was about when I realized it was me.

"I'm here," I smiled. "I'm okay," I reassured them.

"You were really sleeping deeply," Patricia advised. "We were both up and dressed, and you still weren't moving. I don't know how you can sleep like that." She obviously hadn't slept well again.

"What time is it?" I asked, shaking off the last vestiges of sleep.

"It's almost 6:30!" Patricia reported. Well what was all the fuss about? We had been told to stay in bed until 6:30, and I was just following orders. It's amazing how that type of permission can release your mind to relax into it. My companions, however, were up and antsy, eager to hit the road.

"I'll be ready to go in time, don't worry. Breakfast isn't until 7:00. That gives me a half an hour to get dressed and packed." I swung my feet to the cold, tile floor. "Easy, peasy!" Grabbing my cloth and towel, I casually strolled to the bathroom leaving them looking after me in wonder. I smiled, all they had done was put themselves in a tizzy to hurry up…and wait. Before the half hour passed, I was washed, dressed, packed, and waiting outside the breakfast room with them, poles and pack parked in the corner waiting our departure.

The brothers laid before us platters of thick slices of toast, bowls of fruit, and kettles of hot water and hot milk to make coffees and teas of our choices. They were as cheerful and helpful at 7:00 am as they had been the previous day, and I knew this would be a stop I would always remember affectionately.

Out into the morning sun we strode, casting pilgrim shadows on the grassy shoulders of the dirt track. In the distance, fertile, furrowed red fields of earth waited the planting of crops. Or perhaps the seeds were already sown, just patiently waiting a little more sun and rain to pop their shoots above the ground. Newly-leafed trees rustled softly in the gentle breeze, and we enjoyed the mild morning as we walked.

Michel reminded us that he had just retired with four weeks of holidays due to him, so he bragged smugly that he was getting paid to walk the Camino. He found the Camino freeing and spiritual, but not the religious sort of spiritual. He enjoyed the architecture, the people, the food and wine, and the music, where he found it.

He told us about the two women he would be bringing back to the Camino. We knew he wasn't talking about his girlfriend, a blow-hot, blow-cold relationship that he seemed unsure of continuing.

"She would never do this," he said. "She likes to travel, but it's good hotels all the way. She couldn't handle the minimalism of the Camino. You two seem to be handling this journey well. My friends are about your age, and I'd like to ask you what I should tell the ladies to bring in the way of female things." I don't think he was blushing; with his fair colouring he usually seemed a little pinkish about the face.

"Sunscreen and moisturizer," Patricia and I suggested simultaneously.

"Tell them not to worry about makeup and hair products. The less they carry, the better. They'll enjoy it more if they're comfortable and not worried about appearances," I added.

"But they might want to dress up a little in the cities," Michel mused.

"I use my Buffs to do my hair different ways without having to worry about blow dryers or curling irons. And makeup you'd just sweat off. But sunscreen; they'll want sunscreen. I have this little skirt I can pull over my leggings to make me feel more dressed up. And my Buffs add colour. I love my Buffs." *Oh really?*

"I save one shirt that I never walk in, so when I put it on, I'm off duty," I contributed. "I also brought a chiffon swimsuit cover. It's light, doesn't wrinkle, and put over my black tank, looks pretty dressed up. Only thing is the shoes; let's face it…there's no feminine way to do boots and trekking sandals! When I get to Santiago, I'm going to pick up some mascara and a pretty pair of shoes for my days there."

"And real underwear!" Patricia added with enthusiasm. "Something girly!" Okay, so now maybe Michel was blushing and maybe he was sorry he had asked.

"When are you bringing them?" I asked, changing the subject.

"Next spring. Who knows, maybe this will be a retirement business for me. Escorted Camino tours. Could be worse," he shrugged as he broke into song, set a good pace, and led us onwards.

Before we knew it, we had arrived at El Burgo Ranero, and a refreshment stop was in order.

"I hope the bathroom is clean. Yesterday there wasn't even a seat on one I used. You'd think they would take better care of us since they rely on our business," Patricia complained. After a cold glass of fresh orange juice, I took advantage of the facilities, thankful for the toilet seat and bonus, the toilet paper. That was another thing to advise Michel to tell his ladies: always have some tissue in your pocket 'cause many of the bathrooms don't supply that.

The trees lining the *senda* provide scant shade, but lovely company just the same. Suddenly a call came from behind, "Bikes!" We jumped to the side just as three cyclists, bikes laden with panniers, rolled by, their tires crunching in the gravel, calling out *"Buen Camino"* as they went.

"I just wished they'd use bells or horns or something. Why do they even come on the trail when there's a perfectly good road right beside us. It's not like it's a different route six feet away!" Patricia huffed. So, it seemed she was still a little cranky today. I purposely dropped my pace and her frustrated demeanour translated into faster steps as she fell in beside Michel. I whispered my apologies and hoped he would pull more joy out of her than I had.

The downside about starting later is that by the time we trekked the twenty kilometres to Reliegos, we were walking in under a relentless sun. At the outskirts of town, a colourful bar beckoned with vibrant orange plastic chairs and swirling umbrellas. Cognizant of the climbing sun and the creeping clock, we needed to get back on the road if we wanted to get a bed in Mansilla, so we finished our drinks and pressed on.

Winding out through the little town we passed a row of colourful little bodegas, built into the side of the hill, festooned with wild flowers. These clever little huts were dug into the clay banks and then fires lit inside, firing the clay like pottery in a kiln. The end result was a sealed, dark, cool wine storage, the contents of which the owners guarded with locked, wrought iron gates.

Just over an hour to walk, the narrow *senda* was dusty and hot as it ran alongside a motorway. We jockeyed for position in a steady stream of pilgrims and cyclists. It appeared the closer we got to the larger centres, the thicker the numbers on the path. The oppressive heat washed over us, robbing us of energy and even of conversation as we focused on the path, the way markers and our feet.

"I really don't know if I should stay a second night in Leon when we get there," Patricia agonized. She pulled this issue again out of her mental backpack. "If I want to go to Finisterre, I need to go faster. I know I said I would stay with you at the hotel, but maybe I should go ahead. Would that be alright? I know we were going to share the cost of the room. Maybe I could bus to Finisterre, or maybe I should skip it. But if I want to go there, I need to move ahead faster than you plan." I assured her that I would roll with whichever decision she made, and that she had to make the choice that was right for her. Deep down inside, I was also thinking that I needed to make sure no one else was making my choices for me. I needed to make my plans and stick to them unless it was me who wanted to change them.

Walking in through the industrial outskirts of Mansilla, we realized the lateness of our arrival had put us in jeopardy for finding a bed. Crossing the concrete bridge, we entered the town and turned off at the first *albergue* we found. While they had no beds for us, they were happy to serve us crisp salads and cold drinks to slake our thirst. Around us, a bevy of Italians were in party mode, having secured beds for themselves and for their incoming countrymen. They cheered each new arrival like a sporting event. According to the *hospitalero* at the *albergue*, it seemed that we were running into the same "no room at the inn" scenario as we had before Burgos.

"What do you think?" asked Patricia, sliding her Buff off her head, freeing her silvery hair to whatever fresh air could be found. "The next place that might have beds is another six kilometres; that would make this a thirty-three-kilometre day and would put us there around 4:00," she mopped her brow. "And if there's no bed there, it's another four and a half; another hour in this heat."

"What about hopping the bus to the next town?" I queried. "That would get us there sooner, and we'd know sooner if we had to go on further."

"Well that puts us only twelve kilometres from Leon. Perhaps we should just take a taxi into Leon and get a head start on this crowd from there," suggested Michel. "It seems," his gravelly voice continued, "that there's a bit of a bottle neck when we get to the big cities. Where did you plan to stay in Leon?" he questioned.

"Patricia and I planned to spend one night in an *albergue* and a second in a hotel, but now her plans are up in the air about staying a second night. For my first night, I really want to stay at the convent *albergue*, Santa Maria. It's run by the Benedictine nuns. The *albergue* is attached to a cathedral, and they have sung vespers and a pilgrim's mass." Patricia and Michel seemed unimpressed.

"I think Michel's idea is good," drawled Patricia. "I don't want to go on in this heat just to find no bed when we get there. Let's go to Leon by taxi and get settled for the night. That way we can walk around and see a bit of the city in case I don't stay the second day with you. Alright?"

Michel went to see about a taxi and returned to say it would be about twenty minutes. Then he turned to his guidebook and found another option for a place to stay.

"I'm going to call the San Francisco de Asis and see if the brothers have a bed there for me. Would you like me to reserve beds for you?" he questioned. Patricia agreed, but I said I was going to go with my original plan. The hotel I had reserved for the second night was very close to the convent, so staying there would make transferring easy. I wouldn't be wandering around the city looking for the hotel, which would be safer, especially if I was going to be on my own. I battled against sadness at the risk of losing them and reminded myself that I was totally capable of being on my own. Right?

While Patricia went to use the washroom, Michel sidled up to me.

"Do you think she will stay or walk out with me the next day? I'm only going to stay the one night. Last time I did the Camino, I took a bus out of Leon in the morning as far as Trobajo; that's about four kilometres, and it got me past the industrial part of the city. She seems a little nervous to walk alone, so she could walk with me," he suggested, somewhat sheepishly, as if he felt he was stealing her away from me. *Funny how no one seemed to worry about how I felt about walking alone,* I thought. By this point, I was tired of the back and forth. I was starting to happily envision a peaceful hotel room, all to myself. More importantly, I knew the hotel room had a bathtub, and I was looking forward to a long, luxurious soak.

"She will have to make her own decision," I replied. "Whatever she chooses will be fine with me."

"Let's go wait down the block so these pilgrims don't see us get in the taxi," he cautioned as Patricia returned. What was all the cloak and dagger about? Those people were all kicked back with cold beers, knowing they had a place to sleep tonight. We'd already walked twenty-eight kilometres today. If we walked on, and there was no bed, we'd be faced with the same choice of taking a taxi or walking on, but hotter and more tired than we already were. As the van pulled up to the curb, we loaded our packs in the back and climbed into the cool interior.

"We have been busy today!" laughed the driver. "It is too hot for walking with big packs, and there are many towns without beds," he confirmed. "You will have no trouble finding a place in Leon. There are many, many *albergues* in the city." Reassured that we'd made a wise decision, we relaxed into our seats, watching the industrial area fly by as we entered the busy centre of Leon.

Fifteen minutes later, the taxi came to an abrupt halt in a circle crowded with taxis and busses. In the centre, an impressive fountain encircled by colourful floral displays shot jets of water up into the blue sky, a refreshing mist settling on the hot pedestrians on the sidewalks. Thanking our driver, we shouldered our packs and huddled up to form a game plan: bank machine, my *albergue*, their *albergue*, and ice cream! The last item was, of course, Patricia.

Trying not to look like a back-country hick, I trailed behind the others, taking in the beautiful old stone buildings gracefully ignoring the glass and steel structures looming behind them. Even the streetlight standards were beautiful, festooned with wrought iron curlicues and mythical beasts. The wide streets were more pedestrian than vehicular, with collections of café tables and chairs spilling out the doors of restaurants and bars, and waiters delivering frothy glasses of beer and crusty slabs of breads and cheeses to lounging customers.

Although we took the precaution of guarding each other as we withdrew funds from the automatic bank machine, there was a feeling of security in the area. Signs warned of video surveillance and uniformed men patrolled in pairs. We had agreed to find my *albergue* first since I had no reservation. That way, Patricia had reasoned, if there was no room, I could come with them and try there. It was only mid-afternoon, so I was hopeful we had arrived early enough to get a bed. Asking assistance from two well-heeled Spanish matrons, we were guided down a winding, narrow street fronted by a dazzling array of storefronts, mostly closed due to the siesta.

We entered the convent through large double gates and found the *hospitaleros* registering pilgrims at a shady table in the corner of a walled parking area. Samantha welcomed us with a beaming smile and assured me yes, there were still many beds. The young Spanish beauty's cascading curls fell to the shoulders of her voluptuous figure, the appeal of which she seemed totally unaware.

"We are a convent you know," she said, eyes sparkling. "So only ladies on the bottom floor and men on the top floor. If you are married," she looked quizzically at Michel and Patricia, "and you have your wedding certificate, we have a special area for couples. Her attention returned to me. "And there," she gestured across the way, "is where you can have supper. The pilgrim's supper is nine euros and is very good, I promise you. If you need laundry, you give your clothes to Michele, and he will run the machines for you. You pick them up when they are dry. And at 7:00 we meet here for Vespers; the nuns will sing, and there will be a pilgrim's blessing. It is very beautiful. You will enjoy."

"For breakfast," the information continued, "you can also have it here. You go up those stairs and have your breakfast before you go." I was impressed at the amount of information she delivered in English in her charming Spanish accent. I told her that I was to stay at the Hotel Pax the next night, and she pouted sweetly that I would not stay with them again.

"I was told that it was not allowed to stay in an *albergue* two nights in a row unless you were sick or hurt and a doctor advised against moving on."

"Oh," she smiled, waving across the pavement to another *hospitalero* massaging an older pilgrim's feet, "if we have room, we can keep you again. But the hotel, it too is part of this convent. You see, it is just there, on the other side of that hedge. You will be happy there. They have bathtubs!" A woman who truly understood!

Passport registered and stamped, she crushed me in a joyful hug. I went to join Patricia and Michel only to realize they were taking seats to register as well. I found my eyes filling with tears as I rested a hand on Patricia's shoulder while Samantha stamped her book. I hadn't realized how much I didn't want to be parted from them.

"Well you know," Michel called out, "they have everything we need here, they have room, and we can all stay together one last night. Then, if Patricia stays with you, I will go on alone in the morning, but if she wants, she can come with me. I will just call the monastery and cancel my booking," he said cheerfully. He obviously felt he was giving me a gift, with the hopes that the return would be he'd have a walking partner in the morning. Dinner tickets in hand, and reminders of the mass, we scattered to our designated bunk areas to stow our gear and grab quick showers.

Out in the courtyard, we found Michel charging his phone. I thought we were fast in the shower, but it seems he was even faster. I asked them to wait just a few minutes longer while I checked over at the hotel about my next night's reservation.

"They said I can bring my bag for storage there when I leave the convent in the morning, but that the room won't be ready before 1:00. And yes, yes, yes! There is a bathtub! Apparently, the room has three beds in it." I left that information hanging as we traced our steps, back through the warren of narrow streets to the wide avenue.

"Now!" exclaimed Patricia, "Let's go find ice cream!"

"And the cathedral," we reminded her.

"Yes, and the cathedral. But first, ice cream!"

Spotting a frozen yogurt shop, we scurried inside, eyes wide at the assortment of topping choices. Cups of creamy yogurt in hand, we stepped back out into the sunshine.

"I really wanted chocolate. I guess they just don't make chocolate yogurt," mused Patricia.

Ahead of us, the street opened up into a wide square, a setting for the central jewel, the thirteenth century Santa Maria de Leon cathedral. Also known as the House of Light, its ornate towers framed an impressive rose window, and I had to wonder how these mammoth works of art and architecture were constructed so accurately without the benefit of machines or modern-day technology.

The massive doors were locked behind iron gates, with visiting hours posted for later that evening, so we snapped photos and explored the shops bordering the square. Young families strolled by, their uniformed children fresh from school, animatedly sharing their day's events. Elders rested on the benches lining the front courtyard of the cathedral, deep in conversation, or quietly enjoying the fading sun as they watched the crazy tourists.

Spotting a pharmacy sign, I pushed through the door and enquired about Epson salts. The man behind the counter seemed to have difficulty understanding what I was asking. I threw in a little French; "*sel de bain?*" No luck. He disappeared and came out with a white-coated young woman.

"Oh yes. One moment please." She disappeared as well, but quickly returned, "We have some at our other store. If you come back in one hour we will have them brought here." I asked her how big the package would be and what the cost would be. "You will see when you come. If you do not want what we bring you, that is okay. You can choose." How civilized! I advised her that I would come back in the morning.

Joining the others back in the square, I discovered Patricia scooping chocolate ice cream from a cardboard cup. She grinned triumphantly. I shook my head and wondered yet again where she put it all. We casually strolled back towards our *albergue*, stopping from time to time to check out stores newly opened now that siesta was done.

Back at the convent, more pilgrims were lined up at the registration desk. We found seating at a table by the receptacles and quickly claimed them, charging our phones while we checked and sent messages. Michele, the older *hospitalero* who had shown us our beds earlier, clapped his hands and announced that the dining room was now open for supper.

Michel, Patricia, and I joined a long table of happy pilgrims as waiters placed carafes of water and bottles of *vino tinto* among us. First to arrive was a crisp salad, with curls of carrot, half of a hard-boiled egg, spears of white asparagus, and a dollop of tuna, all lightly dressed in vinegar and oil. This was followed by grilled white fish, simmered in a golden sauce, accompanied by golden fries. Dessert was a creamy rice pudding, liberally sprinkled with fragrant cinnamon. Nothing was really new, but each dish was beautifully presented and well prepared. I was well satisfied by the time we trouped back outside to wait our escort to the adjoining church for Vespers.

Annie, another *hospitalero*, arrived and herded us out through the gates, up the narrow roadway, and through large wooden doors into a tiled vestibule that echoed with our chatter. We were greeted by a tiny, bespectacled nun in traditional, black habit. In heavily accented English, Sister Celestine welcomed us and, clasping her hands over the long rosary that hung around her neck, divided us into groups based on our languages. Then she asked for a volunteer, and I found myself handing out multilingual service books, ensuring that everyone got the one they could read. Sister Celestine then explained the service and led us through practice responses and a dry run of a hymn we were to sing in Spanish. Satisfied that we were prepared, she led us silently through another set of doors, indicating where we should sit as we entered the hushed sanctity of the church itself.

A couple of clicks and the altar area lit up in stages, revealing panels of golden scroll work set against the backdrop of rich, dark woods. Before us, on either side of the aisle, were the choir stalls, which began to fill with an assortment of nuns, all ages, colours, shapes, and sizes. Like a girl helping her grandmother, a younger nun assisted an older one, cane in hand, through the door and into her chair. In the midst of the hush, three priests proceeded into the church and the service began.

I tried to follow along, comparing the English writing to the Spanish spoken as I strove to add to my vocabulary. A young nun, plain in looks, her small, white-framed face overwhelmed by heavy, black-framed glasses, spoke in a clear, lilting voice from a side pulpit. The three priests sat in their heavily decorated vestments, nodding sagely, observing her progress as they waited their cue to stand and proceed with the service. Authoritative words spoken, the chalice raised, blessed, and served, the language was different, but the rituals very similar to our communion services back home.

The nuns broke into song, voices – some strong and clear, others tremulous and strained – raising in joyful celebration of their beliefs. I felt moved to tears as I often am by powerful music and swallowed a lump building in my throat as they moved from one piece to another in the Vespers program. Sister Celestine suddenly stood, turned to us, and like a conductor before a choir, led us as our hesitant voices stumbled through the Spanish words for the hymn we had practiced in the vestibule. When we were done, she beamed at us like a proud mother, and we resumed our seats.

The priests stood and intoned the pilgrims' blessing upon us, and although we may not have understood the words, their intent was evident as they prayed for protection for our journey, strength in our faith, and a safe return to our homes. Amen's all around, the priests proceeded out a side door, the nuns disappearing as quietly as they had arrived, and Sister Celestine led us back to the world outside.

Quietly we walked back down the street to the convent *albergue*. While some retired to their beds, Patricia, Michel, and I rested on benches against the court-yard's stone wall, still warm from the sunshine of the day.

"So, I've made a decision," Patricia began. "I think I'll bus out with Michel in the morning if you really don't mind. As much as I would like a rest day, getting here early today gave me time to see Leon and still get a jumpstart on my schedule." Michel and Patricia looked at me expectantly.

"Absolutely," I replied. "You have less time than me. I'd like more time to explore the city, and this is the first real rest day I've scheduled. Anyways, if I get to Santiago early my hotel won't be available."

"You could come with me to Finisterre," suggested Patricia, as Michel waited the outcome.

"Finisterre is not for me," I said. "I just want to take my time and enjoy the journey to Santiago. I don't want to rush or miss anything I want to see along the way just to make time for Finisterre. It's important to you, so, you need to travel faster. Michel is on that same agenda, so as long as you both choose to, you can travel together. We can keep in touch by cellphone, and you can let me know how you're doing. You go with Michel. I'll be fine, really," I assured her.

Patricia let out a long sigh. "Maybe we should walk down to the *mercado* and get some chocolate and bananas for tomorrow then." We all laughed and accompanied her to the store.

"I'll be getting up the same time as you in the morning, and we'll have breakfast together before you two walk up to the bus stop. That will give us the chance to say goodbye properly, until we see each other again." Hugging us goodnight, Michel walked up the stairs to the men's dorm, and Patricia and I walked down into the ladies' dorm. We snuggled into our bunks and whispered softly back and forth. I was reminded of sharing a room with my sister when we were young. The whispers slowed, then dropped off, and I slept.

Seven kilometres in – Looking back at St. Jean Pied de Port

Tranquil Larrasonana (between Zubiri and Pamplona)

Colourful canola outside Pamplona

Map of the world planted to welcome pilgrims of the world

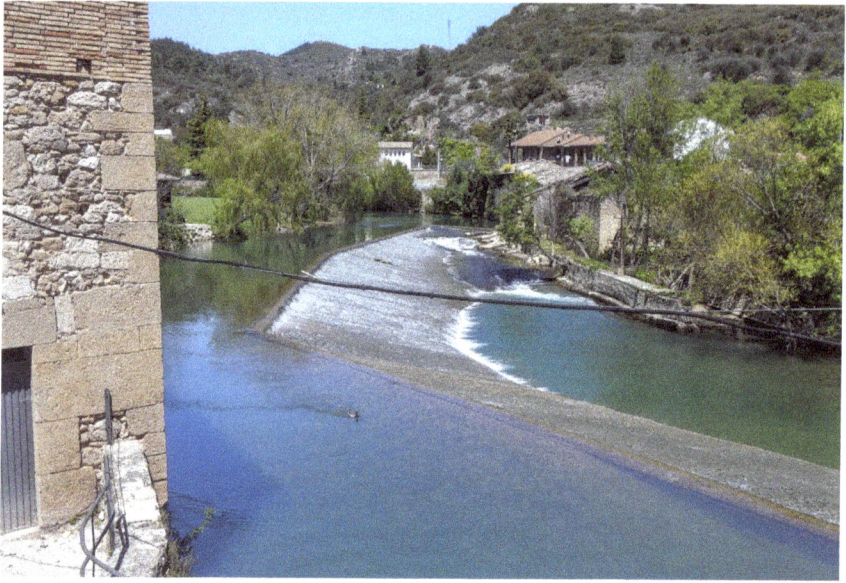

A cool welcome to Estella on a hot, hot day!

John and Armin pause by a lonely boot left behind at Edwardos on the road to Los Arcos

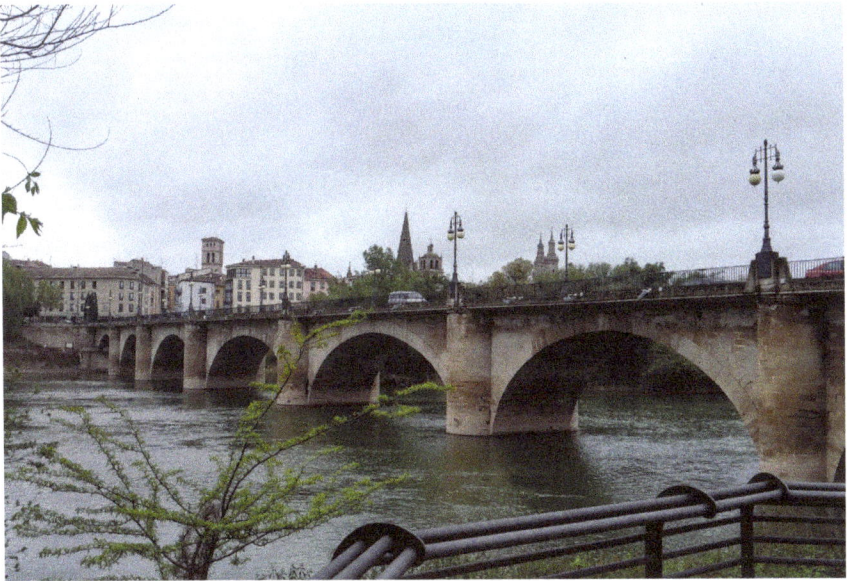

Crossing the Rio Ebro into Logrono

Stormy skies only enhance the brilliant greens of the fields

Laundry on legs!

Typical albergue bunk room

Technicolour walk along the Camino's undulating senda

The 13th century Catedral de Santa Maria dwarfs the old city of Burgos

A solitary tree echoes the loneliness of the endless meseta

Searching for dry ground on the boot sucking trek from San Bol

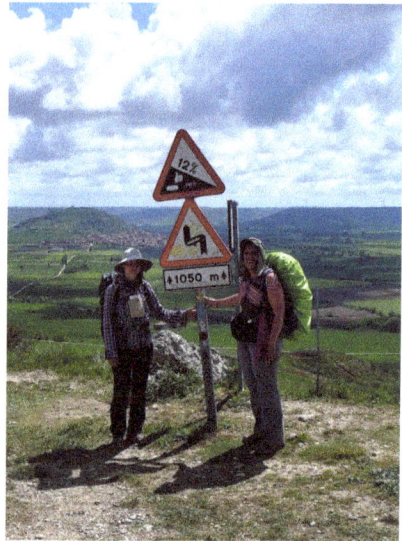

We made it! A challenging climb outside Castrojeriz

The Impressive 11th century Romanesque Iglesia de San Martin in Fromista

Meseta madness! Flat out for Bercianos

The Gothic Pulchra Leonina Cathedral (also known as the House of Light)

The cosmopolitan city of Leon, a contrast of old and new, where history meets the future

Amidst the progress, an ancient pilgrim finds rest

The Cruz de Fero where stones, representing burdens, are laid down

The rain in Spain doesn't always fall on the plain!

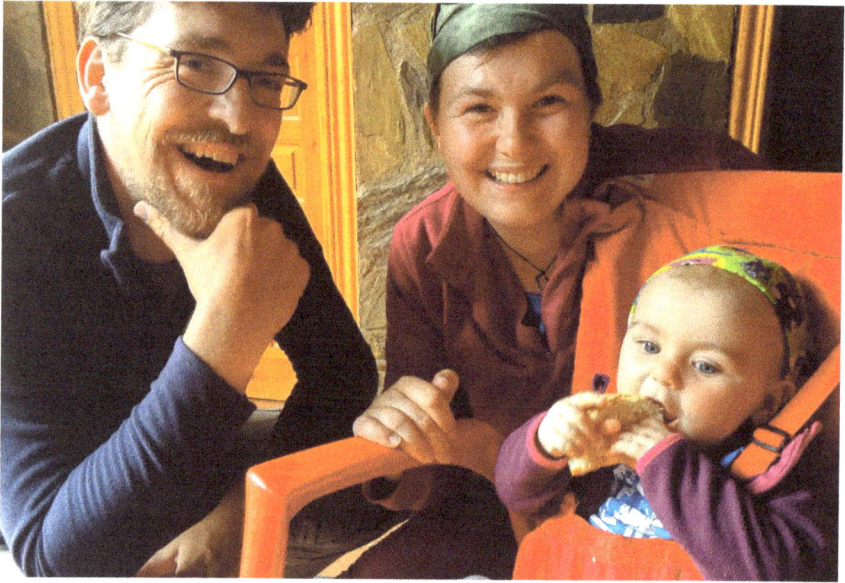

Andi, Ester and Camino Bambino, Irma

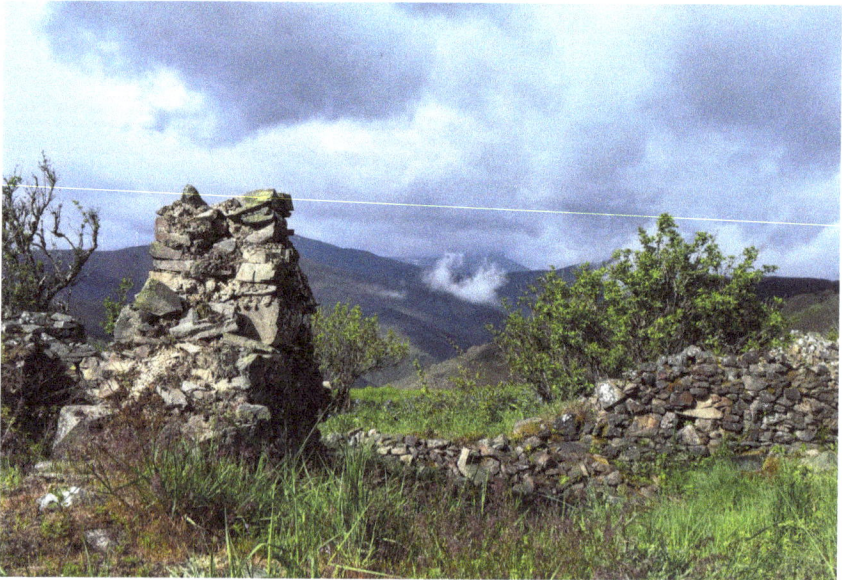

Misty mountains, guarded by sentinels of the past

Picturesque Villafranca del Bierzo perched between the rivers and the hills

The whimsical pallozas of O'Cebeiro

Dawn breaks in rural Galicia

Ornate cribs, resembling mausoleums were built off the ground to protect the corn

The "stairway from Hell!" Luckily, the refuge of Portomarin is in sight

The "Final Five" reach the first marker indicating under 100kms to go!
(Left to right: Paul, Zbigniew, Roxey, Ana and Catharina)

Medieval bridge crossing the Rio Furelos into Melide

A supper of pulperia and peppers de pardron await

Pilgrims' mass at O'Pedrouzo the night before entering Santiago

Arrival at the Santiago Cathedral – the Praza das Praterias

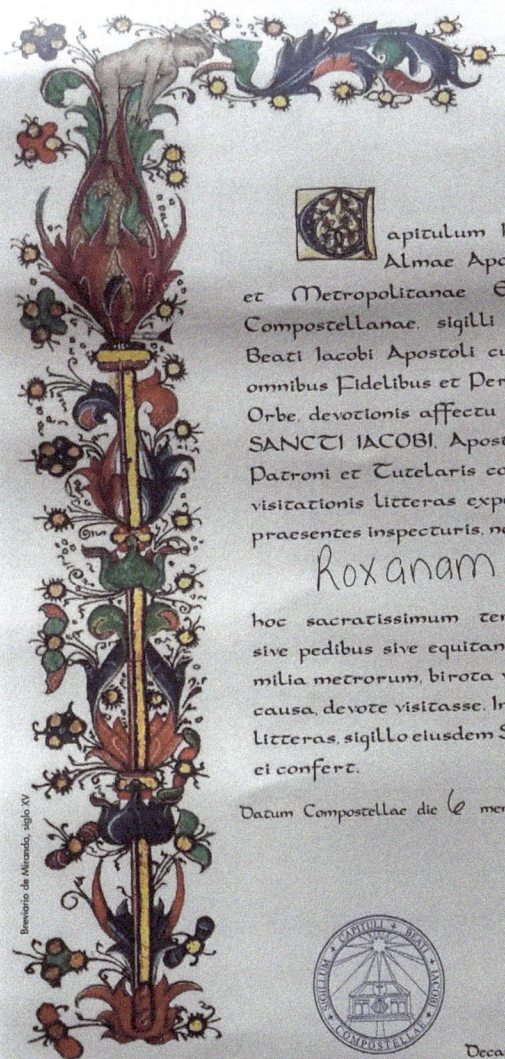

Capitulum huius Almae Apostolicae et Metropolitanae Ecclesiae Compostellanae, sigilli Altaris Beati Iacobi Apostoli custos, ut omnibus Fidelibus et Peregrinis ex toto terrarum Orbe, devotionis affectu vel voti causa, ad limina SANCTI IACOBI, Apostoli Nostri, Hispaniarum Patroni et Tutelaris convenientibus, authenticas visitationis litteras expediat, omnibus et singulis praesentes inspecturis, notum facit: Dnam

Roxanam Edwards

hoc sacratissimum templum, perfecto Itinere sive pedibus sive equitando post postrema centum milia metrorum, birota vero post ducenta, pietatis causa, devote visitasse. In quorum fidem praesentes Litteras, sigillo eiusdem Sanctae Ecclesiae munitas, ei confert.

Datum Compostellae die 6 mensis Iunii anno Dni 2016

Segundo L. Pérez López
Decanus S.A.M.E. Cathedralis Compostellanae

Journey finished – My Compostela

The High Altar at the Cathedral – A golden St. James looks on

The Botafumeiro waits to swing

The Cathedral at Santiago Like a partially wrapped gift waiting to be revealed, even the scaffolding of the restoration could not deter from its beauty. Whether you were there for religious reasons, spiritual reasons, or just to enjoy a very special place, it filled you with its magic.

The morning sun streamed through the narrow windows set high in the dorm wall, spotlighting the colourful backpacks parading down the wall. Their female owners, in a variety of states of dress, some still rubbing sleep from their eyes, tumbled out of their bunks, preparing to lift them for another day. Today, while Patricia pulled on her hiking pants, I dressed in street clothes, such as I had; leggings, a clean t-shirt, and my trekking sandals. My boots would take the day off, securely tied to my pack until tomorrow. Since I wouldn't have my pack, I tucked everything I would need for the day in my front pack and tied my jacket around my waist.

"Are you ready?" questioned Patricia. I nodded and shouldering our bags, we climbed the shallow stairs to the courtyard. Samantha greeted us with a wide smile, and remembering I was relocating to the hotel, showed me where to stash my pack for the day. I followed Patricia up the narrow staircase to a crowded breakfast room. Pilgrims filled the benches on either side of the room-length trestle table, covered with a bright yellow plastic cloth. At the sideboard, a bearded *hospitalero* poured hot coffee and hot milk for me. Hugging my large, ceramic mug, I settled down on the bench next to Patricia, watching as she chose a thick slice of toast from the basket in the middle of the table.

"The preserves," Samantha announced, "are made by the nuns, and they are very nice." No label, no idea what the fruit was, except something gold. The jam was very good. As I spread a second slice of toast, Michel appeared at the head of the stairs.

"Michel, Michel!" called Patricia (*as if he could have missed us in the narrow room*). "Come sit here!" she ordered, patting the bench beside her. Cup in hand, he swung his long legs over the bench, folding them under the table where he rested his elbows. He looked up from under his thick, white eyebrows, his sensitive eyes adjusting to the light.

"So, you are good to stay on your own? You won't change your mind and come with us?" he asked.

"No. I'm really going to miss you both, but I want to take this day. Maybe I'll see you further down the road. By the time I get to Santiago, you may be returning from Finisterre, and we might see each other there." It was a long shot, we all knew, but we upheld the pretence that this was not a final goodbye.

"Maybe I should stay..."drawled Patricia. *Here we go again. More waffling!*

"No," I said, "you made up your mind, and I'll be fine. You go with Michel. We'll stay in touch." My words were brave, but I wasn't sure I wanted to walk up and see them board the bus and drive away. Placing our rinsed cups on the drain board, we clambered down the stairs. I lifted Patricia's pack to her shoulders and embraced her in a sisterly hug. "Keep yourself safe," I ordered.

"I will take care of her," Michel assured me as he engulfed me in a fleece-covered hug. "It has been good to know you. Maybe we will walk again together one day." I nodded as they turned and, with a final wave, disappeared out the massive courtyard doors. Again, I was on my own.

The streets of Leon were still waking as I strolled out, feeling strange not to have a twenty-pound pack on my back. My feet felt light. The trekking sandals allowed my toes to breathe where my boots had not. Storefronts still closed, some locals sat at bistros, stirring cups and munching on croissants, while others, dressed for their day's work, hurried up quiet streets to unknown destinations.

In the distance, I made out the figure of a trio of pilgrims, packs on their back as their poles tapped along the street. That should be me, one of three, I thought for a moment. But Patricia and Michel would be long gone by now, and I had the whole day ahead of me to explore Leon.

I walked up to the main avenue, admiring airy fashions in creams and yellows, cosmopolitan mannequins inviting me to return when the stores opened. Tiers of shoes, imprisoned behind glass, called out to me, but I knew I would liberate none of them. Any shopping I would do today would be window shopping. There was no room in my pack for frivolities. As I walked, I watched city workers going about their tasks; mowing, watering, sweeping and climbing down into manholes. Interestingly, I saw no women crew members. On our crew, we had some pretty impressive ladies handling technical jobs, operating massive pieces of equipment, and working elbow to elbow with the men. But all in all,

I crossed the road and looped back past the fountain and up to the cathedral square, bypassing stores devoted totally to candy or pastry or tourist souvenirs. Still too early for the drugstore, I bought a hot cup of creamy coffee from a side-walk cafe and settled on a bench addressing the imposing face of the cathedral. Watching an older couple wrangling energetic toddlers, I wondered what my grandchildren would think of this trek.

"The Camino with kids; might be fun, but probably a lot of work," I mused aloud.

"Oh no, it can most certainly be done," a voice assured me from the next bench. There sat a young woman, with a lush body and short auburn hair, enjoying a cigarette. "My husband and I, we are travelling with our eight-month-old baby girl," she said, taking care to blow her smoke in another direction.

"With a baby? You're doing the Camino with a baby? That's incredible!"

"It's easy," she continued with her nonchalant attitude. "We live in Germany, so it is close. My husband and I, we have done the Camino every year since we have been married. Last year I was pregnant when I walked. So this year, we do it with a child. It is fine."

I asked how they managed it, and Esther (as she introduced herself) advised me that her husband carried their daughter in a baby pack on front, and then carried a small backpack on back for balance.

"I carry a pack with things for the day, but we send a suitcase full of baby things on to our next stop."

"And you stay in the *albergues?*" I questioned.

"Well sometimes yes, but today we are having a rest day. We rented a small apartment, just over there," she gestured vaguely. "It was a good price, and we have a whole suite so everyone got a good sleep last night. My husband is there with the baby as she is now napping. Not all *albergues* will allow babies. You must book a private room. It is for the good of the baby and for the good of the other pilgrims. And you? Is this your first Camino?" Esther questioned as she ground out her cigarette on the pavement.

"Yes, this is my first Camino. I come from the west coast of Canada, so just getting here took me about eighteen hours in travel time to St. Jean."

"We started in Pamplona this time. It was too much to take the baby through the mountains. Are you travelling alone?" she asked gazing across at me from heavy-lidded blue eyes. I told her about my walking companions who had bussed out this morning. "Yes," she agreed, "it is good to get past the industrial section. It is okay to start in Trobajo or La Virgen. You must get on the green bus if you do that. It goes every day but at different times on weekends, so you must check the time. Once you get to La Virgen you again have two choices. I would suggest you go across the land to Mazarife. It is a country road and much nicer than going along the highway." Advice dispensed, Esther rose from her bench.

"Now, I must go. My baby will wake soon, and I must relieve my husband. *Buen Camino*." I watched this remarkable woman saunter casually across the road, so relaxed, so confident, so natural. I wondered if her husband and baby shared her demeanour.

The bells rang out and pigeons took to the sky, forming a feathery cloud around the highest point of the cathedral. It was very peaceful. The sun shone warmly off the vanilla cathedral walls, and a soft breeze played through the tender leaves of street trees planted in boxes spilling over with colourful blooms. I drained my cup, depositing it in a nearby bin, and pulled myself to my feet with a contented sigh.

As I walked down the gentle slope, I noticed in the shadow of the great cathedral, a row of houses across the street. There was a gap, like a missing tooth, where one had been torn down. The walls of the neighbouring houses were covered in a mustard-coloured substance resembling sea foam toffee, and a large steel rod was jammed across the space between them. I later found out that when a building was removed from a row, an insulating foam was sprayed to restore the protection the missing house had previously provided its neighbours. In cases where the remaining houses also needed extra support, rods were placed across the void until a new building was constructed to fill the gap.

A silvery bell jingled as I stepped through the door of the pharmacy. The same young woman who had served me yesterday smiled out from behind the counter. She disappeared into the back and quickly reappeared with a small, plastic bag of Epsom salts. I paid the bill and stashed the salts in my front pack, happily walking back out into the morning, dreaming of a hot, soaking bath that evening.

"Well, hello girl!" a voice drawled from a sidewalk café table. It was Charlotte, my Tennessee friend from Bercianos. I walked over and plunked myself down on the offered chair, just as her husband, Steve, strolled out through the door bearing two complicated ice-cream sundaes.

"Hey Canada! How ya doing? Where are your folks? You here alone?" the heavily accented words poured out from this mountain of a man. "You want ice cream? We're having a treat!" his blue eyes sparkled boyishly beneath his signature bandana. I laughed and told him no, I was good for now. I shared that Patricia and Michel had moved on this morning, and that I was taking a day in Leon.

"Good to rest a little," Charlotte agreed, rubbing her leg. I noticed that she was missing her cumbersome brace. "I take a break from it when I can," she advised, "darn thing sweats so much in this heat, but I need it when I'm walkin'. We're gonna rest here another day too. Got a real nice hotel," she drawled. "Going to do a little shoppn'," she continued.

"Our granddaughter is crazy for football, so we're looking for a jersey for her. We get one every trip," Steve supplied. Thinking of the need to pack whatever you buy, I wasn't so worried for this big, ex-marine. He would have no trouble with a little extra weight in his pack.

"I know you told me last time we met that you did a lot of travelling. What other trails have you done?" I asked.

"Well," Charlotte started, "of course the Appalachian Trail; it's in our backyard," she smiled. "When I retired from teachin', Steve was right behind. We started walkin', and we just haven't stopped yet."

"Wanted to see a bit of the world with my gal, here," Steve added, placing a big, gentle hand on his wife's shoulder. "We been together forty-four years. Got two fine girls and a couple grandkids who are mindin' the farm while we're away."

"We've always been outdoors folk; huntin' and fishin' and all, so doing these big walks was just another thing to share. We started bloggin' our adventures in 2008 with the Appalachian Trail, then in 2009, we did the Pacific Coast Trail."

"Then we did the West Highland Way in Scotland. 'Member that? That was a good one!" Steve broke in, scooping another spoonful of ice cream and chocolate. The couple shared wide smiles as they sunk back into memories of that journey. "After that, it was the Long Trail in Vermont."

"Did that one a couple three times!" Charlotte interjected. "In 2013, it was the Florida Trail."

"And in 2014, it was Tanzania to hike up Mt. Kilimanjaro and go on safari," Steve reminisced. "Then there was Peru and Iceland…"

"Then over to Ireland, and now we're here!" Charlotte finished triumphantly. Was this for real? Where had this couple not been? I shook my head in amazement. "We just love to travel, and we'll keep doin' it as long as we can!" she pronounced, grinning over at her husband.

"That's amazing! I feel like I've travelled the world just talking to you. With my husband in a wheel-chair, our travels are limited pretty much to camping on Vancouver Island, wherever his electric scooter can go. Maybe if we won the lottery we could hire some Sherpas and travel more adventurously," I pondered.

"Well, don't you worry darlin,'" Charlotte said, resting her hand on my knee, "we all just do what we can. How's your man doin'?"

"Oh, Al's doing really well. I miss him though," I remarked wistfully.

"Well another couple weeks and you'll be home again!" Charlotte patted my knee.

"Yeah, it will be good to see the kids again!" agreed Steve. It was obvious that as much as they loved to travel, they too were missing their family.

"See you later girl!" called Charlotte, and I left the happy couple behind, looking back to see Charlotte reach over and wipe an errant spot of ice cream from Steve's cheek.

It seemed the city had just woken up and here it was getting ready to shut down again for siesta. Down the narrow streets, lights were being turned off and shades drawn. The restaurants continued business, filling the passageways with inviting aromas and the clatter of dishes and cutlery. Loud Spanish voices called out to each other as baristas checked orders with roving waiters deftly placing entrees before the waiting patrons. I was starting to feel a little hungry myself and remembered the bar on the square near the convent and my hotel.

Coming around the corner, I saw a number of metal tube-framed tables and chairs set out on the dirt courtyard. I popped inside the bar and looked over the display case. Settling on a *bocadillo* filled with lean sausage and white cheese, I carried it and a cold glass of white wine outside. All of the tables were filled, mostly with couples and clusters of locals. At one table, a man leant back in his chair, a glass of *vino tinto* swirling in his hand. By his clothes I knew him to be a pilgrim and hoped he spoke English.

"Excuse me. I was wondering if you would mind if I stole a corner of your table to sit at?"

"Of course! Please join me," he invited. So not only English, but British. "I'm Paul." He introduced himself and asked where I was from. I told him my name and that I was from Canada. "Oh, I have friends in Toronto," he shared.

"Well, I'm about as far away from that in Canada as you can get. We live in BC," I replied, taking a sip of my cool, clear wine.

"Oh, I have been there, to Whistler."

"Actually, I'm from Vancouver Island, so not on the mainland where Whistler is."

"Right," he nodded. "That looks pretty sparse there," he commented, looking at my sandwich.

"It was all that they had right now. It's between lunch and supper, so the menu's limited during siesta," I advised.

"Well I ordered the special so if you like, you can share mine," he offered generously. The slim, bearded barista called out to Paul and he rose to go in and collect his meal. Returning, he set down his plate scattered with a small selection of sliced cheese, drizzled with oil, accompanied by some rounds of dry bread and a few olives. "This is their special?" he remarked doubtfully. "I would have done better to have what you had."

"Maybe it's their tapas offering, not a meal at all," I suggested. "They won't likely be serving real meals until about 7:00 tonight."

"Sounds like you know what it's about then. You're a pilgrim, are you?" I nodded. "Are you walking alone? How long have you been travelling?" I told him yes, I was walking alone and explained about my husband at home. I shared that I started at the end of April in St. Jean. "Whew!" he exclaimed. "Now I feel like a pathetic git! I've only just arrived and tomorrow will be my first day. I'm staying over there at the hotel," he pointed.

"I'm staying there too. I stayed at the convent there last night," I indicated the adjoining building, "but I'm moving over to the hotel tonight since you can only stay in *albergues* one night."

"You've got it worked out, don't you? Very organized. Where are you staying tomorrow?" he asked.

I hesitated before answering. He appeared to be a decent fellow, probably about my age and friendly. "I'm not really sure. I'm headed to Mazarife, and there's a few *albergues* there, but I don't have anything booked."

"The guy at the hotel booked a place there for me tomorrow night. It's called Tito Poppa's or something like that. Maybe that would work for you." I agreed it might and said I'd check into it when I went over to the hotel. I told him my recent walking partners had bussed out this morning and that I was thinking of doing the same in the morning.

"Aw no, you don't have to do that," he said, "the guy showed me on a map how to walk out and save about twenty minutes on a more direct route. You just go down this road and turn up towards the cathedral, but don't turn towards the cathedral. You keep on going until you get to…" he began to search through his guidebook, "well I have it here somewhere!" He frantically checked pockets, looking for the lost information.

"Sorry, not very organized here," he muttered in disgust. I told him not to worry, and then I told him about Esther and her suggestion to take the scenic route rather than the highway.

"A baby! They're walking with a baby! I can hardly handle the great lump of a rucksack I have. I borrowed it from my son, and it's heavy to begin with, and then there's all the stuff inside. A baby?" He'd finished his wine and stood, asking if I'd like another glass.

"No, thanks. I should really get over to the hotel and see if my room is ready. I want to see about getting some laundry done too," I advised.

"Oh laundry. I guess that is another thing I'll have to learn about. It's good to talk to someone who's been at this a bit. Do you think you'd like to walk out together in the morning? Between the two of us, we should be able to sort it out." I agreed that might be a good idea and took careful note of his appearance to ensure I'd recognize him in the morning. I schooled myself to remember details to help recognize him when I saw him next. Paul's swarthy clean-shaven face was crowned by a half-wreath of short, grey hair. He had a medium build, was about my height, and it seemed, had a preference for blue clothes.

"I'd like to head out about 7:00. Would that work for you?" He nodded. Best laid plans can go awry on the Camino so I suggested, "We could meet here, but if I'm not here and you want to go, just go. I'll do the same. What colour is your backpack?" I asked, seeking another clue for the morning's half-light.

"Blue. I'll see you here then, at 7:00," and with that he disappeared into the bar to chase down another glass of wine.

Pushing through the glass and brass front doors of the hotel, I entered the marble-floored lobby and approached the dark wood desk. The young man behind the desk advised that my backpack had been brought over for me already. He disappeared behind the door and came out, dragging my pack. Embarrassed by its size and weight, I looked at his pristine suit and tie and offered to take it from him.

"No, no. It is my pleasure to help you," he insisted. He scanned my credit card as he explained the facilities of the hotel, going into great detail about the restaurant hours. I looked at the posted menu and realized I would not easily afford eating there.

"Where can I get some laundry done?" I asked.

"Oh laundry, you can get that done over at the convent. You go through this door here, you see, by the elevator, and then down that little path to the back of the convent. They will do your laundry for you there. And now here is your key," he smiled.

Too funny! Last night I slept at the convent for five euros and had supper there. Today, I would take my laundry back to the convent to be done, return to their dining room for supper, but sleep next door, at the hotel, in a private room with a bath for eighty euros.

I rode the smooth elevator up to the second floor where the doors opened right across the hall from my room. Floor to ceiling windows invited fresh breezes into the hallway, setting long, sheer curtains dancing. Opening the door, I walked into a cool, softly decorated room offering my choice of any of three beds. I chose the one closest to the window, from which I spied Paul, still nursing his wine at the bar in the square. I took in the stormy clouds gathering about the skyline of the historic buildings and wondered how long it would be before the barista would have to pull out the maroon awning to protect his guests. In the centre of the square stood a large fountain, water burbling gently above a pair of stone cupids, their smiling faces weathered by the passage of time. Off to another side, I saw another bar, but this one looked pretty lonely, the preferred choice of locals being the one where I had met Paul.

Inside I pushed open the bathroom door and was confronted by not one, but two toilets. Well, actually, the second turned out to be a bidet (not common in Canada), but I was amused at the two of them, sitting there, facing off across the tiled floor. And yes, there it was; a wonderfully deep bathtub! Making a date with the tub for later that night, I pulled my used laundry from my pack and went down to the convent to do laundry.

"Hello again!" smiled Samantha. "Did you get settled in your hotel? We sent your pack over." I assured her it was all good and asked about laundry. She directed me back down the three shallow stairs by the entrance to the ladies' dorm. There I met Eugene, who took my laundry and got it going in a washing machine. He told me that when I returned, it would be folded and waiting in the blue tub. Euros paid, I went back out into the courtyard and joined an elderly pilgrim from the States.

Sharon said she was having trouble with her feet, and this was her second night at the convent. I told her I was staying in the hotel tonight. We shared stories from our journey while I waited for my laundry and soaked up the sun. I advised, given the expense of the hotel's menu, I would eat at the convent again, and we agreed to meet for supper. Having gone to the vespers service last night, I just wanted to have supper, a long, hot bath, and tuck in early for a good start the next day.

At supper, I realized the menu was the same as last night's, so I did some creative ordering. Rather than picking a first and then a second course meal, I asked for two firsts; a salad and pasta. I still had trouble wrapping my head around a full plate of pasta as an appetizer! The conversation at the table was lively, with all new players in the game, but after my second glass of wine and a dish of fragrant rice pudding, I was ready to call it a night. Bidding farewell to Sharon and my tablemates, I collected my laundry, crossed the square, and returned to my hotel sanctuary.

Pulling my Epson salts from my daypack, I ran the bathtub full of hot, hot water. While the tub filled, I set out my clothes for the morning and tucked my street clothes back in my pack. I peeked out the window at the growing clusters of people congregating happily around tables at the bar and returned to the bathroom.

Testing the water with a toe, I sighed, sank into bliss, and sighed again. I didn't have a book, so this seemed the perfect time to call Al and bring him up-to-date on my progress and find out how he was doing. I could hear him smile as I told him about the bath; he knew me so well. He was amazed to hear about Esther and her husband travelling with a baby, but agreed that at that point in life, kids are pretty portable. Our kids were all doing fine (more or less). Amanda and Matthew had come for a sleepover, and they'd made spaghetti together.

"Your tomatoes are thriving," he advised. Al was taking his watering responsibilities seriously. We talked about the minutia of his days, all of which seemed so suddenly foreign from a bathtub in Spain. Al assured me he was doing fine, but he and Kirby were missing me. The 10th of June seemed a long way away for both of us, and we ended the call with "love you's".

Towelling down with thick, thirsty white towels, I slipped in between the crisp cotton sheets, pulled up a soft blanket, and prepared to sleep. Then, the party really started.

Out in the square, the rain had backed off, and more and more chairs and tables had been dragged out onto the packed earth. Obviously, the popular bar was really popular, as more than a hundred locals gathered for food, music, and laughter out in the square. Still wanting the cool evening breeze, I pulled the window closed to just a crack and, with a resigned sigh, pulled out my earplugs. Silly me! I had thought with the lack of others snoring in my room I wouldn't need them. Despite the earplugs, at 2:00 in the morning, I could hear the party still going strong. I rolled over on my good ear thinking, if these people wouldn't take that afternoon siesta, they'd go to bed at a reasonable time and we'd all get some sleep. Feeling somewhat cheated of my enjoyment of my private room, somewhere through the night, I finally drifted off to sleep, and somewhere through the night, the party finally ended.

Despite the boisterous block party, I did manage to get some sleep the previous night – but most of it in the final four hours before my alarm peeped. Unlike most North-American hotels, my Leon room was not equipped with a coffee maker, so I started the day with water and a banana, both of which I had purchased on my rounds of the city centre yesterday. Between bites, I finished tucking the last of my belongings in my pack.

Done dressing, back in Camino mode, I slathered my feet with Vaseline and pulled on my socks, preparing my feet for another day in sturdy hiking boots. Ever hopeful that last night's stormy skies would give way to sunshine, I covered my face with sunscreen, pulled on my coat, shouldered my pack and left the comforts of the hotel behind.

A few minutes early, I waited for Paul at our appointed rendezvous point. Ten minutes past the hour, no Paul in sight, I decided to go in through the *albergue* gates and grab a cup of coffee from the automatic coffee machine, just inside the compound. I returned, and sipping the hot, sweet mixture, waited. No Paul in sight, I guessed he was either sleeping late or had decided to go off on his own. Plans change all the time on the Camino, so I wasn't surprised, wondering only if I'd see him again somewhere along the way.

I trekked down the lane towards the main street, watching for a mid-sized Brit with a blue backpack, but saw none. Struggling to remember what he had said about the short cut out of town, I decided to forego the bus and try to walk out on my own.

My husband has always said that I have an uncanny knack for going the right way, with little or no direction. Back in 2000, before his MS put him in a wheelchair, we had travelled to Portugal, renting a tiny red car to tear around the country. Travelling up to Lisbon, we crossed the Vasco de Gama bridge and entered a daunting six-lane traffic circle. As Al drove in loops, I consulted our map, establishing that our hotel would be in the general direction of the hospital. On our next round, I told Al to make his way to the outside and take my chosen exit. Ahead was an intersection where we would have to turn left or right. Focused on the busy road, Al wanted to know which way we should turn.

"Turn left," I said, although there were no addresses in sight, "it just feels right!" He turned left, moved into the outside lane, and pretty much drove into the arrivals area of our hotel. As the car rentals guy, who had been waiting our arrival, drove off with the car, Al just looked at me and shook his head.

"I don't know how you do it!" he smiled, "but I'm glad you do!"

Smiling at the memory, I crossed the thoroughfare, rather than turning up the main road towards the cathedral. As I walked in the shadowy morning light, I marvelled at the contrast between the imposing, ancient fort wall, heavy with moss, looming over my head, and the modern, multi-levelled apartment building across the road. I tapped alone in the quiet, still feeling I was moving in the right direction, but marking my path in case I needed to backtrack. Suddenly, a block away, a pilgrim crossed the road in front of me. I hurried to the corner, and sure enough, there was a yellow arrow.

Reassured, I picked up the pace, coming to a huge intersection with an ultra-modern glass and steel structure on one corner, and across the street, beautiful lawns and gardens fronting a structure from the past. A triangular flower bed, bordered with crisp, green hedging, offered a brilliant display of purple and white lupins. In the background, a majestic building rose, all intricate stonework and arched windows. I followed the wide sidewalks inviting me to move further into the garden. Soft, mauve wisteria trailed from sturdy pergolas. The monumental building turned out to be the Parador de San Marcos, formerly the Convento de San Marcos. I recognized this as the "fancy" hotel where the travellers in the movie, The Way, stopped for a night of indulgence. The site has a colourful history, taking the original twelfth-century hospital building through major additions and reconstruction during the 1500's, and serving as a dreaded prison during the Spanish Civil War. Now a luxury hotel, its current polished marble floors and genteel existence was enjoyed by guests with the coin pay for opulence at its finest. In my well-worn pilgrim's attire, I commiserated with the solitary brass statue of an exhausted pilgrim reflectively resting at the foot of a stone cross. Neither of us would have the chance to experience the life offered inside those ornate doors.

Pushing on, I crossed a bridge and followed a trickling flow of pilgrims along dismal city streets as we left the city of Leon behind. An hour or so later, walking in through La Virgin del Camino, I stopped at a bar, tables and chairs spilling out on the sidewalk, as an enthusiastic waitress flagged down passing pilgrims. At her invitation, I placed my order and left my pack under a table, going inside to use the washroom (which rated an eight on my informal washroom survey, having a toilet seat, toilet paper, hot water, and soap, but no paper towels). Returning to my chair outside, a large, frothy cup of *café con leche* and a cheese and sausage *bocadillo* was delivered with a smile.

At the foot of the hill, a rough, red-dirt track offered an alternate route to the gravel walkway paralleling the roadway. A small cluster of pilgrims gathered at the junction, comparing notes and weighing options. While others walked on, I turned off on the rutted road, hoping I was making the right decision. Worst came to worst, I could backtrack. I'd just have to walk a longer day if it came to that, I thought, eying the gathering clouds.

At Oncina del a Valdoncina, a bright blue geodesic dome appeared, as did a tall, t-shirted Spaniard generously providing refreshments by donation. This was about the fourth "pop-up" refreshment stand I'd come across on the Camino. Warm despite the ominous skies, I removed my coat and stuffed it in my pack, then savoured a plastic cup full of fragrant sliced strawberries. Water, juice, pop, fruit, cheese, bread, nuts, tissues, and even pilgrim passports, this friendly *hospitalero* offered it all. I put my coins in his donation box and poled up the dusty dirt road that led out among flat fields of wild grasses and bright blooms.

It was so quiet. And I was so alone. There was literally no one in sight as far as I could see, and I could see forever. Soft breezes danced through the wildflowers, releasing herbal fragrances into the sky. The only sounds were buzzing insects, chirping birds, and the soft thuds of my own footsteps. Sinking into the serenity, I remembered Esther and thanked her for her advice to take this route. Calm and peace, time for reflection as the road wove up and down gentle hills.

Suddenly a barrage of bells and male laughter broke the silence. Cyclists, dressed in matching flashy spandex called out "*Buen Camino*" as I stepped to the side and the cluster raced by. I thought of my sister-in-law, Rita, who religiously followed the *Tour de France*. In a moment, they were gone. And suddenly, I was alone again.

Lazy horses munched grass in a fenced yard, giving this passing pilgrim only the merest attention. The two-street town sat silently as, directed by a yellow arrow painted on a brick wall, I took the left-hand road to Fresno del Camino's town square. There, lounging on a bench under a weeping tree, sat Paul, along with two other men. So, he didn't end up walking alone after all, I thought.

"So, there you are!" he exclaimed. "I waited for you, but you didn't show," he scolded. I protested that I had been there by 6:50 and had waited (aside from my dip inside the gates to pull coffee from the machine) until 7:15. "Naww… didn't see you. Thought you slept in," he chided, his mates joining in his teasing. Munching my banana as I walked, I laughed and waved goodbye.

Shortly after noon I arrived in Villar de Mazarife, bypassing two *albergues* before coming to *Tio Pepe's*, situated in the town centre, right across the street from the church. Here, for less than twenty euros, I would find my bed, my supper, and my breakfast the next day. A matronly, dark-haired woman was cleaning glasses behind the bar. With a friendly smile, she stamped my pilgrim's passport with a flourish and led me up a narrow, winding staircase. She indicated the door to my room, and then showed me where the shower and bathroom was before disappearing downstairs to resume her work.

Knocking gently, I pushed open the door to my room and three sets of "deer in the headlight" eyes focused on me. It turned out I would be sharing the room of four bunks with three men, all from different countries, only one of whom spoke English. I took in their surprised faces, looked at the remaining top bunk, shrugged, and dropped my pack in the corner. The men relaxed a little as Alard, my Dutch translator, made introductions. I collected my kit bag and clean clothes and headed to the shower. When I returned, "done and dusted", as I fondly remembered John saying, the room was empty. I took a little time to nest, sorting out things for the next day, and then went down to the bar.

I ordered a glass of white wine and carried it out to the sunny, flagstone terrace, encircled on three sides by the *albergue*, a pair of wide wooden gates at the far end closing it off from the street. Suddenly the barista appeared bearing a little plate of cheesy scalloped potatoes. I thanked her for the little tapas treat, still surprised that these little freebies were quite normal practice. Behind me, beneath the overhang of the building's second level, two young men were busily setting up equipment.

"The children will have a fiesta tonight," she advised before disappearing back inside.

"Oh, so you did take my advice." A voice startled my siesta. Esther, the young woman I had met in Leon was just crossing the patio, baby bottle in hand.

"Hi Esther. I did not know I would see you here. How was your trip today?" I asked.

"It has been good. We took the bus to the edge of Leon and had a nice walk today. My baby is sleeping, and I just want to get some hot water to make her meal," she advised. On her return trip across the deck, she paused to ask how I'd found this *albergue*, and I told her the desk clerk at my hotel had arranged it for me. I told her of my shared room upstairs, and she laughed when I described the reactions of my bunk mates to having a lone female in their midst. Her little family had a private room in the wing across the courtyard.

"When my baby wakes up we will come out and you will meet them," she assured me. I pulled out my guidebook to explore options for the next couple days' walk.

"Oi, there you are." Now Paul had arrived. "So, you are staying here as well," he commented, setting a glass of red wine on the table next to me. "Are you upstairs? I'm sharing a room up there. Not too bad. You have the same book as me. Are you planning tomorrow? Where will you stay do you think?" He fired questions without waiting for answers. I told him I hadn't planned for tomorrow yet. "Have you had a look about the town? Not much doing, but a nice church across the way," Paul offered

Outside, in the courtyard of the church across the street, I saw a gathering of well-dressed Spaniards.

"They make a first communion," our *hospitalero* supplied, stepping out the door behind me. Suddenly firecrackers started exploding all over the street, echoing between the stone building walls as two mischievous boys lit and tossed them in the direction of startled pedestrians. "There will be a big party," she supplied, crushing her cigarette before returning inside.

More firecrackers banged and popped as a small girl, dressed in a long, filmy gown burst excitedly through the church doors. Adults poured out around her, her short-skirted mother, adjusting the crown of flowers on the girl's long, black curls as a bevy of relatives patted her shoulder and kissed her full cheeks. Obviously, the star of the event, the little girl was all smiles, enjoying the attention, twirling in her long dress and stomping her shiny, white shoes.

I headed down the road to the *mercado*. Despite siesta time, the door was open and inside, three Spanish women, one in an apron behind the counter, stood chatting noisily. Not wanting to interrupt, I selected a bag of almonds, a roll, and a banana for the next day. Eying the display case, I asked if I might buy a small slice of cheese. Feigning confusion, the clerk held up a package of cheese slices, more than I wanted and more than I wanted to pay. The two other women threw up their hands in disgust, Spanish words flying fast as they berated the clerk into removing a large wheel of cheese and cutting me off a manageable slice. Paying my euros, I thanked the now smiling ladies as I left, their "*Buen Caminos*" following me out the door before their excited Spanish conversation resumed.

After stowing my goodies in my pack upstairs, I returned to the patio to find more preparations for tonight's party underway. Chairs and tables had been cleared from the centre of the patio, and I anticipated some dancing as I watched a sound system and lighting being installed.

Across the open space, Esther appeared through a doorway, a tall, thin man following behind with a baby secured in a Snugli against his chest. Reaching my table, Esther introduced Andi, who carefully unzipped the baby pack, revealing his daughter.

"And this," he exclaimed with pride, "is Irma!" Clear blue eyes smiled up at me from under a cap of red-gold hair, very much like her mother's. Without any hesitation, Andi simply placed Irma in my arms. Worried that she might make strange, I was delighted when she reached up to play with my necklace, cooing and making wonderful baby noises. Yes, it is so," Andy proclaimed with authority, "she is a very friendly baby. She is a perfect baby!" Obviously, this man was in love with his little girl. I was reminded of my son and his little daughter.

"Only not so perfect at 3:00 in the morning," Esther assured more realistically, rolling her eyes. "She is right now teething. Irma is mostly a happy baby, but the teeth are coming." With an ingenious little red coat that somewhat resembled a straight jacket, the parents anchored the little girl into one of the plastic chairs, an instant highchair, before handing her a small, frozen cucumber. Amazed and impressed with their chosen solution for sore gums, I imagined how my daughters-in-law would have reacted if I had handed a frozen cuke to my grandchildren. "I'm going to get drinks. Roxey, do you want anything? No... okay just for Andi and me, then."

As Esther returned with their drinks, Paul pushed through the door and asked to join us at the table. I introduced Andi, Esther, and Irma.

"Oh, so you meant it. They do have a baby. And what a beautiful little girl you are, aren't you?" he cooed at Irma. How is it a baby is able to reduce perfectly reasonable adults to complete gibberish? A hit with the pilgrims missing their families and a baby pilgrim a rarity with the locals, Irma delighted us all.

Lighting cigarettes, Andi and Esther stood off to the side, looking on approvingly as Paul and I kept Irma entertained. Paul asked Esther (who had a better command of English) questions about their previous Caminos and her recommendations for future stops. Enjoying her role as the experienced leader, Esther made suggestions, Andi inserting comments along the way. Sometimes the young couple would disagree on a point and launch off into a discussion between themselves in German before coming back to us with an agreed stance in English.

Esther, it turned out, was an x-ray technician, and Andi, a former chef, was now a caregiver at a seniors' hospital. In Germany, both parents are entitled to "paternity leave", which allowed them time to bond through their Camino adventure in their daughter's early months.

Andi's gentle eyes shone out from behind heavy-framed glasses, shadowed by a cap of light-brown, unruly curls. His quietly serious attitude, with its underlying current of humour and gentleness, made him a natural for dealing with the elderly patients.

Esther, meanwhile, was quick and matter-of-fact, a perfect fit for a technical trade. While her smile and concern for her baby and husband spoke of a generous nature, she seemed a non-nonsense sort of girl. She addressed motherhood with the same practical approach she probably took to her work, but she was genuinely not looking forward to leaving her baby behind to return to her job.

The men were off on a discussion about football, and Esther and I weighed *albergue* options for the next few days.

"I would not stop in Hospital de Orbigo. Last year, we went to the town behind Hospital and stayed with Christine in Villares de Orbigo. It is only a couple more kilometres. We will be staying there as well." Not finding it in my guidebook, Esther consulted her agenda. "I have her number right here. I can call her and see if she has room for you if you like. You will like it very much, I am sure." Internally I warred with wanting to be independent, trying to do things for myself despite the language barriers. Seeing my turmoil, she spoke again.

"I can do this or I can give you the number. Whatever it is you would like. Just make a decision." I knew she was not being rude; it was just her direct approach that demanded a response, one way or the other from me.

"If you could call, that would be great." I sighed. It has always been hard for me to accept help from other people. Being the one most people in our family rely on, I was used to being the one to organize things and to take charge. Taking a backseat was a foreign thing to me. Allowing myself to be helped rather than being the one to be helped was a real challenge. Esther would never know the work it took me to turn this small task over to her. Perhaps this was the Camino working on me. Paul, having overheard part of our conversation, asked if she could book him a bed too.

"It is done," she announced, placing her phone in her pocket. "And now for the next couple of days, here are my suggestions. I can help with your bookings if you want me to." It would have been ungracious and somewhat foolhardy to let the gift of knowledge fall by the wayside in the name of pride, so I allowed her to suggest *albergues* for the next three days. Paul was right there, adding his name to the reservation list. It looked like he was going to be part of my world for a while.

We wondered, looking around at the party preparation activity on the patio, how the evening was going to go as the noise level increased. The little German family crossed over to their wing just as the gate at the foot of the patio opened, and two stock cars were driven into the courtyard. So not a dancing space, but rather a display area for the family's stock cars. Our *albergue hospitaleros* came out from the bar, joining the young drivers to admire the shiny vehicles, the father pounding his son on his shoulder proudly.

Where was Al at a time like this? He would so be loving this! Back in the day, Al used to drive stock cars, and our first date was actually taking my sons to stock car races. While I cringed as cars sped around corners and collided, the boys hollered and hooted, happily bookending Al and I in their enjoyment of the sport. A successful, if a bit unique, first date led to a great relationship between Al and the boys.

Out in the courtyard, the music was turned up, the flashing lights turned on, and our quiet little patio filled with young people. Called to supper inside the relative quiet of the bar, I ended up at a table with my Dutch roommate, Alard, and a retired couple from the States, Grant and Sylvia. Sylvia had been fighting a bad cold for days now, and I have to admit, I did my best to put distance between us. I didn't relish the idea of carrying her cold for the remainder of this journey.

Across the room I spied Andi and Esther at a table, Irma happily chewing on a soggy rusk. Paul was filling wine glasses at a table over by the window, the three other men sitting with him laughing at some great joke.

Every time the patio door opened, music and laughter pumped in through the door. Food and beverages carried out, the door would close, and the sound level dropped to where conversation was possible again. As plates of chicken and the ever-present fries were delivered to our table, our waitress cocked her head at the patio door and reassured us that the fiesta would end at 9:00.

While pilgrims lingered over last drinks, daylight faded from the sky, and the street outside the windows became heavy with shadows. Finally, well fed and with a couple of relaxing glasses of wine in my system, I bid my tablemates goodnight and climbed the stairs to bed. Tapping on the door, I made sure the coast was clear before entering our empty room. I quickly changed for bed, lining up my clothes for easy access in the morning, and climbed under the quilt.

A few moments later, there was a tap on the door as first one, then another, and finally the third man crept into our room and, with snaps, zips, and rustles, changed under the cover of darkness. Despite the bass pumping through the closed window from the party below, I heard a muffled curse as someone's toe made contact with the bunk frame. The loud "shh's" and smothered laughter made it apparent they thought I'd slept through their considerate entrance, and I remained silent and still in appreciation of their efforts.

Laying awake in the dark, I listened to the pounding music and revelries of our *albergue* family's young people. There was no snoring in our room yet, so I could only assume my roommates also lay awake in the din. A couple of exasperated mutters from the bunks below confirmed my guess. I tapped my cellphone, displaying the time as 10:45. My earplugs in place, I rolled over onto my good ear, smothering as much of the noise as possible. I wondered how Esther, Andi, and Irma were dealing with the noise on their side of the compound. I also wondered if Paul's room, like ours, hung over the noisy courtyard, or fronted the quiet street.

Fatigue taking over, finally I slept. For a while. Suddenly, revving engines and squealing tires broke through my slumber as the cars peeled out of the courtyard and down the road. Well at least that's over, I thought, seeing 12:40 on my cellphone. But no! Now it seems an impromptu car race was taking place through the narrow streets of the tiny town. I could envision the two cars, jockeying for position in the darkness, careening around tight corners between shuttered buildings. I heard them race away, then circle back, only to race away again on their spontaneous racetrack.

Two party nights in a row made for two sleepless nights in a row, and I was glad tomorrow would be a short walk. Groaning, I rolled over, pulled my pillow over my head, and tried again to sleep.

What a night! Gentle snores filled the room as I scrambled under the covers to switch my sleeping shirt and leggings for my trekking clothes. Sitting up, listening to the men groaning as they turned over, denying the daylight pouring in through the window, I pulled my socks on. Sliding down the side of the bunk, I grabbed my cellphone and my front pack, before slipping into my sandals and out the door. Down in the bar, I took a seat at an empty table by the window, gratefully accepting a steaming hot *café con leche* from the barista.

"The breakfast is for free this morning," she smilingly advised. I guessed the *albergue* was doing penance to its pilgrims for the noisy night.

"Ah! There you are," Paul called across the room, catching the eye of the waitress before joining me at my table. "That was quite something last night, wasn't it? I thought those cars would never stop. I'm only late because there was someone else in the shower and then I couldn't find my book." Perhaps my first clue to Paul's competitive nature; we hadn't agreed to meet this morning, so he wasn't late, but in his mind, he was because he hadn't arrived first. "I thought I left it on the table in my room, but it's not there. Maybe I left it back at the last hotel. Maybe if I give them a call, they can send it ahead for me to our next stop," he worried, patting his pockets like the book might miraculously appear.

"Did you go through your pack?" I asked, remembering his inability to find the written directions the first day we met. "You said it had a lot of pockets. Maybe you should check it again."

"Right. Will do," he agreed, taking a long sip of coffee. "What's for breakfast then?" he asked. Just then the waitress arrived with baskets of hot, crusty toast and two types of spread; one fruit and one tomato. "I love this tomato spread!" Paul remarked.

I walked up to the bar to get my coffee refilled, waving at Alard and our two non-English speaking roommates as they settled at a table across the room. It was surprising to having felt more protected than threatened sleeping as the only woman in a room with three unknown men. No way that would happen back in the real world.

"Looks pretty stormy out there," Paul muttered, glancing out the window at the threatening sky. Thankful that at least it was not raining yet, I agreed. I told him I would be keeping my poncho handy, but would settle for covering my pack with its shell for now.

"It's a short walk today, innit?" He continued, "Should be there by noon, I'd think." He beckoned the waitress over and ordered another espresso. Finishing my coffee, I rose to go upstairs to collect my things. "I'll be right there. Won't take me long," he assured me, downing the hot liquid and chasing up the stairs behind me.

Hitting the bathroom one more time and making one last sweep to make sure I'd left nothing behind, I clomped down the stairs, clutching my poles. No Paul in sight, so I stood in front of the *albergue*, inhaling the damp earth morning air, listening to the bird call, the only sound in the now quiet streets. Suddenly Paul exploded out the door, a huge blue backpack strapped to his back.

"I found my book right where you said it was! It was in one of the pockets all the time. This is a bloody big pack my son loaned me. It's heavy even empty!" he said, adjusting his straps. "Right, we're off!" he announced.

"I wonder where Andi and Ester and the baby are?" Paul questioned.

"They probably didn't get much sleep last night. Their room was across the patio, but on the ground level, so the fiesta was likely noisier for them than it was for us," I suggested. "They may be starting later."

"Right, that was a bad night. First the big street party in Leon and now this. I hope it's not like this the whole way!" I assured him that most of my nights so far had been quiet, and Esther said the *albergue* we were staying in tonight was very nice, so hopefully a better sleep all around.

We set off down the hill, passing the closed *mercado*, and made our way out of town. On either side of the dirt country track, fields stretched to the horizon. Behind a wire fence, a gentle cow tossed her head, her brassy bell clanging as we passed by. Paul and I used the peaceful walk to get to know each other. He was a retired businessman from Hull, the northern part of England. I told him I had been born in England.

"My dad was in the Canadian navy, and in those days, the families were allowed to travel along. Each of us were born in different ports: my older brother, Dan in Halifax; me in Weymouth; my younger sister, Joan, in Plymouth; and my baby sister, Jackie, in Victoria. She could have been born in Singapore, my dad's next posting, but my grandmother got sick, so dad brought the family home. No, I've never been back," I said answering his question of a return to England.

"Well you must come up and see us some time," he invited. "Me and Mary would be happy to have you stay. We have loads of room, and it would work for your hubby since it is all kitted out for wheelchairs courtesy of our lovely Daniel." Paul told me of his son, Daniel. In efforts to improve Daniel's quality of life, Paul's wife, Mary, focused her energies on lobbying for services to support young adults, like him, challenged with complex disabilities. What started as an action group grew, with local council support, into a formalized charity. "Mary did a brilliant job and the people carrying on her work are very professional. You can check it out at *Dannysdream.org.uk*." I pulled out my cell, tapping in the contact as we walked.

Paul and Mary did their best to take Daniel everywhere, cramming as much life into the time they had with him as they could. Paul said that was why he was so strong, from carrying an adult around so much. Sadly, in 2010, Daniel suffered a seizure and died suddenly. Paul's voice became choked and his eyes "got blurry" (as he called it), still grieving as he spoke of his son. His pain and the storm raging within him matched the ominous clouds above his head.

Finding the balance between honouring his need to grieve and wanting to lift his spirits, I asked about his other son.

"Oh yes, that's Paul Andrew. He's married to a lovely Malawi girl, Thandi. He met her while working there. She had a young son when they married, a great lad, and now they've had two more boys."

"Couldn't you have least reversed it and had Paul as his middle name?" I teased him about naming a son with his own name. He paused his steps, looked at me as if I were crazy.

"Well no, that wouldn't be the same at all, now would it?" he asked incredulously.

"Well doesn't it get a little confusing with you both being Paul?" I laughed. He shook his head in wonderment at my question.

"No. I am Paul and he's Paul Andrew."

"So, you call him Paul Andrew, the whole name, all the time?"

"Of course! That's his name innit, you daft girl!" By this point we were both laughing, and the moment of darkness had passed. The clouds were lifting too.

The dirt road led us into the outskirts of Villavante, the town still sleeping off an obviously rough Saturday night. Under drooping strings of flags, workers were busily picking up a multitude of broken bottles, using leaf blowers to corral plastic cups and paper streamers.

"Must have been some party," Paul whistled. "Maybe it was better we stayed where we did!"

Leaving the clean-up crew behind, we had caught up with a couple of men, one from New Zealand and one from Korea. The young Korean pilgrim had a verbal GPS. He was actually in constant communication with his young wife at home, and she was talking him through the trek, supplying information and directions. Of course, the men were all dazzled by the technology; boys and their toys. I stepped up my pace and left them to talk gadgets, myself focusing on the scenery around me.

After a couple hours, we reached the turn off to Hospital de Orbigo, where the alternate highway route merged with our cross-country choice. Entering the town, we discovered the Puente de Orbigo, a multi-arched medieval bridge, one of the longest of its kind in Spain. It was built in the thirteenth century and was one of the highlights of the Camino. The roadway over the bridge is called the Paso Honroso due to a famous jousting tournament that took place there in 1434. Apparently, a spurned knight threw down his gauntlet challenging all comers until he had broken 300 lances, whereupon he, along with his trusted companions, journeyed to Santiago to offer thanks for his freedom from his unrequited love. It appears that the romance and pageantry of the event survives. In addition to colourful pennants waving from posts along the bridge, we noticed viewing stands in the fields at the town end of the bridge. Jousting tournaments and medieval fairs were still a big part of the town's culture.

Paul noticed an announcement for noon-hour mass at a nearby cathedral and advised he wanted to go. It was always a little weird being one of the few non-Catholics on the trail, and while I honoured their religion, I didn't feel the need to stop this day. Given our emotional conversation earlier this morning, I wanted to give Paul the space he needed to pay tribute to his son. I'd suffered too many family deaths in my life and found the best way through was time and space. I told him I'd walk on and meet him in Villares.

Passing through Hospital, I walked out into the countryside where fields were supplied with cleverly run irrigation ditches. The concrete channels had gates and switches enabling the farmers to redirect the water, pulled from the river, as needed. I continued in solitude down the straight dirt road, finally coming to a thick growth of tall, straight poplar trees, their spade-shaped leaves whispering in the wind. I had realized it was windy out on the flat terrain, but here, among the trees, waving to and fro in the breeze, it sounded like a rushing river. Leaving the brief grove behind me, I entered a silent town, two streets wide, with no sign of life in sight.

The *albergue* was easy to find; it's tall, mustard-coloured wall depicting whimsical white paintings of lines of laundry painted on its walls. Pushing open the huge wooden gate, I entered a sun-filled courtyard, boxes on the balconies trailing flowers and greens to the stone patio below

"Oh, you are here!" a stout woman with short blonde hair exclaimed as she came out of a door in response to my call. It seemed she was expecting me specifically, but maybe that was the way she greeted everyone. She wiped her hands on the towel tucked into the waist of her black skirt and motioned me over to the desk. My Canadian passport registered, and my pilgrim passport stamped, I followed her black boots up the stairway into a sunny room of four bunks.

"When you are settled, come down and have coffee," she suggested. I was so ready for coffee! Having the room, and indeed the whole *albergue* to myself so far, I took a leisurely shower in a large, airy bathroom, and changed into shorts and a clean t-shirt. As Christine poured me a cup of robust coffee, more pilgrims pushed in through the gate. She left me enjoying the sunshine while shepherding two lanky young women up to share my room.

Refusing my offer to help, I just sat and kept her company as Christine set about peeling vegetables. She told me that she had walked the Camino two years ago and had fallen in love with it.

"I saw this place was for sale and I talked to my husband. We decided to buy it and set up an *albergue* for our retirement. But we had a problem," she continued. "In Belgium, the retirement age was sixty, so I retired first and came to set up the *albergue*, knowing he was only a year behind. Then, a couple of months later, the rules changed back home and retirement is now 65. So now my husband lives there and works, and I live here and run the *albergue*, and it will be another three years before he can retire."

"An unfortunate turn of events. It must be hard to be apart so long," I commiserated.

"I go home for long visits and then they just put up a sign in Hospital saying the *albergue* here is closed. It works out, and it is not forever. Oh, here you are!" Christine exclaimed as she rose to greet another arriving pilgrim couple and Paul.

After signing in, Paul shuffled over saying, "She says we can get lunch at the bar across the street. There are two bars, but she says to go to the one on the right. Give me time to have a quick wash, and we can go over." He climbed the stairs, following our hostess to his room, and I settled back to wait.

"Right," he said, startling me from my semi-coma, "Let's get something to eat and a cold beer!" Crossing the street to the correct bar, we were welcomed by a robust Spaniard who placed a small plate of sausage slices and crackers on the table before we had even ordered.

Apparently the tall, leaning poles I'd seen in the fields earlier were hops plantations. The locals produced their own line of beers, and it was a field to table endeavour that was meeting with some success. Paul and the barkeep entered into a lengthy discussion weighing the pros and cons of the different beers offered, and he asked if I had a preference. Not really a big beer drinker, I did appreciate a cold glass once in a while, and told him I liked a pale ale. Rolling his eyes at my lightweight taste, Paul quickly ordered a blonde ale for me, and a more hearty lager for himself.

"Yorkshire men drink real ale; none of that light stuff! One day you'll come to Hull, and I'll take you to a real pub. Then you'll taste some real beer! Should we have something to eat as well?" he questioned, not really needing my response before ordering plates of cheese, olives, bread, and octopus. Digging in with gusto, he snorted in derision as I picked at the plate. "I love this stuff!" he exclaimed, spearing another piece of octopus before glancing up at the television broadcasting football results.

"It was lovely," Paul answered my question about the mass. "All in Spanish, of course, but it's all the same. Good to sit and think about my lad."

"I've been to about four masses along the way. It doesn't really matter that I don't understand the language. The music and the singing still seem familiar, and the pattern is much the same as in our church. We don't take communion every mass, just once a month. I'll definitely take communion in the cathedral at Santiago. There will be so many pilgrims there, no one will notice a protestant or two in the mix!"

Answering his question about my reason for doing the Camino I explained, "For me this is a spiritual journey. It's a chance to leave the real world behind and focus on who I am. My life at home is so busy and full of responsibility. I don't get the chance, or more honestly, don't take the chance to just be. I wanted to re-establish my connection with God and discern my purpose." Thinking Paul would be embarrassed by my personal revelation, I was surprised to see him nodding, gazing at me intently. I went on to say this was the first time I'd ever done anything like this and would likely be the last.

"Oh me, I travel all the time. My business made it necessary, and after I sold it, I had the bug." I was a little vague about his business; something to do with shipping. I wasn't surprised to hear that although very good at the mechanics of business himself, he had surrounded himself with a strong staff who kept him organized.

"Did well when we sold the business, so that was good. We did several trips with Daniel. Went to Medjugorje a couple times. Do you know it? It's a holy place in Bosnia Herzegovina similar to Lourdes. Do you know Lourdes?" I nodded, telling him of our visit to Fatima when Al and I visited Portugal.

"My mum was from Italy, and the family has property down there, so we go there from time to time. Mary's people are up Scotland way, so we're always gadding off up there. Of course, we visited Paul Andrew and Thandi while they lived in Malawi." He rallied, calling out for another beer. He shrugged as I waved away his offer for another glass and carried on. "I'm hoping to do the Camino again next year, with my eldest grandson, Chama. And then later, when they're older, the younger lads, Eugene and Francis, as well, of course."

It was easy to see that Paul was very family-centered, and that it was a very tight-knit family. There was no distinction in his love between his adopted grandson and his two youngest grandchildren, and he and Mary's world was wrapped around their son's family. Paul was an open heart, despite his protestations as to the tough nature of Yorkshire blokes.

Back across the street in the sunny *albergue* courtyard, we welcomed Andi, Esther, and Irma. Christine, like a mother receiving children home after a long absence, was beyond herself in greeting them. Apparently, they had stayed there last year and were some of Christine's first guests while she sorted the whole *albergue* business out. She was excited to meet the new addition to their family. During their last stay, Esther had made a German apple cake and shared the recipe with the older woman.

"Guess what I have made you for dessert," Christine proudly announced. "Apple cake!"

As Andi peeled Irma out of her baby pack, her little arms began waving all around. I put my hands out to her and without hesitation, she leaned towards me, a drooly smile complimenting her sparkling blue eyes.

"She knows you already!" Esther pronounced. Thinking of the protective parental approach of my own children, the fact that Andi and Esther would hand their baby over to a virtual stranger was a huge surprise. But then that's the way it was on the Camino; we were really all one big family, it seemed.

"As soon as she saw you, she started kicking to get out," Andi confirmed, rubbing his battered midsection. I suggested she was meeting so many new people, she was probably just excited to see a familiar face. "No!" Andi insisted, "you are her Camino granny!"

I offered to take Irma while they got settled, and we played together in the sunshine until Esther returned with her lunch. Settling Irma into her makeshift highchair, Esther called up to Andi for Irma's "baby cape" and he rushed down the stairs with a plastic smock.

"She loves to eat, but she is a messy girl," Esther advised as Irma bounced like a needy fledgling. "Look here," she said poking a finger inside her daughter's mouth, "this tooth is almost here and there are more coming." I made the proper amount of fuss, acknowledging this great achievement on Irma's behalf and sat back enjoying her obvious delight in food.

Having a baby around made me miss my grandchildren even more. Matthew was four, and Alayna was three, so not babies any more, but still very fun to watch as they discovered new things in life. Each family lived a distance away in different directions, so we didn't get to see them as much as we'd like, but being in the middle, our home was often the location for family gatherings. Our grandchildren were totally enamoured with Al, and for him, not ever having had babies in his life, they were his joy. Often, while visiting, one or the other would take off with Grampa's walker, rolling it down the hallway and laughing at having committed such a crime, but quickly returning it when he needed it.

When going for long walks, they loved to sit with him on his scooter, and it was always a special treat to scramble up into Grampa's lifting chair. Grampa had all the best toys!

Christina called us into the dining room, and we sorted ourselves along the cloth-covered table, pulling up chairs as we sat. On the table, between jugs of water and unlabelled bottles of *vino tinto*, baskets of crusty bread peeked out from beneath chequered cloths. None of the plates matched, none of the cutlery matched, none of the chairs matched, but then none of the people really matched either. It was a noisy, colourful, friendly collection of reaching hands and animated conversation as, like a family, we settled down to eat.

Christina tapped her glass and called us all into order, expressing her pleasure at having us all with her this day. Respecting all forms of spirituality, there was no formal prayer, just warm wishes for a safe and meaningful journey, and then the plates began passing.

A welcome break from all the chicken and chips, in addition to a fresh salad, Christine had prepared *pinchos*; metal skewers of grilled meat and vegetables, which we placed over scoops of flavourful rice. Irma, sitting on her daddy's knee, charmed the table as her mommy shovelled spoons of rice behind the budding teeth. By the time the much-anticipated apple cake was served, the sun had begun to slide down the courtyard walls. Esther complimented a beaming Christine on her reproduction of the German specialty cake, and we all applauded the cook as wine glasses were topped up.

Upstairs in my room, my roommates were snuggled in under the comfy quilts, still feeling cold. I guessed as much as the Spanish temperature felt overly warm to my Canadian senses, it felt a bit chilly to their South African norm. The chattering between the two finally dropped off, replaced by soft, dragging snores. I pushed in my earplugs, saying goodnight to my family photos on my cellphone and rolled over to make up for the past sleepless two nights.

The light filtering in through the linen curtains, my young roomies were up and chattering happily. While my day's walk would end in Murias de Rechivaldo, about twenty kilometres away, Althea and Eugenie would be travelling almost nine kilometres more to El Ganso.

Pots of hot coffee greeted the early morning risers, more chairs empty than filled at this point. Esther was in the breakfast room assembling a tray to take to their room.

"Today we will have a short day and tonight we will rest in Astorga," she advised. "We will see you in Rabanal." We gave each other a hug, and she disappeared out the door with her family's morning meal. I looked forward to reuniting with the little German family again in a couple of days.

Christine bustled over to pour coffee and offered me golden slices of toast and homemade yogurt. What a treat! Although she charged a set price for the bed, Christine asked only a donation for the meals as you left. Smart move on her part; anyone with a shred of fairness would properly compensate her for the flavourful, home-cooked meals. Putting my money in the box, I trundled back upstairs just as Paul, freshly showered, thundered his way down.

"Go on. I won't be far behind," he said, racing into the breakfast room. I collected my pack and poles and headed out, sharing a warm embrace with Christine before passing through the *albergue* gates.

The town was silent, the streets empty, the two bars across the street shut up tight. The paved road soon became a dirt rural track, taking me past farm houses and barns. Cows jostled for position on their way to be milked, the soft clanging of bells and mooing heralding their progress.

I came up behind a large woman, talking animatedly on her cellphone. Short, unnaturally red hair set off the fair complexion of this middle-aged woman as she spoke loudly into the phone. It seemed she was talking to her dad, and I left her to it as I continued the climb.

Suddenly a flock of birds filled the air, and just as suddenly, disappeared. Then it happened again. Where were they coming from and where did they go so quickly, I wondered. At a dip in the track, a murky pond filled the shallow bowl at the base of a tall, red clay wall. The canyon side was perforated with hundreds of small holes, almost as if it were ventilated. Suddenly the holes exploded with life, and there were the birds again. They swooped around the trees, dipping low over the stagnant water, and disappeared back into the wall. I guessed these were some sort of swallow, but they never hung around long enough to be identified.

The red dirt track continued to wind up and down, pastures and crops stretching out to distant tree lines. The pilgrim traffic was light, and neither the woman I'd passed, nor Paul had caught up yet. The road dipped and rose and fell again creating pockets and twists, like a gentle roller coaster that would easily disguise the proximity of nearby pilgrims. They could simply have been just around the last corner, and I'd never have known it.

In silence I poled along, enjoying the peaceful trek as the path began a gentle climb, and small evergreens joined the tall grasses along the roadside. Pilgrims were congregating at another pop-up refreshment stand, hosted by a small stone house set back off the road behind it. I waved as I passed, accepting cheerful *"Buen Caminos"* as I walked on.

Although the skies held scattered clouds, it was still very warm and my jacket soon found its way into my pack. Seeing San Justo de la Vega in the valley below, I began a slow descent, arriving at a monument where other pilgrims stopped for photos. Not understanding the Spanish explanation of the cross, I continued on my way, heralded by a wild-haired busker sitting roadside, idly strumming his acoustic guitar. No one else in sight, I decided to err on the side of caution and not stop, so I smiled and waved, noting his friendly invitations turn to angry curses as I disappeared down the hill.

Passing quickly through the small town of San Justo, I kept moving, my goal to get to Astorga early enough to have some time to explore before heading to my day's final destination. I walked along a paved roadway, fields giving way to rural homes with busy gardens, brilliant blooms cascading over fences and rock walls. Large, shaggy dogs barked warnings out from behind wrought iron gates.

As I was nearing Astorga, I found a bright green structure that resembled some sort of amusement park ride. The complex bridge took pedestrians through a maze of switchbacks, up and over a mass of train tracks, repeating the twists and turns on the other side, descending to continue the Camino into the city.

Looking up above the Roman walls, I could see the soft stone buildings of the city. I wound my way up the narrow sidewalk, clinging to the walls as I dodged beeping cars that sailed downwards around tight corners. Arriving up in the old town, I was welcomed by a unique pilgrim sculpture. The bronze statue's coattails flew to the wind as the bearded man clung to his hat, hoisting a clumsy suitcase over his shoulder. Glad for my modern backpack, I was sure that carrying any weight in that position for any length of time would have resulted in shoulder injuries.

To my left, beside the La Ergastula, a glass canopy ran the length of the museum's wall. Diverting from the path, I climbed the viewing stairs. Beneath the protective barrier, colourful tile floors and walls were revealed, remains of Roman baths, unearthed by gentle archaeological excavation. I wondered how much more of the ancient city lay yet undiscovered beneath the cobblestones.

Astorga is known as the European birthplace of chocolate and is famous for its chocolate museum. I had received a text from Patricia and Michel two days ago saying they had arrived and stayed overnight here. Patricia crowed that they had chocolate gelato…twice. Knowing her addiction far outweighed my own, I hoped there was still some chocolate left to try.

In the corner of the tidy central square, I found a chocolate shop and was amazed by the selection jammed into the tiny store. If I hadn't had to pack everything, this would have been a great opportunity to pick up some really good, and in some cases, very unique chocolate for those waiting my return at home. The prices were very reasonable, and I selected a large bar of dark chocolate and hazelnuts. Despite its size, I knew, being honest with myself, that I wouldn't be bearing its weight for too long.

Back out in the square I took a seat at an outdoor café and enjoyed a frothy cup of *café con leche* and a cheese and tomato *bocadillo*. Finished with my lunch, it really didn't seem right not to join Patricia, in spirit at least, in a gelato. I strolled around the square, spooning in creamy chocolate as I took in the store-front fashions.

"Oy! There you are! Where did you get to now? I thought you must have taken a wrong turn when we left this morning. Never saw you along the way," Paul chided. I laughed and told him I kept looking back for him, but never saw him either.

"I met a lovely girl from Sheffield along the way. Her name was Andrea. Did you meet her? Really nice. You'd like her." I told him I'd passed a woman but that she had been talking on her phone, so I didn't actually get a chance to meet her. "She's a bigger girl; short, dark hair?" he queried. I agreed that was probably the same person and suggested maybe we'd meet somewhere along the way.

"Did you get something to eat? I had bacon and eggs at the café just there," he indicated to the tables pouring out the door of a nearby café.

"Oh! I wished I had known that. I would have much rather have had bacon and eggs than a sandwich!" I protested.

"Well then you shouldn't have run off this morning!" Paul laughed.

"I didn't run off. I just left earlier than you did." I retorted.

"Just like in Leon, when you didn't meet me," he teased. I gave up. There would be no convincing him that I had waited as promised, and we'd never know how or why we missed each other that first day.

Changing the subject, I asked him to take my photo in front of the town hall at the end of the square. Its Baroque edifice boasts three towers, the highlight being the central bell tower, with a mechanical man and woman who, upon the hour, strike the middle bell with hammers. Checking my cellphone for the time, we didn't want to wait another forty minutes just to see that, so we set off together, admiring the vast square with its rows of stucco and stone storefronts.

We followed yellow arrows down a narrow street, coming out into another square where the impressive Episcopal Palace of Astorga and Cathedral of Astorga sat side by side, welcoming worshippers within their walls. The two buildings were so close, that from our perspective, they looked like one massive church, except for the distinctly different architectural styles; one creamy brick with pointy turrets, the other heavy dark masonry block and flying buttresses. I noticed a heavy wooden door ajar on the Episcopal Palace. I stuck my head in for a peek and discovered a group of people huddled around a priest at the front of the church. Paul, treading immediately upon my heels, ran into me as I came to a full stop.

"Wassat?" he questioned. I whispered there was a mass in progress. "Right, I'm going in then," he announced as he slid in through the gap. I knew that the memory of Daniel held a lot of importance for Paul on this journey, and that he took every opportunity for mass that he was able.

I felt a little silly loitering around, twenty-pound pack on my back, near the doorway of the church, so I took myself across the square, leaned the pack's weight against a warm wall, and stood in the sun, people watching to pass the time. I wondered what part of this lovely city Andi, Esther, and Irma were staying in and almost wished I had decided to stop here. Then I would have had time to find and explore the chocolate factory…but that might not have been a good thing.

My feet were starting to get sore, and my legs tired of standing still, so I decided to carry on, knowing we were just over an hour's walk from our destination. The guide book advised this was a bit of a boring stretch, so I was sure it wouldn't take Paul long to catch up. As I walked out of the city, I noticed two very modern apartment buildings, three stories high, built of glass and metal, with a tiny stone-walled house, the rooftop growing grass, jammed in between them. I smiled at the obstinate little house, refusing to let its history cave to the future.

The journey to Murias de Rechivaldo was as unremarkable as promised, travelling as it did, a gravel pathway paralleling a minor service road bearing a steady stream of vehicles. Heavy power lines on my right, and rumbling transport trucks on my left, I poled my way down the trail, taking note of the occasional farm house along the way.

Finally, at the top of a gentle slope, I entered the tiny town of Murias de Rechivaldo. I passed a couple bars with pilgrims enjoying cold drinks at their roadside tables, a church, and a couple of houses before coming to the town's last building, the *albergue* that would be my home for the night. I walked in through the gate to see a dark flagstone floor with doors leading right and left and a sunny, grassy courtyard populated with empty chairs before me. A large German shepherd lay dozing across the mat before one of the doors. I was uncertain as to which way to go.

Suddenly, a tall, young Spaniard crossed the courtyard to the registration area. I told him my name, and he crossed it off the reservation list.

"And Mr. Paul? He is with you too?" I advised that Paul had stopped for mass in Astorga and would be along shortly. Amelio (as he introduced himself) spoke gently to the dog, who resignedly stood and moved away from the door, only to collapse again a few feet down the wall. Amelio chuckled as he held the door, motioning me inside to a large room, filled with wooden bunks.

"You are almost first, so you may choose. You may choose for Mr. Paul also," he smiled. "The showers are beside the kitchen, one is for men and one is for women." Answering my final question, he said that breakfast would be served in the morning, but no other meals were available at the *albergue*. "I would suggest Café Felix. The food there is good. You will enjoy." I'd learned to trust the recommendations of the locals.

Dropping my pack against the wall, I selected two bottom bunks, side by side in the corner, just inside the door. Putting some strategic placeholders on both beds, I went out into the courtyard, crossing over to the shower room. Double duty done, shower and laundry, I pulled on my shorts, shirt and sandals and went to look for a laundry line. A doorway in the back wall of the courtyard led out to a large, grassy area where a few lonely items clung to lines, flapping in the breeze.

I scouted out the kitchen, looking for coffee, but finding first, a large wicker basket full of fragrant oranges. Amelio, busily wiping tables in the adjoining breakfast room called out.

"You can have one if you like," he said, and I quickly selected an orange, slicing it up on the side counter. I closed my eyes in appreciation as the juicy, sweet fruit slid down my throat. I offered to pay for the orange, but Amelio, enjoying my delight in the fruit, waved my coins away with a shy smile.

"There you are," Paul called, just entering the gate. "Did you get them to save my bed?" I nodded. "Is it a bottom bed or do I have to go up top?" As Amelio stamped his pilgrim's passport, I told him he had a bottom bunk, right across from mine. "Right. Very professional. Good to have an advance guard!" he laughed.

As he headed off for a shower, I took a cup of coffee out to the courtyard, pulling a chair out into the sunshine. I noticed the woman I'd passed earlier in the day sitting in the shade. Crossing over, I introduced myself.

"I'm Andrea," she stated. "I can't do the sun, and my bag hasn't arrived yet, so I'm just waiting here." Her fair skin obviously would suffer in the sun, so at her invitation, I collected my coffee and joined her. "I checked with the *hospitalero*, and he says the bags will be here soon. I hate sitting here all sweaty, but I can't do anything until they arrive." Andrea was a nurse in Sheffield, and it had been her dad she was talking to earlier when I'd passed. "I have a brother in town, but my dad relies on me, so it's a bit hard having left him behind. I like to check in with him from time to time and morning is best."

"I understand what you mean," I supplied, sharing my concern for Al, left behind at home. "I try not to worry, but it's always there, at the back of my mind. When I talk to him, and he says he's all good, I kick myself for being such a worry-wart!" Andrea laughed warmly, saying it was good to have someone important in our lives, even if it meant a bit of worry.

We shared notes about the journey, laughing at some of each other's stories, waving at the freshly showered Paul as he crossed back over to the bunk room before resuming our gab fest. She reminded me so much of my younger sister in so many ways, and it seemed I had known her forever.

"Oh look, a taxi just pulled up!" Andrea exclaimed, "That will be the bags." Before rushing off to claim her bag and claim a shower, Andrea and I made a date to meet later for supper. Paul joined me in the sunshine; revolving door people.

"So, you've met Andrea, I see," he remarked. "Nice girl, that one." I agreed. "I'm just going to give my clothes a bit of a wash up," he said, heading for the laundry tub. I told him where to hang them to dry and took my guidebook out on the lawn. The warm sun on my back, gentle breezes rustling through the grass, it wasn't long before reading became dozing as I nodded off.

"You won't burn?" questioned Andrea, rousing me from my impromptu nap. Sitting up and brushing dry grass from my shirt, I assured her that my skin took a lot of sun before burning. "You're so lucky, that," she remarked. "Ready to go get some supper?"

As we entered the courtyard, I spied Paul, sitting at a table, talking on his cellphone. I motioned that we were going to eat, and he waved us off, indicating he'd be along. There were only three choices for supper, and I hoped Amelio had filled Paul in on the Café Felix. If not, I was sure he'd enjoy a glass of *vino tinto* or two along the way as he tracked us down.

Inside the small café, Andrea and I pulled up stools at a table in front of the window. A Spanish matron was busy getting drinks, chatting loudly from behind the bar with the local couple seated at the table beside ours. Wide smiles split their faces as the conversation lobbed back and forth, and we smiled too, following the good-natured verbal tennis match. Finally, wiping her hands on her apron, she came out from behind the bar, crossed to our table, and handed us some menus. The menus were in Spanish, and as we struggled to decipher what we might be ordering, a helpful voice came from across the room.

"The first line is chicken, the next is beef, the third is pork, and the last one is rabbit," a slender pilgrim in a long skirt translated. "I had the rabbit. It was very good. He," she motioned to her bespectacled partner, "had the pork and really enjoyed it. Everything comes with salad and bread, the standard fries, and of course wine or water. Everything was really good. Whatever you choose, you can't go wrong."

"I just want water. I had a bit too much wine last night and paid for it with a headache this morning," Andrea said. I would have liked a glass of wine, but I didn't want a whole bottle to myself.

"May I have a glass of white wine?" I questioned our beaming waitress. Smiles aside, I knew she was not understanding my request. "Can you help?" I asked our translator and she broke into halting Spanish, not fluid, but much better than I could have done. "Thank you," I repeated as our waitress walked away, and I settled back in my chair, anticipating a nice, cool glass of white wine.

The kitchen door burst open and the cook bustled through with our main courses as the waitress approached with a tall bottle of water for Andrea and a tall bottle of white wine for me. I'd only wanted a glass, but I guessed it got lost in translation, or they just didn't do it that way. Oh well, I thought as I tipped the cool wine into my empty glass.

"Here you are!" exclaimed Paul. "I had to stop at two other places before I found you." He pulled up a chair, and I called for another glass so he could share my wine, but he waved it away. "I've already had a couple on the way here. I was chatting with another fella from our *albergue*, and he's going to join me for supper," he advised as he ordered a beer. I knew he was a red wine guy.

When he asked, Andrea shared that she was also walking on to Rabanal the next day, but she was staying at a different *albergue* than the one Esther had reserved for us. She said that her fly day was June 6th, the day I had planned to arrive in Santiago, so she needed to step it up after Rabanal. Sorry to know that we wouldn't be travelling together much longer, I enjoyed her company while I could.

Leaving Paul talking football with his newly-arrived dinner partner, we strolled down the road to our *albergue*. After promises to keep in touch, we hugged goodnight and made our way to our bunks.

I was still thumbing through my guidebook (the closest thing I had to satisfy my reading addiction), when Paul pushed noisily through the bunkroom door.

"Right. I'm just going to get my laundry," he said. "Don't want to forget anything in the morning." I laughed; morning confusion seemed his norm.

By the time he rolled into the bunk across the way from mine, the overhead lights had dimmed, and I hovered on the edge of a sleepy abyss.

"Thanks for saving my bunk," Paul whispered loudly.

"No worries," I countered, popping in my earplugs. "See you in the morning."

I leapt into the abyss.

As requested the night before, I reached over and tapped Paul's arm. He sprang awake and ran for the shower. In the shadowy bunkroom, I finished dressing, tucked my belongings into my pack, and stepped out into the morning.

Crossing the courtyard to the breakfast room, I looked up to see beams of sunshine labouring through the gloomy clouds. Enjoying the luxury of time to spread out the journey, today's would be bit shorter walk than yesterday's, although it would be a steady climb of 400 metres.

I bent to scratch the dog behind his ears, and he responded with a gentle sigh. I was the first in for breakfast, and Amelio waved me over to a table in the corner. At my nod, he carried over a steel pot of hot coffee, poured my cup half full, then filled it with warm milk from a second pitcher. I settled into my chair, glancing through my guide as I waited his return. Amelio placed a plate of warm, buttery toast before me and then, with a flourish and a shy smile, placed a bowl of fragrant orange segments beside my plate. Smiling my thanks, I spooned jam onto my toast and took a deep sip of my coffee. Peeling the last of the sweet orange segments into my mouth, I refused Amelio's offer for more coffee.

I thanked him for his generosity and departed just as a flurry of pilgrims, including Paul, arrived. Stopping at the bunkhouse, I grabbed my poles, slung my pack on my back, and pushed out through the battered wooden doors, wondering if I'd catch up with Andrea somewhere along the way.

Soon, Murias de Rechivaldo was part of my past, as I trudged along the red dirt track that paralleled a country road. Ahead of me, silhouetted pilgrims marched through the dawn, pausing to bathe in sporadic shafts of sunshine as they walked. The going was easy, a gradual slope on an even trail, and I revelled in the warmth, despite the looming clouds. I appreciated the quiet solitude; alone, but not lonely. There was distance and yet reassuring presence between me and the closest pilgrim.

I passed through tiny Santa Catalina de Somosa, but chose not to stop, continuing on another hour to the fragile town of El Ganso. Here, despite the buildings of crumbling stone, lay a pilgrim favourite; the Cowboy Bar. The tiny bar, no bigger than a single-car garage, was entered through wide, double doors, and inside, a collection of "all things cowboy" hung from the walls and ceiling. It was bizarre; a confusion of saddles, hats, ropes, stirrups, chaps, posters, and more! It was almost hard to find the bespectacled and moustached Spaniard who was doling out drinks. He tugged proudly on his leather vest as he offered a steaming coffee.

Out in the courtyard, comprised of three small, round, metal tables and a collection of mismatched chairs, Paul was already seated, munching on a slice of toast.

"Oh, there you are. Do you want a piece?" he asked, motioning towards his toast and tomato spread. "I love this stuff!" he said, breaking a corner off for me.

"No, I'm good," I thanked him. "Had a big breakfast and I have this banana," I replied, perching on an empty chair with my coffee.

"I missed you back in the town. I just grabbed a quick coffee and then came after you, but you were gone." Funny how that happened; I left first and he arrived first. He must have hit the road while I was getting my things together in the bunkroom; probably one of those pilgrims, just ahead in the distance, I had been following all morning.

"Right. One more espresso, and I'll be good to go," he announced as he scurried back inside the bar with his cup. I took the opportunity to visit the "gals'" room only to find it too held to the old west theme; no toilet paper (lucky I had napkins in my pocket), no soap or towels, and not even a toilet seat. Two points!

The Camino *senda* was now paralleling a paved road, lightly trafficked with trucks and delivery vans. As we picked our way along the gently climbing trail, we reached wide, muddy portions that forced us out onto the pavement.

"You like those sticks?" Paul questioned. I told him I did.

"I find they help the circulation in my hands, and when I'm climbing or coming down, they can be a Godsend. Are you thinking of getting some?"

"Oh no! Yorkshire men don't use sticks!" he exclaimed.

"Well, you might find them useful when we start hitting the big climbs again."

"Naww, totally unprofessional for a Yorkshire man to use sticks!" he jested derisively.

The trail took us back behind a sparsely treed division from the roadway. Tall, pale-pink, plumed flowers shaped like feather dusters caught my eye, and as looked more closely I noticed crosses entwined in the fencing along the path. I remembered reading about the Via Crucis in my guidebook and was moved by the variety and number of crosses we passed. Like back between Logrono and Navarette, pilgrims had taken twigs, adorned them with laces and ribbons, and pinned their prayers to the fence.

Here it was, just coming on noon, and we were walking into Rabanal del Camino. Esther had made reservations for us, saying they had stayed here every Camino and highly recommended the *Albergue* Neustra Senora del Pilar.

In through the arched wooden gates, we found ourselves in a flower-filled flagstone courtyard, a large cage of cooing birds just inside the gate. Two rows of white plastic tables and chairs were busy with diners devouring plates of food. At the last table before the entrance to the bar, a stout Spanish matron was busy registering guests.

Crossing our names off her list, she stamped our pilgrims' passports and recorded our national passports. The *hospitalero* led us past the bar, through a hallway (which was actually the bathroom), and in through the door of a massive bunkroom. Most of the wooden bunks were set up in pairs forming clusters of four. You could roll from one bed right over to the other. Directing Paul to a bunk near the door, she led me down the aisle towards the back and proudly offered me the bottom of a single set rather than a double. In a room of forty beds, this was a gift, and I smiled my appreciation.

In the next bed, a pleasant-looking woman nodded, adjusting her glasses as she wrote in a book. I smiled back at her. She appeared younger than me, but her short hair was silvered like mine. She didn't seem to want to talk, so I took her lead and busied myself with my own nesting process.

"Do you want to go out and see the town?" Paul questioned appearing at the foot of my bed. "I was talking with a fellow across the way, and he was telling me we have a big climb tomorrow."

"Well yes," I agreed. "Tomorrow is Monte Irago and the Cruz de Ferro. We will climb about 400 metres in just over an hour, and then after the second summit, we will descend steeply, almost 600 metres again."

"D'ya think it would be good to have sticks then?" he asked uncertainly.

"Well, it sure wouldn't hurt!" I advised. The woman in the bunk next to me nodded seriously in agreement.

"Okay. Let's go have a look then. But it better not get back home. Yorkshire men don't use sticks!"

As we exited the enormous bunkroom, I counted two toilets and two showers in the hallway and wondered how comfortable I'd feel showering in what was basically a thoroughfare to the bunkroom. Out in the courtyard, Esther, Andi, and Irma had just arrived. Loudly greeted by our Camino *hospitaleros*, Irma was already being passed around, everyone exclaiming about the beautiful baby girl. She was a hit everywhere she went!

"We meet again." Andi smiled. Remembering that because of the baby, they had to stay in private rooms, I asked where their room was, and he indicated the balcony to the left of the gate. "We stay there. It is small, but it is okay." They shared a bathroom with three other "apartments". I considered it might just be worth packing a baby when I thought of the two toilets between forty beds.

"This little one has to have a nap," declared Esther, reclaiming her daughter. "And we too will rest. Maybe we will see you later for supper?" she questioned. We said we'd see them then and walked out the wide gate against a tide of incoming pilgrims. Our bunkroom would be full for sure.

Wandering up and down narrow roads, I was enchanted with banks of flowers and fragrant lilac bushes claiming their space against walls of stone and decaying wooden doors. We visited a small chapel, devoid of any ornamentation aside from the fading frescos painted on the ceilings. Ancient, scarred benches faced an austere pulpit, so out of keeping with the opulence we had seen in most churches along the way.

A bucket in the corner of a nearby shop held a small assortment of mismatched trekking poles which caught Paul's eye.

"Do I need two do you think?" Paul questioned, testing a blue metal pole for weight. "You have two, but there's no match here. Does it matter?"

"As long as they're both the same height, it doesn't really matter the colour or design. If it works for you and is built well enough to support you, that's all that matters," I assured him.

"Right. Well maybe I'll just try it with one. I see fellas walking with just one stick, so maybe one will do." Despite his earlier reluctance, Paul seemed happy as we strolled back up to the *albergue*, his new stick tapping along as we went.

Back in the bunkroom, to my delight, the set of bunks on the other side of me had been claimed by my Tennessee friends, Charlotte and Steve.

"Hey Canada," Charlotte called out, rubbing her leg just freed from its brace.

"How are you doing girl?" asked Steve, bending down to see between the bunks. We shared notes on our journey and spoke about tomorrow's climb.

"How will you do with your leg?" I asked.

"Oh, we'll get there. It might not be pretty, but we'll get there!" Charlotte exclaimed. "Did you bring a rock from home for the cross?" she asked.

"Actually," I said, "I brought a sand dollar. I thought that was more representative of my island home."

"A sand dollar?" she questioned. I reached into my pack and gently removed the seashell I had wrapped in tissue and carried safely all these miles.

"Micah 6:8," she read as she turned it gently in her hand. "You know your bible girl?"

"Yes. This is my mantra: Seek justice, love kindness, and walk humbly with your God."

"That's right," nodded Steve sagely as he examined the shell his wife had passed to him. "Good words to walk by." He returned the sand dollar, and I passed it over to my unknown friend so she could see it. I really was going to have to get her name. She just seemed so quiet! She handed it back with a soft smile and then laid down, pulling her covers up. Introductions would have to wait.

"Looks like we're going to be bunk mates tonight!" Steve crowed as he rolled easily from his bunk to Charlotte's.

"Oh, stop that, you old fool!" she exclaimed, slapping his shoulder playfully.

I laughed, gathering my things to brave the shower. Cleaner, I found the quiet dining room where I could prepare a cup of instant coffee. At the end of the long trestle table, a woman with short auburn hair sat in solitude. A waitress deposited a plate of pasta and bread before her.

"*Dank je,*" she intoned seriously. So German, or maybe Dutch, I thought. The other end of the table busy with other diners, I motioned questionably toward the empty bench across from her. "*Ja*" she nodded, and I slid in.

In the centre of the table, there were games, puzzles, and decks of cards. Sensing that conversation was not likely between us, I picked up the cards and entertained myself with a few games of solitaire. My silent companion was focussed on her meal, and I played on. Finally, my coffee finished, I rose to leave. "Goodbye" she said hesitantly, and I wondered if I had missed an opportunity to make a new friend.

Out in the bar, they had zipped a canvas wall across the opening to the courtyard, closing the bar off into a snug common room. The clouds had finally broken and rain was pouring down, bouncing off the flagstones outside. Pilgrims, crowded into the suddenly smaller gathering place, found seats along the bench-lined room. A lucky few had seats close to a small, pot-bellied stove that was pumping out heat. Late stragglers, who had gotten caught in the rain, hung soggy clothes off the nearby racks, hoping the heat would reach them and provide them with dry socks for the next day.

"Hello!" exclaimed Esther, automatically handing baby Irma across the table to me as she pulled up two chairs. Paul, suddenly appearing, slid in next to me, depositing a glass of red wine in front of each of us. He may be a bit of a tease, but no one could fault his generosity. Andi carried drinks over from the bar and took his place next to his wife. Immediately a crowd gathered to see the baby, and it was time to play "pass the baby" again. Good thing Irma was so easygoing.

"How was your day?" Esther enquired.

"She made me get a stick," Paul accused. I looked at him.

"I did not make you get a stick. I told you it was a good idea. You made the choice yourself!" I argued.

"Ah, but Yorkshire men don't use sticks. I would never have got one if you hadn't bullied me into it!" his blue eyes sparkled mischievously. Rolling my eyes, I cut my losses and shut up.

"Probably you will find it will help you tomorrow," Andi suggested. "Ah, here is our meal." Saved by the dinner bell!

I offered to entertain Irma while Andi and Esther enjoyed heaping plates of pasta, rich with tomato sauce and liberally sprinkled with slices of spicy sausage.

"This is good," Esther advised between mouthfuls, "really, you should have some." Convinced, we put in our orders. They finished their meal, and then reclaimed their daughter as ours arrived. We hadn't realized how hungry we were.

As we were finishing, the woman I'd met in the dining room slid in next to Paul, reaching her hand over for Irma to grasp. She said a few words and then Esther and she were off.

"She is Catharina, and she is Belgian. She speaks Dutch, but I can go there with my German," my multi-lingual friend advised.

"Does she speak any English?" I asked.

"*Ja, ik* speak English good!" Catharina proudly announced. Okay, so it was going to be a bit of work, but we could communicate. It would appear I had acquired another Belgian friend.

Andi got up to refill their drinks, and Paul brought another glass of wine for each of us, Catharina included. I tried to refuse it, but he insisted we needed a night cap. I asked Andi what they were drinking, and he searched for English words, deferring to Esther's better command of English.

"It is a shandy. It is a mix of beer and lemon drink. Pop, you say. It is quite refreshing. Here, try it," she offered, sliding it across the table. I thought how easily people shared on this trip, and how little we worried about germs. Taking a sip, I found it very nice and told her I might order one at our next stop.

"That will be Acebo. Do you have a room there?" I told her no, but that there were quite a few places in the guidebook, so we weren't too worried.

"I haf no room there also," said Catharina, and I suggested she should travel with us, and we'd get a place together. Her stern expression dissolved, and she beamed at me. "Ya, we go together."

"Right, that's it then. We have another partner!" Paul announced. Little did we know we were slowly building a solid family unit, five of us who would finish the Camino as one.

"And now, it is time for this one to sleep." Esther gathered Irma from her daddy's arms, and they rose to climb the staircase to their room. We pushed out from behind the table ourselves, Catharina trailing behind as we headed to our bunkroom. I touched Catharina's shoulder and whispered we'd see her in the morning.

"Ya in the morning. Ve valk."

Pulling the door softly open, we entered the sleeping room, a variety of soft snores filling the near darkness as we each sought our beds. I dragged off my pants and quickly donned my leggings, tucking my feet inside my sleeping bag. As I rummaged under my pillow for the earplugs I had stowed there, I glanced across at the woman lying in the bed across from me. Her eyes were open, and she was watching me with a smile.

"Roxey," I whispered touching my chest.

"Ana," she replied softly, doing the same.

"Buenas noches," I whispered.

"Buenas noches," came the soft reply.

Better late than never I thought as I rolled over and settled in to sleep.

Daylight streamed in from the skylights between the rafters in the bunkroom ceiling, and pilgrims rolled out of bed, pulling on pants, socks, and shoes, racing for the limited bathrooms. Ana and I smiled good morning as we rolled our sleeping bags and tucked our belongings in our packs. Steve was helping Charlotte adjust her complicated leg brace. As I left the room behind me, Paul was busily packing his bag at the foot of his bunk near the door.

Out in the dim hallway, pilgrims lined the benches. As I moved towards the bar to order coffee, I noticed a tall, slim man with a crown of white curls and a tidy white beard that wreathed his face. He was bent to the task of tightening his boot laces, but he looked up as I passed and gave me a friendly smile. I murmured, *"Buen Camino,"* and he nodded as Paul rushed up and joined me at the bar.

"Good morning! How was your night?" questioned Esther. The curly-haired matron in the black and white apron greeted Esther gaily, asking after the bambino. Esther and Andi would always take back seat to Irma on this trip it seemed.

"Our room was good, and we slept very well," she advised. "Irma was a little fussy. I think she is cutting another tooth. We just gave her a cold cloth to chew on, and she went back to sleep. Andi is with her, so I will bring breakfast. Did you bring a stone for the cross?"

"Naw, I didn't. This one," Paul lightly tapped my shoulder, "didn't remind me we were meant to bring a stone. Not very professional of you, I must say," he chided me. "I guess I'll just have to pick something up along the way."

Obviously, some pre-arrangement had been made, as the barista quickly assembled Esther's tray with two tall, creamy mugs of coffee, a plate of toast and cheese, and a bowl of scrambled eggs.

"We will see you tonight at El Acebo perhaps. We are staying at the new place. Maybe it will suit you and there will be rooms?" she smiled as she departed with her tray.

As we drained our cups, Catharina and Ana appeared in the doorway. Ana cocked her head in question, and I suggested she join us. Paul swung his new stick, keeping time with the three of us for a while, but as usual, picked up speed and pulled ahead.

The morning was filled with rosy sunshine and rainbows. In the distance, low hills lined with white windmills beckoned. The tall turbines seemed to be churning the mist, dispelling the clouds in favour of the sun. We walked along a gravel country track, a low stone wall the only barrier between us and a herd of docile horses, eagerly pulling grasses from the hedgerows of green. We walked without talking, each in our own world, though just a hand's reach apart. My thoughts filled with family and friends at home, and I asked my morning blessings on them each.

The track began to climb, and Catharina, dressed in sombre sage, dropped back a bit, letting Ana and I take the lead. Ana's large, brown eyes smiled out from behind black-framed glasses. I guessed she was a few years younger than me and thought she really reminded me of someone I knew; if only I could remember who. Her turquoise coat matched the stripes on her pack and her shoes, but she didn't strike me as the fussy type, so I decided this coordination was more a matter of chance than design.

An hour later, we came into Foncebadon, a collection of stone and wooden shack-like houses. Off to the left, packs and poles adorned a rustic porch, and we peeled off in search of a bathroom. Inside the low-ceilinged room, rough benches ran along plank-topped tables where pilgrims clustered, cups in hand. Although the rain had stopped, the air was still chilly and a cup of hot coffee was welcome.

As I waited my turn for the washroom, I noticed a mini-*mercado* in the corner of the bar. Chocolate bars, gum, bags of nuts and dried fruit, along with laces and tissues and sunscreen; it was a surprisingly comprehensive selection. Among the offerings I noticed small tubs of peanut butter and immediately thought of Steve. Yesterday, while we were talking, we spoke of what we were missing from home. Steve had said he really missed peanut butter, and the closest he'd been able to come was Nutella. I was tempted to pick up a couple of containers for him in case he and Charlotte bypassed this bar, and he missed out on it. Then the voice of reason broke through; if you buy it, you carry it! And the reality was I had no way of knowing if I'd even see them again.

Packs and poles in place, we struck off up the hill, the gravel track now transforming into a more challenging grade of loose rock and shale, still slippery with the mud of yesterday's rain. Thankful for our sturdy boots and long pants, we dodged wide areas of greasy mud and standing water, taking care to find firm footing before taking another step. Either due to the warming day or the exertion of the trail, coats were soon unzipped. Below us, Catharina's face was serious and purposeful as she focused on her footing.

The tree-lined trail opened up to reveal remarkable views of soft, green hills and the tiny town we had come from, already far below in the valley. Shafts of sunshine did battle with circling clouds, lighting up some of the panorama like spotlights. Emerald green pasture land rolled down the shoulders of the hills to the floor of the valley, broken only by sporadic copses of newly-leafed trees and the occasional low, rock wall.

"Beautiful!" exclaimed Ana with an appreciative smile as we turned back to the trail and continued our climb. The terrain, much like a dry streambed, was finally improving, returning to a loose gravel, interspersed with hard, packed mud. On the shoulders of the trail, colourful clumps of flowers scrambled up the shale slope in explosions of whites, yellows, and purples. The beauty took my mind from the work of the trek, and we quickly climbed the last few metres to reach the first peak and the Cruz de Ferro.

Located at over 1,500 metres above sea level, the weathered pole, crowned by a simple black cross, stood at the top of its own hill of stones. I was surprised to see a paved road and parking lot off to one side. Then I remembered the barriers my husband often encountered, those that prevented his wheelchair from reaching what others so easily experienced. My disappointment with the modern imposition turned to thanks that anyone wanting to see the cross would have that opportunity.

A collection of pilgrims gathered under cobalt blue skies, respectfully waiting their turn to climb the hill and leave their stone. The tradition is to climb the hill, built by the offerings of pilgrims past, and contribute your own stone. It's meant to be symbolic of laying down your burdens as you ask blessings on the rest of your journey.

Leaving my pack and poles by the fence, I climbed the hill carrying my sand dollar from home. As I climbed, I was undecided if I would break the offering or leave it whole so future pilgrims could see "Parksville, BC, Canada" and my mantra written on it. The sand dollar could remain whole and mark my place long after I finished my journey and returned to my home. I was undecided.

Despite the people at the foot of the hill, the summit was surprisingly quiet. Gentle breezes buffeted around me as I placed my hand on the pole. I said a brief prayer, raised my sand dollar, and broke the fragile shell, releasing the five tiny, white triangular bones contained within, honouring the legends of freeing the "doves" of God's love and peace. I brushed an errant tear from my face, surprising myself in how moved I was by this simple gesture, and made my way back down.

Paul was running from person to person, asking if they had a pen that would write on rock. He frantically tried one, then another, reminding me of the line, "*A horse, a horse! My kingdom for a horse!*" from William Shakespeare's *Richard III*. Finally, success! Pen in hand he bent to write a message on a flat piece of shale and carried his words to the top of the hill, prayerfully laying it at the foot of the cross. I knew he was doing something important; probably in regard to Daniel, so I quickly snapped a photo of him placing the stone, knowing it would be appreciated by him somewhere down the line. Following in Catharina and Ana's footsteps, I set off down the trail, leaving Paul to his moment at the cross.

There was a bit of a dip before the final climb to Alto Altar, and as I bypassed Manjarin, I noticed the clouds were gathering once more. Low, stone walls with taller faces that may have been hearths in ages past, were all that remain of this abandoned village. The lowing cows, their bells clanging gently as they pulled grass from the lush, sloping meadows, were the only indication that anyone lived nearby. I came to the colourful *albergue* operated by a single *hospitalero* and wondered how many had stayed there the night before, enjoying the rustic "charm" of mattresses on the floor and an outhouse out the back.

At the summit, the clouds were getting serious, and the sun had lost its battle. A moment ago, I was hot in a sleeveless t-shirt; now I scrambled to pull my poncho over my head and my pack. The vivid blue skies of the Cruz de Ferro were gone, and the world became grey and wet again. The descent into El Acebo was very steep, dropping 500 metres in less than five kilometres, so attention to footing again became crucial. I braced my downward leaps over broad rocks running with wet and wondered if Paul was glad he had picked up a walking stick after all.

It wasn't really rain, but a mist so heavy that pilgrims before me were quickly swallowed from sight. Focusing on the track, I laboured downwards and suddenly found myself levelling out, faced with a street of stone houses, surrounded in the mist. Ana and Catharina had been just ahead of me, and they waited at the first bar where pilgrims sheltered around tiny tables, narrowly tucked under the dripping roofline. Inside I received a steaming hot cup of coffee from a surly barista and went out to the cold, where the reception was warmer.

"They have rooms here," Ana announced, waving her hand at the second storey up a questionable flight of wooden stairs. "And there are more *albergues* in the town." Paul pulled up, quickly dropping his pack beside me and ran in through the doors to get an espresso.

"Right," he said. "Where are we staying?" I repeated Ana's suggestion that this place had room, but I was doubtful about the welcome we would have given the demeanour of the operator. To some running an *albergue* is a calling; to others, it is just a job. The attitude can make a huge difference. I said I had read in the guidebook that there was a parish *albergue* at the lower end of town. The beds were by donation, and there was a communal meal and evening prayers. That seemed to interest everyone, so we downed our cups, shouldered our packs, and struck off into the mist.

As we trekked down the hill, we spotted a sign of a new hotel, complete with a pool. This seemed a little incongruent given the age and dilapidated state of most of the buildings in this tiny mountain town. We found the parish *albergue*, but the sign on the door stated it would not open for another hour, and there was no place to shelter from the onslaught of the rain.

"Let's just see what else there is," I suggested and we filed along, down the hill. All of a sudden, before us, was a modern, new building; glass, chrome, pennants on poles, and yes, those were tiki huts! How bizarre! We trudged up the paved driveway in our sodden boots and entered the pristine lobby. A young woman with long hair, fixed by a sparkling headband, stood behind a podium, ready to welcome incoming guests. Without hesitation at our sad appearance, she advised us that half of the hotel operated as an *albergue*, and the other had regular, private rooms. She went on to say they provided laundry, and that the pilgrims meal was a set meal at a set price, served in the dining room. Following the wave of her hand, we saw plush banquette seats and linen-draped tables set with silver and glass. We were sold! Check us in!

Passports stamped and euros paid, we mounted the wide, carpeted stairs that led to the *albergue* side of the hotel. Unlocking our door, we discovered eight, light-wood bunks, complete with soft blankets and puffy pillows. The lone occupant of the room seated on a bottom bunk by the window was Moira, the woman from Atlantic Canada I had met what seemed like years ago. We each chose a bunk, mine a top one by the window above Ana's, Paul's a bottom one by the door. Catharina took the last bottom bunk, and we wondered who might fill the remaining top two.

We headed for the showers, going down the hall, down a short, wide staircase, and up another after crossing the landing and down another hall. Lots of light and room, no waiting for showers. As we peeled off our top layers, I showed Catharina the looseness of my pant waist.

"*Das es* from here?" she questioned, asking if I had dropped that much size on the Camino. I nodded. I was surprised that while I always seemed to be eating and drinking a lot of wine and beer (by my standards), I was still dropping weight. Funny what walking twenty-odd kilometres days over hill, over dale will do! "*Dey vill* fall down! *Haff* you a belt?" she asked, cocking her head.

"No," I said grinning, "but I have some extra boot laces. I can tie them between the belt loops and have fashionable bows at my hips!" We laughed.

"They do laundry down in the basement," Moira offered when we returned to the room. "They're big machines, so we could share and save. I offered to run the laundry down and get it started, so everyone sorted the clothes they wanted washed and placed coins in my hand.

A hotel maid helped me load the machine and advised I should return in thirty minutes to transfer them to the dryer. She returned to the huge ironing press. The fragrance of slightly singed cotton filled the room as it was lowered on crisp white sheets.

Upstairs I was told Paul was down at the patio bar, the rain having stopped for a while. The German family had arrived, and Andi was enjoying a beer and a cigarette while Esther and Irma slept. Sitting on my quilt dragged down to the floor by the window, I did a little journaling and fired off some texts to Al. I noticed the other two beds strewn with belongings.

"A woman from France and a tall man from Stockholm," Ana supplied at my questioning look.

"*Ya*, he is Santa Claus", intoned Catharina sternly, and everyone giggled. Must be that man I'd seen this morning, I thought. Realizing it was time to transfer the clothes, I headed downstairs. I quickly thrust the clothes into the dryer, popping coins in the slots.

Out on the deck, Andi was gone, and Esther sat lounging, enjoying her own cigarette as Paul nursed his glass of wine.

"This is Zigniv," Paul introduced and the gentle man shook his head. "No, I mean Zabiniv. No, that wasn't it either. I'm sorry, I just can't get it straight," a frustrated Paul apologized as I pulled up a chair. The white-haired pilgrim at the next table raised his glass to me in courtly fashion.

"Zbigniew," he supplied.

"Yes, that's it," Paul agreed, (as if there was any doubt the man could get his own name right). I laughed. "He is from Stockholm," Paul advised. "But he's Polish," he continued, "and he's in our room."

"Join us for a drink," Esther suggested lazily, careful as always, to blow her smoke away from us. "Andi has gone to have his shower while Irma is sleeping."

"You have to come and see the pool!" Ana invited, Catharina in tow. We followed the path to the back of the hotel. There it was! An outdoor pool all pristine blue. The deck was strewn with white tables and chairs, shelter provided with shaggy, straw beach umbrellas. There was not a soul in sight. I reached over and streamed my fingers through the frigid water and found the reason. As lovely as it was to look at, it was way too cold to enjoy! Of course, we didn't have swimsuits anyways, and I was sure skinny dipping would be strongly frowned upon.

Back down in the laundry room I pulled toasty clothes from the dryer and folded them into a soft pile, matching socks as I found them. Upstairs, not knowing whose was what, I laid the clothes out on the first bed inside the door for everyone to sort and claim their own. I took my things and organized them into my pack; Ana did the same. Paul opened the door and seeing the laundry, happily pushed a pile in his pack before grabbing his guidebook and heading back down to the patio.

"Mine *sockens es not* here," Catharina advised seriously upon her return. "No more *es* mine pants." She held up a pair of pants that were obviously too short for her.

"I don't know," I muttered, "I brought everything. I checked the machines carefully, and I don't think I dropped anything."

"*Dese es* not mine," Catharina repeated soberly, holding the gray pants up before her. A quick check with Moira confirmed they weren't hers either.

"Paul." I thought. I went to the window and called over the railing to the patio below. "Paul, can you come up for a moment?" Andi had changed places with Esther, and the three men looked up at my call. I heard an exasperated sigh and male laughter and something about "women". In through the door Paul sauntered.

"Well, I don't know," he replied at our question, pulling the clothes he had jammed in his pack. And yes, there was a pair of Catharina's missing socks, and another, and the third.

"Well these aren't mine!" he exclaimed pulling a pair of pants from his pack.

"What about these pants?" I asked, holding up the orphan pair.

"Let me see…yes, those are mine," he said handing Catharina her pants in exchange. "They were on my bed," he blustered. "Not very professional, Roxey, to put them on the wrong bed. You got us all mixed up. I thought you were more organized," he mocked.

We all just laughed, and with the rightful clothes in the rightful packs, we joined the others down in the dining room. I sat between Esther and Ana, Irma safely ensconced in a highchair at the head of the table. While waiting our meals, conversation revolved around where to stay for tomorrow.

"I don't so much enjoy Ponferrada," advised Esther, drawing on her Camino experience.

"No, it is too…industrial," Andi agreed, rubbing his bearded chin, searching his vocabulary for the right English word.

"I have a reservation in Ponferrada," Moira advised. "I want to explore the fort there." Ana nodded; that was her destination too.

"We have reserved in Columbrianos, the town just behind Ponferrada," Esther advised. I searched my guide book. "No, you won't find an *albergue* listed there. It is new. I have the number. I can call if you would like me to see if they have room?" We all nodded, including Zbigniew. Looked like we had another member for our tribe. Pulling a cigarette from her pack, Esther walked out onto the deck to make the call.

Plates started arriving just as she returned, and everyone had one in front of them except for me. It looked and smelled delicious! I caught the eye of the uniformed waiter and asked. Seeming confused that I had not yet received my meal, he disappeared through the swinging doors of the kitchen.

"Please eat while it's hot," I encouraged the others, munching on a slice of crusty bread while I waited.

Finally, a gloved hand placed a dish of steaming chicken in a rich sauce before me. The fragrance hit me wrong for some reason. Maybe my palate had changed with all the plain food I had been eating. I shook my head and pushed my fork into the tender meat. It tasted way better than it smelled. After the plates were removed, glasses were refilled, and we enjoyed slices of dark, chocolate torte together. Really, this was a great place. Maybe a little out of character for the Camino, but we had a nice room, good showers, clean laundry, and a great meal…I thought.

Tucking into our beds, we wished each other goodnight. I rolled over to get a good sleep…I thought.

Shortly after midnight, I awoke to deep rumblings. It wasn't thunder, it was my belly! Waves of cramps rolled through me as I struggled to drop as quietly from my bunk and ran for the bathroom. Down the hall, down the stairs, across the landing, up the stairs…down the hall; I just made it. Obviously, something I had eaten had not agreed with me. Maybe it was just too rich.

Back in bed, I felt much better and snuggled down to sleep…I thought. Another mad dash for the bathroom, and I knew this was food poisoning. The night was spent between brief naps and rapid races. I wondered how I would manage the day.

Catharina tutted when I explained my night. No one else in the room had any problems. A quick check identified that I was the only one in our group who had chicken.

"Perhaps it sat too long. Yours was the last to come," Ana commiserated with concern. "Will you be okay?"

I advised I thought it was through me by now, and that I'd see how it went. As I joined the others for breakfast, I declined anything but a banana and clear tea. Hopefully I would keep that down and be on the way to recovery as well as Columbrianos.

Leaving the resort behind us, we each found our pace and were sorted by twists and turns of the trail into singles and pairs. We were travelling together, but apart, each allowing the other privacy for thought and meditation. Except I was with Paul.

"This town is quite different, isn't it? he questioned, taking in the tidy houses. The skies above still brooded with yesterday's clouds, although some bright patches of blue held promise.

"Are you feeling okay now?" he asked as we picked our way down a stony trail exiting Riego de Ambros. I told him I was feeling better. "Good. Not very professional getting sick on the Camino you know," he scolded. "Maybe should have had the beef, not the chicken." *Hindsight is twenty-twenty*, I thought. "My meal was fine, and Zgivniv had fish. It was okay."

"His name is Zbigniew," I corrected.

"Well no matter. You should have had the fish. Your mistake having the chicken."

"How was I supposed to know the chicken was bad?" I countered. My tummy rumbled in agreement.

"How long have you two been married?" a female voice enquired. I suddenly realized we weren't alone.

"We're not married! He just treats me like we are." I looked back at Paul gingerly stepping stones behind me. "And I pity his poor Mary!" I retorted to the woman who had walked her way between us. I heard a loud laugh behind me as Paul crowed his success in getting to me. The woman laughed too, pushing past, to put this quibbling couple behind her.

We were, by now, deep in the hills, and our progress took gentle rises and falls. To the left of the rough path, the side of the hill fell off sharply, and I looked down across treetops to the other side of the gorge. Likely there was a river down there, but I couldn't hear water, just Paul tapping along behind me.

No one had passed us lately, but I could hear by the hum of voices ahead that we were catching up to someone. Our descent to Molinaseca took a steeper pitch for a while. I guessed that was what had slowed those in front of us down enough for us to catch up. A steep drop and loose gravel under foot; a good reason to slow down and take caution. We noticed a paved road curling around the hill, and it appeared that some pilgrims had chosen that more tame path to trod.

A short while later, we crossed the roadway into a pretty river town, the first buildings a graceful stone church and a bar, its patio strewn with chairs and tables, umbrellas folded waiting the heat of the sun. Crossing the arched bridge, we came to a cafe right on the edge of the river. Inside, my first stop was the bathroom, but thankfully, there was no mad dash.

Carrying a plate of toast and a cup of tea out to the sunny tables by the front door, I found Paul sipping an espresso.

"Oh right. You didn't have breakfast. Are you okay then?" Teasing aside, he really did care. "I'm just going to get another coffee.

"Hallo, my friends!" a voice called out. It was Zbigniew. He must have been just behind us. Despite the heat, Zbigniew wore a long-sleeved orange shirt. He accessorized jauntily with a black-and-white-striped scarf and a royal blue bucket hat that matched his sparkling blue eyes. "The sun does not like me," he supplied as he pulled up a chair and sat down. Waving away our suggestion of coffee, he pulled out a bottle of water and a bag of cookies. "I wait to eat at Ponferrada."

Given my sleepless night, I was being lulled into lethargy by the peaceful river. Looking around at the pretty town, I wondered if this wouldn't have been a better place to stop last night. But then, that would have meant another two hours' walk through yesterday's rain. Wanting to get moving before I slid into a coma, I left the men in masculine camaraderie, going over their entry route into Ponferrada.

The Camino followed the major road out of Molinaseca and by now it was a sun-baked concrete sidewalk that I trekked. The steady downhill path took me past small farm plots and struggling forests. I walked alone, wondering where everyone else in our little group was. Before long, the scrub brush turned into suburbs, and I saw a large city ahead on the hill. Ponferrada (Iron Bridge) was a modern city with a few ancient twists, the renowned twelfth-century Templar castle being one of them.

I followed a straight, red track that looked like the red dirt of Spain, but it was actually painted concrete, hot and hard on the feet. Maybe they wanted you to think you were still on the "trail" as you entered this busy city. I remembered different entry options mentioned in my guidebook, but I found the easiest way was to follow the backpacks before me. But wait! Those backpacks were crossing the road…that one was going straight. Now what do I do? I caught up with the single backpack before me and recognized a German woman I'd met before Burgos.

"This is a short cut," she claimed as we skirted a busy corner and made our way across a long bridge, a rushing river passing below. Was this the "iron bridge"? Not sure. We carried on upwards, dodging traffic as we searched for signs of the Camino. Were we lost? Not sure. The German woman suddenly broke across the road, making for a market offering ice cream. I saw the castle before me on the hill. I reasoned that since it was a national monument, the main square would be nearby, and the Camino always touched on the main square. I could get my bearings and go from there. I waved farewell and trudged up the road, wondering if the shortcut had been to ice cream or the Camino!

Climbing upwards, I finally found a Camino marker and, passing under a stone arch, the castle lay before me. The imposing structure had been the focus of recent refurbishment, but it still spoke of ancient times, especially in comparison to the sprawling modern city behind it. On one wall, ivy climbed, softening the rock edges and lending a bit of gentle nature to its hard walls. On a concrete wall just in front of it, someone had added their own embellishment – graffiti. The contrast between the two walls couldn't have been more apparent.

The Plaza Mayor was busy with pilgrims taking their mid-day meal. Tired from my lack of sleep and the heat, I decided to push on and located what I thought was a Camino marker. I followed the wide stairs downwards, not seeing anther arrow. I decided to give it a little more time and, at the bottom of the stairs, I happily discovered an arrow, sending me in the direction of a bridge. I felt a shimmer of success, until a group of Korean pilgrims stopped short in front of me. The men began a heated discussion, lots of finger pointing at maps. Finally, they reached some sort of consensus and turned back in the direction from which I'd come. Now what? Maybe they're looking for an *albergue*; not the way out at all. I held my course.

Crossing the bridge, I found myself walking along the river in a park-like setting. I walked past a school, the children's voices reminding me of my grandchildren, and I missed them anew. Dappled sunlight streamed through the tall trees along the river, and on I walked. A couple strolling hand-in-hand, their dog tugging at its lead, moved towards a bench, and on I walked. Two young men were kicking around a football, and on I walked. Finally, I ran out of walkway, with only a gravel road and what looked like some sort of warehouse before me. Then I spotted a yellow arrow pointing up the hill beside the building. And on I walked.

Struggling up the steep gravel hill, I broke out on the edge of a busy highway. Now what? Was that a backpack up ahead? Yes! I crossed at an intersection and entered the courtyard of something that seemed to be an abandoned hospital or school. The arrows led me through an arch, back out the other side, and down a residential road. I continued to follow the signs, now tall, metal crosses with hands and shells at the top, depicting a pilgrim's hand holding a staff.

There it was! "Welcome to Columbrianos." So now all I had to do was find the *albergue*. I was looking for San Blas. Poling my way through deserted streets, suddenly, there came Paul!

"Right! There you are. Have you found it yet?" Sure I was now going to be accused of not locating the *albergue* professionally, I just laughed and told him it was just down the road. And it was. In through the shady patio we were led and up to a room with eight bunks. The floor to ceiling widows opened onto a narrow Juliet balcony overhanging the street. Across the street, on an island in the middle of a triangle of three roads, stood a tiny church, its front wall adorned with a charming mural. Behind the church, a tall pole stood, topped proudly by a stork's nest. Someone had finally found a way to beat the storks nesting in the belfry. They always nest at the highest point, so the church had simply erected a taller pole for them to choose. Smart move.

"Hello my friends." In walked Zbigniew, Catharina hot on his heels. Catharina looked at the bunks and tutted, not happy with something. A short discussion with our *hospitalero* later and Catharina was shepherded off to another room. I wasn't bothered sharing a room with these men by now, so I unpacked my bag and headed for the shower.

Down in the lounge, I ordered a cold beer and took it out to the sunny backyard.

I collapsed into a wicker chair and propped my feet on a short wall as the barista arrived with a plate of bread and cheese slices drizzled with herbs and olive oil, my complimentary tapas. Paul sauntered out from the lounge, bearing a mug of beer and his own tapas.

"So, you made it!" Esther's voice broke through my unplanned doze. I stood and we hugged. Paul offered to get more beer. "No, I am going to shower and get some laundry done," she declined. "Roxey, could I ask of you a favour? Irma is so comfortable with you. Would you be able to look after her while we shower and do laundry?" Would I look after our delightful Camino *bambino*? Of course!

Andi came out bearing his baby girl, a blanket, an assortment of colourful, chewable toys, and a bottle of water and bag of rusks. We were in business. I spent the next hour cooing and playing and having a wonderful time as Paul looked on from the patio.

"Roxey has the baby," Catharina stated as she arrived. My serious Belgian friend walked over, crouched down and reached her hand to Irma. She was charmed when the tiny hand closed around her finger, and she babbled at the baby in Dutch. Irma just smiled and drooled; teething will do that.

"You come for walk?" she questioned. By now Zbigniew had joined Paul, and they had switched to wine.

"I just have to wait for Andi or Esther."

"They come now," she announced as the young German couple strolled out to the lawn to retrieve their daughter.

It was a short walk; there wasn't much to see or do in this small town. It was siesta and everything was closed, so we returned to the *albergue*, settling into the chairs on the covered patio lounge, waiting for dinner. We looked an unlikely family, seniors to infants and everything in between. Our happy host wrote down our dinner orders and produced two bottles of wine for the table. Still favouring my stomach, I also asked for a jug of water.

"It's funny," I said, "we all went through Ponferrada in different ways, and yet, here we all are, together!"

"Absolutely!" toasted Zbigniew, raising his glass. We all clinked glasses and laughed. Out came our *hospitalero* with an amazing plate of beef steak and chips. When he placed one in front of Zbigniew, he refused, passing it over to Catharina since she had ordered the same.

"Oh! No, no, das is yours!" she protested. He insisted and, looking somewhat flustered, she accepted.

"Please eat," I suggested. "It should not get cold waiting for ours." And wait we did. Ten minutes later, out came another appetizing plate, this time for Zbigniew. Paul looked confused.

"Why is it taking so long? Why aren't they bringing them all out at once?"

"Well they're a new *albergue*, and they may still be sorting things out," I explained.

"Yes, and look how nice the food is. It's good? See! It will be worth the wait," Esther pronounced.

We were on a roll now. Paul and I had both ordered the fish, and the two plates came out together. Now I was feeling badly for Esther and Andi having to wait. Irma was happily gobbling down the pureed food her mommy spooned into her waiting mouth.

"I will take Irma for a walk while you eat," I suggested, knowing what it is like to juggle a baby while your food gets cold.

"That will be wonderful! Now about tomorrow. May I make a suggestion for all of you?" Esther asked. She and Andi were staying two days at Villafranca, our next night's stop. They had booked a small apartment and would use the time to let Irma get a good rest.

"There are many nice *albergues* in Villafranca, but I would choose the one behind all the others. It is the last one in the town and will set you up well for leaving the next day. La Piedra is run by a young couple, and they are very good. I have always enjoyed staying there. We would stay there this time, but for Irma."

"Esther," I said between mouthfuls, "I notice you are using the wrong English word when you are speaking about places." She cocked her head inquisitively. "You say behind, when what I think you mean is after."

"Don't correct her. Esther does much better than all of us. She speaks so many languages. You shouldn't criticize," Paul chided.

"I'm not criticizing. I know this important to Esther, and I want to help," I replied.

"It is okay, Paul. Roxey is right. If I can make my English better, why would I not? Roxey, please explain."

"Okay. If you say behind, that means something is in front of it, like this glass is behind this bottle. When you are talking about places, and you get to the first one, the next place is the one after. After, not behind, does that make sense?"

"Oh yes, that makes perfect sense. Thank you for helping me," she smiled.

"And here is our supper," Andi crowed, rubbing his long fingers together. Esther efficiently wiped Irma's hands and face, and I removed her baby cape and carried her off for a tour of the town.

Not a tear nor a minute of alarm, Irma seemed totally comfortable in my arms. We walked through the balmy evening, up one street and down the next. All of a sudden, a car whizzed by, and she jumped in my arms laughing like the funniest of things had just happened. I turned her toward the road as another car went by; same reaction. We spent the next twenty minutes or so, watching cars go by as if it was the greatest show on earth.

I turned and stepped off the shallow curb and all of a sudden, I felt a painful pull in the arch of my right foot. Oh no! Not this close to my goal! Walking gingerly, every step radiating pain, I held Irma close and returned to the *albergue*. Not wanting to share my injury, I pasted on a brave face and walked over to my chair. Irma was all giggles as her daddy held out his arms. Little arms flailing, Andi had to recover his glasses before she settled comfortably in his arms.

Our *hospitalero* came with the bill after ensuring we were wanting nothing further to eat or drink.

"Roxey, you look at it and figure out what we all owe. She can be very organized and professional sometimes, you know," he reassured our dinner partners. I tapped his shoulder with the bill in reproof.

I looked at the tally carefully, working out the items and said I thought there was a problem. The total just didn't make sense. Doing a quick tally, I found we had been undercharged by about fifty percent.

"Let me see," said Paul, and examined it himself. "Esther, you have a look," he said passing the bill.

"I think Roxey is right."

"We have to tell him," I insisted. "They're just starting out. They provided us with good beds, a nice place to rest, and a great (albeit slow) supper. It wouldn't feel right taking advantage of them."

"Yes, I think Roxey is right," agreed Zbigniew; Catharina nodded in agreement.

"It's one thing to get a good deal; it's another to profit from someone else's mistake," I said.

Paul called our *hospitalero* over and showed him that the bill was wrong. Our *hospitalero* maintained it was right, and Esther slipped into Spanish to explain the error. Finally, it dawned on our young host that he had not charged for enough suppers. His eyes shone as he thanked us for our honesty…and another bottle of wine arrived on the table.

Irma was fussing, ready for bed, so I walked Esther up to their room while Andi stayed with the others and had another glass of wine. Using the handrail for support, I tried to keep as much weight off my foot as I could.

"Do you remember when you asked me if you could help me make the reservations when we were back in Mazarife," I questioned Esther. She nodded. "All of my life, I have been the one that everyone goes to for help. When something goes wrong, I'm the one who fixes it. I am not used to being the one helped. It was strange, almost hard for me, and that is why I was so reluctant to answer."

"I knew there was something," Esther responded, touching my shoulder. "It should not have been such a hard decision for you. I just wanted to help."

"I needed to find the strength to let you help me, to be the one receiving help for a change. I have a favourite hymn from our church called the "Servant Song". It speaks of allowing me to serve you, but at the same time, allowing me the grace to let you be my servant too."

"That is beautiful. And today you helped me with English and Irma!" she declared as she passed the baby for a final goodnight hug. "Tomorrow, Andi would like to cook for you and Paul. We would invite all the others, but our place is not so big, and you are Irma's Camino grandparents. We have known you the longest. We would be happy if you would come. Paul has already said yes to Andi while you were walking with Irma."

"Of course," I said. "It would be happy to have supper with you. What can we bring?"

"Andi has everything worked out, and we will shop when we get there. You can bring some wine if you must bring something. We will call your cellphone when we arrive and give you directions to find us. Good night and sleep well." She hugged me and melted back into the darkness of their room.

When I entered the room, I went to close the door so I could dress in private before the men returned. There was no door! Maybe that was what bothered Catharina about the room when we first arrived.

I changed into my sleep clothes and pulled up my covers. As I drifted off to sleep, I wondered how I would manage the walk tomorrow. Maybe I could just put lots of tape on my foot and I'd be okay. I couldn't stop now. Not this close! My thoughts in turmoil, I finally gave into sleep, never even hearing the men return.

I awoke and swung my feet to the cool, tile floors. As I stood, a sharp tear of pain told me my right foot was going to be a problem today. Limping carefully to the washroom, Paul in the bunk across from me and Zbigniew, just around the corner, were still buried in their covers.

I popped a couple of ibuprofen and searched through my pack for some K-tape my son had armed me with for the journey. Paul disappeared to shower and I found my scissors, cutting lengths of the blue, adhesive tape. Not knowing quite how to wrap my foot, I guessed supporting the arch was the main objective. I had my socks pulled over the tape before Paul returned. I didn't want to alarm anyone and have them insist on medical attention that would slow me down, severing me from this group of people who had already become so important to me. Today I would just take it easy and stop to rest and elevate my foot if I needed to. Later, I would contact my son for his advice.

Down the stairs I crept, using the handrail and placing my feet carefully. Our *albergue* didn't provide breakfast, however the bar across the street's door was open wide, welcoming the early morning pilgrim trade. I just wanted coffee for now and settled at a table with Catharina, stirring the frothy milk into the dark coffee below. In through the door strolled Paul, and up to the bar he went, ordering toast and an espresso. Next came Zbigniew, smiling, but obviously early morning was not his best time.

Catharina waved as she pushed out the door, eager to be on the road. Gulping down his coffee, Paul returned to the bar for another espresso. We sorted through our various guidebooks, identifying the main route that would take us up and down some minor hills before a steady climb to Villafranca. Paul rose from the table and returned to the bar; this time coming back with a cup of camomile tea.

"You're having an identity crisis I think," I laughed. You have two cups of espresso to jack yourself up and then a cup of camomile tea to calm yourself down! And," I continued, "you're not sure if you love being English or would rather be Italian! You talk lovingly of Hull, and then you say you'd rather live in Italy. You sing Italy's praises, lapse into Italian phrases, and go on about their food and wine." By now Zbigniew was laughing and Paul was blustering with protest. "Then you are all about the beauty of the English countryside and your beloved Hull football team. I'm not sure you really know who you want to be."

"Well, I can love both. You can blame my mother for my love of Italy, but Hull has been my family home for years. We'll never leave," he protested.

"Lucky for you to have the freedom to travel and enjoy then," I suggested and he joined me in laughter.

The busy road of the night before was quiet now. A vigilant gardener was out pulling weeds between garden rows. Two housewives, clutching their cardigans against the morning cool, were in animated discussion across the low, stone wall that divided their laundry lines. Just as the number of houses dropped off, they increased again, and it was hard to tell where one little town ended and another began. In the distance, purple mountains beckoned us onward. Transport trucks racing noisily along the highway separated from our path by a tract of wild grasses.

Paul and Zbigniew pulled ahead steadily. I was struggling to keep up but didn't want to push myself. Soon, I was walking alone. I tapped along, transferring some of the weight from my foot to my pole. The trail continued to follow the roadway, undulating over gentle rises and falls. Pretty perfect walking conditions when you had a tender foot.

Suddenly, the track deviated right and I found myself on a dirt road, budding vineyards on either side. Down a gentle slope I went and before long, I was entering Cacabelos. I bypassed Prado del Tope, a well-known wine store built on the site of a former seventeenth-century hospital that had cared for pilgrims past. This area was famous for its wine and even boasted a wine museum depicting production processes over the years. Today I wasn't so much interested in wine as I was in finding a chair where I could sit and rest my foot for a while.

Travelling down the main road, a variety of options made finding respite easy. I stepped into the cool darkness of a bar and asked if it was possible to have two eggs and toast.

"It's possible," the friendly man behind the bar said and laughingly called my order into the kitchen. I don't know if he found the breakfast order odd at mid day, or if he was entertained by my attempt to request it in Spanish.

Delivering a cup of cold, fresh orange juice to my table, he ran a heavy hand through his silvering thick hair and asked where I was from. "Oh! Canada! I have a cousin who lives there." Unfortunately, I had to admit that I did not know his cousin, Manitoba being quite a distance from my home, but he didn't hold it against me as he returned with my plate of eggs.

Back out in the street, I saw an elderly man, impeccably dressed in polished shoes and a sweater vest, standing by the door of a small museum of religion. I poked my head in the door and passed my pilgrim passport to this welcoming guardian of relics of the past. The building was very small, but filled wall-to-wall with an impressive collection of paintings and statues depicting saints and religious events. One almost life-sized statue of Jesus riding on a donkey caused me to pause. The soft colours of the robes and the detail of the animal's fur seemed so real. Unfortunately, I wasn't able to understand all the things the curator was trying to tell me, but I appreciated the artistry no less. A gentle Madonna, enrobed in blue, her shining eyes and gentle smile, seeming to reach across the centuries to embrace my soul. I felt quiet, at peace, and somehow renewed. I pressed some euros in the collection box, accepted my stamped passport back from the smiling curator, and stepped back out into the sunshine.

Across the bridge, trudging up the side of the busy roadway, heat was already becoming an issue, and I strove to maintain a steady pace to accommodate my tender arch. A stout matron, hair tucked tightly under a kerchief, cardigan buttoned snugly across her ample chest, kept pace just ahead of me. Her straight skirt revealed thick, woollen stockings and sturdy shoes. Under one arm she'd tucked a soft, leather purse; a string bag of produce hung from the other. Upward we climbed in companionable silence, she with her load and me with mine.

At the top of the hill, I saw pilgrims ahead, their colourful packs disappearing over the other side. I stopped to take a drink of water. Eyeing the steady stream of cars and trucks, I prepared for the downhill trek. Suddenly there was a small, brown hand on my arm.

"No, no senora. You go that way," my small companion directed. I gestured uselessly after the departing pilgrims. "No. You go that way senora," she insisted. I nodded, and she smiled and waited. I looked in the direction she had suggested and found nothing to indicate this was the way. Still she stood there, waiting. Fine! I'll go this way. I could always backtrack when she was gone. I struck off down the dusty dirt track, and she waved me off before turning on her heel and disappearing down the shoulder of the road.

All around me ran rows of budding grape vines, a striped patchwork quilt of green rows on brown. The sun beat down, and a copse of whispering trees drew my eye down the curved farm track. I soon found myself enjoying the serenity of the country road, winding my way through vineyards and fruit tree orchards. Reaching up, I grasped a handful of juicy red cherries from a leafy branch. I spat stones in the dirt as I passed field after field, spying the occasional farmer out pruning their vines.

Eventually the road ran through a small collection of rundown buildings, jammed up against the hills on either side of the gravel road. Since I had no idea where I had gone, I had no idea where I was, so I just kept walking, following the dusty undulating country track.

Finally, I came around the corner and Villafranca del Bierzo appeared before my eyes. A large, squared-off stone church lay nestled between green hills, like a jewel in a setting. White plaster and stone houses supported by tall stilts, clung to the cliffs. The small city rolled with the terrain, all valleys and hills, and I continued downward following the curve of the impressive fifteenth-century Castillo Palacio de los Marqueses, stone turrets thrust towards the cobalt sky. Bypassing a bustling commercial area and a cheerful playground set amongst municipal gardens abundant with lush roses and carefully trimmed hedges, the Camino led me down to a river. Multi-storied buildings clung to the hill, and umbrella-filled decks hung over the rushing waters. I hoped one of those was my *albergue*.

Crossing the arched stone bridge, I followed the arrows until, just nearing the outskirts of town, I saw the sign for La Piedra. Inside the door, I dropped my pack, happy to relive my aching foot of some of the weight. A tall, thin young man greeted me and checked my name off in his registrar.

He must have noticed me limping gingerly, and he slowed his pace as I followed him up the twisting staircase. Two floors up he indicated the small communal kitchen, the showers, and washrooms, as well as small a lounge with a computer for pilgrim use. At the top of the next flight of stairs, Paul hung his head over the railing

"There you are! We were getting worried," he said. "You are the last to arrive."

The *hospitalero* led me across the bright yellow room, indicating the top bunk in the corner, above Catharina's was mine. Paul and Zbigniew both had bottom bunks. Ana's pack hung from the top bunk across from mine. Looking at the narrow rungs of the ladder, I cast my eye around the room.

"Is there any chance I could have that empty bottom bunk over there?" I asked.

"No, I am sorry. That one is reserved," our *hospitalero* advised.

"Well, is it possible that they take this top bed when they arrive, and I have the bottom bunk?" I was close to whining now and not proud of it.

"No, I am sorry. I have already given your group some bottom beds and must save that one for another group."

"But I'm just not sure I can handle the ladder with my sore foot," I protested, close to tears.

"I am sorry, Senora. This is the way it must be." He placed a consolatory hand on my shoulder before disappearing down the staircase. Paul and Catharina gathered around me.

"Your foot es hurt?" Catharina questioned, clucking comfortingly as I explained the pull in my arch.

"You can have my bed," ever generous Paul offered. But his bed was butted up against the staircase and I knew sleep would be difficult with the comings and goings of the large room. So, it seemed I was doomed to the top bunk.

I gathered my clean clothes and limped back downstairs to the showers, then back upstairs freshly dressed. Gingerly, I climbed the ladder and found, if I left my shoes on and stepped more to my toes, it wasn't too bad. Catharina watched my progress with concern, shaking her head as I climbed back down. I rattled off a text to my son, explaining my situation and asking assistance in proper foot wrapping technique.

"Are you okay to come out for a drink with us?" Paul asked. "We're not supposed to meet Esther and Andi until 7:00. There is a coffee shop just around the corner," he said, explaining that since it was built into the rock face of the hill, our *albergue* didn't have any sort of gathering area of its own.

On the walk over, we had shared our evening plans with Catharina, hoping she wouldn't feel hurt by being excluded from the invitation. She waved our worries aside, however, saying she would probably find Zbigniew and join Ana to share an evening meal. It was so great how we could all be so honest and no one got bent; everyone just seemed to go with the flow.

Settled around chairs on the small patio between a rock wall and the roadway, we were joined by Ana who had been off exploring on her own. Paul told Ana about my foot. At her worried glance, I told her I had it wrapped and was being careful with it. I expressed concern at how far it might be to Andi and Esther's apartment though.

Conversation over small cups of coffee ran the gamut with regard to our home lives. Ana was quiet as usual, but seemed to enjoy our company. We got, somehow, around to grocery shopping and were discussing the differences in how goods were sold in our respective countries. Catherine adjusted the burgundy sweater hanging around her shoulders as she set about explaining something about buying eggs in Belgium. At the vacant looks on our faces, one searching the missing information from the other, she gave a big sigh. And started again.

"*Des* chickens *es en zhe* top (she waved above her head)…and *dey* lay *des eggz*" (chicken clucking noises made)…and they come…" She rolled her hands giving the impression of something tumbling down. "*End* you take your bag, and you pick *ze eggz* and put *zem en ze* bag," she finished triumphantly, looking expectantly at each of us. Still nothing! We couldn't figure it out. One more time! She went through the whole story again, more hand motions, more chicken noises, and we were laughing so hard we had tears running down our faces.

"Okay, this is what I get from this," I said, wiping tears from my cheeks. "They keep the chickens in the store, where they lay their eggs, that come down a conveyor belt, and you choose and box your own eggs. Is this right, Catharina?" She folded her arms across her chest, looked at me in disgust, and gave a derisive snort. Still not sure if we'd gotten the story right, we all dissolved into laughter, the corners of Catharina's lips losing their fight not to smile.

Zbigniew sauntered up, hatted and scarved, looking like a man about town. He pulled a bottle of wine from a bag, offering it to fill our empty coffee cups.

"Where did you get that?" Paul asked.

"There, at the *mercado*." Zbigniew waved his hand towards the large building we had passed earlier.

"Oh," I took Paul's lead, "we have to get wine for supper. Guess we have to get going soon. Did you get an address yet Paul?" He checked his cellphone.

"Yes, it looks like it's close to the fort, across the bridge, and back up by the park. They're expecting us in an hour."

"You take taxi?" questioned Catharina, looking pointedly at my foot.

"We should be okay. We have lots of time, and we'll just take it slow," I assured her.

"Okay, but no *nee, nee, nee en ze* morning!" she warned. We all laughed at her translation of whining.

Zbigniew settled into Paul's vacated chair, and we waved farewell to our friends, off in search of wine.

"Probably red," Paul suggested. "It seems everyone drinks red with everything here." I nodded my agreement.

"What about picking up some beer and lemon pop to make shandies?" I suggested. His turn to nod.

Paul insisted on carrying our purchases. We crossed the bridge and walked up to the park. Laughing children's voices filled the air as vigilant mothers watched from benches. Sidewalk cafes were filled with locals and pilgrims enjoying drinks and food in the warm evening air. Even the bustling traffic had slowed, the cobblestone roads quiet as well. We walked one way and could not find the markers Esther had explained in her text. Then we tried another; Paul's battery was fading. Finally, I asked an elderly man where to find the street she had mentioned. He motioned back the way we had come, and the hunt began again. I was just starting to think Catharina may have been right about taking a taxi, when Esther appeared around the corner of a building at the end of the street.

"There you are. I thought maybe my directions were not good." Gallant as ever, Paul said she did just fine, and we looked at each other conspiratorially, a silent pact made not to admit we had been lost.

"Here they are," Esther called out as she welcomed us through the door. The small apartment was hot and steamy, Andi happily cooking at the two-burner stove in the galley kitchen along one wall. Irma was playing on the floor next to a small couch. A table set for four, accompanied by an old wooden highchair, sat against the back wall, its windows overlooking the street. Pretty tight confines, but better than a bunk in the corner, I thought.

"This is great!" I exclaimed. Paul handed Esther the wine and beer, and she happily set about making shandies as I bent to pick Irma up.

"We have also a bedroom with a baby bed, and of course the bathroom. It has no tub, but we can wash Irma here in the sink, when I do the dishes!" Andi laughed, stirring a bubbling pot.

Paul and I sat on the couch, while Esther perched on the arm. Irma, bouncing on my knee, was busy playing with Paul's watch. He slipped it off and much to Esther's horror, handed it to the baby.

"She can't hurt it!" he laughed, as she promptly folded the links into her mouth.

Andi called out to Esther, and she returned with an appetizer of figs wrapped with lean sausage slices.

Seated at the table, Andi ladled creamy mushroom and onion soup into crockery bowls. We tore pieces off a crusty loaf and dipped it into the fragrant chowder. Heaven! We heaped compliments on our abashed host and cleaned our bowls, preparing for the next course. Haven given up Paul's watch, Irma had moved on to a rusk of bread and was busily blowing bubbles and making baby noises.

"She has two new teeth," pronounced her mama as she hooked a finger under her daughter's top lip to reveal two little white pearls. "And there is more coming soon!" Amazingly, Irma continued to be a happy baby, with none of the fussing and crying teething usually generates. Andi returned to the table, handing her a frozen wedge of cucumber, and she went right to work, gnawing on the icy spear.

"I thought you may be tired of French fries," Andi explained as he placed plates of a vegetable rice concoction. "I have not all my spices. But I think it will be okay." It was more than okay, and we happily lifted our plates for refills.

"And we have a special dessert!" Esther announced, inviting us back to the couch. Andi dragged a kitchen chair over for him and for Esther, as she brought over a plate containing two wedges of cheese and some grapes. "The cheese is very special to this region. We get it always when we come here."

"We will stay here two days and then we will start again. We will arrive in Santiago on the 8th. That is two days after you, I think," Esther said. We nodded confirming I would be flying out on the 9th, and Paul on the 10th.

"That is perfect," Andi smiled.

"We would like you to join us for supper at a very nice restaurant in Santiago," Esther continued. "We can call you when we get in and let you know when the reservation is for." Knowing Catharina would still be with us, I suggested she make the reservation for one more.

"Of course," responded Esther. "And now, for tomorrow, where do you stay?" I told her that we planning on Ruitelan, and she advised there was only one place there and it was good. I suggested I was thinking of Hospital da Condessa. "I would suggest you go on to Fon Fria. That is a nice place; we will stay there. In Triacastela there are many good options, and then you will be near Sarria. In Sarria, the new pilgrims begin. They are the ones who choose to walk only the last hundred kilometres. You will find them rude, I think." Andi nodded in agreement.

"They are in a rush and push past everyone; the Spanish men are the worst. They think they are entitled and do not wait in line. All you can do is be patient with them," she offered.

By now, the sun was beginning to set, and it was looking like Irma was ready for sleep also, so we thanked our gracious hosts and hugged them goodbye.

"See you in Santiago." A light evening shower started to fall as we made our way back to our *albergue*.

Up in our room, the others were waiting. The men decided to go across the street for a last night cap. I told the girls that Esther had recommended the *albergue* in Ruitelan. Ana smiled and said she had a reservation there. I told Catharina I'd go make a reservation for us if she liked.

I asked the *hospitaleros* to call ahead to Ruitelan to reserve a bed for Catharina and me. They were happy to help, saying they knew the brothers who ran that *albergue*, and we would enjoy staying there. The men came back from their drink, and asked if we would mind their booking the same place.

"Of course not," I smiled. It was heart warming they wanted to stay together. Once Paul confirmed that he and Zbigniew had beds at the same place, everyone wrote down the name of the *albergue* and the phone number in case we got separated through the next day.

Checking my phone, I smiled, finding foot taping instructions from my son. Even long distance, he was trying to take care of me. I pulled my blanket down onto the floor and followed the diagrams he had sent, cutting the K tape and applying it securely. I put my socks on so that my night's sleep wouldn't disturb the tape. Leaving my sandals on, I climbed the ladder carefully, stashing them at the end of my bunk for my descent in the morning.

Despite the damp and the snoring, I drifted off to sleep knowing we had beds for tomorrow, and that we would all be together at day's end. We were now the "Final Five", and we would all share meals, rooms and more for many days to come.

Lying on my bunk in semi-darkness, I pulled my leggings off and wriggled into my pants. Due to the chilly damp, I'd slept in my walking shirt, so after checking my taping, I was ready for the day. Putting my sandals on to protect my damaged arch from the ladder rungs, I gently crawled over the side of the bunk. Catharina was up, dressed, and efficiently tucking things into her pack. Ana was just disappearing down the stairs. Across the room, Paul, kit in hand, was headed down for his morning shower, while Zbigniew was still in bed, covers pulled up to his chin in denial.

Zbigniew was a bit of an enigma to me. His thick, flowing white curls framed a leathery face that had lived a lot. His sparkling blue eyes were often full of mischief and laughter, however a shadow of sadness never seemed to leave them. His charming accent was born to him in Poland, then flavoured by three decades of living in Sweden. Zbigniew was a gentleman, with old-country manners bespeaking a renaissance style. Regardless of his tall, slim frame, it was apparent, by the care he took in wrapping his legs and by the fact he ported his pack, that he struggled with some challenges. He never seemed to rush; an elegant stork, moving with long, relaxed strides. Zbigniew held no appreciation of early rising and was usually the last of our group to finish dressing. I got the feeling he'd much rather lounge in the morning, sharing coffee and bright conversation with friends. I was looking forward to getting to know him better and finding out what had brought him on this journey.

Downstairs, Catharina and I joined the dance in the bustling reception-area-turned-breakfast-room where pilgrims juggled cups of hot coffee, vying for use of the toaster that really only warmed up the bread. At a table with Ana, we reserved spots with bowls of cereal and glasses of juice while pulling cups of yogurt from the vending machine.

To put the rain shell on or not to put the rain shell on was the main topic of conversation. One brave pilgrim, seeking a weather report, opened the front door to the sound of rushing water and then with smiles we realized it was river noise, not rain noise. As we were clearing our dishes into the kitchen bin, Paul hurriedly arrived to claim the space we were vacating.

"Walk on… I'll catch up," he cheerfully called.

Zbigniew's status still in question, we shouldered our packs, walking out to rain-drenched cobblestones and mist-shrouded mountains. Erring on the side of caution, Ana and I had pulled our rain shells over our packs. Catharina's pack sent ahead, she traveled with a small canvas daypack in which, knowing her practical approach, a rain poncho lay waiting its turn to walk.

Morning tentatively broke over the hillside with a promising glow of sunshine that transformed the clouds into puffs of yellow and pink cotton candy. We crossed the bridge, left the rushing river behind and poled past sleeping farms, up a gentle climb. Yellow arrows beckoned us along the roadway curving around the side of the mountain. As the mist turned to drizzle, I looked ahead and saw pilgrims snugging rain covers over their packs and dragging ponchos over their heads.

My new taping technique working, my steps fell into a comfortable rhythm and Catherine gradually pulled ahead, joined by Paul who had quickly caught up. Corralled between the protective steel barriers that created safety from the ravine drop on one side and oncoming vehicles on the other, Catharina and Paul trod on before me, without ponchos, bare legged, and seemingly oblivious to the light rain.

Two hour's walk later, in Trabadelo, seeing abandoned poles and packs tucked under the porch of a rustic bar, I pulled off my poncho and left my pack to wait with the others. Through the rough plank door, I was met with the muffled hum of conversation and the sudden whoosh of the espresso machine as the young man behind the bar delivered another cup of steaming *café con leche* into cold, waiting hands. The barista's brilliant red sports jersey seemed a sharp contrast to the aged stonework walls, slab floor, and heavy, dark timbers of the low ceiling room. Through the dim lighting, I saw Paul, Zbigniew, and Catharina huddled around their coffees at an oilskin-covered table, wet jackets slung over their tall wooden chair backs.

How did Zbigniew do that? He was the last to leave, yet here he was before me! Must have been when I took a bathroom break at Pereje. And where had I lost Ana? Must have been zoned out. After a quick stop at the washroom, I collected my coffee and joined the others.

"Did you sleep well?" Paul asked.

"Noooo," answered Catharina, searching for English words. "Too much *snorkeling en das* night!"

We other three looked at each other blankly. "Oh," the light dawned, "you mean snoring," I suggested.

Perplexed by the difference of my pronunciation and hers she agreed, "*Ya, much snorkeling.*" We all burst out laughing.

"Catharina, the word is 'snoring,'" Paul gently corrected. Cocking her head, the difference finally seemed to sink in, and she smiled.

Paul and Zbigniew lingered, ordering second cups of coffee while Catharina and I went out to brave the rain. We stepped out of the warm bar to find the rain had slowed to almost a stop, so I stowed my poncho and we shouldered our packs, just as another cloud burst pelted down. Catharina, rolled her eyes in disgust. Off came the packs, out came the ponchos, and on we walked through the depressing drizzle. At some point, Catharina drifted off behind me as I strode on, determined to get to Ruitelan and out of the rain.

Passing through Vega de Valcarce, I resisted the invitation of restaurants offering hot pies and tasty desserts. Maybe I should stop, just to have a hot drink and warm up. But no, I didn't think anyone would appreciate my dripping all over their floors while I divested myself of layers of sodden clothing. Then too, I would have to put the clammy, wet stuff back on and that would just be disgusting.

As I left the town behind me, the rain pounded down harder and the roadway became a river. I suddenly noticed, a pilgrim walking by my side. Despite the layers of rain protection, she seemed familiar and I realized it was Ana. I murmured it wasn't far now, wondering if I was trying to reassure her or myself.

"I hope," Ana replied quietly. In silence, we trod on.

I was starting to feel the damp through my boots. My pant legs were sopping wet, clinging around my calves, and my poncho, having reached maximum water saturation, was plastered against my body. My cold hands ached from the death grip I had on my rain-slicked poles. I focused on the road in front of me, willing myself to keep going, one foot in front of the other; she kept time with me. Around another corner we trekked, seeing the first signs for Ruitelan posted on fences behind which a herd of sorrowful cows stood dripping in the rain. The hills ran with instant streams, and the pasture they stood in looked marshy and dismal. On we marched in the deluge, finally coming to the first buildings of the one-street town. I looked ahead and saw hanging over the age-old buildings, an expanse of modern vehicular bridgework spanning the heights between the mountains, dwarfing the tiny hamlet.

Congratulating ourselves upon our arrival at the old white building proclaiming itself as the only *albergue* in town, we followed the path around the back to find the door locked and a sign saying that the *albergue* would open in another two hours.

Suppressing a groan, I turned to find Ana, as miserably drenched as I was, holding her cellphone and asking if I would take her picture.

"They all think I'm having a lovely time in sunny Spain. They'll never believe this if they don't see it!" she laughed, her glasses awash and water dripping off her elbows. As I took the photo of my soggy new friend, I too started to laugh.

We squelched across the street, in search of shelter and a hot drink, pushing open the door of a darkened bar. One of the two stocky Spanish grandmothers pulled her cardigan tightly around her shoulders, muttering at disgust at the water pooling around our boots and huffed off into the kitchen. The younger of the two approached us, smiling, gesturing to the stair rail across the room where we could hang our dripping ponchos. Having mopped a few floors in my life, my guilt was offset only by the need to be free of the clinging wetness. Settling into the round chairs nearest the door, we wrapped our numb hands around the little cups of heaven that was Spanish hot chocolate.

"You set a good pace," Ana commented. Our first real time to talk, we easily unloaded our stories. By the time our cups were drained, I knew she was in her mid-fifties and retired from a banking position in Porto Alegre, Brazil. Her newly-married daughter, Marina, lived in England.

Ana spoke wistfully of visiting her daughter in England on the way home, and from the shine in her soft brown eyes, I knew how much they missed each other. I asked, since she was retired, and her only child lived in England, why she stayed in Brazil. She softly replied that her elderly parents lived near her home and relied on her visits. I understood that feeling of wanting to be in a different place while duty, combined with love, held you hostage somewhere else. She faced a tug of war of not wanting them to need her, and at that same time dreading the time they would not be there to need her.

Ana had started her Camino in Pamplona and was not firm in her plans to walk to Finisterre or stop at Santiago. Her fly out date was the day before mine, so she had to decide to move faster or forego Finisterre.

The bar quickly filled with newly-arrived pilgrims and the blame for the wet floor was no longer ours alone. Catharina arrived, quickly followed by Paul, who ordered red wine and wondered if there was any chance the TV would be broadcasting an important football game from England.

As opening time for the *albergue* approached, there was a hurried collection of discarded gear and a rush for the door. Doubts crowded my mind; not having been able to leave packs to hold our place in the rain. I sure hoped our reservation stood. Several people surged through the doorway before us and more pushed from behind. Some frantically called out to the friendly-looking Spanish man, panic in their voices as they clamoured for beds.

"Please, I am not a woman, just a man, and I can only do one thing at a time!" the *hospitalero* called out, smiling despite the chaos. Well he won the hearts and cooperation of at least half of the pilgrims with that statement! Quietly, I stepped forward.

"We have a reservation for four beds," I said, proffering my passport and indicating my amigos behind me. Seeing a way to clear out four at once, he registered us, indicating the room for six across the hall and saying he would take payment later. I told him one other in my group had not arrived yet, but Ana, moving in our wake was quick to be registered next. She too, had a reservation, but not in our room. Our *hospitalero* directed her to a "ladies dorm" next to the reception area.

Our room of three sets of bunks had a lovely, tall window that opened onto the street where we saw Zbigniew jauntily striding up the road. Having missed out on a bottom bunk the day before, I claimed the one in the corner just as he came strolling through the door.

Catharina and I met Ana in the hall, and in turn, life-restoring hot showers were taken. It seems there are never any hooks for your clothes or dry places to change, so in the interest of getting the next person in the shower and keeping our clothes dry, we took turns dressing in the toilet closet.

Returning to the room, we found the reason for Zbigniew's delay. He had stopped at the local *mercado* to purchase cheese and wine. He slipped out to the common room and came back with glasses, and pulling out a decorative little knife, divided the cheese for all of us. Catharina contributed a banana, Paul mints, and I added my bag of dried apricots; a veritable buffet! We toasted our survival of the rain with cups of wine, doing our best to ignore the sign stating that eating in the rooms was prohibited. Somehow it seemed okay since we were all partaking and no one was left out.

Having fortified ourselves with our illicit bounty, we set about nesting. It appeared that despite the shortage of Camino beds, we four would have the room to ourselves, leaving two top bunks empty. Catharina and I quickly adopted the extra quilts to speed up the warming process after our cold, wet walk. I unpacked my bag, reassured as I pulled out dry clothes, that the water proofing had done its job.

"Oh no!" Paul shouted. Now what had he lost? He kept losing things only to find them after a few minutes of panic. But no, his sweater really was missing. Sure that he had left it behind that morning, he arranged a taxi to take him back to Villafranca to look for it.

"Does anyone want to come for a ride?" he asked. I was just starting to warm up and as I looked out the tall, wood-framed window at the sodden world, I was in no rush to go out again. Also, I knew I would find it disheartening to travel by taxi in minutes the distance I had walked for hours in the pouring rain. No one else seemed interested in going either, so Paul cheerfully wandered off down the hall to wait for his taxi.

Zbigniew, Catharina, and I lounged in our beds, snuggled under quilts, chatting comfortably. I asked Zbigniew how it was he lived in Sweden, knowing he had been born in Poland.

"Well," his words dragged out. "I moved there after prison."

"You were in prison? Why were you in prison?" I asked, instantly regretting my inquisitive reaction. I would never have asked anyone that back home, but somehow the Camino freed us to discuss previously taboo subjects.

"It was political. I was a political prisoner. I was a journalist and what I wrote was a truth they did not want to hear. They took me from my family, and I was in prison. I was in prison for five months." His eyes clouded at the memory.

"Did they treat you okay?" I asked.

"No! I was tortured both mentally and physically. The only good and light was when my wife came to visit. It was a while before she found me. They took me and did not tell her where I was."

"So how did you end up in Sweden?" my curiosity overtook my tact.

"The communist regime wanted me to leave my country of birth. We had no rights and could not get jobs. Political militias took away everything that I wanted for my family. I ran the risk of more prison. After struggling to stay in the country, I was forced to leave. We were issued passports without the right to return to Poland. So, I took my wife and my baby son, Piotr, and we go to Sweden. I leave all the rest of my family behind. I leave my mother behind." As emotion took over, Zbigniew's English became fragmented. Catharina sighed her concern in the corner.

"So, you never get to see your family?" I asked in shock.

"Oh no!" he rallied. "In 1989, Solidarity won and the communists lost power, so I could go back to see my family. But for me, my son, and my daughter, they grew mostly in Sweden, so I don't take them back to Poland to live. Just for visits. And then, when their mother died last year…" So now I understood the sadness that always seemed to haunt his eyes. I understood it well, having gone through a similar loss. "My son and my daughter, Maja, are my world…and my grandchildren," he smiled sadly. "And now," he said raising his glass of wine, "I walk, I travel, and I meet new friends." Like the day, his rain was over and the sun shone valiantly through the clouds.

How amazing, I mused, to meet these people from all over the world, with all these stories and life experiences. It was a trip of discovery in more ways than one, and my respect for this courageous man was profound.

When he returned waving his sweater triumphantly a short while later, Paul and Zbigniew decided since it had stopped raining, they'd go for a walk, which was code language for a search for more wine and somewhere to watch the football game.

I learned very quickly that all Europeans seem crazy about football. I walked across the hall to check with Ana about moving in with us, but she had settled already and was happy to be with all women. I told her the guys were trying to find somewhere to watch the football match, and she confessed that she couldn't possibly really be Brazilian since she didn't like football!

Catharina joined Ana and I in the common room where journals were written and Wi-Fi accessed for updates to and from home. Tomorrow's walk involved a demanding climb through O Cebreiro, to the highest point in the Camino. Given that, I had planned to make a shorter day stopping at Hospital da Condesa. Ana and I put our heads together over our guide books considering the options. Ana felt we could go further and Alto do Poio was only 18.3 kilometres of walking. Esther had recommended Fonfria, but we were concerned that with the demands of the climb and the forecast rain, the additional four kilometres would be too much for some in our group. We were now a group! So with a compromise between my shorter plan and Esther's longer recommendation, Ana called ahead to Alto do Poio and reservations for five were made.

Our *hospitalero's* brother, the cook, chased everyone out of the common room to prepare for dinner.

"The cows come," Catharina, gazing out the window, announced in her heavy Belgian accent. Not really sure what she was talking about, I joined her. Sure enough, those same soggy cows we had passed earlier were being driven home by a small truck at their heels. As the lead animals trotted into the compound beside the building next to ours, a momma cow all of a sudden broke form, her creamy calf quick on her heels. There was a lot of laughter as we watched frustrated bystanders attempt to herd the cow and her little one back towards the gate when finally, after another pause, she finally consented to enter the coral. It was better than the television that unfortunately wouldn't be showing the coveted football match. Cellphone updates from Hull would have to do.

The common room doors opened, revealing the family-style wooden table, flanked by plain, backless benches, laid out for thirty hungry pilgrims. As I took my place beside Ana, the brothers cheerfully served us an amazing cream of carrot soup accompanied by baskets of thick, crusty bread, and followed by salad platters bearing layers of lettuce, tomatoes, crescents of soft, white cheese, and the proverbial canned tuna. The main course, creamy, pasta carbonara was washed down with goblets of *vino tinto*.

The cook (now upgraded by the pilgrims to a chef) bashfully entered the room to rounds of applause. As the table was cleared, the brothers bid us goodnight and reminded us no one was to get up before they heard the music in the morning, at which time breakfast would be served. Payment of five euros for the night's bed and a donation for supper and breakfast would only be accepted then. Given the quality of the supper, donations were likely to be high.

We tucked into our rooms, snug under fresh quilts, wondering what music would wake us from our dreams.

My face jammed into the soft pillow, I cracked an eye to see if anyone else in the room was hearing what I was hearing; no one was stirring. The potential Camino hallucinations they warn you about had finally got me! I could hear angels singing *Ave Maria*. Suddenly, Paul's balding head popped up like a prairie dog. Catharina turned over and muttered a Dutch oath, looking askance at the door.

"Niiiiice," smiled Zbigniew widely as he rolled on his back and pushed his unruly white mane back from his brow. So it wasn't just me! They heard it too. Then I remembered our *hospitalero* brothers saying everyone was to stay in bed until they heard the music. We had drifted off to sleep last night wondering what "the music" would be and now we knew. Well, it could be worse!

Out of bed we rolled, feet hitting the rough, planked floor, heads habitually bent to prevent banging them on the bunks above. Paul hopped down from his top bunk, grabbed his kit bag, and scurried down the hall, racing for the single shower. Still wasn't sure why our English friend found it so important to start the day with a shower when we knew we'd all be bathed in sweat in no time. But, to each their own Camino.

Zbigniew lay back, eyes closed, enjoying the music as Catharina and I systematically pulled on clothes and packed our bags. Paul burst back in through the door, hurriedly finished pulling his trekking pants over his shorts, and scrambled to get the rest of his things together. Zbigniew, now in a sitting position on the end of his bed, was carefully wrapping his troublesome leg. Catharina and I shuffled out the door to join our misplaced Camino sister, Ana, in the dining room. Louie Armstrong's *Wonderful World* filled the room, and the three of us shared a morning hug.

Hot coffee, hot milk, granola, toast, jam, juice, biscuits, cakes, and even fruit. It was as good a breakfast as the meal at last night's supper had been. As I looked around at the relaxed and appreciative faces of those enjoying their creamy coffees, I knew that the donations would reflect the true value of the meals. Sight unseen, or taste untasted, donations beforehand might have been minimal, but all of us knew that the hospitality we had experienced with the brothers in Ruitelan was extraordinary, and it would take a chintzy pilgrim not to pay their due.

Out into the mist-shrouded world we walked, climbing now the wet and muddy path to O Cebreiro, the Camino's steepest climb since the Pyrenees. Anticipating the work ahead, and remembering my Camino mentor's recommendations, I had caved and had my backpack ported along with the others to our next stop at Alto de Poio. Although I still carried a small daypack, I felt naked and alone without the big hug of my pack and I worried that the bag might not be there when I got there.

I got over missing the weight though, as enveloped in already clinging, wet rain ponchos, we continued to climb the steep and slippery slope, driving our poles into the mud for support as we went. Rising above the valley floor, we followed the remnants of an ancient Roman road, sharp-edged rocks exposed by weather and time. I couldn't help wonder what it would have been like to march an invading army along this track, pushing and dragging carts up the mountainside. I could almost hear the nervous horses neighing as they sought firm footing, and the heavily laden soldiers grunting with exertion as they put shoulders to wheels stalled by rocks and mud.

Stoic Catharina, challenged by the grade, had as usual dropped back. We knew she would catch up when we hit level ground where her determined stride would probably leave us watching her day pack march away, at least until the next climb. I could hear murmurs from the Korean couple just ahead of me and as I caught up, I realized they were chanting each other up the hill. She would recite a verse, and he would reply. Now I can't say for sure their words were prayers (not speaking Korean myself), but they certainly had the cadence of psalms being read in church. I pushed myself, straining to catch their rhythm and enjoying the beauty of their connection and devotion to their God and to each other.

I turned back to Ana, who, glasses speckled with raindrops, was working to keep up.

"They're praying," I answered her quizzical glace. She smiled gently, and we followed in the chanters' wake, focussing on the melody of their words rather than the challenge of the climb. The path finally flattened out, and as we drew abreast of the pausing couple, I thanked them for their prayers, telling them they had helped me up the hill as well.

"God be with you," said the smiling couple, with shallow bows. It's funny that as much as we are different, we are more the same.

Passing the standard chicken coop that welcomed us on the outskirts of every tiny town, we paused at La Faba, but the line at the small coffee bar was so long, we continued our climb. Right behind us a tall, young man strode along with his music blaring. I looked at Ana who merely smiled and shrugged. Even after 600 kilometres and thirty days as a pilgrim, I had not achieved the peaceful tolerance of my Brazilian friend.

One of the unwritten rules on the Camino is that you use earphones and don't inflict your choice for music on other pilgrims seeking a more natural, reflective journey. I slowed my pace and let him pass. As I had learned, a small pause is all it took to part ways with someone you didn't want to share the trail with. When we arrived at Laguna de Castilla a short while later, I was glad to see him and his blaring music walk on.

Laguna was the last outpost in Castile for a meal. We pulled off our dripping ponchos and hung them on the hooks wisely provided outside the door. Inside, the inviting sound of coffee steaming into mugs welcomed us. Our orders of bacon, eggs, and toast had just arrived at our table as Paul and Catharina staggered through the door, wiping raindrops from their brows. After putting their breakfast orders in at the bar, they dragged battered wooden chairs up to our table and plunked themselves down beside us. I pushed my plate across the table towards them offering my remaining bacon and toast while they waited for theirs. My favourites, the eggs were gone. The freshness and rich, deep orange yolks spoke of free-range chickens strutting around the backyard.

"Quite a climb!" Paul exclaimed as he reached over and downed a strip of bacon.

The grandmother behind the bar welcomed a small, dark-haired boy of about three who had just run in, arms outstretched, from the living quarters at the back. I was missing my grandchildren and envied the tight hug he gave her, his dark curls disappearing into the folds of her cardigan. The last time I had spoken to Al, my grandson was visiting, and he'd asked if I'd like to talk to him. After a brief pause I said no. It was heart wrenching enough to hear Al's voice so far away. If I heard Matthew's voice, I'd be done for.

Weather aside, the climb hadn't been as bad as I had expected to this point. Had I just built this section up to be some big thing in my mind or had my strength and endurance improved that much? I'm sure not having my twenty-pound pack on my back probably made a difference. No one had seen Zbigniew yet, and we hoped the climb wasn't giving his leg too much trouble.

Resuming our wet climb, the trail wound its way up and around the mountain, gifting us with spectacular views of the valley below. Suddenly two women appeared on the trail, clipboards in hand, not seeming to be deterred by the rain. In my sodden state, not knowing enough Spanish to know what they wanted, I waved them away. Paul stopped and I saw him signing a board as we reached a marker announcing we were now entering Galicia. We stopped for soggy photo ops as we waited for him to catch up.

"It was a petition," Paul shared, although he seemed a little vague about what is was for. I wondered what importance some random pilgrim's signature would hold on a mountainside in Spain. Maybe it was about installing some rest stops or toilets along the path; that would be helpful.

"They were gypsies," Ana warned sagely, having a bit better handle on Spanish than the rest of us. The dark clouds in her eyes suggested she had experienced negative aspects of the gypsy culture before. I had been warned about pick pockets in Paris using just this type of charade to hold your attention while their partners relived you of your valuables. What did they think they might get out of toiling pilgrims? We didn't even have our packs with us and our valuables were buried safely inside our pockets under our ponchos. Even if they had gained access to my pack, the best they would have found was my previous day's laundry.

We continued up the hill and wandered into the foggy hamlet of O Cebreiro. I have to admit I was disappointed. I had anticipated a crown on the mountain; a bustling village waiting to welcome us. Instead we found a silent collection of about twenty mist-enfolded buildings. Other than one bar displaying souvenirs, everything looked pretty locked down. Excepting a straggling pack of soggy pilgrims, there was no one in sight. The church (as we had often found along the way) was locked, and the cobblestone streets ran with rain. In conflict with the forbidding stone-faced houses, off to one side I spied a couple of mystical structures and realized these were the Celtic *pallozas* I had read about. Their round, low-built stone walls, topped by sloping thatched roofs, were meant to house and shelter animals in ancient times. I wasn't sure if they were still in use, but I really wouldn't have been at all surprised to see a hobbit pop out one of the tiny wooden doors.

Our climb was not yet done, and finally we approached Alto do San Roque, where the altitude of 1270 metres made it the highest point of the Camino, this side of the Pyrenees. For my companions who had started their journey in Spain, this would be their mountain-top moment. Unfortunately, it was saturated with rain and the promised "spectacular views" were no-shows. Paul pushed on, disappearing down the trail into the mist.

Ana, Catharina, and I crossed the empty roadway and, buffeted by wind and rain, took photos of each other posing with a huge iron sculpture of a bare-footed pilgrim (San Roque?) holding his hat on his head with one hand as he too leaned into the wind. Standing to his waist height, we looked pretty sad in our soggy ponchos, but we rallied smiles for the camera just the same.

Despite the raincloud surrounding us, as we began our descent, we could see rays of sun piercing the clouds and striking the valley floor below. We arrived at Hospital da Condesa, the place I had originally thought to stay, and found only one lone building, but the hot coffee and use of a real bathroom were a welcome respite from the drizzle.

The trail continued to lead gently downwards, winding around hills and through glens. With every building, our hopes were raised that our trial was over. This looks good…no, this is not it. Keep going. Really, it should be any moment now. The markers sent us down a narrow trail that again, surprisingly, began to climb. Up ahead, on a ledge above the path, we saw the stone wall of a structure, and we knew this was where we must now climb. Breathing hard, pounding up the steep, loose-gravel grade, we crested the bushes to find two dreary buildings hunkered down in the onslaught of rain, facing off against each other on either side of an asphalt road.

Under the sagging awning dripping with rain, a sad collection of bright orange plastic chairs and tables jumbled up beside the *albergue* door provided sporadic shelter for a collection of fussing chickens seeking respite from the weather. Two big black dogs, their shaggy coats slick with water, lumbered towards us, barking as they came. Cautiously we approached and as the gap between us closed, the dogs, having asserted their power, ran off towards the scruffy backyard of the *albergue*. Gingerly, I dodged murky puddles and tentatively toed a chicken out of the way to drag the heavy wooden door open, Ana and Catharina following on my heels.

Inside the low-ceilinged great room there was a buzz of conversation from pilgrims seated on long wooden benches on either side of a huge trestle table that pretty much filled the room. We shook the worst of the wet off our ponchos and pulled them off over our heads, balling them up in a pile by the door. Squeezing along the wall, we located the *hospitalero* behind the bar. She wiped her hands on her apron, happily crossed our reservation off the list, took our money, and stamped our passports.

Just then we heard Paul call out; he had made it here before us and shouted from across the table that he had already checked in and that our packs hadn't arrived yet. Great! That was what I had been afraid of. Summoning my inner-pilgrim power, I intoned, "The bags will come...the bags will come," and looked up to see Ana smiling at my new mantra, mouthing the words herself. This was the first time she had ported her bag too, and she appreciated my inner struggle between doubting and trusting.

Paul managed to extricate himself from behind the table and trailed behind as our *hospitalero* showed us to our beds. Rather than taking us through the doorway leading upstairs, the stout Spaniard woman led us back outside, through the chickens and the rain, to a door on the side of the building. We entered the sleeping quarters, a big L-shaped room with rows of metal bunks lining the cold, damp, tiled walls. We were advised for the thirty beds there were two toilet rooms that also contained the showers, both of which were already in use. That didn't really matter since our bags were not here yet (the bags will come...) and we had no dry clothes to change into.

Paul showed us his chosen bunk near the uncurtained window, the glass as wet on the inside as it was on the outside. Having nothing else to use to lay claim to bunks, we spread out the scratchy woollen blankets at the foot of our chosen bunks to assert our claim. Placing my hat and gloves by the pillow, I reserved the bunk above mine for Zbigniew rather than leaving him stuck with the remaining bunk by the drafty door. We hadn't seen him all day, but we knew he'd show up; his bag was coming here along with the rest of ours...the bags will come...

Not having much else to do but wait for the tardy bags, we shuffled back into the dimly lit great room and carried cups of steaming hot *coffee con leche* back to the tables where we squeezed in between those already seated. There was a small brick fireplace burning brightly in the front corner of the room where an old woman in a kerchief and cardigan was enthroned in a big stuffed chair, defiantly blocking the heat from the rest of the room. Searching warmth, I sidled down towards that end of the bench and smiled at her. She made absolutely no response to my friendly overture. With my characteristic need to think the best of everyone, I decided maybe she didn't see too well.

Chilled by the lack of welcome rather than warmed by the fire, I slid back up the bench to find Ana had ordered soup, Catharina a slice of tortilla, and Paul, a bottle of red wine. While I mused over the limited offerings of the sticky menu card in the middle of the table, Zbigniew strutted through the door, his signature blue hat and striped scarf somewhat drooping, but stylish just the same. Paul put a glass of red wine in his hand and once he was registered, we took him out and showed him our dismal sleeping quarters.

"Not here yet," I replied to his questioning search about the room for our bags. The bags will come...

Finally, the bags did come, and there was a scramble to hit the shower and change into dry clothes. My turn to be first, I promised to be quick. When I opened the bathroom door, I was appalled. The walls ran with moisture and mould grew in the crevices around the shower stall. The floor around the sink and toilet was thick with dirt, hair, and Lord only knows what. I decided I might come out dirtier than when I went in, so I opted just to change, struggling to keep my dry, clean clothes off the floor, putting my worn clothes in a plastic bag to launder at the next possible chance.

"Was the water hot?" Ana questioned. I just rolled my eyes and told her what to expect. Both she and Catharina went in, changed, and came out in record time. I should have pushed for Fon Fria, I thought.

In the corner, a large, bearded man lay snoring noisily in his bunk, the sounds reverberating off the tiled walls. If this was an example of the volume just this one pilgrim would generate, we sighed at the thought of a sleepless night.

"Is this all there is? Is there nowhere else?" pondered a discouraged Zbigniew.

"Well there's another building across the street. Let's go check it out. At least there may be more food choices for supper." Ana suggested, and we pulled our coats around us, piled out into the driving rain, and ran across the road to the other building.

Inside, we found a warm, bustling room, with a cheerful Spaniard pouring drinks behind the bar. We crowded around a wooden table in the corner, resting our weary backs against the alcove walls as Zbigniew sauntered over, putting bottles of wine and glasses on the table. It was his generous custom to share wine with the group, and we happily obliged him. He would always say we could get it next time, but it was a challenge to beat him to it.

The discussion got around to the deplorable conditions at our *albergue*. We watched more wet pilgrims arrive only to be escorted up the stairs behind the bar.

"I'm going to see if they have any rooms over here." Paul challenged. "That bloke back there was snoring so bad I thought the roof would come down. A night like that and I'll be too knackered to walk in the morning."

"*Ja*, but already you *haf* a bed. Already you *haf* paid," Catharina reminded him.

"I don't care. If this is better, I'm moving!" And off he went. We continued in quiet conversation, enjoying the warmth and swapping stories of the day's challenges. It was amazing how a warm room and a glass of wine could improve the day. In through the door blew Paul, his monster backpack slung over his shoulder, and up the stairs he disappeared.

"It's great!" he announced, returning jubilantly to the table. "There's only three beds in a room and they're real beds, not bunks. I got the last one, although the others haven't come in yet," he continued. "It's only fifteen euros and the supper is a proper meal."

"Did you get money back for other bed?" questioned Catharina. "If no, you pay twenty-one euros to sleep."

"Yes," he chortled with glee, "but I get to sleep in a proper bed while you lot have to sleep in those nasty bunks and listen to that snoring git." Ana and I exchanged looks. Catharina looked perplexed. Zbigniew sighed and refilled his glass.

Okay, so that was enough said; but no, Paul went on and on, gloating, rubbing in details that spoke of his landing in a much better place. I was hurt by his heartless taunting, and I'd reached my limit.

"You know," I said, gazing into the wine I swirled in my glass, "a friend once told me if you belonged to his church, you would be lifted up to heaven at the end of days. Even if you were Christian, if you didn't belong to that particular church, you would be cast down into the fiery pit of hell. He seemed pretty smug about belonging to such an esteemed organization and went on and on about it. Then I asked how he was going to feel about sitting up on a fluffy white cloud, while all those he said he loved and cared about, roasted in the fires of hell."

With that, I looked at Paul, drained my glass and, sorry to leave my friends in an uncomfortable atmosphere, walked out the door to the fiery side of the road. Not very pilgrim-like, I will agree, but I felt too good to feel bad about that one.

Back in the great room, I was sitting at the end of the bench closest to the fire (granny didn't seem to mind too much and yes, I think she might just have smiled!), writing in my journal. Rosario, a woman from Uruguay Ana had introduced me to earlier, was in earnest conversation with the *hospitalero* who was busily peeling potatoes. I asked if she was staying here and she said yes, but that she had a private room upstairs. I cocked my head and asked if there were any more private rooms available. Rosario translated our Spanish hostess' assurance that all the beds were taken. Well, at least I tried.

It was still ugly outside and getting darker as the day died its natural death. The door blew open and Catharina and Ana walked in, shook off fresh rain, and joined me at the table. They reported that Zbigniew was staying with Paul until the evening meal was to be served there, and then he'd join us.

We ordered wine, staving off the chill with its warmth. Tired from the work and the stress of the day, we resignedly ordered the pilgrims' meal. We were very pleasantly surprised when steaming plates of boiled potatoes and succulent braised short ribs were placed before us. Not French fries…real potatoes. And meat in a fragrant gravy, not swimming in grease. It was so good. I wiped the plate with a piece of crusty bread, not wanting to leave a drop behind.

Zbigniew finally pushed in through the door and joined us just as we were finishing a bottle of robust red. We poured out the last glass for him. He ordered a hearty meat sandwich and, having had all I could eat, I pushed my dessert his way.

The bill paid, we trekked out to the other side of the building (no chickens to dodge in the dark), climbed into our bunks, pulled scratchy, but warm blankets up to our chins, and wished each other a good sleep. None of us mentioned our missing *compadre*.

In the darkness, as I listened to everyone settling into dreams, I prayed for patience with Paul, wished him well in the other *albergue*, and asked for forgiveness of my mean-spirited treatment of him. And then I took it back. And then, missing my friend, I sighed and repeated my request for forgiveness…and drifted off to sleep in the snore-free room.

Despite the less than appealing bunkroom, I slept soundly at Alto do Poio, however nothing about the *albergue* invited us to linger in the morning. The first pilgrims out of bed tried to be quiet, but every sound echoed off the damp tiled walls and the room was emptying quickly. Zbigniew swung his legs over from the top bunk, dropping to the floor beside me.

The world was wrapped in fog as we stepped out the door; chickens and dogs nowhere to be seen. Catharina and Zbigniew led the way as Ana and I trundled along behind them. A narrow dirt track paralleled the asphalt roadway, quiet except for a passing truck or two. Where was Paul? He could have been very close behind or before us and we wouldn't have seen him. The fog was thick, the procession of pilgrims quickly disappearing ahead of us.

In less than an hour, we entered the sleeping hamlet of Fonfria and stopped at the local *albergue* for breakfast. While I waited for my cup of creamy *café con leche*, I explored past the bar, travelling a short hallway to come upon a glorious great room, filled with deep couches clustered around a stone fireplace and soft-coloured wall hangings. If this was any indication of what the bunkrooms would be like, I kicked myself for not pushing for Fonfria.

Today would only be a short day of walking; a bit of a rest without actually stopping. We had time to linger over our steaming cups and crusty, chocolate-filled croissants. Gathered at a table with Ana, Catharina, Zbigniew, and Rosario, we looked out the window to see Paul trudging along.

"*Kijk, Paul komt,*" announced Catharina, but he went right by without coming in.

At first I was hurt that he hadn't stopped, but then I thought he might have bad feelings about the way we left things the night before. He probably needed some time and space to sort things out. I looked across the table at Ana who just shrugged. Hopefully we would get past this and come together again. I missed Paul's quick wit and even his teasing banter. I missed my friend.

Remembering it was my youngest son's birthday, I prepared to send him a WhatsApp message.

"*Ve sing for him,*" Catharina offered. Whoever had thought this Belgian woman was stern was missing a huge side of her delightful personality. Despite the language barriers and her lapsing into Dutch from time to time, we were forming a fast friendship. Her prickly exterior hid a surprising sense of humour and a heart of gold.

With a quick run through to make sure everyone knew the words, we recorded "Happy Birthday" for Scott, the whole bar, not just those at our table, joining in.

"We should now sing again each in our own language!" declared Zbigniew, but amid much laughter, it was decided that one international musical fiasco was enough for the day. I wasn't sure what my Scott would think of the call and smiled when he texted "LOL". Catharina was texting her own son, reminded of missing him as well.

"*Het is mijn zoon, Patrick. Zeg hallo,*" she commanded, thrusting her cellphone in my face. It was then I realized she was "face timing" her son, not texting. Thankful that Patrick's grasp on English outweighed his mother's, I greeted this young man I'd never met before. He laughed, saying it sounded like we were having fun, and I passed the phone back to his beaming mother.

Zbigniew and Catharina pulled ahead, Ana and I walking apace, while Rosario hung back to share the trail with another friend. We came to a collection of stone farm buildings. Ana explained that on such farms, the house and the barn were one, with the people living upstairs and the animals below.

"The heat from the animals warms the living space, and the farmers always know their animals are safe, so it works," Ana advised. I said I wasn't sure I could get used to the smell, and she laughed. Sure enough, as we passed by the largest building, we spotted pots of flowers on the railings of the windows above, and peeking in through an open half door below, we met a creamy little calf, bawling for its mother. A big dog lumbered towards me, and I carefully stretched out my hand. After a couple of sniffs, he decided I was okay, and he came in for a scratch behind the ears. We walked through the farmyard to rejoin the trail, and my four-footed friend followed.

"You have a new pet!" Ana laughed.

When first I met Ana in Rabanal, I found her somewhat withdrawn; maybe just shy. Since El Acebo, our friendship had gently grown, solidified by our trials in the rain on our way to Ruitelan. Her peaceful serenity was a good balance to my more forceful disposition, and we enjoyed sharing the trail, even if we strolled in silence. I was in awe of her serenity.

"Here is the little one's mother," she suggested as we approached a herd of gentle milk cows, grazing happily on lush green grasses in a field encircled by low, rock walls. Ahead we saw Catharina's backpack disappearing into the forest. It seemed

Zbigniew was taking advantage of the downward slope and was well in the lead

Below, the fog was lifting, revealing a sunlit valley, quilted in shades of green. In the distance, a tiny town beckoned, and we sauntered along casually, knowing we would arrive well before noon. The gravel *senda* continued downward, winding its way through a tunnel of trees, and following fence lines as we came to Fillobal. A bustling bar invited us in for coffee. Apparently rice pudding was their specialty, and I ordered a dish to go with my coffee. When it arrived at the table, Ana cocked her head in question.

"Rice pudding with cinnamon," I advised. "It's really good," I reported after my first spoonful. She quickly made her way to the bar.

Just then, Rosario popped in the door. "What are you having?" she questioned Ana. They both returned with bowls full of the creamy concoction. Ana and Rosario, both being from South America, were able to find common ground in their somewhat different languages. The Portuguese Ana spoke was different than that of Portugal, and different again from the Spanish dialect Rosario used, but the similarities made conversation easy for them and I left them to it, drifting off, gazing at the gardens outside.

The rest of the morning was spent in a gentle descent to the valley below and before we knew it, we were arriving in Triacastela, named for three castles that no longer existed. We wound our way past rustic shacks, the standard welcoming chicken coops, and an amazing gnarled tree. Before us, the road divided in two, and choosing to go left, we bypassed an ancient church and graveyard before finding the *Albergue* Complexo Xacebeo, and Paul waiting our arrival.

"Our room is up here. This place is great!" Paul exclaimed. We registered quickly, paid our euros, and climbed a wide wooden staircase from the lobby, which looked more like a high-end living room back home. On either side of a stone-faced, dancing fireplace, soft, low-slung couches complimented a polished coffee table, stacked with magazines.

"You see those doors on either side of the fire?" Paul questioned, looking over his shoulder as he led us up the stairs. "You put your boots in there and the heat from the fire will have them toasty warm and dry by morning. Very professional!" he chortled.

"Here they are!" he announced leading us into a large room where Zbigniew and Catharina had already claimed single beds. "I'm up here," Paul indicated a top bunk. "And I saved those lower bunks for you." He seemed to be trying to make amends. We all stood and looked at each other, then suddenly came together in a group hug. "I missed you guys last night," Paul murmured. No explanations required, no apologies needed; our Camino family was restored.

Rosario claimed the last bottom bunk, and we headed for the showers. After last night's disgraceful bathroom, I welcomed the large, clean shower, enthusiastically peeling the day's clothes from my sweaty body, thankful that there were good laundry facilities here as well.

Everyone clean, boots baking, and laundry hanging on the lines, we strolled out into the sunshine to explore the town. Rosario, who seemed to be coming down with a bad cold, elected to spend the afternoon sleeping to see if she could shake it off.

Between the two streets, Triacastela was well equipped with coffee bars, bank machines, and a store or two, ready to deal with the pilgrim trade. We noted the restaurant, also owned by the operator of our *albergue*, for supper this evening. The menu looked inviting, and the prices were reasonable.

In a tiny store, we spent some time, delving through the t-shirt supply. Zbigniew always wore long-sleeved shirts, his skin being very sensitive to the sun, but the heat, called for a reprieve. Among much giggling, Catharina, and I held first one, then another for his consideration. Then we found the perfect one; bright orange, with a cartoon pilgrim on the front. Eyes rolling with indecision, he finally conceded and bought the shirt, and we rejoined Paul and Ana in a search for a *mercado* that was still open.

We slipped in the door of the market one street over, just before they closed for siesta. We quickly gathered cheese, chips, bread, olives, sausage, and wine, and carried our booty back to the *albergue's* communal lunchroom. The adjoining kitchen was empty, so we grabbed a cutting board, a knife, glasses, and plates and slid down the polished benches around the broad, white table. Zbigniew and Paul filled glasses with wine and opened bags of chips while Ana and I sliced cheese and sausage. Catharina sliced bread and put olives in a bowl. A family again, we happily passing food up and down the trestle table, chatting about the day, and planning the stops ahead.

Sarria, the last substantial city before the hundred-kilometre minimum mark, was just over eighteen kilometres away. At that point, many new pilgrims would join the Camino, ready to achieve their Compostelas by walking only that final distance, so it was likely that Sarria would be busy. Pouring through our guidebooks, I suggested we go five kilometres further and settle in Barbadelo for the night. An *albergue* that was a seventeenth-century restored farmhouse, complete with its own chapel, had caught my eye. Ana took out her phone and made our reservation.

"I was thinking I would like to go to Samos and see the monastery," Paul mused. Founded in the sixth century, I had read about this being one of the largest and oldest monasteries in Europe. The idea of seeing it called to me, but that alternate route between Triacastela and Sarria would add another seven kilometres to the day's walk. That wasn't so bad, but I knew I'd want to spend some significant time there, probably staying the night, which would separate me from the group. Paul was good with just cruising through and having a look. "I'll meet you in Barbadelo, don't worry," he reassured us.

"My pictures no take," Catharina advised sadly as we cleaned the dishes. It seemed her cell's camera memory was full. She was the only one with an iPhone, so we were a bit at a loss as to how to help. I assured her I'd send all my photos to her when I got home. She was thankful for that, but understandably she wanted to take her own if it could be managed.

"Sarria is a bigger city. Perhaps they have an electronics store there," I suggested. Ana agreed, and we formed a plan to hunt down a memory stick for Catharina when we got there.

At 7:00, we wandered down to the small church, its yard filled with mausoleums and headstones depicting the familial history of the town. Inside, the church was sparsely decorated, but the ambience no less holy than that found in the larger churches. A robed priest made his way to the front and led us all in the by-now-familiar cadence of the Spanish catholic service. I followed Ana's lead, watching as she and the boys crossed themselves at appropriate times. Catharina had settled stiffly in a back pew.

Back into the still warm evening, I stopped back at the *albergue* to see if Rosario would be joining us for supper. She still looked dreadful, but said she was feeling much better. I was torn by the desire to give her a supportive hug and my selfish avoidance of illness. Erring on the side of good karma, I gave her a hug and led her down the stairs.

We joined the others at a big, round table in the busy back room of the restaurant. Waiters rushed around tables taking orders and plopping bottles of wine and water indiscriminately on every table as they passed. Zbigniew had met the couple sitting behind us and was delighted to find they were also from Stockholm.

When our orders arrived, everyone enjoyed the plentiful food. Paul insisted I try some of the cheese that came as his dessert. Full, but in the interest of harmony, I took a slice and agreed it was delicious. He pushed more my way, and I laughingly told him I was full. Paul was still insisting, but instead, I grabbed his plate and offered some to Zbigniew's country-men. The whole table erupted in laughter that a protesting Paul finally joined in, and more wine was poured.

The sun had set behind the mountains, and the air was growing a little cooler by the time we returned to our *albergue*. Zbigniew was opening another bottle of wine to share on the couches, but I declined, sipping my water and enjoying the camaraderie by the fire. Gradually the wine and the heat of the fire lulled me into a contented drowsiness. I climbed the stairs, wishing those who remained below a good night and sought my bed and sweet dreams.

We girls gathered our things, commiserating with Rosario, who was still feeling under the weather. She said she would sleep a bit more, and then walk a shorter day. Leaving her to healing slumber, and the boys to their final packing, we made our way down the wide staircase and pulled toasty dry boots from the cupboards beside the fireplace.

We sauntered down the road to the same restaurant we'd had supper in the previous night. It was just as busy, filled with pilgrims fuelling themselves for the day. Ordering croissants and coffee, we sat back, discussing our plan to solve Catharina's photo problem.

Now I will be the first to admit that I am not tech-savvy. Catharina's best hope was Ana, but even she had little experience with iPhones. It seemed to be an issue of memory, so logic told us that we just had to find a memory stick, transfer some of her photos, and she'd be good to go again.

The boys came in the door and found seating nearby. Paul ordered his standard espresso with a camomile tea chaser. Zbigniew ordered orange juice, still struggling to wake up.

"You not wear new shirt?" Catharina interrogated Zbigniew sternly.

"I save it for Santiago I think. If it gets too hot, I may wear it sooner," he reassured her.

As a plate of toast and tomato spread was delivered to their table, we finished our coffee and made ready to hit the trail. Zbigniew was a lone walker, and Paul was taking the alternate route, so waiting wasn't expected.

"I wrote down the name of the place you chose, Roxey," Paul advised. "I will get there later than you, since my route is longer, but I will get there. Don't let them give my bed away!" We assured him we would save it for him and told him to enjoy the monastery and take lots of pictures. Zbigniew, eyes brighter by now, waved us off.

At the edge of town, we turned right, striding purposefully, trekking poles tapping in rhythm. Leaving the paved roads of Triacastela behind us, we followed a dirt road, winding its way gently upwards, curving along stone-walled pastures and leafy stands of graceful trees.

Although it was cloudy, the sky was breaking up, and it promised to be a warm, sunny day. Mist hanging in the forests would soon fall victim to the sun's searching rays. The trail climbed steadily. Reaching the silent hamlet of San Xil, we knew we had passed the half-way point of the 300-metre climb to Alto Riocabo.

I pulled off my coat and stuffed it in my pack, Catharina shaking her head at the crazy Canadian who got hot so easily. She snorted in derision and, pulling her coat zipper up, continued up the hill. Ana laughed and fell in behind me, but I noticed she kept her coat on as well. Up and up we climbed until the trail levelled out, and we knew we had arrived at the summit.

The views were as spectacular as promised. Blue skies stretched endlessly above us as we looked down onto the patch-work quilted valley below. A thin layer of mist hung between the blue above and the deep purple hills below. As I turned to replace my water bottle in my pack, I saw with a smile, Ana and Catharina pushing their coats into their packs.

It was sort of like that story I remembered from childhood about an argument between the wind and the sun as to who was stronger. No matter how hard he blew, the wind could not get a traveller to take his coat off. Simply by shining, the sun won the argument. In life also, it is amazing the power shining gently can have on the world, despite all the anger and hurt that seems so prevalent. More people should shine; less people should blow. Okay…mountain top reflections over, we headed down.

Dropping steeply down the other side of the mountain, we envied Paul's more level route, but not the extra distance he would walk. While our view had been the valley from the mountain top, his would be the impressive monastery. There were so many ways to walk the Camino, even between the same two points.

We stopped for coffee in Pintin. Catharina and I carried cups of *cafe con leche* to the table as Ana returned from the bathroom, rubbing her hip.

"Little sore?" I asked, and she nodded.

"Must have slept on it funny last night," Ana mused.

"Mine hips *es* not hurt," declared Catharina. "*Dey* is not real, so *dey doz* not hurt," she beamed.

"What do you mean your hips are not real?" I asked, wondering if something was being lost in translation.

"Before the Camino, I haf new hips made," she smiled triumphantly, her round apple cheeks bunching happily.

"What? Are you trying to tell me that you had a double hip replacement surgery just before you came on the Camino?" Ana and I stared in wonder at our older friend.

"Ya! Dey is plastic!" she laughed, thumping her new body parts soundly. "I *haf zem* just before Christmas. Like Christmas present!" We shook our heads. All this time and we were still learning about each other.

I was impressed by the constant pace Catharina kept. An ex-nurse, I was surprised to learn she was sixty-five. Her skin and copper hair defied that number, and her strength on the trail spoke of a younger person. Catharina didn't carry her pack, and she slowed down on the hills, but she just kept going and going. On the level, she could leave us in the dust (or mud, given the weather we were having), and it wasn't long before we were looking at her small pack get smaller again.

From here the trail rose and fell across the undulating countryside. Through tunnels of shady trees we walked, the path still moist from earlier rains. We enjoyed the stroll in companionable silence. Birdsong filled the air, and the ever-present wind gently ruffled the leaves of the trees; nature's conversation.

The way became punctuated with small farms and then gated homes, and we knew we were getting closer to Sarria. I had been warned that the personality of the Camino would change here, with the pilgrims known as "Camino Lite", those who for one reason or other, chose only to walk the last required hundred kilometres. I knew it would be busier, but I hoped the Camino wouldn't lose its peaceful power to noise and commercialism.

We crossed a bridge and entered a river-side plaza bordered with shell-shaped metal fencing. Thirsty pilgrims sought the shade of wide awnings in front of bars as they enjoyed the rushing coolness of the waters below. Following arrows, we wound our way through commercial streets, searching the rows of storefronts. Spotting something that looked cell-phone oriented, we pushed in through the heavy glass doors, waiting to speak to the crisp, young woman behind the polished granite counter. Around us an array of phones were on display, so we were hopeful. Ana's Spanish the strongest, she took the lead. As the discussion progressed, Catharina and I exchanged questioning looks. Didn't sound too hopeful after all.

"She said they just sell plans and phones here, but if we cross the street, just down the way, there is an internet store. She thinks maybe we can get a memory stick there."

"*Gracias!*" we all called as we exited the glossy, air-conditioned salesroom. Dodging heavy traffic, we crossed the road. In through the battered wooden door we went, entering a musty little store, with no one in sight. Craning our necks around the corner, we saw a row of young men, busily engaged in fighting oppressors on video screens. A tall, bespectacled man with a scruffy beard came out of the back, pulling headphones from his dark curls. Again, Ana explained our problem, Catharina and I standing by for morale support. Once again, it seemed, we would not find help here.

"He says try the Euro Store, just up the hill. We should be able to buy a memory stick there." Although we did find several entertaining novelty items, no memory stick for an iPhone was found.

"Enough! *Ve go!*" Catharina decided, frustrated with the fruitless search. "*Ve haf* beer!" This seemed a perfectly reasonable alternative to solving the problem with her phone for now.

Climbing higher, we left the modern commercial district behind, the paved roads becoming cobblestone and tile. On either side of the roadway, *albergues* and bars abounded, brightly coloured signs inviting pilgrims within. A noisy group shared beers and songs on one corner, and we smiled and waved away their invitations to join as we passed. Spotting a quiet bar, we sidled up to the counter, perusing the menu posted behind. We each selected paella and ordered beers delivered to our tables in tall, frosty glasses.

"Ana," I asked, "you said you used to work in a bank. Is it usual in your country to retire so early from such work?"

"No," she answered slowly, "not usual. I used to love my job, but then we got a new manager and everything changed. It got to be that my sanity was not worth the money, so I retired." Kicking myself for having raised what clearly was a painful subject, I apologized. She shook her head like trying to shake off a shadow and her usual peaceful smile returned.

"I am myself getting close to retirement, and I am not sure what that will be like. My husband and I get along really well. We love to go camping, and that puts us pretty much alone together, in pretty tight confines, but we handle it really well. It will be nice to do what I want to do on any given day, but I'm used to being busy, so I'm not sure how that will feel for me."

"*Ya*," Catharina said, "was every day, I up early in *ze* morning, go to work; work all day in *ze* hospital. Now, I can walk every day. Also, I take care of dogs when people go. I must watch *ze* money more now too," she finished with a sigh.

Our food was very flavourful, but too much, and we all left some on our plates as we pushed away from the table. It didn't do to eat too heavily. We still needed to walk, not sleep.

Out the door, we continued to climb the hill towards the cathedral. A steady stream of pilgrims would be searching for places for the night. Already we were noticing the "fresh" pilgrims. While it was hard not to smile at their eager excitement and to criticize their trendy city clothes, it was important to remember this was their Camino too, and there was room for all.

We sought the more quiet, reflective *albergues* rather than the boisterous hostels, more suited to a sporting event than a pilgrimage. Don't get me wrong. We laughed and played and partied on a comfortable scale. We just had been on the trail too long to handle the fresh crowds. I wondered what it would be like when we finally arrived in Santiago and then went home, back to the real world. Would the world suddenly seem too noisy, too fast? I guessed it was going to take time to reacclimatize to our old lives.

Leaving Sarria behind us, we followed a narrow path, beaten down by years of parading pilgrims. Tall grasses and overhanging branches enclosed the trail, providing a buffer from the adjacent road and shelter from the hot sun. Soon the path turned away from the road, leading us through tranquil woods, to a babbling stream, winding its way through the cool shade. Stepping from flat rock to flat rock, we crossed the sparkling water, and continued into the forest. Unexpectedly, the trail began a steep incline. Dwarfed by tall, thickly trunked trees, we climbed, filtered sunlight dappling the trail before us.

Suddenly, we broke out of the forest, coming out into the blinding sun in a large, grassy meadow. On a rutted farm track, we skirted the large field to the corner, followed it down the other side, and then trekked back towards the forest, basically drawing a box around the field with our footsteps. Why couldn't the path have gone straight down the first side and saved us all that work, we laughed.

Across the shallow valley, the highway crossed an impressive bridge supported by pillars rising from the greenness below. Sprawling farms, crops just bursting through rich red dirt, spoke of harvests to come. As we entered the town of Barbadelo, we passed the first *albergue*, the umbrella-topped tables full, the bar doing a busy trade. On we walked, passing a cluttered, open-fronted souvenir shop, its enthusiastic operator calling to us to stop. We laughed and said we might be back later and walked on, looking for our *albergue*, Casa de Carmen. Ahead, we saw a gracious building, its white pillared arches draped with purple wisteria. A well-dressed woman, her hair in an old-fashioned French roll, stood ready with a clipboard.

"Casa de Carmen?" I questioned. With a disgusted snort, she waved her manicured hand up the hill. Finally, the last building in town, there it was. The rambling farmhouse was paired with a newer bunkhouse, but care had been taken to maintain the character of the seventeenth-century farmhouse in the design of the new structure. To one side, flowering succulents spilled over a stone-walled garden, behind which a tiny plaster chapel stood. Across the path, a cool-clear fountain ran, spattering the rocks below and inviting us to cup our hands and be refreshed.

As we walked in through the wide farmhouse doorway, a smiling woman came out of the kitchen, wiping her hands on the apron tied over her dress. Angelina welcomed us to Case de Carmen, taking ten euros from us each as she stamped our passports. She asked if we would be having supper there, and not wanting to walk back to look for other options, we agreed we would. Another nine euros paid, she showed us the sunny dining room, the walls painted sherbet orange and gleaming wooden tables and chairs, clustered family-style within. Supper would be at 7:00 she advised, leading us out to the bunkhouse, stopping along the way to ruffle the head of a massive, shaggy white dog.

In the foyer of the bunkhouse, low comfy couches surrounded a square coffee table, creating an inviting conversation pit. Down the hall we went, passing three large, clean shower/bathroom combinations, and through two large, lavender-painted rooms, each holding bunks for twelve pilgrims. Then she led us through an open doorway to a cozy little cell of six bunks. Between the beds on the outside wall, a screened door opened onto a sunny porch, complete with plastic chairs.

"You are the first here today. You get the choice of this first," Angelina beamed. Well she didn't need to ask twice! As we dropped our packs on the beds, we asked about laundry, and she advised we could wash things in the washrooms, and then there were lines above the gardens for drying.

When I returned from my shower, I found Zbigniew had arrived and was enjoying wine with Catharina and Ana on our "stoop".

"There you are!" exclaimed a hot and sweaty Paul as he pushed out onto the porch. "This is nice, isn't it? But I don't see a bar. Where do we get a drink?"

"Here is our drink." Zbigniew smiled and held up the wine. The man was always prepared!

"Right, shower and laundry," Paul decreed. "That was a bit of a walk that. I was sort of regretting it until I saw the monastery. It was huge! Very nice. Stayed for a bit of the mass, but I didn't want to be too late. Did you pay for supper?"

"We did," I waved, including Catharina and Ana. Zbigniew nodded in agreement as well. "But breakfast may be an issue," I continued. They don't start serving it until 8:00, and it costs five euros. Maybe they don't really want to do the breakfast thing. That's really too late to have breakfast, and it would have to be a pretty good breakfast to be worth five euros." Nods all around indicated we would be walking out without breakfast in the morning. Morgade, being just over seven kilometres away, looked the best choice for breakfast we agreed.

Ana and I put our heads together over our guidebooks, planning our stops for the next few days. With the extra pilgrims on the Camino now, we weren't going to leave beds to chance. The others were quite happy to leave the decisions in our hands.

"Very professional the two of you," Paul pronounced, grabbing his kit bags. "Haven't messed up yet. Except for that chicken place," he taunted and escaped out the door towards the shower.

"Our goal is to be in Santiago by June 6th. What do you think of alternating longer and shorter days?" I asked.

"Ya, des is good," Catharina nodded, Zbigniew agreeing in turn.

"Okay, Ana. What about Portomarin tomorrow? It would be about the same walk as we did today; about eighteen kilometres. There is a fair bit of up and down, but it's pretty steady from the looks of things," I suggested. She looked at my book and nodded.

"Yes, and there are lots of *albergues* there, so it should be easy to find a place. They are all about the same price; ten euros. Is that okay?" she asked. Everyone nodded. "There is one that is six euros, but it has 110 beds!"

"Oh no!" exclaimed Catharina, recoiling visibly along with the rest of us. "Das es too big!" We agreed, envisioning row on row of bunks, thirty and forty to a room. We were so done with that! Ana tried a couple *albergues* listed and was advised they were "*completo*". Next on the list was a place called O Mirador. Ana called and the reservation was made.

"Perhaps we should reserve more days," Ana suggested given the number of places that were full in Portomarin. "Where should we stay next?" Portos looked good, just a bit further than today's walk. Ana started dialling; no room at the inn, either one. We decided to back up a bit and try Eirexe, two kilometres closer. One *albergue* was full and the other said she had one room with four beds and one private room. Problem was the private room was twenty euros, while the other beds were ten. Ana covered the phone with her hand while we discussed the options. It would mean one person would have to pay more, but they'd have a private room. None of us really cared about the privacy, but if we didn't take it, the next place we could try would be another hour's walk.

"Let's just take that, and we'll work it out somehow," I suggested. Agreement all around and another reservation was made. The next logical stop would be Melide. It would be a longer day, but I was really pushing for it because they were famous for their octopus, and I really wanted the opportunity to try some regional fare.

"Look! This one has an elevator; no stairs, no matter what floor we end up on."

"That is good!" agreed Zbigniew, rubbing his knee. "I like that one!" Phone call made; reservation made.

"That should hold us for a while. We should really only need two more stops before Santiago at that rate." The weight of those words settled upon us, and we grinned at each other. We were getting close.

Paul bounced back into the room and commended us for our professional handling of the travel plans. He headed out to hang his laundry. Zbigniew and Catharina wanted to take a bit of a rest before dinner, and Ana and I wanted to explore the gardens.

Slowly, we meandered along the terraces, checking out the lush roses and trying to identify plants unknown to us. Finally, we sat on a bench and just breathed in the fragrance of the garden. There was lavender and mint somewhere around here; we could smell it.

"It's hard to think we're a week away from being done," I mused. "This trip seemed to take forever to come, and there were days walking it that felt like an eternity, but now the end seems to be coming too fast." I looked over at Ana and witnessed tears trickling down her face. "Oh Ana! Please don't be sad. When it is over, you go to England, and you'll see Marina. I will go home to Al and the rest of my family."

"I do not want to go home," she stated soberly, her tear-filled eyes gazing into mine. I reached out and took her hand. I knew that she planned to remain in Brazil as long as her parents were there. I thought from our earlier conversation she had made peace with that decision. Her sadness was apparent as she looked past her visit with her daughter and travelled in her mind back to Brazil. I remained quiet and let her talk.

"In my country there is so much poverty and so much corruption. The government says they are working to improve the lives of the people. But the people are no better. They live in shacks, have rags for clothes, and cannot feed their children. It is so…so…so heart-breaking!" She sobbed. "My heart is broken when I see my country," she muttered quietly. Her sadness was so raw, I just wanted to wrap her up and take her home with me.

"I know it can be hard to see people suffer. Even in Canada, there are people without homes; even in my own small town. I don't think things are as bad as what you describe in Brazil, but in Canada, children do go to school hungry, and their parents work so hard, but just can't make it better. I try to help where I can, mostly through my church. You do what you can do, even if feels like it's just a drop in the bucket."

"You can't fix the big picture, but while you remain in Brazil, is there somewhere you can help? If not the church, is there some sort of school or clinic where you can help? If you can make one person's life, one person's day better, you are helping. And when you help, you feel good and you are empowered to do more. Is there somewhere you can go to read with children? Can you help grow a garden for food or collect clothes for those who need them? There are so many little things you can do, and really, for people in need, they make a huge difference. I don't want to sound like a bleeding heart, but I really believe each of us can make a difference."

"Roxey, I can see what you are talking about, and I can try to find something to help. Even if am not happy with the situation there, I love my country. I will try to make something better there. It will take time to think how. But I will try!" she smiled. "You are a good friend, and I am so glad I found you on the Camino."

"You are like a younger sister to me. It is funny. If either of our paths had changed by one day, if we had not spoken to each other that first night, we might never have known each other. How amazing that such friendships can be formed. We are a Camino family for sure!" I pronounced. Embracing, we returned to the *albergue*, arms around each other's waists, like good friends do; like sisters do.

"There you are!" Paul exclaimed, bursting the tender moment. "We're just going over for supper. Are you ready?" We walked in through the arched doorway inside the reception of the old house. Passing the kitchen door, I spotted an old-fashioned wood stove, the cooks busily stirring huge pots and turning meat on a griddle, chatting loudly as they worked.

In the dining room, we took up the centre table, only three other tables being occupied. A young woman with a halo of black curls brought a basket of thick, crusty bread wedges to our table. Already waiting was a carafe of cool water and two bottles of red wine, labels optional. Settling around the table, the men filled glasses. The waitress came around, asking our choices between a chicken dish, one with beef, or a piece of local fish. Regardless of our choices, I was sure the entrée would include French fries.

Looking around the room, we noticed a man sitting by himself. A hushed conversation between us, and Paul crossed the room, inviting the lone pilgrim to join our table. A wide smile on his face, the tall, clean-shaven man collected his bottle and glass of wine and pulled up a chair next to Zbigniew. I raised an eyebrow inviting the couple across the room, but they smiled, happy to stay where they were.

"Thanks for asking me to join you," Dennis introduced himself. "I started walking in Leon with some other folks, but they decided to stop in Sarria; they liked the larger town. I'm from Chicago," he supplied as we dove into the crisp, colourful salads placed before us. "What do you think about this Camino?" he asked loudly, coming up for air between mouthfuls. "Don't you think the whole thing is one big commercial grab!" he suggested.

Oh no! Don't you try to take the spiritual out of my Camino, I thought.

"It's all about how many pilgrims you can push through a town and how much you can get out of them," he insisted. Our new tablemate appeared to be full of air, much like the windy city he hailed from.

I suggested it was more a matter of sustaining the small towns and villages we had walked through to ensure they would be there to support the pilgrims of the future. He looked at me like I'd grown another head. Our waitress circled the table, depositing appetizing dishes before us and returning to the kitchen for more.

"I've been making a list of what should change on the Camino." Slicing into his slab of beef, he had our attention. "First," he said swallowing a chunk of meat, "cellphones. No cellphones should be allowed. They shouldn't be strolling along the countryside, talking to home. Also, people couldn't call and book *albergues* as they went. They should have to travel by the seat of their pants, like true pilgrims."

"Well, I have to take issue with that," I stated. "I agree I'd rather people saved their cellphones for private conversations, but without mine, I'd be lost. It's my communication with home, my flashlight, my clock, my camera; it's everything. And if we didn't call ahead and book *albergues,* we might not be able to stay together as a group." The others nodded.

"But this is supposed to be a pilgrimage. You're supposed to leave it to chance and leave your other world behind!" he argued, leaning back in his chair arrogantly.

"My husband is at home, and if I couldn't communicate with him, either by text or voice, I wouldn't know if he was okay. Then what sort of frame of mind would I be in?" I responded.

"Well, that was your choice, to leave him behind. If you weren't ready to make that choice, maybe you shouldn't have come," Dennis suggested smugly, wiping the last of his gravy with another piece of bread. He licked his fingers and picked up his wine, looking over the top of his glass at me.

Catharina looked stricken; Zbigniew, muttered under his breath.

Do something! Ana's eyes screamed at Paul.

She's got this, Paul's eyes responded. The waitress arrived, hovering uncertainly with bowls of ice cream.

"If I had any choice, my husband would be with me. He's in a wheelchair." Dennis sat forward and swallowed hurriedly. "This was important for me to do, and my husband supports me. I don't think that it's too much to expect that we would have some sort of communication for peace of mind for both of us. He's dealing with MS and that's enough without his having to worry about me as well. Maybe you should rethink your list."

"No thanks," he sputtered as he waved the ice cream away. "I think I'm done for the day." He stood suddenly and drained his glass. "*Buen Camino*," he saluted sarcastically and stalked away. In shocked silence, we all exchanged glances, then burst into laughter.

"And to think we invited him to our table!" Paul said. "Sorry for that Roxey." Zbigniew poured out the last of the wine into my glass.

"No worries. I think there's probably a good reason why he was walking alone." We started laughing again, wiping tears from our eyes. The waitress, smiling as she came, placed a fresh bottle of wine on our table that we hadn't even ordered.

"Actually, I'm pretty tired. Why don't you guys take this wine back to the *albergue* and relax in the lounge?" I suggested.

"Good idea," Zbigniew agreed, picking up the bottle and his glass.

Waving the others and their wine glasses on, I crossed the path and ducked into the small chapel. It was about the size of a walk-in freezer and cool like one too. The deteriorating plaster of the walls and rounded ceiling spoke of many years past and many prayers heard. On the scarred wide-planked floor, a simple Madonna stood beside the altar where votive candles sat ready for lighting. As my tiny flame danced to life, I sat on the short, backless bench and gathered myself reflectively. My thoughts included thanks for the safe walk of the day and the love and support of my Camino family, as well as prayers for the continued well-being of my family at home.

I added to my prayers that all on the way treat each other with respect and with compassion, remembering not to judge and to allow each their own Camino. Amen.

Out in the warm night, I bent to scruff the white monster dog behind his ear. The gentle giant sighed contentedly. Inside, Catherine and the boys had comfortably settled into the low-slung couches. Waving off another glass of wine, I chose instead to join Ana for an early night. As quietly as I could, I changed into my night wear, trying not to disturb her.

"Are you good?" Ana's soft voice lifted from the darkness of her bunk.

"Yes, I am good." I assured her, slipping into my bed. "Sleep well my friend."

"*Boa noite*," she murmured, already drifting off.

"*Buenos noches*," I responded as I too settled in to sleep.

Morning mist hung over the valley. The sunrise had begun to paint the sky, all soft golds and pinks. It was magically silent except for the occasional crow of a rooster and the rhythmic tap of pilgrim poles. Leaving Casa de Carmen behind us, we strode side by side, the gravel crunching below our feet. Passing along the back of a collection of farmhouses, we were surprised to be greeted by a long-eared mule who gently nuzzled our hands, looking for more than the scratches we offered. We were hungry too, so we bade him farewell and continued along the wooded trail. Thick fingers of ivy clung to the trunks of the trees and trailed over the path, grazing our passing heads.

In contrast to our usual travel, we stayed together, walking a few feet apart, but quiet. Each of us seemed lost in our own world this morning. Perhaps the boys were fighting off the residue of last night's extra bottle of wine. It never ceased to amaze me how much wine we could consume and still get up early and walk kilometres through the day.

Touching my wrist beads, each in their turn, I held my family members in my heart and in my thoughts, wondering how they were doing on the other side of the world. This isolation from all of them was just foreign to me. It was probably good for me, but it was still strange. How fast that first hour flew by; hardly noticed at all as I travelled on automatic pilot, immersed in my thoughts.

The trail now became a road, and it dipped gently down to a sprawling building, windows aglow in the shadowy morning light. Ahead I saw Paul, bare-legged in his shorts, push in through the doors of the bar. The rest of us piled in after him, anxious to wrap our chilled hands around hot mugs of *cafe con leche*. Looking at the menu chalked up on the wall, I chose an egg, cheese, sausage, and tomato bocadillo, thinking that should be plenty of protein to carry me through the day. Ana and Catharina ordered the same. After passing us cups of foamy, hot coffee, the barista suggested we go up the stairs and take a seat in the dining room; our food would be delivered. In the large, open room, sat Paul and Zbigniew, coffees in hand, waiting for their orders as well.

"So today we will see our first hundred-kilometre marker," Paul announced.

"Yes," Ana agreed. "We should have a picture there."

"Well, we'll all have to stay together," I suggested. "We don't know when or where that's going to happen, and we don't want to miss anyone for the photo." The girls looked pointedly at Paul, who had a knack of pulling ahead, and then at Zbigniew, who seemed to disappear mysteriously along the way, only to reappear at our destination.

"*Ya, ve* stay together!" Catharina warned sternly, waggling her finger at the men.

"Well if I get ahead," Paul continued, "and I see the post, I'll just wait there for you lot to catch up."

A young man in an apron, marked with sauces and smears of his trade, shouldered a large tray bearing our breakfasts. He plunked the plates down on the table, allowing us to sort out who got what. The sandwich I had ordered was enormous! Catharina and Ana just sat and looked at theirs, each of us wondering how we were going to eat it all.

"We should have shared," I laughed, sinking my teeth into the warm, crusty bread, catching a run of egg yolk with my finger as it made its way down my chin.

"That looks good," Paul said, comparing his standard toast and tomato spread with our sandwiches. Zbigniew had a plate of bacon and eggs and was busily dipping thick-crusted bread into the orange yolks.

"Would you like some of mine? There's more than I can eat," I offered, Catharina and Ana offering the same.

"Naww, this is good," Paul waved our offers away and munched on his toast.

Ana looked at me and shrugged. *Well his loss was our gain*, her eyes seemed to say. It was interesting how much the two of us communicated non-verbally. Often, I would catch her eye, or she mine, and a whole conversation would ensue without a word being spoken. The connection between us was strong.

Despite her protestations about the amount of food, Catharina managed to polish the sandwich off. Ana and I each wrapped the remainder of ours in napkins; food for the journey. When I got back to the table from the bathroom, Paul was already gone. So much for staying together.

Still climbing, the road became a path once more, and we followed low, moss-covered stone walls skirting fields of wildflowers and tall grasses. We entered a thickly treed stretch where the path suddenly ended and we were faced with a stream. It appeared that over the centuries, water had found the path of least resistance and had adopted the Camino trail as its own. As a solution, large, flat rocks had been placed, bridge-like, down one side of the babbling brook. We stepped gingerly, one stone to the next, until the stream took another turn, and the trail resumed. Coming out of the forest, a glorious sunrise filled the field before us, shafts of sunshine cutting diagonally from the tops of the trees to the grasses below. Tall blades stood in silhouette, backlit in gold by the rising sun. A bird called out and another answered.

No signage evident, we weren't sure, but we thought the tidy hamlet we were entering was Ferreiros, and we kept a sharp eye out for a marker and for Paul.

"What do you think that is?" Paul queried, resting casually on a low stone wall, ankles crossed, arms folded across his chest, forehead glistening. I smiled thinking he'd hurried on ahead, so he could look like he'd been waiting for us; the sheen of sweat gave him away. In the yard behind a humble farmhouse, stood a little brick structure, raised off the ground on a stone platform. The gabled ends were built of stone, with intricate ornamental posts on the top. On one side was a small wooden door, rusty iron hinges holding it fast. "Is it a burial site, like a mausoleum or something?" he queried.

"The size is right," I agreed, "but I read about these. They're specific to the Galician region. This is a corn crib; a storage hut to keep the corn away from wild animals. That's why it's raised off the ground," I advised. We agreed that it was a pretty fancy corn crib and continued on through the town, admiring the roses and calla lilies that poked out through wrought iron gates.

We came around a corner, and there it was! The first marker under one-hundred kilometres; 99.930 to be exact! Each of us wanted a photo, and we took our turn, leaping across the shallow ditch, to stand proudly beside this symbol of the home stretch.

"We need a photo of all of us," I exclaimed. "I'll find somebody!" and I hurried off looking for someone, anyone to take the picture. Returning to the group, I found them gathered around as Catharina tried to attach her cellphone to a selfie stick.

"That can't be right!" muttered Paul as the telescoping pole dropped forward suddenly on its hinge.

"No! *Es* not good!" agreed a serious Catharina as she adjusted knobs. Feeling better about the fit, they tried it out, and she brought it down to check how the picture turned out. "Humph!" exclaimed our Belgian friend in disgust. From my vantage point on the road side of the ditch I wondered what had happened.

"Let's have a look," Paul said, twisting the camera to see. "Well that's the other side of the road, now, isn't it?" he said perplexed.

"Oh, it's backwards!" laughed Ana. Paul and Catharina looked on sheepishly as she removed the camera and turned it around. Zbigniew sighed and walked over to sit on the wall on the other side of the road. Suddenly, a trio of Camino cyclists came around the corner, screeching to a quick halt when they found us scattered all over the roadway.

"Could you please take our picture?" I said rushing up to them and thrusting my cellphone at them. I had no shame! "This is the first marker under a hundred. Could you please take our photo, and then, we can take yours for you. You'll want to have a photo of this marker too!" I assured them.

"Okay, okay," the laughing young man stepped off his bike and took my cellphone in hand. Jumping across the ditch, we arranged ourselves around the marker, smiling wildly, and being silly. I bent and pointed to the number, Zbigniew doffed his hat, and Catharina plunked her leg up on the front of the marker, like a woman trying to attract a cab.

"I took two, so one should be okay."

"Do you want me to take yours now?" I asked.

"Naww, that's okay," he said, but then his buddies joined in the spirit.

"Yes, yes! We should have a photo!" They abandoned their bikes and jumped the ditch for their turn. Waving them off as they pedalled away, I turned to the others promising to send the photo by WhatsApp as soon as we had Wi-Fi.

That happy task done, with no excuse for us to stay together, it wasn't long before Paul climbed out of sight. The brilliant blue horizon stretched endlessly across fields of green and yellow and lavender, rolling easily over the gentle hills.

The trail continued to climb, and we were once more in a forest, sunlight dappling the muddy track through the whispering leaves of a tree-formed tunnel. Ana pulled up ahead and disappeared over the ridge through a halo of green. Catharina, Zbigniew, and I picked our way along, trying to dodge the worst of the mud. We came out of the shade and the ground, no longer protected from the sun, was dry once more.

The climb had been gradual, and it hadn't really felt like we had been working our way up a mountain, but we found ourselves at the summit of Alto Momientos. The view was breathtaking, as the lush valley spread before us, fields and forests, surrounded by misty rolling mountains. Of all the parts of Spain I had seen, I found myself falling in love with Galicia, perhaps because it reminded me so much of home.

Making our way down the mountain, we came to Mercadoiro and stopped for a cold drink. Zbigniew, it appeared, was having trouble with his legs. He ordered a coffee. It took longer to drink, which meant a longer rest. We three girls strode out as he waved us off. We were glad to see him taking the time he needed to rest when he did. I thought that's probably why he disappeared the way he did, pacing himself to have space from the group so we wouldn't be aware of how much he was suffering.

The next part of today's route would take us steeply down towards our goal, Portomarin, a 350-metre drop in about five kilometres. We'd need to watch our step and take it easy to reach our destination safely. As we approached the top of the hill, we found a Spanish farmer, carefully tending his vineyard. We made to go past him, following the asphalt road around a corner, but he called out and signalled to the opening in the trees running alongside the fence. Backing up, we waved him our thanks and started down the steep gravel trail.

Ahead of me, brilliant blue water peeked invitingly through a frame of trees at the bottom of the hill. We continued down, coming to a sharp turn that suddenly took the trail down a steep stairway.

Now when I say stairway, these were not your ordinary stairs. Rough cut from the clay and stones of the hill, about fifty irregularly shaped stairs led downwards between two ancient walls of moss-covered stone. Some were very definite, some more a blur of shale and mud, making footing tricky. To make matters worse, some were very shallow, but most were deep – more than a foot deep, and often two in some cases. It was more like rock climbing (in reverse) than stair climbing. Picking our way down was a long and slow process, and nobody rushed the pilgrim before them, realizing the danger of the difficult descent.

Reaching the bottom, Ana was first behind me. She gave a relieved smile and a "thumbs up" as she reached the flat surface and crossed to where I stood waiting. We looked up to see bare-legged Catharina, lips pursed, solemnly focusing on each step. We worried if this would prove too much for her new hips and held our breath as she safely dropped another level. Finally, at the bottom, her upper lip was beaded with sweat, but her worried expression softened when she realized she had made it. We wondered how Zbigniew, already having trouble with his legs, would handle this challenge.

"He's there!" I called, seeing Zbigniew's signature blue hat in the midst of the bottlenecked crowd above. We watched as pilgrim by pilgrim, he got closer to the bottom. As he took the final last steps, we were there to welcome him with generous hugs.

Crossing the asphalt road, sparkling blue water called to us. On the hill high above, sat the picturesque town of Portomarin. We crossed the bridge spanning the water and came to the foot of another steep staircase. Despite the number and steepness of the steps, they were way more reasonable than those we had just descended. At the top of the staircase was an arch, the gateway to the town, and to our reprieve from the heat of the sun. Arranging themselves on the stairway for a photo, Catharina, Ana, and Zbigniew reminded me of abandoned toys, strewn behind a toddler as he made his way up to bed.

Finally, up the stairs and through the arch, the sight of orderly streets and well-kept gardens welcomed us. Following the posted map, soon found ourselves in the cool lobby of our *albergue*, O Mirador.

"There you are!" Paul called. "This way, our room is this way," he beckoned us down the hall. Pulling a rough cotton curtain aside, he motioned us forward, waving his hand across a cell of six well-built wooden bunks. "We have these five, and that top one by the door may be for someone else. The shower room and toilet is just down the hall; one for women and one for men. When you're settled, we can go upstairs and get you registered," he offered. Grabbing our shorts and clean t-shirts, along with our toiletries, the girls hurried off to the showers to wash the dust and sweat from our skin.

Paul and Zbigniew were resting on their bottom bunks when we returned, and the five of us climbed yet another staircase, coming out into a busy bar, where wide, opened doors led to a sunny patio where locals and pilgrims lounged under umbrellas, sipping drinks.

Each of us paid our euros and had our passports stamped and registered, joining Paul out on the deck as our names were entered. Last to register, the barista asked me how I had found the big staircase. I told her it had definitely been a challenge, especially for the two older people in our group. I wondered aloud why Esther had not warned me about it since she had come this way before.

"Oh, if she came last year, your friend would not know the path had changed. Long ago, to make it a bit easier, the pilgrims were directed to use the road. But on the road, there is a sharp turn and last year there was a terrible accident. No one was killed, but many pilgrims were injured. So now pilgrims are directed back to the stairs. It is harder, but it is safer!" she finished. My thoughts went to Esther and Andi and their precious cargo, and I quickly sent a text warning them to take care on the big staircase as they approached Portomarin.

"Are you hungry? Paul asked, "the food looks really good here!" We cast longing eyes at appetizing dishes being delivered to neighbouring tables. Finally, it was decided that we'd order a big pizza and share its cheesy goodness among us.

"Do you fancy another drink?" questioned Paul, draining his beer.

"I want to go see the city," Ana said and Catharina and I agreed we'd like to join her.

"Well, we'll come find you when we're done. Zig and I are just going to have another," he advised, signalling the waiter. Probably a good thing, I thought, for Zbigniew to have a bit more of a rest.

Walking up the cobblestone streets, we sought shade under the colonnades fronting storefronts as we climbed to the square. There, the impressive Romanesque fortress church of St. John stood, stark in its simplicity. I had read how, when the valley was flooded to create the water reservoir we had crossed, the church had been disassembled, each brick numbered, and then it was painstakingly rebuilt on the higher ground of the new town site. Built both as a place of worship as well as for defence, it stands in solitary strength, boasting four towers, battlements, and a vaulted nave with an impressive rose window. The cathedral would open in an hour, so we browsed the shops, killing time as we waited the opening of the massive wooden doors.

We discovered the boys circling the cathedral. The doors were open now, so we trooped inside, Paul, Zbigniew, and Ana crossing themselves as they entered. Catharina, hung back, not being a "church" girl.

I rested myself on a smooth pew, polished to softness by worshippers of the years. Inside the austere building, the outside simplicity continued with soft-coloured stone, gentle arches, and minimal ornamentation. A gentle Madonna graced a side altar, while a vivid portrayal of Christ on the cross hung behind the main altar. Paul crossed the floor and took a seat beside me, and we sat in quiet, reflective silence I could tell he was thinking about Daniel. A lone tear slid down his cheek, and I was reminded that for all his bluff and bluster, Paul was a deeply caring man. I patted his shoulder, rose, and left him to his thoughts as he collected himself.

Back out in the sunshine, the troops reunited, and the quest for supper was on. The variety of offerings made by the string of cafes was confusing, and having had the pizza, no one really wanted a big meal. Finally, we decided we'd make a picnic. Time to spare, we lounged on the deck, assembling a list and waited out the siesta closures before heading out, leaving the men to hold the fort.

Strolling back up into town, we visited a large *mercado*, choosing salty olives, robust, red tomatoes, fresh, crisp cucumbers, and crusty loaves of bread. Catharina hovered at the deli counter, seriously pondering her selection of an assortment of cheese and sliced sausage for our picnic. We also picked up two large bottles of water. If we didn't drink it tonight, we could all fill our walking bottles for tomorrow. Inside the euro store next door, I purchased a sharp serrated knife, paper plates, napkins, and clear plastic cups.

"Wine! We will need wine," Ana laughed as we rounded a corner to the street below. Looking past another *mercado*, my eyes feasted on an expanse of green lawns, punctuated by huge, spreading, shady trees, the sparkling blue water of the reservoir a beautiful backdrop.

"Oh! This is nice. Why don't we bring the boys here? The sun will stay with us long into the evening here, and the view is amazing!" Ana and Catharina smiled their agreement as Ana and I stepped inside the store in search of wine. Catharina, our other purchases in hand, waited on a bench outside. We surveyed the variety of wines offered, red being the best choice since everyone liked red. We knew there was no need to choose the pricier bottles; we got good wine for under five euros easily.

"Maybe one more!" Ana suggested, and selected a third bottle. Happy with our purchases, wine bottles clanking softly in their bags, we sauntered back to the *albergue* and found the boys waiting our return. We separated the food and wine into day packs, each of us carrying part of the load. Before leaving the room, I liberated a rough gray blanket from my bunk, stuffing it deep inside my bag. Giggling like teenagers breaking curfew, we climbed the stairs, strolling back out through the bar and out onto the roadway.

"Where are we going then?" Paul questioned, and we told him to wait and see. When we arrived at the park, the men strolled out towards the wall overlooking the water. "This is great!" called back Paul.

We spread the blanket on the soft, green grass, kicked off our shoes and set about preparing our picnic. Ana sliced the bread while Catharina separated slices of cheese and sausage, laying them on paper plates. Zbigniew spilled oily olives from their plastic bags, and I sliced up wedges of tomato and cucumber. Paul opened the wine and pouring it into plastic cups, handed us one each in our turn.

He went to sit down on the edge of the blanket and suddenly sprang up like a scalded cat.

"Ouch!" He danced backward only to jump forward again. "There's something sharp on the ground. Prickles or thorns or something!" he warned jumping to the safety of the blanket. I reached over to run my hands through the grass and found small burrs, either something from the grass itself, or some sort of seed husk from the spreading trees above. I looked askance at him and he blustered, "Well they're sharp!"

Laughing, we all settled in to enjoy our meal. We passed paper plates and built rustic sandwiches, offering each other the local treasures we had collected. We spoke of the day and the challenge of the stairs. We spoke of our families, and of our homes, enjoying this unfettered privacy to learn more about each other.

I compared Galicia with home, saying the area was comfortable to me; forests and streams and rolling hills. Being the only one in the group still working, Zbigniew asked about my work. I explained my job as an administrative assistant in the city's public works division.

"Sounds very professional," Paul quipped, refilling glasses.

"Absolutely!" agreed Zbigniew. Ana told us of her home in Brazil, and the topic of food came up. She shared stories about outdoor cooking, primarily meat dishes, but admitted she didn't do much cooking, living on her own as she did.

"Catharina, do you cook?" Paul enquired. She looked confused. "Are you a good cook then? Do you make special meals?"

"Noooo," she responded seriously. "I *haf* not man so why I cook!" she asserted with a snort!

The laughter continued as we moved from topic to topic, opening our lives before each other. The warmth of the wine suffused us with a happy, relaxed spirit, and the warmth of the sun added to the lazy, carefree atmosphere of uninhibited friendship. We had seen the worst and the best of each of us. Like brothers and sisters, we could say just about anything, secure that any damage done would be just as quickly repaired.

Suddenly, Ana got up and walked away, crossing the road to a tiny *mercado*. A few minutes later, she returned beaming, bearing more wine! Seriously, we had gone through the first three already? Basking in the intoxication of friendship as much as in the wine, we sprawled across the blanket, thoughts and words drifting aimlessly among us in the soft evening breeze.

"Maybe we should save the corks for earplugs!" Ana suggested giggling. I held two corks up to my ears as Paul snapped a photo. As Zbigniew poured the last of the wine, I noticed that although he had said he was saving his new t-shirt for Santiago, the cartoon pilgrim hiked across his bright orange chest, honouring this special event.

The day slowed down, the sun dropping lower in the sky. Conversation lulled into companionable silence. Ana and I, curled like cats on our corners of the blanket, idly picked at blades of grass and pulled leaves from sprigs of clover. Catharina and Zbigniew sat back to back, one supporting the other like bookends without books. Paul, lying on his belly, casually reached out to toss an escaping ball back to a grateful child.

As wonderful as this was, deep sighs all around, we decided it was time to return to the *albergue* before we relaxed ourselves into comas. Tucking the remains of our picnic into bags and shaking the grass from our purloined blanket, we sorted the empty bottles and garbage into a nearby bin, and arm in arm (for support or in friendship?), wove our way back to our bunks.

In the top corner bunk, all we could see was the dark hair of our new room-mate, already fast asleep. In drunken giddiness, we "shushed" each other noisily as we stowed our bags, made quick trips to the bathroom, and scrambled into nightwear. Hugs all around, each of us sought our bunk and snuggled in under covers. Soon the room was full of silent dreamers, enjoying memories of this very special day.

Peeking out the window from my bunk, the lake below was hidden in a valley of mist, making the landscape look like a blurred water colour by Monet.

Having switched my night shirt for my t-shirt and pulled on my trekking pants in place of the leggings I slept in, I slid down the side of the bunk, dropping softly to the cold, tiled floor, smiling at Paul as he rummaged through his bag on the bunk below. I wondered what he'd misplaced now. Our mystery roommate was already gone, I noticed, as Catharina pushed her way back through the curtain that formed our door. Ana was tugging on her socks, and Zbigniew was methodically rolling tape around his knee. For some reason, we were all moving a little slowly this morning, exchanging sheepish grins as we remembered our wine consumption of the evening before.

We joined the parade of pilgrims, quietly walking out into the silent cocoon of fog. Crossing a small bridge, the dirt track followed a sluggish river. We climbed a gentle hill through an increasingly dense forest. All was silent. All was serene…until…

"Si, Si! Chatter, chatter, chatter…" a stocky young woman, dressed in shiny pink spandex leggings, carrying a bright pink backpack decorated with a cartoon kitten, strode along, talking loudly and animatedly into her jewel-studded cellphone. Her disposition was as bright as her clothing. Her shoes, basic cross trainers, were obviously new to the trail. Welcome to "Camino Lite". We looked at each other and smiled.

The hill climbed and we paced ourselves, following along behind the chatting camiga who seemed to start a new call every five minutes. Not understanding enough Spanish, I was sure she was enthusiastically describing her "pilgrimage" to friends and family at home. Frustrated with her disregard for her fellow pilgrims and Camino etiquette, we switched into low gear and pulled ahead, Paul taking the lead and very quickly disappearing ahead of us into the fog.

The trail followed an asphalt road, taking us gradually upward, first on one side, then crossing the pavement, travelling past a chain-link fenced industrial plant, and meandering back to the other side again. About an hour and a half later, we came to Gonzar and the Café Descanso del Peregrino, a bustling café brimming with pilgrims clamouring for breakfast. As we waited in a cafeteria-like line, we noted the increase in new pilgrims, easily evident by their attire, confirmed by their loud and impatient behaviour. Paul had secured a table on the outside patio, and we jostled for chairs, asking disgruntled novices to remove their coats and small packs so we could sit down. Eggs, toast, and coffee; a good breakfast hurriedly choked down in a bid to escape the confusion of the café.

Up ahead, we saw the fog peeling back like a roll of cotton batting, revealing vibrant green grasslands. We continued to climb past the ancient village of Hospital de la Cruz. The trail next led through Ventas de Naron, where a tiny stone chapel patiently witnessed the passing parade. Ana and I poked our head in the doorway of the chapel, hoping to get a stamp in our passports.

We had been told that during the last hundred kilometres of the trek, two stamps were required each day; one from the place you spent the night, and the other from a church, tourist information centre, or other such location providing stamps. This was required as proof that you really walked the day, however it would become evident that there were still ways to cheat the system. What we couldn't understand was why, if this were a religious pilgrimage, people thought to earn the Compostela without really walking. If they believed in the religious significance of the document, didn't they realize that Someone would know they had cheated?

Inside the cool darkness of the chapel, tiny candles lit up the crucifix behind a simple altar draped in homespun cloth. Almost invisible at a desk to the side, an elderly man, gazing off into the rafters, sat waiting. We each said a small prayer, and then crossed to the desk, where we signed our names in a book and the curator stamped our passports in the spot we held open. I dropped some coins in the collection box, and, his hand resting upon my shoulder, received his kind blessing. Back out in the sunshine, Ana pulled out her water bottle.

"Isn't it amazing that he does that and he can't even see!" Confused, I looked at Ana.

"He's blind?" I questioned. She nodded. "I felt he was looking right into my soul when he looked at me," I mused.

"Perhaps he was," she responded softly, "but he couldn't see your face." How had I missed that?

We finally reached the summit and began the downward journey towards Ligonde, where ancient stone houses shouldered the road. As we approached an *albergue* with a *"cerrado"* sign, a small curly-haired black child in denim shorts and a numbered t-shirt came running out to us.

"You buy an orange? I have nice oranges. You like an orange?" His smile was brilliant as he offered up his fruit for our inspection. He quickly passed an orange to a smiling Catharina who had, as usual, caught up with us on the downhill. "You come see. I have more!" he tugged excitedly on my hand. Laughing, I let him pull me across the lane to a tall table holding a large basket of fragrant oranges.

"Can you pick one for me?" I asked as I lifted him up, his tiny bare feet dangling in the air. He pulled an orange out of the basket and I placed him back on the ground. His young father had just appeared in the doorway of the closed *albergue*. Taking the offered fruit, I handed the little boy a coin, but he seemed confused as to what to do with it. "Give this to your daddy," I suggested, and he happily ran over to his father, his prize waving proudly in the air. "Quite some salesman you have there!" I laughed.

"He is good at selling, but not so good with the money yet," his tall father smiled. We waved good-bye and I wished we were staying there. It would have been nice to spend some time with the young family. I was missing my own so much.

"Too bad the *albergue* is closed," Ana echoed my own thoughts. An *albergue* being closed usually meant one thing; bed bugs. The scourge of the pilgrim trade, *hospitaleros* took the nasty vermin very seriously. If a pilgrim reported bites in the morning, reputable *albergues* closed their doors until they could be fumigated, and the pilgrims' clothing and bags washed and cleaned. Unfortunately, some were less ethical and allowed unsuspecting pilgrims to carry the pests from their infected *albergue* to the next. It was good to see this *albergue* was taking their responsibilities seriously, and I hoped they would be back in business soon. They wouldn't be able to live on orange sales for long, no matter how charming their salesman was.

We left the roadway, taking a dirt trail a few minutes further, arriving at the outskirts of Eirexe. Passing a church yard and a couple of houses, we came to a hub, roads going off in five different directions. Three building stood at different points in the hub: a bar, our *albergue*, and another *albergue*. That was the town.

Our *albergue* was a two-storied, white plaster farmhouse set atop a foundation of soft, golden rock. Large, deeply set windows were pushed wide open; the creamy curtains billowing in the breeze seemed to beckon us in. The gravel courtyard was set with square metal tables, flanked by metal tube chairs. A huge, thickly leafed tree cast cooling shadows across the patio. A stout Spanish woman, in a printed house dress, came out the door on the left. This was obviously the family's residence, while our beds would be found by entering the door on the right.

Paul came running up the path behind us, just having come out of the bar. Our hostess led us into the cool, tile-floored reception area and asked who was going to take which room. Pushing open the door by her desk, she indicated a room containing two wooden bunk bed sets, complete with sheets and comforters.

"I had a thought, and since Zbigniew is not here yet, this is a good time to ask you. We have four beds at ten euros each, and one at twenty. I was thinking… and I don't want to put any pressure on anyone…but what if we all paid twelve euros and offered Zbigniew the private room. A little more for us; a little less for him. It seems like the heat and the walk is really taking a toll on him, and he might benefit from a night in a real bed." I looked hopefully at the others. "He might not even want it, but I figured now would be the time for us to talk about it, before he gets here. I'll happily take a top bunk." Taping my foot was helping, and these bunks had decent ladders, so I wasn't so worried about my foot.

"I think that's a really good idea," nodded Ana. The others quickly agreed, and so we claimed the bunks, removing the weight of that decision from our friend. Our *hospitalero* had placed a big wicker basket by the door to our room, stating a very reasonable cost for laundry. Although hand washing the bare essentials on a daily basis helped, we weren't going to turn down the opportunity for proper laundry services. We each took our shower, changed into clean clothes, and filled her basket.

Finally, Zbigniew came strolling up the pathway. We showed him our room, and told him what we had done with regard to the private room. He shook his white mane in disbelief.

"No. It is not necessary," he protested, but we advised him it was already a done deal. He swallowed deeply, and held out his arms, and we joined in a group hug. "You are more than my friends! You are my family!" he exclaimed.

"So, go have a shower and dump your laundry and join us on the patio for a beer!" Paul instructed, turning away before his face could give away his emotions.

Paul and I walked across the street to the bar to find out if we could bring glasses of beer back to our *albergue* patio. The proprietor looked at us like we were crazy even asking.

"But of course!" he announced, filling a tray with tall, sweating glasses and a side plate of crackers. Paul carried the tray and I assured the young Spaniard that we would return the glasses and tray.

At the *albergue* next door, young people had spilled out on the wooden deck, taking advantage of the shade provided by a stand of tall trees. They raised emptying glasses at our passage and playfully suggested a beer heist. Back on our patio, Zbigniew had joined Ana and Catharina at a table. I chose to lay on a nearby bench, wanting to get some sun on my back for a change. The beer and warm sunshine lulled me into a drowsy state of contentment, in the background, musical chatter and the quick rap of a knife blade against a wooden board. Fragrant hints of bread baking and garlic and onions being sautéed escaped the kitchen. I hoped the meal we would be served in the bar would be as good as our *hospitalero* family's meal smelled!

Rousing myself, Ana and I went through our guidebooks, considering options for our last two nights before Santiago. It was pretty much all downhill from here with a few hills thrown in just to keep it interesting. Our walk to Melide would be a longer day, so we settled on a shorter day for our next day, making Arzua our next stop.

"How 'bout this," I asked, tracing the words in the guide with my finger. "They have a place called Don Quijote! All the *albergues* are the same price and offer much the same facilities. This one has fifty beds; some have less, some have more. But I like the name," I laughed.

"*Ya, et es* a good name," Catharina agreed. "I *haf* another name also," she announced shyly. Now what did she mean by that? Like an onion...no, that's too nasty...like an artichoke, Catharina seemed to have many layers, and while the language barrier posed a challenge, each day we were learning something new about our Belgian sister.

"What do you mean you have another name? Like from being married, or before you were married?" queried Paul, as confused as the rest of us.

"Maybe she means a nickname," I offered. "Like my real name is Roxana, but

I go by Roxey."

"Roxana," they rolled my name around.

"My other name *es* Netty," Catharina announced. Okay, so not a derivative of Catharina as far as I knew.

"So is that what your family calls you?" Paul questioned, still confused. "Or your friends?" We all stared intently at her, waiting for an explanation.

"*Ya, es* for my family." So maybe a pet name; one reserved for the closest in life. "You can call me Netty!"

"Netty." We all tried out the name for size. She beamed happily at us, hearing our voices give life to her special name. We realized this was a gift from Catharina…I mean Netty. She had, in its giving, confirmed the importance of our relationships with her. We truly were becoming a little family.

"We could do O Pedrouzo for the last stop. That would break the remaining distance in half, and we'd have two twenty 'k days in a row," I suggested. "If we don't stop at O Pedrouzo, it looks like the next *albergue* would be A Lavacolla. It would make the last day into Santiago really short, but it would mean putting in a thirty-kilometre day before that."

"No… *das es* too much!" Catharina stated; Zbigniew quickly supported her opinion.

"It would seem a little crazy to go for a big push when we've been pacing so nicely 'til now," I remarked.

"Twenty, twenty sounds good to me," Paul agreed. "You girls just make the reservations and tell us where we're stopping. You have kept us well organized. Very professional!"

"Absolutely," pronounced Zbigniew. Ana and I sorted through the *albergues* on offer in O Pedrouzo, selected *Albergue* Cruceiro de Pedrouzo, and made the call.

"Isn't that tomorrow night's place?" asked Paul.

"In Melide? Same name, almost," I agreed. "Just drop the de Pedrouzo." Everyone took photos of the listing for our Melide *albergue*. We found this a handy trick to make sure even if separated, we could find our way to our booking and each other.

Done with beer and done with sitting for a while, we three women decided on a walk. We left the men to their beers and talk. Depositing our glasses at the bar across the square, we checked out the pilgrim menu and agreed that it sounded okay. A good thing, since it was the only game in town!

We strolled down the dirt track we had come in on, diverting off to explore the old church and its impressive cemetery. Headstones and mausoleums of every shape and size, some with little alcoves with integral vases full of fresh flowers, spoke of the history of the area. Family names carried from one to the other, dates progressing through a hundred years. This tiny little hamlet probably wouldn't seem like much to some, but to the inhabitants, this was their world.

Continuing down the lane, we discovered a few old brick and plaster houses, one with a remarkable flower garden (likely the source of those in the graveyard). There were some crumbling homes, glassless windows, weeds overtaking the stairs and doorways. And then, suddenly, there was a very new build, a shiny new car parked at the foot of the wrought-iron railed stairs. We could hear the blare of a television or radio from within, and knew that while the ghosts of the past deteriorated nearby, the future was still anticipated.

"I wonder how much one of these houses would cost," mused Ana.

"Are you thinking of moving?" I asked with a smile. Catharina stopped and looked at her, brow furrowed and lips pursed.

"No," sighed Ana. "But I wonder what they would cost. It might be fun to run an *albergue*," she suggested.

"I think it would be fun to come and do a two-week volunteer stint, but I'm not so sure about a full-time commitment," I pondered.

"But you have your husband, children, and grandchildren. I have just one child, and she is in England. Spain is closer than Brazil for visiting," Ana argued gently. I chose not to remind her about her parents since this was all just imagination.

As if this was a reality, we discussed the pros and cons of running an *albergue*. We talked about language barriers and addressing the needs of different cultures. We agreed we would want separate housing, somewhat like the place we were staying tonight. It seemed likely that the real estate cost would be higher the closer the property was to the Camino path, but that the cost would be offset by the likelihood of having more guests. We talked about what we did and didn't like in the *albergues* where we had stayed, agreeing that having the option of a real bed would be more attractive than bunks.

"The showers should have a place to hang your clothes where they don't get wet. And they should have somewhere you can dress, again without getting wet!"

I insisted. "And I am more attracted to the places where we ate family-style as a group, rather than going to a nearby bar for supper."

"Yes, and home cooked meals are so wonderful. You could have a garden and grow your own vegetables, and maybe have a cow so you could have fresh cream, and I could make my own cheese. I would have to learn to cook for large groups." Ana was really getting into this. Note how the "you" statements slid into "my" and "I" statements?

"*Ya*, and chickens for eggs," Catharina suggested seriously.

"But not running free range around the doorway!" I declared and we all joined in laughter remembering the chickens at Alto do Poio.

"And it would be good to offer laundry facilities," offered Ana. "Sometimes you just really need to have everything washed and dried properly."

"I know I really appreciated the bathrooms that had soap and paper towels. I guess all those costs add up, but when I think about the places I enjoyed, and the ones I would recommend to others, those are the sort of things I remember." The girls nodded in agreement.

By now we had wound our way back to our *albergue* and, not having discovered any likely properties for sale along the way, we went around the house to check on our laundry in the backyard. Among trellised grape vines and a tidy vegetable garden, our clothes hung, dancing in the wind, from a free-standing line. The sun and the wind had done their work quickly. It would be nice to have clean clothes again.

Paul approached, sauntering up the road from the other direction, having scouted out our exit route for the next day. He told us Zbigniew was having a little siesta but would meet us for supper. Seeing our laundry, he made his way out to check on his own. As we crossed the foyer carrying our fresh laundry, a different door opened and out stepped a slim, petite woman with pale-blue eyes and shoulder-length greying hair. I felt I knew her but couldn't quite place her.

"Roxey! I haven't seen you since Roncesvalles! It's Angela," she offered at my obvious confusion. "I was with Cindy's group." Now I remembered. She was the one comforting Davina, and I remembered overhearing that she was from Hawaii. The others, suspecting a reunion, melted into our room with the laundry. I walked into Angela's hug. Angela was dressed in leggings and a drifting tunic, soft and gauzy, with a fringed turquoise scarf that complimented her turquoise and silver bracelet and rings. She emanated an aura of grounded peace and tranquility and my mind instantly supplied "earth muffin". Her style spoke to her occupation as a massage therapist and her love of all things meditative and yoga.

"You look so different!" she exclaimed as we walked out to a bench on the patio. "When I met you back then in St. Jean, you were tight and…closed," she searched for the right words. "You look younger and relaxed; more peaceful. I think this walk has been very good for you." A lot of information from someone I didn't know much at all, but I guess I had to accept the validity of her first impression versus how I appeared now.

Angela told me the little she knew about the others in her group. It seemed it had broken up pretty quickly and not being electronically connected to them, she'd lost touch with most of the members. She said she knew Cindy was still on the trail and still walking with Anne-Marie. She'd heard Patti and Theresa had left for home early, and that Shirley had gone off with some guy in Pamplona. *So, not so happily married after all,* I thought.

"Patricia and I walked together as far as Leon," I supplied. "I wanted to stay an extra day to explore the city, so she walked out with someone else. She wanted to get to Santiago faster to do the trip to Finisterre. I've been getting messages as she travels, so I know where she is and that she is safe. I'm also aware of where there may be shortages of chocolate when I arrive. That girl eats a lot of chocolate!" I laughed. "I just got a photo from her showing her arrival at the cathedral in Santiago. We're hoping to meet up there. By the time I arrive, she will have returned from the coast, so it may just happen." I invited Angela to join us later for dinner, knowing my friends would make her welcome.

Later that evening, trudging across the square to the small bar, we filed through the front door and past the bar, pulled up chairs at the central table, and waited the arrival of Zbigniew and Angela. A young Spanish woman in black slacks and a crisp, white shirt passed menus around. Just as the last of us ordered, in walked our sleepy friend, looking like a new man after his shower and snooze. Zbigniew quickly added his order and filled his glass from the wine bottle left on the table.

"How is your room?" Ana asked.

"Oh. Very nice thank you all!" Zbigniew smiled. Just then, Angela arrived and introductions made. Angela was quickly welcomed by the group. She regaled us with stories of Hawaii as we waited for our salad.

A noisy group from the other *albergue* crowded into the dining room, dragging the small tables against the back wall together to form a boisterous banquet. There was a very young girl at the table, and in conversation between our tables, we were advised that Tasha and her father had travelled from the States to do this walk together to celebrate her nineteenth birthday. I was surprised at Tasha's confidence at her age. She seemed completely at ease among all these strangers, and her very fit father advised she set a hard pace for him. She smiled cheekily and said he should stop acting like an old man. Her father gave her a mock cuff to the head, and we all laughed, enjoying the playful exchange, perhaps seeing a little of our own children in Tasha.

The overwhelmed waitress, valiantly keeping up with all the diners, plunked bottle after bottle of wine and water on the tables, so no one minded waiting for the next course. For dessert, *tartes* Santiago, thin almond cakes imprinted with the cross of St. James, were presented with much ceremony.

Lingering over our last glasses of wine, we watched the sun crawl down the patio wall outside. The shadows grew long, and the noisy table grew noisier. Amidst laughter and song, we made our way out of the dining room, bypassing the bar on the way to the door.

There, a line of jean-clad locals leaned, boots on a rail, downing shots of a clear green liquor. At my enquiring glance, a tall Spaniard slid a glass my way, gesturing that I should down it. He and his buddies encouraged me on with smiles and nods. My Camino family crowded in behind me, Paul and Zbigniew accepting their own shot glass, the other ladies declining. I raised the glass and set my lips on fire. Much to the Spaniards' disgust, I took only a tiny sip, coughing at the strength of the drink. I laughingly wiped tears from my eyes and handed back the glass. My new friend pounded me on my back and laughed heartily. While I hadn't made the cut as a drinker of the local brew, I had at least provided some entertainment!

Reluctant to end a good day, we hugged Zbigniew and Angela as they trekked off to their private rooms. Ana, Catharina, Paul, and I readied ourselves for bed, taking turns in the bathroom, fussing with our packs, and finally climbing into our bunks. A gentle night breeze wafted in through the curtains and we settled down to sleep, listening to our amigos from the other *albergue* staggering across the square in a struggle to find their own beds. Finally, all was quiet, and we slept.

Sunlight filtered through the muslin curtains, filling our bunk room with soft morning light. With good morning smiles, Ana and I slid softly to the floor, Catharina just returning from the bathroom. We each took our turn in the bathroom, a quick wash and tooth brushing and we were out.

"Right!" exclaimed Paul as he rolled out from under his quilt. "A quick shower and I'll be right with you!" he assured us. We exchanged smiles knowing that despite his elaborate verbal itemization and organization of each article of clothing set out the night before, something would go missing, and he'd be scrambling again. Taking the opportunity of "girls only" space, we quickly changed out of sleepwear into our walking clothes and were just shouldering our packs as Paul burst out through the bathroom door. We said we'd wait outside for him, allowing him the same privacy we had shared while he showered.

Zbigniew joined us outside, rubbing sleep from his eyes. Still no sign of Paul, Ana and I said we'd walk ahead and save a table for breakfast.

Two kilometres down the road, we came to Portos with plans of stopping at Paso de Formiga for breakfast. To our dismay, the door was closed and the blind drawn, so we resigned ourselves to walking on. Just then, the door opened, and a smiling young woman beckoned us inside. Six tables surrounded by metal chairs filled the small, bright space in front of the bar. Settling our packs on the floor by the back wall, we glanced at the menus and kept an eye on the window for the other three. On the bar I noticed an apple tart that looked too good to deny. I asked for a slice of the pie with a slice of cheese melted on top, thinking this would provide protein for the morning. The barista looked confused so I knew this North American tradition was a new idea for her. Ana liked the idea, however, and she ordered a similar slice to go with her *café con leche*.

The others had still not shown, and I was wondering what Paul had misplaced now. While waiting for our breakfast, I made use of the washroom, coming out in time to see our three *compadres* strutting past. I realized then that the shade was still down on the front door, and they probably thought the bar was closed. I rushed to the door and called out to them, but they just waved and kept on walking.

"I guess they are trying to make up lost time," Ana smiled. "We will catch up with them later. Sit, enjoy your pie." Other pilgrims pushed through the door chatting noisily and calling out their orders to the barista. Draining our cups, we carried our dishes to the dishpans on the side counter and waved our thanks to our young hostess who was busily buttering toast while coffee steamed into waiting cups.

Cresting a gentle rise, we dropped down into a misty valley, seeing Zbigniew and Catharina just ahead. It was funny that while Paul was often the last one out, his strong stride usually carried him off ahead of us. The road took us through a forested area, and I had to stop and take a picture of my three friends as they disappeared into a tunnel of fog. It was almost mystical, and the vision became even more magical as we broke out of the forest to see the sun, burning through the fog, painting the morning sky a soft, pastel pink. Softly backlit trees hung exotically in the mist like something out of an Oriental water colour. Lush green fields stretched out on either side of our trail, and we each fell into private reflection and companionable silence. Catching up to the others, step, tap, step, tap; we moved on, each in our own stride, Zbigniew and Catharina dropping back gradually.

As Ana and I rounded a corner, a tall, broad-shouldered, young pilgrim strutted towards us. It seemed strange to see a backpack burdened walker coming this way, instead of the other. I wondered if he were one of the over-achieving pilgrims who did the trek both ways and was on his way home. As he approached, I noticed he seemed to be carrying a lot of gear. It was kind of confusing, but it looked like he had more than one pack.

"Good morning!" he called out, sweeping a fringe of long, brown hair off his face. "I wonder if you could spare fifty cents for me to get some water and food?" he asked. Wanting to honour the pilgrim code, I realized all of my money was in my pack, and it would be a big production to get to it. Ana stood silently, hands gripping her poles tightly. He smiled at me and suddenly the warning bells came on. I looked at how much gear he was carrying. I looked more closely and none of it seemed to fit; the items looked more like a collection rather than personal gear a pilgrim would choose. I shook my head and said I was sorry, I had no money with me. He fixed me with a stare, but I held my ground and tightened my grip on my poles. Finally, he muttered something under his breath as he stomped off.

"I think that man was a thief," Ana declared soberly as the distance grew between us and the man. "I think if we stopped and took off our packs, he meant to rob us."

"I got that feeling too," I agreed. "The things he was carrying didn't seem right. I'm wondering if he has robbed others already today. I mean think about it. What could fifty cents buy anyways? It wouldn't even buy a bottle of water!" We continued on, feeling thankful for each other's company and hoping that Zbigniew and Catharina were still together.

The trail wound through the soft, green countryside, each corner opening on a new view. Suddenly, on a gentle hill to the side, there was a large, lodge-type structure, built of logs. A shady veranda ran the length of the two-storied building, and there, at a table under an umbrella, sat Paul and Angela, enjoying tall glasses of fresh orange juice. They waved us to join them.

"We missed you at breakfast," I chided him.

"Oh, I was all ready to go, but then I realized my socks were at the bottom of my bag. Then I couldn't find my phone cord, so I unpacked, and then found it on the bed, and then I had to repack!" Paul advised. Ana and I exchanged smiles. Dropping my pack, I went inside to get drinks for Ana and I. It was early yet, but the temperature was already climbing.

"Did you meet anyone along the way?" Angela questioned. We told her about the man we met, and she said she had been accosted by him too. "I just ignored him and walked on quickly. It just didn't seem right to me," she agreed.

"Hallo!" Zbigniew and Catharina waved from the path below. As they joined us, we conferred about the mystery man. They had met him, but just walked on when he approached them. Zbigniew said he had seemed suspicious to them.

"Ya, es not good," Catharina nodded seriously. This was the first time I had ever felt at risk on the Camino. Even when I had walked totally alone with no one in sight, or shared a room with only men, I felt protected. This was just a reminder to us all that while we felt safe in this protective bubble of the Camino, there were still nefarious people out there, and we had to take care and guard each other's back.

Angela and Paul rose to collect their gear, Paul antsy to get going, and Angela saying she had to keep moving since she walked slowly. An open-ended return, Angela planned to walk short days, and we hugged, knowing we might not see each other again.

Back on the trail, Zbigniew again dropped back and we walked on, honouring his need for space. As the day wore on, it got hotter and hotter, so it was a bit of a surprise as we came through a forested tunnel to see raindrops falling into puddles in the dirt track. Catharina cocked her head, struggling to identify the source of the drops.

"It's tree pee," I supplied smiling at her confusion. "Back home, our yard backs on a forest. When it rains, and then stops, we hear the "rain" falling for a half hour or so as the rain captured by the leaves and branches continues to fall. We call it "tree pee". Understanding dawning, Catharina smiled broadly, mouthing the term silently. Ana laughed out loud at her expression as we skirted the dripping area, tucking back into the woods to avoid the muddy puddle.

Soon the countryside gave way to another small city, and we knew we had reached Palas de Rei. Following the shells and arrows, we wound our way through the streets, coming to a large church surrounded by simple gardens of hedging and graceful trees. To one side, there was a beautiful statue of the Madonna, and I paused to take a photo.

Suddenly, I could hear English being spoken. Answering my questioning glance, Ana waved at the heavy, planked church door, left ajar. Inside we found an American priest on pilgrimage had been given permission to conduct a mass in Palas de Rei for his congregants travelling with him. Ana and I settled into a back pew to listen, but Catharina waved, indicating she was going on.

While a Catholic mass, it was still a treat to be able to follow the words. The priest spoke in a smooth, story-telling voice, regaling English-speaking pilgrims with the magic of the Camino. He spoke of the instances he had seen Jesus in the faces and actions of those on the journey, and how He was with us, even when we were unaware. The priest told of small miracles, everyday actions that spoke of the Holy, and how we could be gifts to each other, as well as to the Lord as we followed the path to Santiago. The equally opulently robed Spanish priest hovering in the background nodded in agreement, supporting his American brother's words. As the service moved into communion, Ana and I quietly departed, renewed and ready to continue our journey.

Tapping along the city roadways we were suddenly hailed from behind as Tasha strode up beside us.

"Good morning!" she cheerfully exclaimed. "How is your walk going today?"

"It is good," Ana smiled. "Where is your father?"

"Oh, he was a little slow getting up this morning, so I just left on my own. I will wait for him in Melide!" she happily assured us over her shoulder as she strode away. While concerned for her safety, we had to admire the spunk and confidence of this young girl, and we wished her "*Buen Camino*" as she struck off.

Leaving the city behind, the trail levelled out, and we found ourselves stepping stone to stone as, once again, a small stream had, over the course of time, made the Camino its own. In the reeds thrusting up from the murky shallows, frogs croaked and peeped in a noisy symphony. Stepping from the final flat rock of the spontaneous bridge, we regained the cinder trail as it wound past fenced fields stretching across the gently rolling farmland.

In a shady country setting, we discovered the *albergue* Casanova, where Paul, Catharina, and Zbigniew were already savouring creamy coffees in the courtyard. Ana and I carried our drinks out to the courtyard, sliding onto rough wooden chairs set along the ivy-draped wall of the *albergue*. An array of containers from plant pots to cooking pots exploded in a colourful floral display, lazy bumble bees and butterflies dancing from one bloom to the next. Zbigniew, giving into the warmth of the sun, laid back on a raised walkway, taking a little power nap. To one side, against a rustic shingled shed, an oversized scallop shell leaned, providing a whimsical backdrop for pilgrim photos. We roused our drowsy friend and cajoled a couple, just coming in the gate, to take a group photo of us in front of the huge shell.

"Would you like me to take your photo now?" I asked the middle-aged couple.

"Oh yes!" the grey-haired woman exclaimed as she rooted through her small pack. "Can you make sure this is in the photo?" She held up a newspaper from their home in the States. "They're having a contest," she explained, "looking for the photo the furthest away, but the newspaper has to be in the photo!" She removed her hat and fluffed her hair while her balding husband handed me his phone. He wiped a sheen of sweat off his forehead, rearranged his shirt over his rounding belly, and threw his arm around his wife. They struck up a pose, big grins on their faces, each holding a corner of the newspaper. I obliged, and handed their phone back.

"Thank you. Where are you from?" the big man asked. I told him I was Canadian. "Oh, they have the nicest people in Canada, don't they Evie?" His wife nodded enthusiastically. "What's your name?" I told him it was Roxey, and his whole demeanour changed.

Now let me tell you of the challenge of my name. While I really don't like being called by my full name, Roxana, my nickname comes with its own issues. "Roxey", however you spell it, seems to have been reserved for strippers, hookers, and theatres that show movies of an adult nature. I've often found, especially on the phone where the caller can't see that I'm your standard, middle-aged woman, that hearing my name conjures up all sorts of visions of the illicit, and their tone changes completely.

"Roxxxxxeee! Well, Roxey…thank you so much for taking our photo. Maybe we'll see you around again sometime, Roxeee," he added with an embarrassing leer and a wink, wink, nudge, nudge. It might have felt threatening if it hadn't been so funny. His wife, clutching her jacket around her, stepped gingerly past me, tugging his arm towards the door.

"Come on George. Let's get a coffee!" All of a sudden, she was not so enthusiastic about Canadians.

As they disappeared inside, I could hear him still going on, "Roxxeee…Roxxee Roller," and his flustered wife telling him to shut up.

Paul and Zbigniew just looked at each other and pulled themselves up, ready for a confrontation. I shook my head, shrugging off their chivalrous concerns, and we headed out. Ana fell in beside me, a hand on my shoulder and a questioning smile.

"It's okay. It's crazy, but it happens to me a lot. I'm used to it," I sighed.

Behind me, Paul started humming "Roxy Roller" under his breath. I looked over my shoulder, gave him a look, and he stopped, murmuring an apology. Then I laughed out loud and the rest joined in as we found our pace, ascending the sun-dappled hill, soft footfalls kicking up dust on the red dirt track.

We came upon a cluster of lightly burdened pilgrims, obviously new to the trek and still full of perky enthusiasm. While we walked in reflective silence, they babbled on, their bright voices overwhelming the peaceful forest path. By now the temperatures were climbing into the thirties despite the lacy treed canopy. In single file we followed the winding track, doing our best to focus on the journey and shut out the constant chatter of Camino Lite pilgrims before and aft.

We broke through the trailhead coming out onto the shoulder of a paved road. To my left, a charming old two-storied stone house stood encircled by huge, sweeping shade trees. I fell in love. The gravel driveway led up to the lush, green lawn set with paving stones inviting passage to the wide, black front door. Large pots brimming with colourful blooms took the place of window boxes beneath multi-paned windows, and flowering ivy climbed the stone walls on each end. The solid chimney, thrusting above the terra cotta roof, spoke of cozy fires in large, high-ceilinged rooms. It wasn't fancy, just big and solid and gorgeous in an old-world way. This could be our house! I'm sure everything Al would need could be on the ground floor, easily accessed by wheelchair. And the upstairs? Rooms for family visitors, or guests, or pilgrims! Okay! I gave my head a shake. Maybe it was the heat. An *albergue* in Spain was Ana's dream, not mine. But it was a really great house.

Knowing this would be the last chance for a cold drink before Melide, we stopped again at O Coto, capturing the last empty table in front of a store doing a brisk pilgrim trade in drinks, light lunches, and fresh fruit. Inside I purchased a soda and a basket of cherries. Catharina had also bought cherries, so there were lots to share. Our table, perched on the side of the pavement, was in a tightly congested area, barely clearing the front door of the store. Across the road we saw a large bus, the driver patiently waiting by the open cargo doors, stowing packs for the pilgrims as they crossed the road from the store and climbed aboard into the air-conditioned luxury of their transport.

"Bus pilgrims," a swarthy pilgrim at the next table muttered derisively. At our enquiring looks he explained. "They probably started their Camino at Sarria. They bus a little, then the driver lets them off so they can experience the Camino. Then they meet up again, and he takes them on to their hotel." We expressed our confusion as to how that qualified as a pilgrimage.

Travelling by bus to experience the pilgrimage might have been a necessity for some elderly or disabled people, to be sure, and I personally wouldn't deny them that. Most of those we had walked with today however, seemed totally capable of walking, at least the last hundred kilometres to earn their Compostela. Ultimately, however, it was their loss. If they were going on to Santiago to get their certificates under false pretences, they would always know they hadn't really fulfilled the true meaning of the Camino.

Ready to hit the road again, I went over to the corner to retrieve my pack. Shoving my hand through one strap, I was just getting to heave the weight onto my back when a stout Spanish woman, dressed more like for a day at the mall than a day on the trail, tried to step over my pack in a rush for the door of the store.

"*Uno momento, por favor,*" I said, but she waved at the bus, indicating she was in a hurry and I was in her way. I placed my hand up to stop her. "It is heavy!" I exclaimed, but she still didn't back off, so I rolled it onto my shoulder, barely missing her. She huffed loudly, as if I were the one being unreasonable, and stomped into the store. My friends, standing waiting, just shook their heads.

"Bus pilgrims!" we all muttered together and struck off in a fellowship of righteous indignation and laughter.

For the next six kilometres, we descended steadily, roasting in the hot, hot sun as we travelled a gravel track, often paralleling a busy roadway. Sporadic trees leant some relief, but with temperatures entering the high thirties, it was a daunting trek. Zbigniew, bringing up the rear of our column was gradually losing ground, dropping further and further behind us. I knew he would catch up eventually and plodded on in place between Ana and Catharina.

The track took a turn away from the road and followed a series of high fences, interrupted from time to time by stands selling cold drinks, t-shirts, and other souvenirs. A good indication we were getting close to our destination, we carried on. The trail dipped down into the little town of Furelos, the white plaster buildings jammed together along the narrow road. A bar, tucked back in the shadows, spilled chairs of boisterous pilgrims gathered around umbrella-sheltered tables, cold mugs of beer clutched happily in their hands. Signs advertising *pulpo* enticed passers-by to stop and try the regional octopus specialty.

"Whoooeee!" a young voice called out, and there stood Tasha, waving madly at our passage. Her dad sat tiredly in the chair next to her, raising a half-hearted wave. I'm sure he was wondering where his daughter got her energy. We waved in salute and carried on over a beautiful, medieval bridge.

After five hours on the road, before us lay a wide, paved avenue flanked by modern *albergues*, but not ours. We had absolutely no idea where we were going, and there were no signs to help us on our way. We saw signs pointing the way to the cathedral. We knew our *albergue* was close to the cathedral, so we turned the corner, tired feet smacking the hot concrete beneath our shoes.

I cast a glance back over my shoulder, looking unsuccessfully for Zbigniew. Having a disabled husband, I have learned to walk the tightrope between my need to take care of him, and his need to be independent; a fine line between providing assistance and damaging the frail male ego. I have learned to ask how or if I can help rather than just pushing in and taking over.

I knew Zbigniew was an adult, an experienced walker, and that there were plenty of other pilgrims behind us to lend a hand if needed. I also knew he had already been feeling the heat at our last stop, and that his leg was giving him grief. I was torn. Paul, sensing my dilemma, said not to worry; he'd be along in his own time.

The next turn took us right into the commercial heart of Melide. After the relative peace of the Camino, the noisy city was an assault on the ears and the nerves. Busy streets were thick with vehicles of every shape and size, and pedestrians thronged the sidewalks. The roadway was lined with modern storefronts and offices, with shadowy pulperias displaying tanks of live octopus to lure diners in. Block after busy block we trudged, looking left and right, trying to find the *albergue*. At a busy intersection, we all looked in different directions, searching out our *albergue*.

"There! There it is! Across the street, on the corner!" Ana announced, pointing at a small sign, partially obscured by a streetlight pole. Paul went to push the pedestrian control button, and I looked down the busy road we had just trekked up. Still no Zbigniew.

"I'm going back to find Zbigniew!" I said.

"He'll get here. Let's just go get checked in, and I'll bet he'll arrive shortly," Paul reasoned.

"If we had this much trouble finding the place with four sets of eyes, how hard will it be for him on his own?" I asked. "You go ahead and get our beds. I'll just walk back a ways and show him how to get here." Concerned glances fluttered back and forth between Catharina and Ana. "Really. It's okay. I'll just walk back as far as the bridge and wait for him there."

"Okay then," Paul agreed. "We'll wait here for you." I turned and literally hot-footed it down the hill, turning the two corners that brought me from the busy commercial district back out onto the wide avenue we entered the city on. Just as I was approaching the bridge, there came Zbigniew. I called out his name and his face lit up. He waved tiredly. Crossing the bridge, he threw his arm around my shoulder.

"Thank you for waiting for me." He smiled, swinging his leg with effort. "I am sorry I am so slow. It is so hot!" he apologized as he mopped his sweating brow.

"No worries!" I assured him, resting my hand on his shoulder. "We found the *albergue*, but it was like a treasure hunt. The others are waiting there. It's not too much further; only about ten- minute's walk."

"Good!" he sighed, taking a big slug of water from his bottle. "I am glad there is an elevator there. It would be hard to do stairs right now. We go!" Together we recovered the distance quite quickly since I knew the way now. Joining our friends, Paul pounded Zbigniew's back in welcome; the girls greeted him with hugs. We crossed the busy road with the light, quickly filing into the quiet, cool lobby of *Albergue* O Cruceiro.

At a modern desk, a young, dark-eyed woman greeted us and checked our names off her reservation sheet. Catharina, Paul, and Zbigniew retrieved their packs from the stack that had been ported from Eirexe. I was glad they had that option; the walk alone had been enough for our older friends. The lift wasn't big enough to take us all, so we sent Zbigniew, Catharina, and Paul ahead, and Ana and I followed our *hospitalero* up the wide, granite stairs.

"Your room is only on floor three. Come with me and I will show you." Trudging up the stairs behind her, I envied her youth, her lack of a pack, and her great shoes! She waved us towards a wooden door with a frosted glass inset. The others came around the corner, the elevator just having deposited them on our floor. "The showers and toilets are there," she motioned towards a door at the end of our hall, "and the laundry is there."

Opening the door, we found ourselves in a room with three sets of bunks, one bed already filled by a heavy, red-faced man rubbing his feet. Introducing ourselves, he said, as he wiped sweat from his balding head, he was from Manitoba.

"Oh, another Canadian. There you go Roxey!" Paul exclaimed. "This is pretty good. Only six beds in here." Ana quickly tossed her things on to a top bunk, leaving the bottom bunk for Catharina. Paul hefted his bag up on the bed above "Manitoba". Zbigniew crossed the room and cocked his head at me in question.

"You take the bottom. I'll be fine on the top," I assured him. He lowered his tired body onto the bunk with a deep sigh, and, stopping only to remove his shoes, collapsed into sleep on the mattress. As usual, the *albergue* operators had left the mandatory sheer mattress and pillow protectors (something like what the nets food-handlers in kitchens use on their hair). Standing on the narrow metal rungs of the ladder, I was able to hook the cover on the bottom end of my mattress, but with the bunks pushed into the corner against the wall, I couldn't easily get to the top end of the bed. I dragged the one chair in the room over to the head of our beds, careful not to disturb my snoozing friend. Standing on the chair, the front corner was easy, but getting that last corner on was a stretch. Leaning over the metal railing, I reached over as far as I could, finally securing the elastic on that last corner just as I felt a sharp tear and heard a crack. Not the sheet. Not the chair. That came from me! Wincing in pain, I straightened gingerly, holding my ribs for support.

"Manitoba" was asleep and the others had gone to the showers, so I cautiously crawled down off the chair. Tears flooded my eyes at the pain. What had I done? Had I broken or displaced a rib? If I had, how would I carry my pack let alone walk? It hurt to draw breath. Really, my Camino couldn't end this way! I stood on the cool tile floor, methodically moving my hands over my ribs. Okay, it was tender, but nothing seemed to move out of place. Perhaps I just pulled a muscle. It hurt. It hurt a lot! But I didn't think any major damage had been done. Carefully I pulled my shower bag, quick dry towel, and clean clothes from my pack, wincing with pain at the effort.

Catharina and Ana passed me in the hall, heading to hang their clothes in the laundry. In the shower, I slowly peeled off my dusty, sweaty clothes and let the cool water flow over my body. It hurt to raise my hands to shampoo my hair, and it was only marginally less painful to soap my legs and feet. As I tried to pass my towel over my back, I yelped in pain. Dressing was a slow process, and I was glad there wasn't a line of other *camigas* waiting for the shower.

In the laundry room, I carefully hung my wet clothes to dry, and returned to our room, determined not to share my injury unless it became intolerable. I'd already had food poisoning and the foot injury. I didn't want my friends to think I was a walking disaster zone. Zbigniew was awake. He'd changed his shirt and said he'd shower later. Renewed by his short power nap, he was ready to explore. I quickly popped a Tylenol and ibuprofen and gingerly followed the others down the stairs.

Siesta time did little to slow down the pace of the city streets, however we found once we got off the main thoroughfare, the side streets were much quieter.

Rounding a corner, we found a little bar with a small, umbrella-shaded patio on the street. Paul bade us sit, and sauntered into the bar, returning with a smile as he claimed his chair. Shortly, a tall, bearded young Spaniard, shirt sleeves rolled up into crisp cuffs, approached bearing a tray of amber sweating glasses and a plate of bread, cheese, and sausage.

Roxeee… So, you made it, Roxeee!" Oh no. George was back. He and his wife had been joined by another couple, and as he made a move to cross the street to join us, Evie, like a mother determined to correct an errant child, tugged his arm in the other direction. We waved them off and returned to our drinks.

"Roxey," Zbigniew began, "the tape you use for your foot, what is it?" I told him it was called "K Tape", and it had been given to me by my physiotherapist son. "I see you have not much left," he continued, "maybe we can find some here?" We put searching for a drugstore on our list after our tour of the cathedral square. Pushing our chairs in around the table, we ambled across the road, waving our thanks as the bartender came out to claim the empty glasses.

The Plaza del Convento boasted two significant edifices: the fourteenth-century monastery, now operating as the parish church, and the original pilgrim refuge, now operating as a museum and tourist information centre. The inside of the church was cool and dark. Its austerity was relieved only by the crucifix, the altar, and two huge sculptures on either side – one a knight and the other a monk, kneeling in prayer. We stamped our pilgrim passports and walked out into the bright sunlight again.

Ambling down the avenue, we quickly located a drugstore and a package of "K Tape". It was pretty expensive, but Paul and I suggested we could share the cost since Paul thought it might also help his knee, and my supply was running low. I still needed to support the arch of my foot. I didn't even want to think about my ribs. It seemed the drugs were helping. The pain seemed less, unless I took in a big breath, like with a yawn, or laughed. The guys were returning to the *albergue*, but Ana, Catharina, and I were enjoying window shopping and wanted to get some fruit, nuts, and water for the next day's walk. Purchases in hand, we rode the luxury of the elevator upstairs to our room. "Manitoba" was snoring gently, and the men were nowhere to be found. Out in the hall we checked our laundry, then explored further, finding a sunny common room, complete with kitchenette, its tall windows opening onto the busy street below. Sitting on benches flanking a long trestle table, we took the time to catch up on messages to and from home. I warred with the choice of telling Al about my rib. I didn't want him to worry unnecessarily and promised myself to confess if it got much worse.

"Right! You lot ready for some octopus?" Paul chimed in through the open door. Zbigniew followed him in through the door, and they fanned flyers out on the table for our inspection. "These are the places the girl downstairs recommended. And this," he pointed, "is the one the fellow at the bar down the street gave us." Well that explained where they had been. At our knowing smirks, Paul raised his hands in defence. "Well that guy was asleep in our room, so we had to go somewhere!"

After a quick stop for another round of drugs, I joined the others back out on the street. Sidewalk cafes and bars were doing brisk trade. We located our chosen *pulperia* and were directed to a table deep within its dark recesses. We passed a glassed-in kitchen where we saw a sturdy Spanish woman using hefty wooden tongs to dip live octopus into scalding hot cauldrons of water. I watched as she dipped and raised the octopus once, twice, three times, then with black-handled utility scissors, snipped it into bite-sized pieces before coating it with olive oil and tossing it out on wooden boards to be liberally sprinkled with coarse salt

Gingerly, I slid into our booth next to Ana as the men consulted with the waiter before ordering two bottles of wine: one white and one red. Meanwhile, we three ladies perused the plastic-coated menu, determining that you paid by the size of the board the octopus was served on. Returning with the wine and clinking glasses, our waiter suggested we order a medium board, and if we wanted more, we could order more. Sound advice, we agreed, adding a platter of fried *peppers de pardron* to compliment the baskets of thickly crusted bread already delivered to our table. Deciding to err on the side of caution with regard to mixing alcohol and drugs, I limited myself to one glass of cool, white wine before switching to water and lemon.

The *pulpo* arrived, hot and steaming, laid out on a round wooden board. Tiny green peppers sizzled on the accompanying plate, and suddenly we realized how hungry we were. A bit tentative at first, I found the octopus very good, and the peppers even better. Between mouthfuls of bread, *pulpo*, and peppers, we demolished the food and ordered more. It never ceased to amaze me how much I was eating, yet my pants got looser every day.

It was uncomfortable sitting in the booth so long, and I felt the need to change my position. The wine was gone and the men wanted to order more, but I suggested we pick some up at a *mercado* on the way back to the *albergue* and enjoy it in the common room. The ladies added that it would be cheaper too, so in good-natured agreement, the men followed us out the door.

We strolled arm-in-arm, mellowed by food and wine, through the sultry evening. Music wafted out from second-storey windows, soft Spanish conversation following in its wake. The men slipped into a busy *mercado*, rejoining us on the sidewalk, bottles of wine held triumphantly aloft.

At the *albergue*, with glasses borrowed from the kitchenette, we settled into low-slung chairs around the common room. Finding it easier to sit straighter, I perched on the corner of a bench as we mulled over the highlights of our day and planned the next day's journey. If anyone noticed I wasn't drinking, nobody mentioned it as the evening gradually slipped away into night, and bed called us each in turn.

As we left Melide behind, we stopped at the tranquil Romanesque *Igrexa Santa Maria*. Soft, muted frescos adorned the walls of the small, peaceful chapel. After stamping our passports, the young priest accepted our donations and blessed our journey for the day. We walked out into the sunlight, adjusted our pack straps and poles, and started our day's Camino once more.

The quiet countryside was laced with small rivers providing refreshing coolness in the climbing heat. Winding our way through shaded forests, we noticed the type of trees changing, spotting more and more of the blue-green eucalyptus, planted as part of a growing pulp industry. I had heard about these new plantations and had anticipated the medicinal fragrance associated with eucalyptus, but really, I noted no difference in the air. The leaves of these trees did not look like what I understood to be eucalyptus either. Rather than round, coin-shaped petals I knew from flower arrangements, these were longer, narrow leaves, and I wondered if it was a totally different type of tree.

By the time we reached Boente, an hour or so later, I noticed my sinuses were packing in and my throat was scratchy. Seeking the shade offered by a wide, green awning, we settled into chairs at the bar fronting a quiet *albergue*, and I thankfully savoured a glass of cold, fresh orange juice.

The riverside trek paralleled a road and as the path joined the roadway leading to Castenada, the pressure on my ears was becoming painful. My eyes were watering, and my nose was running, and still there was the pressure. I pulled a tissue from my jacket pocket and did my best to abate the flow as I stoically trudged along behind Ana.

Through the sleepy little hamlet, the Camino started a gentle climb towards Portela. The summit meant only a hundred-metre difference in altitude, but as we climbed, so did the pressure in my head. My ears were ringing, and my balance was challenged as we crested the hill and started the drop down to Ribadiso. My head was pounding, and my eyes and nose ran a tiresome duet. I frantically dug in my pocket for anything resembling another tissue and considered stuffing one up my nose to stop the flood. Nothing! I pulled my sweat cloth from my hip and used it instead. I was dropping behind my friends, staggering slightly, my balance rocked by the pressure. This was too sudden for a cold; it had to be an allergic reaction to something.

In my sorrowful silence, I berated myself for my weakness. My foot was taped, my ribs ached, and my head was exploding! Here I was, almost at my goal, probably in the best overall physical shape I had ever been, and my body was systematically falling apart on me. I had conquered mountains and snow storms, dangerously slippery slopes, drenching rains, blazing flatlands, and endless treks across the country. Surely I could conquer a running nose!

I decided this was definitely an allergic reaction, but I wasn't sure to what. I trudged across a lovely stone bridge spanning the burbling Rio Iso, but I was in too much pain to appreciate the medieval structure. I knew Ribadiso was just around the bend and remembered its claim to fame was one of the oldest pilgrim hospitals still existing. But I knew that "hospital" translated to "*albergue*" and I didn't hold out any hope I would find any help there.

Catching up to the others, already seated at an outside bar, I let my pack slide sluggishly to the ground. Turning to face my friends, their expressions told me I probably looked as bad as I felt. Ana quickly pulled out a chair to catch my collapse, rushing inside to fetch me a cool drink. Catharina clucked in concern, her nursing training kicking into practical assessment gear.

"*Wat es* happening?" she questioned, handing me a napkin from the rack on the plastic table. "Your eyes *es* red." Well that didn't surprise me with the amount I had been rubbing them.

"Do you have a cold?" enquired Ana, rubbing my shoulder compassionately.

"No, I don't think so." I said, remembering Rosario's cold back at Triacastela. "This came on too fast. I think it's more an allergic reaction." The men looked on in sympathetic silence, at a loss as to how to help.

"I don't know what it is though. I've never had this kind of reaction before." I rummaged through the pockets of my pack, finally locating the baggie holding an assortment of drugs. Thankfully, I pulled out a silvery blister pack of anti-histamines, glad that although I had shared them along the way, I had left one for myself. With that and a Tylenol, I hoped I would be able to pull it together for the last hour's walk to Arzua. There, I was determined to find a drugstore and replenish my supply.

"I should have known something was wrong when you dropped back," Paul apologized. I gave him a weak smile and waved away any guilt.

"What is different?" mused Zbigniew, his long fingers stroking his chin as he looked to the sky for answers. We all pondered that question.

"The eucalyptus!" cried Ana. "We have seen a little in the past, but now there are full forests growing."

"I thought eucalyptus was supposed to be good for you though?" I queried. "But I guess you're right. That is what's different since this all started."

"Will you be okay to go on?" questioned Paul thoughtfully.

"Yes, I think so." I smiled valiantly through my streaming eyes. Catharina cautiously pushed the remaining pile of napkins across the table to me and after wiping my eyes with one, I jammed the rest in my pockets for later.

Everyone finished their coffees and I drained the last drops of my juice. I still had one full bottle of water, so I figured I'd be good for the last hour's walk. The drugs were starting to kick in already, and I sighed resignedly as I pushed to my feet. The sun blazed down upon us and, as I watched the others wipe sweat from their faces, I drew comfort that part of what I was experiencing was just plain old healthy sweat and not a sign of illness.

We tromped down the wooded path, Paul taking the lead, the girls bookending my position and Zbigniew bringing up the rear. I appreciated their concern and realized while giving me space and "privacy" to deal with my symptoms, they were, in effect, standing guard around me and would not abandon me.

Everywhere I looked, the eucalyptus stood sentinel, offering most the protection of their shade, but me, the challenge of their pollen. I braced myself and determinedly trudged on with my friends as we crossed through a tunnel under a roadway back onto the track. I knew that Arzua lay at the top of a hundred-metre ascent, which was nothing compared to previous climbs, but right now, just putting one foot in front of the other was an accomplishment for me.

Entering the town, a wide, store-fronted avenue stretched out; a long, straight ribbon of pavement, disappearing over a gentle hill. Within the first few buildings, we found the *Albergue* Don Quijote, but having started early to beat the main heat of the day, we had arrived too early to check in. The *hospitalero* allowed Ana and I to drop our packs in the foyer, directing us to the café next door for lunch. Glad for the respite from the heat, everyone settled into chairs, guzzling water with minimal conversation while we waited for our meals. Although I had ordered a grilled cheese sandwich in a bid for the comfort foods of home, I tasted nothing, so it was a bit of a waste, other than providing fuel for my tired body.

Between mouthfuls, we discussed our plans for Santiago. I had already made a reservation before leaving home and had a hotel room with a bath tub waiting. I had figured that I would be so done with *albergues* and sharing bunks in rooms with a cast of thousands by then. Now, as my friends scrolled through options on their cellphones, my spirits sunk at the thought of being separated from them.

Paul checked my hotel and found a room for himself, but when Ana announced she'd found a more reasonably priced monastery *albergue* might have rooms, he asked her to get him one too so they could stay together. As if I weren't feeling bad enough! I considered cancelling my room and joining them. Ana paused, made the call, and turning to the group, she translated the details.

"They say they have four singles for some nights. They have room for me and for Zbigniew for our two nights. For you Catharina, you would have a room for two nights, and then you would have to move your things out until 1:00 for the third night, and then you would have to share with another woman. Paul, you would have to do the same for the third night, and you would have to share for your last two nights. It gets busier towards the weekend. The bathrooms are all shared." Ana looked at the group waiting their decision.

Catharina's mouth worked as she sorted through the details. "Ya, *des* is okay for me," she agreed hesitantly, probably not impressed with having to share with a stranger.

"Bit of a bother isn't it?" queried Paul, pausing in his decision. "Okay, Ana, say yes for me," he instructed. She turned back to the phone and made the confirmations.

"So . . . we'll all be together, except for Roxey," she announced, somewhat sadly. All eyes turned to me.

Deciding to stop feeling sorry for myself and wanting my friends to feel good about their plans, I rallied, "But I will have a bathtub! I'm so looking forward to a long, hot soak in a tub! And we can spend all day together, so it doesn't really matter where we sleep," I assured them. Deep down I still wished we could all be together, but given the apparent shortage of beds in Santiago, I decided to stick to my original plan.

As we finished our meal, a taxi pulled up. The sprightly driver ran around to haul packs from the trunk, transporting them efficiently into the coolness of the waiting *albergue*. We saw Catharina, Paul, and Zbigniew's packs sail by. Finally, the *hospitalero* pushed open the *albergue* door, and seeing us through the café windows, beckoned us inside.

The lobby was nicely appointed and quite modern looking. Stamping our passports and taking our money, our *hospitalero* escorted us through a swinging door into the bunk area. She said we could take any beds we liked. We explored the options of the three rooms, all open to a wide hallway along one wall, and each containing about two dozen bunks. It was bright, clean, and had the bonus of lockers and chairs between each pair, as well as blankets and pillows on each bed. The last room backed on a long window which looked out onto a sunny, walled patio, strung with lines for laundry. We weighed the merits of fresh air from the screened windows against the proximity to the noise and activity of the laundry area and chose instead, a quiet corner in the first room.

The ladies' shower room was large and bright, toilets stalls lining one wall, shower cubicles the other, with well-lit sinks and mirrors taking centre place. I took one look at myself in the mirror and decided not to do that again! Stripping my sweaty clothes off my skin, I stepped under a blessedly full and hot stream of water. I let the warmth ease the soreness and the steam open my sinuses. I knew others would be waiting, but this was too good to rush. It was medicinal. Almost spiritual! But my pilgrim conscience finally kicked in and after rinsing the soap from my hair and body, I regretfully turned off the stream and wrapped my towel around me.

There was never a place to hang dry clothes, so as usual, I'd protected them in my dry bag (along with my valuables) and changed in a toilet stall. My short hair required absolutely no maintenance, so I slathered some moisturiser on my face and I was done. "Done and dusted", I fondly remembered John saying. Not for the first time, I wondered how his Camino had gone. I knew my friend would be safely home in Ireland by now, and I hoped he had made it through the door of glory as he had planned.

Back in our room, Ana and Catharina, wet towels turbaned around their hair, were sorting laundry.

"You look a bit better," Ana commented. I nodded my agreement that I felt better. "We are doing laundry. Give us your things and have a bit of a rest," she suggested.

"*Ya,*" Catharina agreed. "*Das* boys go walking," she explained the men's absence.

"Paul's looking for a drugstore," Ana supplied at my questioning look. "We'll go there later," and, dismissing my protests with a wave, she gathered my clothes, and they headed off to the laundry room, leaving me no excuse but to do as directed.

"Okay," I muttered, "just for a few minutes." I laid back in the shadows of my bottom bunk, closed my eyes, and was gone. What seemed like a short time, turned out to be an hour's nap; unheard of in my experience. I do not nap! Ana and Catharina sat on rigid-backed wooden chairs, each at the end of a set of bunks, focused on catching up with their journaling and emails.

"Hi," I tentatively offered. Their chins rose from their phone screens, and smiles spread across their concerned faces. I swung my feet to the floor and sat up, testing my condition. Not great, but doable, I surmised. "Do you want to go for a walk?" Reassured by my question, they led the way out the swinging door, onto the wide sidewalk. Zbigniew and Paul sauntered casually towards us.

"Oh, you're alive!" Paul exclaimed. "Right, so I have found, not one, but three drugstores. Very professional locating!" he pronounced. "But, it is siesta, and they are closed. Two of them will open at 7:00. Will you be good 'til then?" I nodded. "Right! Zig and I are going back to the *albergue* for a bit. You lot pick out a place for supper and come back and get us," he instructed.

"We will wait there for you," Zbigniew agreed, resting a reassuring hand on my shoulder. I assumed the bag he held contained a bottle of *vino tinto* and the time waiting was going to be spent sipping wine and swapping stories on the sunny back patio.

The main strip of Arzua was obviously focused on pilgrims, lined as it was with modern bars, cafes, *albergues*, and shops offering an assortment of souvenirs. I spotted the drugstore symbol hanging from a stucco building just to the left, up a hill twisting towards the residential part of town. Anticipating standard pilgrim offerings, we walked down the gentle hill, checking menus and prices as we went. Some offered better selection, others better prices, and some more inviting premises. We walked several blocks down one side, then back up the other, weighing one eatery against the other, but making no decision.

We walked past the town square, its flagstone courtyard encircled by colourful flower gardens and shady trees. Elderly men sat on a bench, deep in conversation, ignoring the pigeons strutting around their feet. A noisy family group gathered happily at a sidewalk café next to the church, the children laughing and scampering around while parents gently chastised them to no effect. A young couple sat on a shady wall, the girl wistfully twirling her long, dark hair around her finger, the blue-jeaned young man plucking randomly at his acoustic guitar in a timeless form of courting.

Looking at shoes and handbags in one window and colourful blouses and jewellery in another, this was the safest way to shop; everything was closed. We stopped to admire pastries in the bakery window, and cheeses in another. The town was famous for its cheeses, a claim illustrated by statues on the corner of the square: one a young peasant woman offering a stone basket filled with wheels of cheese, another, a pair of youngsters, playfully wrestling a resistant calf. The church stood tall and serene, casting long shadows over the bars on the street below, where, aromas of garlic and onions invited us to step inside.

Climbing back up to the main street, the stores were just beginning to open. We stepped inside a small gift shop, absently checking out the souvenirs, each lost in thoughts of our families back home. Only two more nights to Santiago, and then it would not be long until we were headed home. Eagerness to see our loved ones warred with not wanting the journey to end.

"Look! *Es* here Roxey!" exclaimed Catharina. She pulled from the glass display shelf a puzzle depicting the route of the Camino. She and I had seen one like it mounted on the wall back in Villafranca, and I had expressed the hope to find one like it for my husband. His limited mobility turned his interests to things like crosswords and puzzles, and I thought it would be a very appropriate gift for him. I checked the price and hefted the weight.

"How will you fit that in your pack?" questioned Ana.

"*Ya, es* big!" agreed Catharina seriously. Turning it over in my hands, I considered my options. Pulling out my phone I took a photo and put it back on the shelf.

"I will look for it in Santiago. They're sure to have it there if they have it here in this small town." Nods all around, then we were back on the sidewalk, headed for the *albergue*. In contradiction to their plan, the men were seated outside, enjoying a beer at a bar a few doors down from our nest for the night.

"There you are!" Paul called out. "Ready to go to the drugstore?" *So ready!* The drugs and the rest I'd had earlier were wearing off and my eyes were beginning to water again. I wanted to nip things in the bud before they got too far out of hand again.

As we walked, we answered Zbigniew's question; no, we hadn't picked a place for supper yet. We discussed options as we walked, pausing once or twice to consider posted menus. Halfway down the road, we veered up a hill to the left, taking a side street I hadn't noticed before. Buildings here were very old; fraught with fancy embellishments that spoke of times when craftsmanship was more important than speed.

Pushing in through the glass door of the tiny drugstore, a young woman, thick dark hair resting on her white lab coat, looked up from behind the counter as our group filled the space. Knowing Portuguese was spoken widely in this area, we stood waiting patiently while Ana explained my needs to the chemist. In the background, the men were quietly inspecting the wares on display, raising tins to their faces, grimacing like boys, before replacing the fragrant boxes back on the shelves.

The young woman, taking in my visible symptoms, disappeared to the back of the store, returning with a small box, the contents of which she explained to Ana. While Ana's Brazilian Portuguese was a bit different than the regional dialect here, I trusted her translation that I take one pill only every twenty-four hours, but I was concerned that something that potent might have negative side effects. Conveying my concerns that I was very sensitive to drugs, Ana asked if the chemist thought it would make me drowsy (her more politically correct translation of my "stoned") and unable to walk. The young woman assured her that I should be fine to walk in the morning.

Out in the street, I advised my friends that I wasn't sure how I was going to react to these drugs. They reassured me, promising they would not leave me behind. I took the pill right then and there, stashing the remaining pills in my fanny pack, and hoped for the best.

Back on the main strip, we again addressed the quandary of where to dine. Once again, we walked down the street, and back up the other side. We returned halfway down the street, only to decide against the eatery we thought might work. Undecided, we returned to the block our *albergue* was on only to choose the bar three doors down for supper. Laughter in his eyes, Paul asked if we were sure, or did we want to do another loop.

"No, no!" Zbigniew protested. "How many times will we walk up this street?" We laughed as we pulled up chairs in the street front dining area, telling him we were done and this was it!

A young waitress came out of the door, placing menus before us. Ana started reading the Portuguese side and our waitress' dark eyes lit up. Suddenly they were off in an animated conversation as the rest of us just sat back smiling, enjoying their excitement in sharing their language. Ana explained that the girl was actually from Portugal, just working in Arzua for the summer. With her "insiders track" Ana had ferreted out the best choices for us, and soon plates of hot, aromatic fish, chicken, and pork were laid before us.

Raising my hand in denial as Paul went to fill my glass, I told him I'd rather not mix drugs and alcohol. I was already feeling much better; not at all spaced out or sedated. Things looked good for the morning, and I joined in the laughter and conversation as we took turns sampling each other's meals. Dessert was offered with coffees, but again, the drugs being an unknown entity, I declined the extra boost of caffeine, settling for the minor dose that came with the chocolate sauce on a Spanish torte.

Evening was falling and, as usual, the streets were filled with pilgrims and locals alike. Music and laughter poured out of bars and cafes as appetites were met and spirits were raised. I wondered what this little town was like in the winter. I knew pilgrims travelled all year, but numbers would be drastically reduced in the colder months, heavy rains and snow taking their toll on enthusiasm.

We lingered contentedly at the table, discussing the walk for the next day. It would be about a twenty-kilometre walk with gentle rises and falls except for one short burst of altitude and then a steady drop down into Pedrouzo. This would be our last stop before entering Santiago. The thought settled heavily on the table before being gently lifted on the wings of laughter among friends as we joked about what we would do when we reached the city.

Zbigniew spoke of celebrating with wine, Ana glowed in anticipation of seeing her daughter in England on the way back to Brazil. I dreamt aloud of sinking up to my neck in a hot, bubble bath. Paul said he wanted to make arrangements to go to Finisterre or Muxia, or both, and Catharina puzzled over the details of booking a bus trip home to Belgium.

Then, more seriously, we talked about the arrival itself; of getting our certificates and going to the cathedral. Being Catholics, the religious aspect was more resonant for Ana, Paul, and Zbigniew, although I knew I would find some common footing in the service as well.

"I will be proud to get my certificate." Catharina looked seriously into her glass. "But I can only believe what I can see and what I can touch. I will come for the beauty of the church and for my friends."

When I had asked Catharina why she was doing the Camino, she'd smiled and said she just like to walk. Well that was totally fine too, wasn't it? Everyone was doing their own Camino for their own reasons. I realized that of all the "Final Five", I knew the least about Catharina. Originally, language had been a bit of a barrier, as had her somewhat formal demeanour. But those gates had come down along the way. Catharina smiled with pleasure at our acceptance of her words. I guessed she felt somewhat at risk, going out on a limb to confess her scepticism regarding religion to a group obviously doing the trek for spiritual, if not religious, reasons.

Our acceptance spoke to the unconditional power of our friendship. We could say and do just about anything without fear, and I felt in my heart that these were some of the most honest relationships I had ever enjoyed. We had seen each other's physical and emotional warts and all, but still we stood together.

The bottle was drained, but there was still the one Zbigniew had purchased waiting unopened at the *albergue*, so we moved our party down the street –three doors. I was feeling tired and so was Ana, so we begged off as the others took glasses from the kitchen, heading back to the patio with the wine.

"So, you won't join us?" Paul chided, as he turned to go.

"Either I party with you, or I walk tomorrow," I held my ground teasingly. "Which would you prefer?"

"Well I want you to do both of course!" he laughed. I gave him a quick hug and told him to go join the others; I'd see them in the morning. "I'm glad you're feeling better," he called over his shoulder.

"Don't party too hard, or you won't be walking tomorrow!" I laughed.

"I think it is good we sleep tonight," Ana gently intoned. I agreed, and once tucked into our opposing lower bunks, we carried on a quiet conversation, like sisters do, until sleep overtook us and silenced our words.

A good night's sleep put me in fine form for the sunrise. The drugs seemed to be working, and best of all, didn't seem to have any unwelcome side effects. Across the aisle, Paul, on the other hand, seemed to be moving more slowly this morning. As I rounded the end of the bunks, I saw Zbigniew too, stretching and shaking sleep from his body, delaying the inevitable departure just a few moments more.

I joined the girls, stuffing the last of our belongings in our packs. The men were still dragging on their clothes, and we knew they'd be a while. We told them we'd stop for coffee at the first place we found open down the road, and they could find us there. Catharina dropped her tagged backpack by the front desk, knowing that it would be waiting for her at O Pedrouzo when we arrived. Ana and I, like turtles wearing shells, carried our packs bearing all our belongings, our home away from home, by now comfortable with the weight.

The rosy dawn lit the sky; the road below, devoid of traffic other than a few straggling backpacks. We strolled down the wide, silent sidewalks, wondering at the difference from the evening before. Shops, bars, and cafes were shut up tightly, shades pulled, lights out, and chairs upended on empty tables. We walked two blocks, and then past the square. On the other side of the avenue, light and chatter poured out an open door. Crossing the pavement, we transitioned from the semi-dark silence into a bright and bustling café.

The wall behind the bar was all bottles and mirrors, above which, it was creatively finished with the raw ends of boards. It was like looking at the butt-ends of stacks of lumber. The ceiling, in stark contrast to the rustic woodwork, was painted in a soft fresco of pale blue sky and fluffy, drifting clouds. It made me think of a casino I'd been to in Las Vegas. A broad Spaniard behind the bar was pouring short glasses of orange juice while coffee steamed into cups on the counter behind him. I thought he looked quite dashing and debonair; neat moustache, meticulously combed hair, striped shirt sleeves rolled into crisp cuffs. Breaking from his animated conversation with the pilgrims at the bar, he called orders to the unseen help behind the saloon-style swinging doors to the kitchen.

Ana and I dropped our packs in a corner, hung our coats to claim the nearby chairs, and joined Catharina at the bar. To facilitate things, a menu with a number-coded set of breakfast choices was posted. I wanted a number two, but not the orange juice. A number one didn't include toast, and a number three didn't include coffee. It appeared to be an all-or-nothing venture. Reasoning that the price difference wasn't huge, even if I didn't drink the orange juice, I ordered number two, as did the other girls. I nodded in the direction of the bathroom knowing the girls would watch for my order.

The bathroom was a work of art! The fanciest one I'd seen on the Camino. Marble and glass, golden fixtures, ornate floral arrangements, framed water colours, and embossed wall coverings; it was worthy of a high-end hotel. Drying my hands with a soft towel, I wiped splashed water off the counter, not wanting to leave a blemish behind me. Definitely a ten!

"You gotta check out this bathroom!" I gushed before noticing my friends were not happy. Glasses of juice waited on the table, but no coffee nor toast in sight.

"They still haven't brought our orders," Ana confirmed.

"Ya, end ozers, ze haf zers!" protested Catharina.

I looked the bar, now three deep in pilgrims wanting breakfast. Obviously, this was the only place open, and the one, now flustered proprietor, struggled to deal with the onslaught on his own. He poured and filled cups and called out to the kitchen frantically as people waved money at him. I saw two plates of toast cooling on the end by the kitchen and took matters into my own hands. Grabbing the plates, I deposited them on our tables, assuming they must be ours. Then, I returned to the bar and pushing my way to the front, captured the next three cups of coffee coming off the counter. Others complained, but I insisted we had been waiting since before they even arrived, and made off with my booty.

"Still we haf not one plate of toast," Catharina chided as we sipped our coffee, keeping an eye on the door for the men. We shared the toast between us, less being better than none, and better than rejoining the fray to get our money back.

Guessing the guys had decided to walk on, we poled our way down the hill, past the church, following the arrows to the street below. A group of young people, clad in jeans and leather, chains hanging from their belts, hung out at a corner bar we had noticed the evening before.

As we approached, one tall, skinny leather-jacketed youth with an unlikely Mohawk hairstyle, tossed his cigarette into the street. He suddenly pounced, picked something up and hurled it at the wall of the building just in front of us. Startled by the violence of the action, I looked at the pavement at the foot of the wall and saw a small pigeon, twisted, but still alive, stunned by the impact. Its bright eyes clouded in confusion, and its feathery breast heaved as it struggled to draw breath. I pulled myself up, glaring at the youth, ready for confrontation, but Ana, placing her hand on my shoulder, pulled me away. Realizing her wisdom, I followed behind, my cheeks running with tears at the senseless destruction of a harmless bird. Catharina tutted quietly, shaking her head at her shame at the youth.

A gentle rise took us out of the town, and I did my best to shake off the ominous beginning. While lush forests graced the distance, this was still primarily farmland. Along the way we saw signs announcing refurbishment projects under way. It seemed those promoting the Camino were trying to upgrade the scenery along the way. They didn't want the pilgrims going away thinking Spain was falling to wrack and ruin; not a good impression for bringing in the pilgrim trade.

An hour or so later, we reached Calzada where a bustling roadside café called to us, promising a sustaining cup of coffee. There, seated on colourful plastic chairs in the dirt courtyard, sat Paul and Zbigniew, enjoying their breakfast *al fresco*.

"Where did you get to then?" enquired Paul. Ana told him we stopped, as we said, at the first café that was open. "Nawww, we looked for you. Didn't see you," he insisted. "Not very professional!" he chided, looking directly at me.

"Well, we were there!" I maintained as I strode off for the café. I'm sure he wondered what had gotten into me, and I promised myself to apologize. As well as food and drink, part of the café was given to souvenirs; another sign of the increasing commercialism of the Camino. I carried my coffee out to the table, Ana and Catharina following in my steps, and settled into the chair next to Paul.

"So only another three hours, and we should be there," Paul stated. Seemed he'd not been bothered at all by my abrupt response earlier. I thought, sometimes, that he enjoyed the fact that I gave as good as I got. "I wonder how big Pedrouzo is. It's Sunday, so things may be closed. Might be a bit difficult to find somewhere to eat," he mused.

"I understand Pedrouzo prides itself on facilitating the pilgrims. It's one of the most popular last night stops on the Camino, so I'm guessing there will be some options," I reassured him. "The *albergue* we're staying in is huge," I provided, consulting my guide book, "and it says there's a whole street of shops, cafes, and bars."

"Right. Absolutely. Very professional research, Roxey," he agreed. I had been redeemed.

Leaving the café behind us, we trekked along dusty dirt roads, surprised to see roadside garbage containers, emblazoned with affirming Camino logos, popping up along the way. Until now I had never seen a trash can. Pilgrims were pretty good about adhering to the unwritten laws about carrying your garbage with you, and none of the bars sold drinks in disposable cups, so litter had been pretty minimal.

The men had pulled out in front as the trail wound its way through tiny, unnamed hamlets. Following a muddy track, we came upon a long, stone wall virtually covered in empty beer bottles. Whether it was an accumulation over time, or the results of a party at the *albergue* the night before, the seemingly endless stream of bottles was impressive and brought smiles to our faces.

Given the increasing heat of the windless day, we appreciated the coolness of the lightly forested trail. Winding between fences and walls, along a gradually climbing track, we savoured the fresh fragrance of the greenery around us. Robust ferns sprang from the shoulders of the roads beneath trees trailing branches, shading our way. Unseen behind a wall of thick growth, we could hear stream water burbling and the occasional belch of frogs lounging on the moist shoreline. Butterflies danced in the warm air, birds called from hiding places within the tall grasses. It was idyllic.

The woodland path continued as we approached our half-way mark – Salceda. Paul and Zbigniew were seated at scarred ladder-back chairs at a brightly painted table outside the popular Bar Verde, enjoying a glass of *vino tinto*. Given the name, I was sort of expecting a "hippie" influenced bar, drawing the line from "green" to eco-friendly. Not really wanting a drink, but needing a bathroom, I wiped the sweat off my brow and climbed the stairs to be greeted by loud, pounding, hard-rock music. The gaudy walls were plastered with rock concert posters and signed photos of the stars that generated the music. An assortment of guitars hung from the rafters above the sticky bar, thronged with boisterous pilgrims. I made quick use of the bathroom, and beat it back out of the noise and confusion, wanting to restore the serenity of our morning's walk. Catharina had settled in a chair and waved Ana and I off as we struck out again.

Following the path at the side of the main road, we reached the outskirts of the town, finding a cool, quiet café, and slipped inside the door. This was more like it. We ordered a grilled cheese, ham, and tomato sandwich to share, and lemonades to wash it down with. Watching the passage of the parade of pilgrims through the wide front window, we saw Catharina approach, obviously searching for us. Either she had finished her wine fast, or she'd decided not to stop after all. I went to the door and called her inside.

"*Wat es dat?*" she asked, indicating the remains of our sandwich before ordering her own. Given the size of the bread, we were surprised to see our slim friend easily polish off her meal in no time. Just as we pushed out the door, the men came trudging up the hill.

Climbing gradually for most of the day, we reached Alto de Santa Irene and began the quick descent to the valley, under broiling sun. The dirt path turned to rural tracks, then we came to a paved road, our passage blocked by a uniformed policeman standing beside a car with flashing lights. Pilgrims bottled up behind us as we awaited permission to proceed, and we wondered if there had been an accident. All of a sudden, a flight of numbered cyclists sped by. The policeman then stood aside and waved us across the road to enter the forest on the other side. Funny; a cycling event.

I thought back to a camping trip Al and I had made, dragging our trailer along a gravel road in a dense forest. Our trip was blocked not once, not twice, but three times by a cycling event, its route winding in serpentine fashion along our direct route. To this day, when we come to an unanticipated roadblock, we look at each other, say "cycling event", and laugh. Al would laugh when he read my message about this tonight.

Tall, straight tree trunks surrounded us, bark peeling to the ground in long, fragile strips. I looked at the leaves of these massive trees and realized this was eucalyptus. Either the drugs were working really well, or perhaps I was only affected the by gassing off of young, growing eucalyptus, and not by the less fragrant old-growth trees.

"Bike!" the warning called out and broke my reverie. Jumping to the side, I just missed getting hit by a racing cyclist and I laughed. More cycling event! The next half hour was a constant struggle to make progress towards Pedrouzo while dodging oncoming racers. Pilgrims behind called out "bike!" the way kids in Canada called out "car!" when playing street hockey. It was good to have someone watching your back.

Emerging from the forest, we were outside a large, modern sports complex, complete with lined and lighted fields, bleachers, and a gymnasium. This was obviously the finish line for the event. The streets were crossed with strings of colourful pennants, and weary cyclists lifted muddied bikes onto vehicle racks.

We crossed the street and followed the sidewalk down the hill into the town's centre. Being a Sunday afternoon, things were pretty quiet, however signs announced pilgrim menus at bars and cafes that would open after siesta. We came to an intersection, the road to the right and left crowded with storefronts and cafes. Before us, a sign indicated the way to the church and, knowing our *albergue* was close to the church, we continued down the hill.

Albergue Cruceiro de Pedrouzo at ten euros a head offered a very modern rest stop for our last night before Santiago. The top floor common room was bright and open and furnished with contemporary, cafeteria-styled tables and chairs. Along the back wall, stainless steel counters and neon green cupboards made for a utilitarian, well-equipped kitchen area, complete with a stove, a bank of microwaves, and sinks. Vending machines hummed in the corner, tiers of bright-coloured packages on display through their sparkling glass faces.

Trudging down the wide staircase, slips bearing our bunk designations in hand, we came to the bunk room, a twisting maze of close to a hundred high-tech bunks, row on row. In addition to our bed assignment, we had been given keys to co-ordinating numbered lockers: one vented for boots and one for possessions. Each sheeted bed had its own plug as well as reading lamp, and the bright green pillows were cheery. Signage hung on chains from the ceiling, directing pilgrims to the showers and washrooms, and alternately to the laundry facilities.

The bunkroom was fronted, floor to ceiling by a glass and metal-framed wall. No curtains or blinds were needed; pilgrims woke and walked with the sun. Doors led out to a large, brown lawn. At the far side of the lawn were laundry lines, the only familiar touchstone to our regular pilgrim housing. It was all very clean, all very efficient, but not much in keeping with the pilgrimage experience. I was disappointed we weren't staying in more traditional surroundings for our last night.

We settled into our little corner, a cell along the back wall of the huge bunk area, Ana and I taking top bunks, leaving the three lower ones for Catharina, Paul, and Zbigniew. As I surveyed the room from my bunk, I was glad we were against the wall. Weary pilgrims resting on top bunks on the inside sets reminded me of cakes on stands, displayed in a bakery window for all to see.

Like a team hitting the floor at a basketball game, we grabbed our shower gear and broke for the showers, agreeing an early supper was in order as soon as everyone was ready. Female chatter kept me company as I allowed the hot water to wash away the dirt of the day. Standing on a wooden platform, like dishes drying in a rack, I appreciated having my feet off the wet floor, and quickly pulled on my clean clothes. The bathroom was equipped with hand dryers, and with a quick blast, my short-cropped hair was dry and shining. I took my wet laundry out to the line, knowing the steady wind would have it dry by evening.

Upstairs, we waited for the men to join us, watching newly-arrived pilgrims check in and receive their bunk assignments. In the kitchen, a Korean couple was busily cooking on the two-burner stove, others looking on with interest. Zbigniew and Paul crested the staircase, and we walked out into the sunshine.

Trekking back up the hill, we were faced with an array of choices for food and drink. Pilgrims filled the street-side patios, separated only by wrought iron railings. We considered the options of one place against another and then walked back to check out the first one we'd passed.

"Oh, we're not going to do this again, are we?" exclaimed Paul, and I knew the men were hoping our selection wasn't going to take the time and work it had the night before.

It was funny how the men deferred to the ladies' choice for meals. It seemed natural, I guessed; women provided the meals at home, so why not choose the eating place abroad. Then I remembered Zbigniew was a widower, and I wondered how comfortable he was in the kitchen, or if he ate out a lot. I knew he had a son and a daughter, but they didn't live close enough to look to his needs on a daily basis. My own husband knew his way around a kitchen and produced some pretty great dishes; I hoped Zbigniew was similarly able.

Finally settling on a lively café, we pulled up plastic patio chairs at an awning-shaded table. The group at the next table gave us a hearty welcome and were full of suggestions as to what to order. Passing friends found each other and hugs and heartfelt greetings were exchanged. The atmosphere was loud and festive; a party in the making.

Wine was poured and bread broken, and I couldn't help thinking this was our last supper as pilgrims together. Tomorrow we would enter Santiago. I looked at my friends at the table and gave thanks that we had found each other to complete this journey together. My thoughtful reflective bubble was popped as a generously laden plate was set before me. Joining in the laughter and accepting a small glass of wine from Paul, we toasted each other and dug into the rich food.

A bit of a siesta was in order after all that food and drink, so we strolled back down to the *albergue*. My pillow propped against the wall, I spent the next hour lounging in my top bunk, scrolling through my photos, and catching up with Al via text messages. Ana's bunk abutted mine, and I smiled to see her doing the same, our toes meeting like bookends at the end of our beds. Looking to the lower bunk across from me, I saw Zbigniew deep in sleep. The others were directly below me; I could not see them. An hour's sitting still was about all I could handle, and when I hit the floor, I noticed Paul was gone too. Like me, he wasn't big on being still. I walked out to the laundry lines and, as suspected, found the brisk breeze had quickly done its work.

Although still warm, the shadows were growing longer, and I headed back in to round the crew up for church. Paul was just arriving when I reached our cell.

"Are we going to church then?" he asked.

At the top of the hill, a soft golden-stoned church stood waiting, heavy arched doors propped wide to invite us in. Although the front of the church was already filled, we found an empty pew and quickly filled the polished wooden bench. Ana, Paul, and Zbigniew, looking to the altar, crossed themselves as we sat. Catharina pulled her jacket around her "unbelieving" body, and I smiled at the protective gesture.

The church was very unassuming; less of the gold and glitter found in the various cathedrals along the way. Graceful stone arches lent structure to the curved white plaster ceiling, dropping wrought-iron chandeliers with soft bulbs mimicking candles. An alcove off to the right was reserved for ornately carved wooden confessionals. On either side of the altar, two small staircases led to tiny balconies where additional clergy or cantors would stand on more prestigious occasions. The chapel's main source of decoration was the golden, pearlescent scallop shell, that filled the whole font wall of the sanctuary, floor to ceiling. Gently back lit around the edges, it was a beautiful backdrop for the crucifix set above a bower of candles and fresh white flowers.

A tall, dark-haired priest approached the altar, beautifully adorned vestments lending formality to an otherwise relaxed face. He drifted seamlessly through a variety of languages, towards communion. A young man in what looked to be a football uniform joined the priest at the front and received the bread, the wine, and the blessing. He then took up a place in the aisle, halfway down the aisle, preparing to dispense communion in concert with the priest at the front. We filed out to join the line, taking care not to trod on Catharina's toes. My communion was no less meaningful for me, despite the fact it was given by a man in sportswear, and I returned to my seat feeling renewed.

The priest returned to the altar and, after disposing of the remains of the communion meal, turned to address the congregation. He called all of the pilgrims up to the altar. We crowded up the aisle past encouraging locals. Differential unease at approaching, let alone touching, the holy table had everyone jockeying for position.

"No, no!" the priest called out laughingly. "Don't hang back. Come closer! Everyone, come closer." And we all edged a little closer, Catharina uncomfortably standing off my shoulder, not knowing where to look. We crowded in until everyone was gathered tightly around the altar.

"You are all pilgrims of this Camino, like we are all pilgrims in the way of Christ," he shared, a wide smile beaming across his unlined face. "We are all together on this journey, and we do not walk alone." He dipped a small branch in a bowl of Holy water. "Tomorrow, you will walk into Santiago and go to the great cathedral. Even when you get there, your journey will not be ended." He stared spraying the assembly with water from the font, turning to ensure that no pilgrim was left untouched. "I hereby bless your journey and ask God's protection on the rest of your pilgrimage. I ask that He reveal to you the true meaning of your Camino so that you will know why you have walked. You are all brothers and sisters on this journey, and all children of God. God be with you!"

"God be with you," we chanted in response, laughing and hugging the closest person to us. When I turned and looked at Catharina, I noticed water on her cheeks. I looked at her tear-filled eyes and knew it hadn't been put there by the priest. Despite her insistence in believing only in what she could see and touch, she too had been deeply moved in spirit.

Back out in the fading sunshine, we headed back up to the café for a night cap. Inside, the atmosphere was boisterous and charged; the party now on the brink of complete chaos. The aura of anticipation was heightened by good friends and alcohol, and it seemed everyone was delaying bedtime on this last night. It was like Christmas Eve; fraught with expectation and excitement. Paul bought a round for the table, but still taking the unknown miracle drugs, I settled for soda and lemon.

Arms around each other, we slowly made our way back to the *albergue* through the warm darkness. Tromping as quietly as possible down the stairs, we found our bunk cell and prepared for bed. Around us, many beds were already full, and the room was humming with gentle snores.

"What time do you think we need to get going?" Paul queried softly. All heads turned to me.

"Well," I paused, "we have twenty kilometres to go, with at least a half hour stop for breakfast. If we travel at about five kilometres an hour, that means four and a half hours. If the cathedral doors close at 11:45, we need to be on the road by 6:15 at least. That means everyone up by 5:45," I figured.

"Oh!" groaned Zbigniew. "That is so early."

"But that is what we have to do to get there in time for pilgrims' mass," argued Ana gently.

"Oh!" he groaned again, folding his long legs into his bunk and pulled his covers over his head as we all laughed quietly. Ana and I carefully climbed the ladders to our beds, while Catharina and Paul slid silently into theirs. Snuggling down under my covers, I checked my alarm once more and then joined the shadowy bumps around me in the darkness of sleep.

Through the dimly lit room, I padded quietly back towards my bed from the washroom. A hushed female voice, words spoken in a foreign language, halted my progress.

"I'm sorry," I whispered, "I don't understand."

"Oh! You speak English," the voice responded from the shadows of the top bunk above a gently snoring bundle of blankets. "I wonder, do you have any Vaseline? I cannot find my tube and I need some for my feet today."

"Of course," I replied, "I'll be right back." Returning to our little corner in the maze of bunk beds, I quickly located my Vaseline, surprised to see Zbigniew's bunk empty. Retracing my steps, I handed off the tube, sending up silent thanks for how well the product had served me on this journey. I told the mystery pilgrim she could keep it; I had already used what I needed for the day.

"De nada," I responded to her thanks. I was again reminded how strangers became friends, sometimes made in darkness that you might not recognize in the daylight, as we came together, pooling our resources to get each other through.

Zbigniew, folding his length upon his lower bunk, was attempting to cut the K-tape to wrap his foot and ankle. His big hands struggled with the rolled tape and the compact scissors. I smiled remembering his disgust last night at the idea of having to get up for 5:45, and here he was, up and taping at 5:15 am. Mindful that some pilgrims (although not many) were still sleeping, I crouched down and quietly helped him cut the lengths he needed. He asked if I needed any tape for the day. I had already taped my foot the night before and told him I was good. He cut off a generous length of the supportive tape and told me to take it in my pack in case I needed more in the city over the next couple of days.

We had begun to divest ourselves of our tools of passage, knowing we would no longer need to rely on them. Without words, our eyes spoke volumes on this last day of walking together, and he leaned over to give me a hug. Patting his back, swallowing a lump in my throat, I stood and joined Ana and Catharina in packing the remainder of our things. Paul, himself just back from the washroom, also had it pretty much together. It was already a day of small miracles!

Shouldering our packs, we left the men to complete their preparations for the trail. Upstairs, in the brightly lit great room, pilgrims were abuzz with excitement. Some were using the microwaves to heat bread or instant oatmeal, others pulling plastic cups of coffee from the vending machines. Poles were adjusted, buckles checked, and laces secured. Given the early hour, we knew nothing would be open in O Pedrouzo, and we resigned ourselves to a bit of a walk before our morning coffee.

Catharina, Ana, and I stood grinning foolishly at each other, then spontaneously huddled for a "girls only" group hug. Ana dashed a tear from her eye, and Catharina suddenly ducked outside "to check the weather".

"Not too much rain," she sternly reported. We covered our packs with the nylon shells, but stowed our raingear, just as the men's heads broke the surface of the staircase.

"Is it raining then?" questioned Paul, wrestling his big blue pack onto his shoulders. "Do we need our ponchos?"

"Catharina says it's only a little rain," I replied, "so we're going to go without for now." Zbigniew, his signature blue hat and piano key scarf jauntily tied around his neck, looked anxious to be going.

"We go?" Catharina asked, her bright eyes shining expectantly in the streetlight glow.

"We go!" we all replied in unison. The silent streets were shrouded in mist, no sign of local activity, just backpack-bearing pilgrims quietly climbing the paved hill back to where we had entered the town the afternoon before. Step, tap, step tap, and the occasional muffled voice was all to be heard. The banners from the previous day's cycling event sagged despondently from the overhead lines, dripping the night's rain as we re-entered the tall corridor of the eucalyptus forest. No need to dodge bikes today, we retraced our steps to the junction that would take us out of the forest and along the roadway in the direction of O Amenal and coffee, four kilometres away.

Having agreed to stay together this last day, Paul stayed in sight as we each found our comfortable pace. I had mixed feelings of sadness and anticipation. Ana, keeping time with me, shared the same feelings. Seeing his bright blue hat walking apace with Catharina's bobbing backpack, we laughed over how Zbigniew had fought the appointed start time, only to be one of the first ones up today. He was obviously feeling the same sense of urgency calling us on to Santiago.

The trail was thick with pilgrims and there was no chance of mistaking the trail despite the dull early morning lighting. We were a parade with a purpose, each with our own thoughts and feelings, but sharing so much at the same time.

Along the way Ana, and I again discussed the possibility of opening an *albergue*. She pointed out homes along the way, discussing their merits.

"This one you could live on the top floor and make the bottom the *albergue*," she suggested. I cautioned it might be too far from any town to attract pilgrims, but she countered with, "If the food is good, and it is set up well, it would be nicer than the modern place we stayed last night." Obviously, I wasn't the only one who found last night's *albergue* a little too clinical for my pilgrim frame of mind.

Knowing this was just talk, and that Ana was committed to her aging parents back in Brazil, I joined in the spirit of the discussion.

"That one has room for a good garden. You could grow your own food and advertise home-grown, home-cooked meals. You could have chickens too." She smiled at my complicity.

"But not a cow. I think I would just buy milk and cheese," she laughed as we walked on.

After about forty-five minutes, we arrived at O Amenal to find the staff prepared for the pilgrim rush. Apparently, the people running this café knew the pilgrims could not sleep on their last night before entering Santiago and that many would stop here today. They knew we would come early, and we would come in the multitudes. Bypassing a collection of plastic chairs and tables under canvas awnings, inside we found a high-tech assembly line, complete with red plastic cafeteria-like trays sliding along stainless- steel rails. The hair-netted staff efficiently handed over cups of steaming coffee and hot chocolate to accompany pre-wrapped plates of pastries, sandwiches, and fruits and cheeses. A bespectacled cashier sat at the end of the counter patiently ringing in sales and counting coins. While the sheer numbers demanded institutional-style service, the food and drinks were fresh and hot, and no less welcome.

Weaving between the tables with our trays, Ana and I joined the others already savouring their coffees. "How are you feeling today?" wondered Paul. "What are you thinking about arriving at Santiago? Has the pilgrimage been what you thought it would be?"

I remembered what Esther and Andi had told me about their first arrival at the cathedral. They had been overcome with emotion, holding each other as they wept and somebody stuck a mike in their faces. A reporter doing a story on the Camino demanded to know how they were feeling at this important moment. As if their body language and their faces didn't say it all? Esther told me how that person robbed them of their moment; that they had been asked to express in words what they just wanted to experience in feeling and spirit.

Everyone was quiet, suddenly focused on their cups and cutlery, obviously uncomfortable, or perhaps just not ready, to answer Paul's question. It went unanswered as we loaded our empty trays into the metal racks, shouldered our packs and moved on again.

"I hope we will arrive in time for the pilgrims' mass," Zbigniew shared.

"Looking at where we are and the time, it may be possible," Ana advised optimistically.

"There is also a mass at 7:00," I suggested, "so if we don't make it there for noon, we can go to that one and then go out for a celebration supper. One way or another, we will get our credentials and do mass in the cathedral today," I assured him.

"I hope we will make it for the noon mass," he repeated.

Seeing Finisterre, the most westerly point of Spain was not essential to my Camino, but for many, this final coastal stop completes their pilgrimage. Some walk the whole distance there and back from Santiago, some walk one way and return by bus, and some choose to see it as bus tourists, not having enough time or energy to do it any other way.

Paul, Catharina, and Zbigniew planned to go to Finisterre by bus tomorrow, Zbigniew's last day in Spain. I knew that today would be his only chance to attend a noon-hour pilgrims' mass. I understood his drive, but I was worried about his body. Ana and I exchanged concerned glances as he and Catharina picked up their pace.

Excitement started building when we came to a marker that announced Santiago, although the city was still a ways off.

"So," began Paul, "now that we are almost there, how are you feeling about your pilgrimage? Was it what you had thought it would be?" It wasn't even over yet!

Perturbed by his repeated question, I told the story that Esther had told me about when they arrived in Santiago only to have their moment stolen. Paul blustered that he would have hated that and seemed hurt at the implication that he was doing the same. Maybe he wasn't trying to be intrusive. Maybe he was just checking to see if we were feeling the same things as he was. Maybe he wasn't sure what he was feeling at all and needed some feedback to sort it out. Chastened by my own insensitivity, I placed a hand on his shoulder and suggested that I was still figuring things out and that maybe I wouldn't even know how I felt when I arrived. Maybe it would take a while to process it all. The others nodded in agreement, and we thoughtfully resumed our journey. Maybe it was good Paul brought it up again; we were all thinking about it now.

With the root of the word "lava", we'd now come to the place where pilgrims of old stopped to wash themselves before entering the holy city. Lavacolla marked our passing the day's halfway point, and the end of the trail recognizable as the Camino for us. From here, planes flew overhead, and we jockeyed for space among pilgrims as we trekked upwards, along urban roads, past light industrial businesses and the area's television and radio stations; all signs of modern life in stark contrast to our journey. Amid the busyness and traffic, we came to the peaceful tranquility of Camping San Marcos. We had been keeping an impressive pace, but we were still easily an hour out from our destination. Reaching the city did not mean reaching the cathedral.

"Should we stop?" Ana questioned uncertainly. I looked at Zbigniew, moving slowly just ahead on the road. He was swinging his leg from the hip in a modified limp, the distance obviously taking its toll. I knew he was determined to make the noon-hour mass, but glancing at my cellphone, I knew we would be very hard pressed to get there before they closed the doors at 11:45 for the service.

"Guys," I called ahead to Zbigniew, Paul, and Catharina, "I need to make a pit stop." They slowed and waited for Ana and I to reach them. "I'm sorry, you can go on without me, but I have to use a bathroom. There won't be any opportunities once we get into the city and no time once we get to the cathedral. I'll never make it."

"Me too," my accomplice, Ana, stated. "I need to stop as well." Zbigniew looked at his watch and tossed his white mane in frustration, a pained expression in his eyes as he looked ahead in the direction of a city we could not yet see. Paul and Catharina, catching on what we were doing agreed that they would like to stop for a drink.

"We cannot get there in time." Zbigniew sighed resignedly. "We will miss the pilgrims' mass. We will stop for a break," he confirmed, wresting control for the decision as he dropped into a green plastic chair at an outside table. I touched his shoulder and he looked up, disappointment all over his face.

"It's okay, Zbigniew. We will do mass tonight. We will go into the city, get our credentials, find our hotels and have time to wash and rest before mass."

"Yes," he agreed, recovering himself quickly, "and I will buy champagne! Netty do you drink champagne?"

"Ya! I can drink champagne." Catharina replied seriously.

"And you Ana?"

"I would love some champagne!" she agreed, eyes shining with unshed tears.

"We will celebrate together our journey, right Roxey?"

"Yes, Zbigniew. We will be done with walking and will be ready to celebrate. Right Paul?" I asked as he arrived at the table with a cup of espresso and sandwiches to share.

"Absolutely! Very professional decision!" he clapped Zbigniew on the back.

I purchased two glasses of fresh orange juice. Outside at the table, I delivered my consolation gift of orange juice to Zbigniew, who raised his glass appreciatively and smiled.

Rested, and with renewed energy and a sense of purpose, we struck out for Mount Gozo, the last pilgrimage station before entering the city. Looking over to the barrack-like housing, I was glad we had chosen to stay in O Pedrouzo and walk in this morning. Not wanting to delay any longer, we descended into the city under the shadow of gathering storm clouds.

Letting Paul, Ana, and Catharina pull ahead slightly, I fell in step with Zbigniew. He had resigned himself to missing the noon mass, but he was not going down without a fight!

"Why do they make the mass at noon?" he asked in frustration. "We would have to start at 4:00 in the morning to make it there in time. Why do they not make it at 2:00 or 3:00? It would be better for anyone wanting to go to church. They could go during siesta. Why do they make it at noon?"

"I don't know. Maybe the priests take siesta too. It's okay, Zbigniew. You and

I have walked all the way from St. Jean for this. It will be amazing whenever we get there. We can go to mass tonight, just like we can go today, but we will be better rested and able to enjoy it more," I reasoned, pulling my jacket on against the sudden gusts of wind. "And after mass, we will celebrate!"

"With champagne! I will buy for you champagne!" Zbigniew insisted.

"Yes, with champagne." I laughed, recharged with his happier energy.

At the foot of the hill, we came to a long bridge that would take us into the city. Surprisingly, while the road surface for vehicles seemed modern and well maintained, the wooden walkway along side of the bridge was worn, with planks loose and in some cases even missing. As I glanced at the rolling water below, I thought perhaps this was to extend the feeling of finishing a journey in the footsteps of pilgrims of the past.

The others were waiting on the other side, near a busy road. Just as Zbigniew and I reached the end of the bridge, tourists unloading from a nearby bus rushed over, cameras pointed in our direction. They were all excited about "real pilgrims" as they snapped our photo. I was appalled! We were the ones to take pictures! We were not souvenir shots for them! Then Zbigniew smiled at me, and we pulled ourselves up, proudly striding forward, prime examples of the enduring pilgrims entering the holy city. With his stylish hat and scarf and rock star demeanour, they probably thought he was someone special. Well... he was!

Joining our Camino family, we walked under ominously leaden skies, searching for the shells and arrows that would take us through the modern maze of the city. This cathedral was supposed to be huge. You'd think you would be able to see it from anywhere. There were large buildings, many-storied apartment blocks, but nothing like a collection of sky scrapers that would block something big from sight. I guessed it was the hills that added to the visual obscurity of the cathedral, remembering that it, like all the smaller churches we had passed along the way, would be built in the centre of the city. Finally, through a break in the buildings, I spotted a spire.

"There, there! Look! There it is!" I exclaimed. We picked up the pace. A few more turns through the maze and the cathedral burst before us, massive, ancient, and breathtaking! Just as we were trying to determine where the front would be, the ominous clouds plaguing our day also burst, and the downpour suddenly had the stone streets of the old city running with rivers.

We quickly found refuge in a tunnel leading around the cathedral. Safely under shelter, water cascading off the wall above, we looked up the road to see a small, dark-haired woman kneeling on the stones of the hill we had just fled down. The merciless rain poured down upon this living statue who did not move despite the watery assault. As we pulled on ponchos and rain jackets, still she knelt in silent prayer for pennies. Zbigniew, moved by her plight, scurried out into the deluge and placed a pocketful of coins in her bowl.

As suddenly as it started, the rain stopped and the sky began to clear and we stumbled out the other end of the tunnel, looking for direction to the pilgrim's office. The guidebook had stated the office was right off the corner of the cathedral, but which corner? Gawking in every direction like small-town tourists in a big city for the first time, we walked across the huge Praza do Obradoiro (the golden square) teeming with pilgrims.

Before us, loomed the twin towers framing the dramatic western entrance, the Portico de Gloria, which is accessed by twin staircases, architectural works of art in their own right. The tower on the left was encompassed by scaffolding and blue wrappings, a restorative work in progress. But that only highlighted the beauty of the intricate stonework, leaving the impression of a gift in the process of being unwrapped. From an alcove between the two towers, a statue of St.

James looked down benevolently upon the pilgrims below, some who had simply sat down or laid upon the stones of the square, so overcome with emotion. The square was encircled by jewels of Renaissance architecture, the Parador (a very upscale hotel), the town hall, and university buildings, located as if kneeling in worship to the vast cathedral.

We followed the cathedral walls around another corner and come upon the Praza das Praterias where stone horses leapt from the waters of a huge fountain. Behind, a massive staircase led to a phalanx of huge, wooden arched doors, the southern entrance to the cathedral. I remembered that the pilgrims' office was supposed to be near this square, so we continued down the wide sidewalk, tucked under colonnades running along store fronts. Bypassing several souvenir shops and cafes, we finally found a tourist information office where we were told the pilgrims' office had been relocated to a building over on the other side of the square, back by the tunnel we had passed through. Confused, tired, but happy, we retraced our steps, necks craning in attempts to miss nothing.

We finally found the pilgrim's office and joined the long line of pilgrims waiting to get their credentials. Ana, Catharina, and Paul were a little ahead of us in the line, Zbigniew and I standing together as we watched pilgrims disappear through the door ahead and come out beaming, clutching the rolled scroll; the prize for walking so many kilometres. I handed Zbigniew my spare water bottle which he gratefully accepted.

"How are your legs?" I questioned.

"Not too bad. It will be good to sit down," he said, leaning against the wall. He handed me a cookie, and I smiled my thanks. It had been a long time since we'd eaten, and it was likely to be a long time until we would again. After about an hour, we saw the others disappear one by one through the doorway, each returning, Compostelas in hand.

"They told us we can arrange for Catharina's bus trip home just around the corner. We will go do that and wait for you in the courtyard," called out Paul. We waved them off and waited our turn. The line before us was finally shorter than that growing behind us, so we took heart. In the gentlemanly fashion I had come to love about him, Zbigniew waved me on ahead of him as the next spot opened at the registration desk.

At her request, I handed my passport and my pilgrim passports over to the middle-aged woman behind the desk. Dropping my pack to the floor, I leaned on the marble counter while she sorted through the documents. At my surprise that she spoke unaccented English, Audrey smiled and told me she was from the States, just here doing a couple of weeks of volunteer work on the Camino.

"I come every year, usually here, but sometimes I help out at an *albergue* along the way. It has become my way of supporting and joining in the Camino."

"So, you started in St. Jean, yes?" I nodded. "And now you have come all the way here. That is amazing! Do you know that less than ten percent of those who reach here started in St. Jean? It is not a common thing." My eyes flooded with tears. She smiled again and scrolled through the lists of the computer.

"I am just looking for the Latin for your name. Ah! There it is," she said, writing my name with a flourish. "This certificate here is your Compostela, and this," she continued as she filled in a second document, "this is a certificate for the distance you have travelled. It is only given to those who started their journey in France. Congratulations!" She rolled and slipped the two documents into a tube and passed them into my waiting hand. Face awash with tears, I looked across at a similarly emotional Zbigniew, and felt a congratulatory clap of a stranger's hand on my shoulder. "Welcome to Santiago."

Out in the sunshine our family waited. We were hugging and crying and hugging some more. Catharina's ticket for her bus trip home to Belgium had been purchased, and the logistics of her departure two days hence had been worked out. The rest of us would be flying out, each in our turn.

We walked back towards the cathedral, going over plans for the next day. Catharina, Paul, and Zbigniew were going on a bus tour to Finisterre. Ana and I were going to spend her last day exploring Santiago and shopping for gifts for our families. We found ourselves back in the Praza das Praterias, where we each had our photos taken; the triumphant pilgrims arriving at the cathedral, tubes of proof clutched in our upraised hands!

Agreeing to meet back at the "horse fountain" at 6:00 for the evening mass, we scattered, maps in hand, to find our rooms. Within a few minute's walk, I passed out of the old city and found myself facing a busy city street, confronted by modern storefronts, rushing pedestrians, traffic and a convoy of busses. Following my map, I quickly located the Hotel Avenida, my home for the next three days. I pushed through the heavy glass door into the hush of a cool, small lobby.

In heavily flavoured English, the young, solidly-built woman behind the desk smilingly pushed the registration book across to me, taking my passport to scan in exchange. As I filled in the form, Acienta explained the way to my room and indicated a doorway to the breakfast room for the morning. Tucking her chin-length dark hair behind an ear, she asked that I lock my room when I went out, leaving the key at the desk for my return.

"Do not worry. The front door is locked at 10:00, but there is someone here to let you in. If you have any more questions, please come see me. I will go home at 5:00, but my colleague will be here and he also will be happy to help you." With that she handed me an ornate brass key, strung with a leather thong.

Pressing the elevator button for the third floor, the doors opened to a narrow, dark corridor with a ramp sloping gently downward, leading me to the foot of a short staircase that wound up and around the corner. At the top of the stairs, I crossed the landing to a door, pulling it open to reveal two more doors. The one on the right was mine.

Inside my cozy room, a soft double bed covered with a green brocade quilt filled most of the room. Dropping my pack in the corner, I crossed the room to push open the window above the small desk in the corner. Before me, a never-ending sea of tiled rooftops flowed off into the distance. Looking down from my fourth-floor room, I saw terraces and patios, some strung with clothes lines filled with laundry drifting gently in the breeze. I heard dogs barking and children playing, the occasional honk of a horn, but for the most part, it was quiet.

The phone on my bedside table rang. Acienta asked if I found my way and if I was happy with the room. It wasn't fancy, but it was clean, it was quiet, and it was mine. All good. She went on to say that the hotel was built from two houses combined into one hotel.

"That is why the elevator cannot take you to the top. You have to cross over on the third floor to the other side. Your side is taller," she explained. I thanked her for her concern and returned to exploring my room. No drawers other than the one desk drawer, but a roomy closet that would more than accommodate my meagre possessions.

Pushing open the door to the bathroom, I was in love! A deep, gleaming white bathtub called to me. Yes, there was a toilet and a sink, of course, but I only had eyes for the tub! Quickly scrambling out of my travel-stained clothes, I turned on the hot water and stepped in under a forceful shower. After I'd rinsed off the grime of the day, I stepped out, rinsed down the tub, and pouring in a bit of my shampoo, filled the tub with hot, sudsy water. I slid down into the water with a sigh. Heaven!

Resurfacing, I reached out and picked up my phone, and amidst steam, bubbles, and tears, brought Al up to speed on my arrival.

"You did good, babe!" he cheered across the miles. "I'm so proud of you!" I shared my plans for the rest of the day and said I'd call him again in the morning.

Back in my room, I pulled on clean leggings, a black sleeveless shirt, and a teal and black chiffon wrap. Although it was still very stormy looking outside, it was hot, and while the heat called for short sleeves, bare shoulders would be frowned upon in the cathedral. Quickly downing the remaining half of my sandwich from the morning, I snapped on my daypack with my passport, phone, and valuables tucked safely inside, and retraced my steps to the lobby. Acienta, busy on the phone, smiled and waved me out the door.

I left the busyness of the modern city and entered the old city once again. At the fountain, Ana and Catharina were already there, Catharina pacing impatiently, waiting the arrival of "the boys". With wide arms, Zbigniew approached around another corner, looking as if it had been him waiting for us all along. With his snow-white hair and beard, freshly washed and groomed, he looked like a misplaced Santa. "Where is Paul?" he questioned.

"There! He comes!" announced Catharina, as Paul blustered up the stairs, full of explanations of his late arrival. Together we climbed the wide staircase to the heavy wooden door and entered the sanctity of the great cathedral.

Everywhere you looked there was gold, statues, paintings, and rich tapestries. It was hard to know where to begin. Totally overwhelmed by the religious opulence, I felt a tug at my elbow. Ana nodded in the direction of the entry to a narrow staircase Zbigniew and Paul were climbing.

I remembered that part of the pilgrim tradition was to go up behind the high altar and "knock heads" with St. James. In the hush of the tight confines, I saw, as I reached the top step, a scarlet-robed priest sitting guard in the corner as each pilgrim approached the golden, scallop-covered back of the statue of St. James. In my turn, I placed my hands upon the statue's shoulders, and rested my forehead against the back of his. I thanked him for the safety of my journey, the people I met along the way, and prayed for all those I had travelled with, and those I would travel home to. As I moved on, Ana took my place, Catharina next in line.

Back down the stairs on the other side, we filed down a lower staircase leading to the crypt under the altar. Here, in a golden casket, were said to lay the bones of St. James. Those of Catholic faith crossed themselves and knelt to mutter prayers. I moved on, joining the men out on the main cathedral floor. In three directions from the high altar, hundreds of pews filled the hallways, most already filled with pilgrims waiting the mass. Given that this would be Zbigniew's only chance to enjoy a mass, and that Ana had no preference, we allowed him to choose seats for us in the section that had a full-on view of the altar.

High above us, huge organ pipes protruded from the walls in a series forming a golden pincher shape, and from them, rich music filled the cathedral. At the altar, a single priest sung, his clear baritone voice giving new life to old words. A procession of crimson-robed priests made their way to the high altar, some remaining standing, others assuming throne-like chairs. It was hard, from this distance to know who was speaking, the foreign words enhanced by hidden microphones. I watched others and took signals as to when to stand, sit, kneel, respecting the religion, although it was not my own. I joined the others for communion, comfortable at least in its similarity to that of my own church worship. My eyes absorbed the endless columns, the pastel domed ceilings, and the gilded angels of every shape, style, and size. Above the altar, six cherub-like angels, probably about ten feet tall each, held the massive golden structure that topped the high altar. I had the impression they were meant to symbolize holding up heaven. From beneath this structure, I spotted the golden statue of St. James I had earlier knocked heads with, gazing passively out upon the gathered masses.

A sudden break in the service and hushed whispering indicated something special was about to happen. A phalanx of monks, robed in deep burgundy, entered the area in front of the altar. One was bearing a large "frying pan", smoke trailing behind him as he went. All of a sudden, I realized! They were going to swing the *Botafumeiro*, the giant incense burner, historically swung to fumigate the area against sweaty and possibly disease-ridden pilgrims. This was a highlight for modern pilgrims but we had been warned it was not done very often, and usually only at noon-hour masses. That was part of the reason the pilgrims' noon-hour mass had been so important to Zbigniew. After transferring the burning incense into the huge, silver *Botafumeiro*, six monks pulled down hard on ropes attached to a pulley system high above on the plaster ceiling of the central dome. Slowly, but surely, the kettle swung higher and higher in an arc across the altar. We saw it as it passed the altar, then it swung out of sight, into the other end of the church, only to make a reappearance as it swung the other way. A hymn, sung by the lone priest, rang out in jubilation.

Slowly, the *Botafumeiro's* arc decreased, and eventually it returned to the centre of the altar where its progress was halted by one of the monks. A loud round of applause rang out in a most un-church-like way, the pilgrims forgetting decorum in the joy of the occasion. We all hugged and mopped up errant tears, our arrival in Santiago and completion of our pilgrimage properly celebrated.

Among music and laughter, we pushed back out into the still warm evening, full of chatter about the cathedral and the service. Our celebration knew no bounds!

"Now we have champagne!" declared Zbigniew, his blue eyes shining, still bright with tears.

Agreement all around. The question was where to go. The streets surrounding the cathedral were thick with opportunity; front window cases lit with displays of live seafood, slabs of fresh meat ready to be cut into steaks, wheels of fragrant cheese tempting a taste, and stacks of fresh mushrooms and vegetables waiting your choice. Apron-clad waiters called out from doorways, playfully mocking the invitations of rival restaurants as clusters of pilgrims weighed options of one against the other.

"We're not going to walk all night again, are we?" Paul questioned jokingly. "Can we just make a decision? I'm famished!"

Suddenly, across the way, there was Patricia and Michel! Patricia was using a bank machine, her back to me. Michel smiled widely and welcomed me into a big hug. He put his finger to his lips as Patricia finished her transaction, chatting away, totally unaware of my presence. She turned towards us and her eyes went wide in surprise.

"Oh! I never thought I'd see you again. When did you get here? We got here two days ago, but then we went to Finisterre. It was wonderful; a really special trip. Did you go to Finisterre? Or did you just arrive? Are you going to go to Finisterre? When do you leave? We leave tomorrow." Same old Patricia, I laughed; non-stop rapid-fire questions asked without time for answers before she went on.

"We just got in today," I advised waving my arm to indicate my waiting friends.

"Did you go to the cathedral? It's really beautiful. We went the day we arrived and then today when we got back from Finisterre, but they didn't swing the *Botafumeiro*. They might not swing it when you go, but the cathedral is still very nice."

"Actually, we just came from the cathedral, and we were lucky to see the *Botafumeiro* swing. We're just on our way for supper," I advised.

"Oh! Well that's good. That you got to see the *Botafumeiro*. We didn't get to see it swing. But it was still nice." She was still talking in circles as usual. "We fly out tomorrow, so we have to get an early night tonight. I have two days in Paris, so I want to get some rest. We're just heading back to our hotel."

I gave Michel and Patricia a big hug, assured them I'd continue to keep in touch, and watched them disappear into the crowded street. Taking a deep breath, I rejoined my friends and asked if they'd chosen a place to eat yet.

"We could go here," Ana suggested uncertainly, and we followed her into a busy tapas bar, filled with noisy, celebratory pilgrims. A waiter pulled us towards a small table jammed in the back of the restaurant, where the noise reached a deafening level, and we all looked at each other, exchanging silent agreement that this was not what we were looking for. Despite the waiter's protests that there was lots of room, we pushed out through the bedlam and back onto the street.

"That was too loud!" Ana said, shaking her hands like she could shake off the confusing noise.

"*Ja. Het was te luid!*" Catharina agreed, slipping back into Dutch in her confusion.

Recomposing ourselves, we meandered further down the Rua do Franco and discovered the O Boteco *Vinos & Tapas Taberna*. It seemed a little quieter than the chaos of the last place, and as we poked our heads in the door, we were graciously welcomed and ushered through a rough stone arch into a peaceful, high-ceilinged room. Sitting at a dark wooden table on matching backless stools, beneath our feet lay sections of glass flooring through which we saw down into tenth-century food storage silos. It was a little disconcerting, having the feeling of hanging in mid-air as you sat to dine, but everything in this ancient city seemed a little magical.

Zbigniew consulted seriously with our waiter and a sweating magnum of champagne was delivered, the contents poured ceremoniously into tall, crystal flutes.

"I toast to our journey together as friends," Zbigniew pronounced proudly raising his glass high. Smiling happily, while eyes threatened tears, we clinked our glasses and agreed we were more than friends; we were family. Around us, interested diners, most of them pilgrims as well, applauded our toast.

A steady stream of Galician specialties; octopus, peppers of the patron, empanadas and more filled our little table and we passed the plates between us, as any family does. Each of us had chosen a dish to share and before long, any hunger felt through the day was forgotten. The champagne was followed by regional *vino tinto*, and by the end of the meal, we were all suffused with a warm, happy aura of contentment.

After a small, friendly skirmish over the payment of the bill (Zbigniew insisted on paying the cost of the champagne before the remainder was split between us), we went out into the sultry night.

It was by now approaching midnight, and the streets were still thronged with pilgrims and locals, enjoying good food, good wine, and good company. It seemed that this celebratory atmosphere might go on all night, and it was amazing to realize that this happened here all the time, with a new wave of pilgrims arriving each day.

Away from the crowds, a soft guitar played, filling the darkness as we strolled around the cathedral, soft up-lighting making it even more mystical in the night. We strolled hand-in-hand, arms around waists, like brothers and sisters in the early years of innocence, not wanting this special day to end.

Finally, in the peaceful darkness, the day's activities and emotions settled upon us, and we realized our fatigue. Ana and I would not meet until 10:00, but the others were to be on their bus to the coast by 8:00. Hugging our farewells, and reassuring each other of our plan to reunite at the fountain for dinner the next evening, we strolled, each headed in the direction of our beds.

At the exit from the old city, a group of gypsy men hung out, smoking and passing a bottle of wine, sharing laughter and conversation. Still in pilgrim mode, my level of caution was relaxed; a group of men, in the dark, a woman alone. I should have been more nervous, but other than calling out to me, no threat was made. I turned the corner and walked the last block to my hotel.

I lifted my hand to ring the buzzer, but before I could press it, the door was swung open by a compact Spaniard.

"Senora Edwards? My colleague said you would come. I am Sebastian. Welcome. Is there anything more you need tonight?" I thanked him for letting me in and told him I was good for the night.

"Sleep well then," he called as I made my way to the elevator. In my room, I opened the window to the night air. I climbed into bed and sunk into sleep, dreaming of golden angels.

Face sunken into the crisp, white cotton pillow, I opened one eye and looked around. Something was odd. Refocusing my one-eyed gaze, I looked again. Yup! I was alone! I rolled onto my back and star-fished out to the corners of my double bed, enjoying the luxury of not hitting a rail, or a wall, or the person on the bunk beside me. It had been over two weeks since I'd slept alone and the feeling, while pleasant, was a little strange. I missed my bunk mates. But the extravagance of a private room, with a private bathroom quickly compensated for the loss of early-morning companionship, especially since I knew I'd be seeing all my friends later in the day.

Throwing back the quilt, my feet hit the floor, the rough carpet a new texture for toes used to tile and wood flooring. I crossed the room to the small window I'd left open through the night. An early morning fog blanketed the city, leaving only the closest tiled rooftops visible to my curious eyes. Pigeons, roosting on the roof ridge across the courtyard huddled together, heads tucked under wings denying the dawning light. I heard doors banging and voices calling as neighbours greeted the morning and prepared for their days. I felt very at home from my perch and thought how curious it was to be waking up in a foreign city as if it were my own.

Stepping out from under the shower's forceful stream, I made a date with the tub for a bath later that night. Towelling off with a thick white towel (a real towel!), I wrapped it around myself and returned to my room to consider options for outfits. Okay. I had grey trekking shorts, pants, leggings, and three t-shirts. The pants were ridiculously loose on me now, hanging in baggy folds around my newly-toned legs, so they wouldn't do. I settled on the shorts and my bright fuchsia shirt, one that I usually reserved for evenings after walking. The fog was slowly rolling back off the city, but it was still a bit cool, so I grabbed my coat. For shoes, all I had were my boots (no!) or my trekking sandals. While not exactly a fashion statement, I would still be in a world surrounded by pilgrims, so pretty much anything went.

"Good morning, Mrs. Edwards," Acienta called from the desk. "How is your sleep last night?" I assured her it was wonderful and asked if she could suggest somewhere to pick up a few items. "This here," she indicated on a map pulled from a colourful pad, "is where we are. Up here is the bus circle. You will go there to catch your bus to the airport. Over here, is the entrance to the old city," her finger followed the streets to the cathedral. "There are shops all around here, but you will find the prices are not so good. If you go over here, this is the shopping area you need."

In the breakfast room, a continental breakfast buffet flanked one wall of the quiet room. Only two other diners were seated at tables, and they were focused on their food and their tablets. I poured myself a cup of coffee, liberally topping it from the carafe of hot milk. On a small plate, I placed a roll, a cup of fresh fruit salad dressed with a scoop of plain yogurt, and some slices of creamy, white cheese. I looked at the bananas and smiled, realizing I no longer had to think to carry food for later in the day. I would have to remember that since I wouldn't be walking so much every day, my body wouldn't need as much food, so I bypassed the pastries completely.

As I returned to the table, a priest and two nuns walked in. How weird was that! Back home nuns did not wear habits, nor priests walk around in cassocks. But, I chided myself, this is a different world and it shouldn't be so surprising to find holy leaders within a couple of blocks of a world-renowned religious destination.

I was looking forward to meeting Ana. I hoped she had as good a sleep as I had, and that the others had gotten off on their bus tour to the coast okay. I smiled remembering Zbigniew and Paul bantering about getting wine for the journey. I hoped Catharina wouldn't be challenged with keeping "the boys" in line. Still plenty of time, I relaxed into a second cup of coffee before returning to my room.

I dashed off a quick text to Al, snapped on my daypack, shrugged on my coat, and then I was out the door again. Back down in the lobby, Acienta was busy on the telephone, but took time to wave as I pushed out through the door onto the narrow sidewalk. A steady stream of traffic separated me from the old city wall so I joined the throng of pedestrians at the corner, waiting for the light to change. All around me, Spaniards were off to start their normal weekday, but I crossed the road and entered the old city, basking in the more peaceful ambience of the ancient world. Shops under the colonnade were starting to open, bright window displays inviting my inspection. Sidewalk cafes were busy, morning customers clustered around tables, savouring large mugs of coffee and plates of flaky pastries.

Up ahead of me stood the imposing face of the cathedral, and, at the foot of the stairs, the fountain. The sculpted horses burst from the falling waters as pilgrims lined up for photos to send home. I stood off to the side, checking out a store window while keeping an eye for Ana.

"Hallo!" she called and when I turned to her voice, she was not alone.

"Netty!" I exclaimed. "I thought you were going with the boys?" Catharina grinned, like a kid caught truant from school.

"I *haf* a big bus ride to go home. Let *zem* go on the bus today. I vill be with you!" she laughed.

"Well alright! A girls' day! What should we do first?" I asked.

Each of us had a couple of "must haves" in mind, with the focus on gifts for family at home. We agreed to do a loop around the souvenir shop rows below the cathedral, then stop for coffee.

Like any tourist destination, the shops were big on t-shirts, and there were a lot of duplications between the stores. It also became apparent that the exact same things could be had at one store, cheaper than another, the further we moved down the block from the cathedral.

Having picked up shirts for my grandchildren in Pamplona, my focus was on the rest of my family. "I'd like to get a gold shell to put on my chain with my cross," I said. " T-shirts for my sons, and earrings for my daughters-in law."

"*End ze* puzzle for your husband," Catharina reminded me seriously.

"Yes, if we can find one that would be great. I also want to get a big bag to carry my gifts and essentials on the plane since I'll be checking my pack in Madrid all the way home. I'll need to carry a change of clothes for travel from Paris." Wow! Madrid and Paris in the same conversation! What a world traveller I was becoming.

"I would like to look for a pair of comfortable shoes for England," shared Ana. "I am so tired of these boots!" she laughed. I told them about the area Acienta had shown me, and we agreed we'd go there later. We wandered up and down the streets, in and out of one store after another. We shared laughter over some of the odd little things we found and carefully weighed our purchases. I found some beautiful silver shell earrings for Amanda (knowing she preferred silver jewellery) and another pair accented with an intense blue that would reflect Jackie's amazing eyes.

Stepping up to a jewellery store window, I looked at the shell charms on offer in the displays and saw exactly what I was looking for. The shells came in a variety of sizes, and I asked the girls which one they thought best matched my cross. Catharina held my cross, carefully assessing one shell against the other.

"*Haf dis* one!" she pronounced, fingering the tiny shell. Although it was almost fifty euros, I had promised this purchase to myself, and other than a change of underwear, slacks, and two shirts to travel home in, intended no other purchases for myself. I handed my chain to the jeweller as she took it to add the charm.

"I *haf* one too!" Catharina declared suddenly, pushing a charm across the counter to join mine. I looked at Ana questioningly, but she smiled and shook her head, no. I thought it would have been perfect if we all had one. But Ana's budget held her own priorities, and I knew she was saving for her visit with her daughter in England before returning to Brazil. I didn't want to embarrass her by insisting on purchasing one for her. We would still be sisters of the shell without it.

As Catharina unfastened her chain, I noticed two little ivory nubs, set in gold, dangling from the necklace. I reached forward to capture them to see what they were.

"*Dey is my grandboyz'* teeth," Catharina announced proudly, her face beaming. At our questioning looks, she expanded as she slid the chain across to the jeweller. "When *ze* baby teeth fall out, *zeir* mother, she *gif zem* to me. So, I *haf* one tooth for each boy." Well how cool was that! Here you think this is some serious, no-nonsense woman, and she can be totally sentimental to the point of carrying her grandsons' baby teeth against her heart. I was still learning about our multi-faceted Belgian friend.

We crossed the plaza and entered the imposing gates of the university. The thick, moss-hung stone walls insulated the courtyard from the bustle of the streets, creating an other-worldly oasis inside. Arched balconies ran around the square above the ornately carved colonnade. Lush sections of lawns interspersed with colourful floral beds and lacy shade trees created pockets of peaceful privacy among wrought-iron benches. Intricately patterned paths criss-crossed the courtyard, all leading to an impressive sculpture of a bygone scholar. A perfect setting for a group photo, we convinced a passing student to take our picture before he strode off through a shadowy door leading to the classrooms.

The sun was getting warmer, and the streets and stores busier. Strolling down the last street before crossing out of the old city, we spied a gelato shop. Like kids in a candy shop, we drooled over the array of colours and flavours before making our selections. The clerk piled the waffle cones generously, and we were hard put to eat the treat fast enough before it melted. Catharina lost all claim to formality as she happily licked the blackberry cream running down her hand and delightedly sucked the sweetness from her fingers. It was heaven, and we were like children again.

Crossing the busy street, we wound our way around the bus loop, consulting the schedules to confirm this as the place to catch the airport bus. Catharina would be going in a different direction, to the train station, and Paul had gallantly promised to get up early and make sure she got to her train.

We found ourselves suddenly in the world of new-age commerce; all things glass and metal, vivid colours and synthetic fabrics. Large, splashy signs advertised the latest and greatest, inviting shoppers to find their dreams within. Catharina marched stoically behind as Ana and I delighted in fashions, selecting a couple of items each and rushing to the changing rooms. Catharina, arms crossed across her chest, stood judge amid the feminine frenzy as we modelled the outfits. Rolling her eyes, she sighed tolerantly as she approved one and sent the other back to the change room.

Bags clutched in hand, we pressed on, still looking for shoes for Ana. Taking in the rows of supple leathers and light canvas, I too wanted new shoes, but my wide feet had been made even wider by the walk, and it would be a while before they resumed their original shape and size. It made no sense to buy shoes that didn't fit, hoping that one day they would. I sighed as Ana slipped on a soft brown pair of flats and made her decision.

By now we both felt a bit guilty, dragging Catharina from store to store, so we decided lunch was in order. At a corner café, we ordered sandwiches and coffees and chatted happily as the busy world rattled by.

"You know, that shirt I got has no sleeves, and it might be a bit cool for the evening," I mused.

"Maybe you should get a scarf," Ana suggested. She had teased me along the way at my inability to wear scarves, an item she considered a staple, and something you could never have too many of. "And you didn't get your bag yet," she reminded me. Catharina rolled her eyes, bracing herself for round two.

Back into the old city we went, haunting the outer ring of shops that offered more fashion and less souvenir-type items. Ana quickly found just the perfect scarf for me and I tucked it into my bag, laughing at her suggestion I should wear it now. A couple of doors down, we spied a huge striped woven bag hanging in the window. "That would be perfect!" Ana pronounced.

"Here! It is here! Look!" Catharina exclaimed. I crossed the floor to find her holding the long-sought puzzle in her hands. The picture showed a map of the Camino, with inset pictures of special places and monuments along the way.

"It will be perfect for Al! Thank you for finding it, Netty!" She preened happily under my praise.

On the way back to our hotels, at the entrance to the old city was an unlikely pub, one that with its high-backed leather chairs, gleaming bar, brass rails, and ale posters, seemed more appropriate to England than to Spain. We sunk into the cool chairs and ordered up shandies to slake our thirst. I insisted on buying Catharina's drink, thanking her for her patience during all our shop hopping. She just raised her glass in a toast and grinned.

As we sat there, my phone pinged; the boys. They were by now, on their way back home, and from the pictures Paul sent, it looked like they had had a great day. I especially liked the photo of Paul with fishing boats in the background and of Zbigniew thoughtfully leaning against a post inscribed with "Let there be peace."

Remembering that we were all to meet at the fountain at 7:00, we went our separate ways to have a bit of a rest before what promised to be a late night. On my way, I passed a perfumery. A well-groomed clerk stepped out from behind the glass counter, asking if she could help. Making the transition from pilgrim to woman came slowly. Having no other makeup along, I wanted some water-proof mascara, tears being a common occurrence for me in these emotional hours. She packaged my purchase like it was fragile china, cushioning the bag with tissue before dropping the small tube inside. Then she reached into a drawer and pulled out a couple of samples of face cream. I smiled my thanks, and she added a few more. I wondered if she was just being generous, or if my skin looked like it needed the cream that badly! I would share a couple with Ana and Catharina tonight.

Three doors to my hotel, I again looked wistfully at the stylish shoes in a shop window. Well, I could look, couldn't I? I have a thing for shoes, especially soft, leather, well-made shoes, but it was the wrong time to try any on. Then, I noticed some sandals on a clearance table. They had colourful elastic straps, the only solid parts being the sole and the heel strap. I tried them on and was pleased to find them comfortable, so I carried them to the till, happy in knowing that the straps would accommodate the current size of my feet, and then shrink to fit my post-Camino size. Yay! No boots and trekking sandals for me tonight!

After a long, hot soak in a tub, I dressed for dinner in my new shirt I had bought this afternoon, and my new strappy sandals. I tied my scarf around my shoulders, letting the width drop down my back to protect my daypack buckle.

The warm evening air greeted me as I re-entered the old city and made my way to the fountain. Ana waited there, but this time she was alone.

"The boys needed a rest. They had wine on the bus," she smiled. "Catharina will come with them. They said to find a place to eat outside and call them and let them know where we are."

The streets were alive with pilgrims; friends meeting friends not seen for days. Lots of hugging, lots of laughter, and even singing. It was like an endless family reunion, with new pilgrims arriving all the time. The celebratory atmosphere lit the soft shadows of the evening with the warmth of friendship and common goals achieved.

Ana and I found ourselves in front of an "Italian" restaurant, offering pizza and pasta and various regional meat dishes. Something for everyone, we decided. We phoned Paul to let him know where we were, settling into a corner, each with glass of wine while we waited for a large table to come open in the street-side patio. Finally, Catharina and Paul arrived; no Zbigniew in sight.

"He's sleeping," Paul advised. "Said he'd be along in a bit. So is this where we're eating," he looked at the menu card doubtfully.

"Yes, there are many things to choose from." Ana handed him the larger menu and his face relaxed.

Our waiter approached, and we carried our glasses out to a large table on the broad sidewalk between the courtyard garden and the street. Paul ordered a bottle of red wine and poured some out for the two of them. Ana and I waved his offer off, indicating the white wine still remaining in our glasses. Uncomfortable with putting the waiter off, we finally decided to order. Paul called Zbigniew again, and he said he was just on his way. I walked up to meet him at the corner.

Our friend arrived, dapper as ever, a jaunty scarf draped around his neck. He enfolded me in a tight hug, telling me about his day as we strolled, arm-in-arm, back to the others. Apparently, they had really enjoyed being tourists for the day.

"We were like the bus people. Off the bus, snapping photos, back on the bus and off again," he laughed.

"Ah! There you are," Paul greeted us. "The food is just about to come. Sit there, between Catharina and Ana, Zbigniew. Here's a menu," he said as he filled Zbigniew's glass, emptying the bottle. Zbigniew stopped to give each of the girls a hug before sitting and pulling up his chair.

Our waiter, followed by another fellow, came bearing large trays, fragrant with the steaming plates of glistening pasta we had ordered. Paul ordered another bottle of wine before turning back to the table, insisting that everyone try some of his *bottocino* cheese slices, drizzled with olive oil and sprinkled with green herbs and slivers of sundried tomatoes.

The second bottle of wine arrived along with Zbigniew's order, and we shared a glass, each relating the happenings of our day. Catharina teased Ana and I about all the time spent shopping, and the boys said she should have come on the bus with them. Laughing, Paul repeated Zbigniew's story of how the bus stopped at first one place then another and how everyone trooped out to take photos before getting back on the bus. Catharina reassured them that she had enjoyed her day with us, and we showed off her scallop charm.

I called over to a man at the next table, asking if he would take our photo as we toasted each other happily. When Paul reached over to top up our glasses, Ana and I both denied refills, happy just nursing the wine that remained in our glasses from the first bottle. He drained the bottle filling Catharina and Zbigniew's glasses and beckoned the waiter to fetch a third bottle.

Evening became night and I leaned back in my chair, looking up at the lit wall of the cathedral. In the sky above, I spotted small crescents of silver wheeling above the chapel towers, realizing they were circling doves. It was magical and I just sat savouring the lively banter between my friends, relishing what a very exceptional time and place this was. I gazed at my friends, committing their faces and small gestures to memory, already preparing for the loss of people who had, in the space of a very short time, become as important to me as family.

As the bells of the cathedral called out 11:00, I was surprised to realize how warm and comfortable we were, outside in shorts and sleeveless shirts, despite the hour. Suddenly, a petite woman in a short, fringed dress and heels, walked up to Zbigniew, greeting him happily as she rearranged a colourful scarf around her deeply-tanned shoulders. Ruth and Zbigniew had met earlier on the trail, but hadn't seen each other again until now.

Paul generously invited her to join our table, ordering another bottle of wine as Ana shot me a puzzled look across the table, and moved over to allow Ruth to pull her chair in next to Zbigniew. I got the feeling that Ana, like me, resented this intrusion on our last evening together. Paul had spent the day with Zbigniew, but this was all we had before we parted.

In her broad, Australian accent, Ruth said she lived now in India, but did the Camino regularly, since her children lived in Santiago. Reaching the city meant also reaching her grandchildren. Well that explained the outfit and shoes. She didn't have them in her pack, they were waiting here for her.

After she drained her drink, Paul refilled Ruth's glass with wine, ever the magnanimous host. Zbigniew's eyes sparkled as she spoke. I wondered if there was more than a passing friendship in the building. Well he was alone in the world now, and it turned out Ruth was single, but I knew Zbigniew's heart still belonged to another. Whatever was happening, it seemed Zbigniew was pulling away from our little family, and that, I wasn't ready for.

The waiter finally arrived with the cheque, Paul suggested we simply split the cheque five ways since Ruth was our guest. I had limited my drinks knowing I was close to maxing out my funds, but I laid my share on the table. I saw Ana struggle with the extra cost as well.

I said I was going for a walk around the cathedral. While the girls rose to join me, Paul reclined, swirling the wine in his glass, gazing up indifferently. Zbigniew and Ruth waved us off casually. Really! Was the Final Five going to end like this?

Blinking back tears, I strode from the table. Catharina and Ana hurried to catch up with me and Ana folded me in her arms. She understood my sorrow and as sobs hiccupped through my body, tears also traced their way down her cheeks. Our hearts joined in hurt and confusion. Catharina, at a loss in dealing with such raw emotion, patted our shoulders comfortingly, clucking her concern.

Pulling myself together, I suggested we walk around to see where the doves were coming from. As we climbed the staircase above the fountain, Paul caught up with us.

"Hey, you lot! Wait for me." He threw a brawny arm around my shoulder in silent apology, and I gave his hand a squeeze in forgiveness.

As we made to turn the corner, we looked back to the plaza to see Zbigniew deep in conversation with Ruth, and our eyes met, silently mourning the loss of our friend. As much as it obviously pained Ana to leave without a proper farewell, she smiled gently.

"Zbigniew knows what he is doing," she murmured softly. I pondered her statement wondering if she meant that he was intentionally separating himself from the group to prevent the need for a painful goodbye. We walked on through the night, now the Final Four.

Rounding the third corner of the cathedral, we found ourselves gazing up at the front of the building, the two towers floodlit in the darkness. Above the towers, dove flew in circles, the glaring lights preventing their rest. In the background, a lonesome harp echoed through the night, creating an ethereal aura around us. I set my phone on video to capture the magical music and the circling doves. Paul sidled up beside me.

"It's very magical isn't it?" I looked at him and nodded. "Are you filming this then?" I nodded again. "And can you get the music? Is it taping the sound?" I sighed, lowered the phone and nodded again. "Oh! So, you can hear me talking! Och! What a git!"

I laughed and started filming again, my friend silent now beside me.

We continued our walk around the cathedral. Midnight chimed as we made our way back to the fountain, only to see Zbigniew still sitting at the table, alone now. Waiting.

"You came back my friends!" he rose, throwing his long arms wide, encompassing all of us girls in a gentle hug. We discussed bus times and flight times and hugged some more, each of us not wanting to let the others go. Reunited as a group, we walked slowly out of the old city towards my hotel.

At the door, we clung together, knowing tomorrow two would be gone. After more tearful hugs and goodbyes, I slipped inside the cool, dark lobby, sad, but happy that we had reunited for a final goodbye.

I would see Catharina and Paul at the fountain in the morning, and we would spend one last day together, but by the time I saw the horses leaping from the waters, Ana and Zbigniew would be gone.

I woke knowing that this would be my last day in Santiago. I lay snuggled in the softness of my bed, waffling between feelings of sadness and those of anticipation and joy. Yes, it would be my last day to explore this special city, but today I would attend the pilgrims' mass at the cathedral, and we would be meeting Andi, Esther, and Irma for supper. More importantly, tomorrow I would begin another journey; one that would take me back home to my husband, my family, and my real world.

I was meeting Catharina and Paul at the fountain at 11:00, so I had plenty of time. After so many days of rising with the dawn, sleeping in would have to be relearned.

By now, Ana and Zbigniew would be travelling, already gone from the city, I thought as I laid back in the half light of another foggy morning. I was surprised at the sense of loss I felt at their absence. Staring at the plaster ceiling, I reflected on the emotional roller coaster that was last night's farewell supper.

When Zbigniew finally arrived, our little Camino family was together, happy and whole. Then Ruth joined our table, and silent frustration flew between Ana and I. Ruth might have just greeted Zbigniew and walked on, but Paul invited her to join us.

Why did he do that? I stormed silently. While it was the bigger, friendlier thing to do, I resented this intrusion on the last of our time together. I had warred between supporting Zbigniew's pleasure at Ruth's arrival and my childish, possessive resentment. My better self was losing that argument when Paul suggested the five of us split the bill that included multiple bottles of wine I hadn't shared, as well extra drinks for this interloper. Not only did I have to share precious time but my dwindling funds as well! "It's not fair!" my immature self had declared, stamping its foot in my head.

In retrospect, I realized that I was more upset with myself than I was with Paul, my only excuse being the intense sense of loss when faced with the possibility of losing Zbigniew.

Paul and I both have strong personalities, so it was likely we would butt heads once in a while. But no matter what the situation, our relationship was more important than making a point or winning an argument. As with any family, conflicts happen; feelings are hurt, but love restores the balance and strengthens the bond.

The loving support of my Camino sisters and the swift resolution between Paul and I had healed the rift even before Zbigniew rejoined us. Once he flung his long arms around us, it was all out happiness and we had finished our last evening in Santiago as the Final Five, reunited again.

Then, of course, the evening finished in tears, as we said goodbye, knowing that two would be missing when next we met. Happiness, excitement, frustration, anger, hurt, sadness, and joy; it was all there in the mix. Our emotions were a reflection of the ups and downs from the start of our journey to the celebration upon our arrival in Santiago, to the bittersweet leave taking we would have with each other, and with the Camino.

Whoa! Pretty deep stuff to start the day with. I needed coffee! I made my way downstairs, waving at Acienta at the desk, and joined other diners at breakfast. Still lots of time, but that meant some space for private discovery before joining the others.

In through the passageways of the old city I went, winding my way up to a set of shops above the main colonnade that led to the fountain. The morning fog was rolling off the city quickly, revealing rows of buildings I hadn't yet had the chance to explore. The shops were just opening, clerks sweeping entrances clear while curious pigeons looked on from the striped awnings above. High fashion and jewellery, leather and gold; this area spoke more of expensive taste than practicality, more of frivolity than budgets. A wall of glass displayed shoes that were more works of art than footwear. I could envision young Spanish brides slipping dainty feet into the beribboned and bejewelled confections, the icing on the cake of what would be their wedding days.

Around the corner I came to a lingerie shop and my own sense of practicality evaporated. I was so done with quick-dry underwear and sports bras! I wanted to feel like a woman again! The silver bell tinkled as I pushed through the heavy glass door and entered the perfumed shrine of femininity. An impeccably dressed and coiffed clerk stood checking lists behind the sparkling glass counter. Items of satin and lace of every description floated above tiers of pearlescent pink boxes on the shelves behind the counter. She smiled, and I faltered, at once self-conscious of my weather-beaten pilgrim appearance.

"How may I help you?" she invited without missing a beat. I told her what I was after, dreading the usual endless trial of finding the right fit. She looked me over, turned to the lovely wall of boxes, pulled out creamy whispers of nothingness, and led me to the change room. And then something amazing happened. Everything fit! She had it in one! This woman really knew her business and her stock. I tossed my over worn gear disdainfully in the wastebasket, not even willing to carry it as far as the hotel, and happily finished dressing.

Still early when I arrived at the cathedral, I stood at the top of the stairs watching for Paul and Catharina coming. Looking down the stone steps to the fountain, something seemed a little different. Then I realized there were uniforms everywhere. At the foot of the stairs, beside a shiny black van, two policemen stood at the ready, their eyes panning the square for suspicious activities.

Nothing suspicious I could see, other than Catharina and Paul arriving on time. Descending the staircase, I met them with warm hugs as they took in the police presence. We realized we had time for a quick cup of coffee in the square, and we settled into chairs as we watched a number of dark-suited men purposefully striding by, one of them surreptitiously speaking into his collar.

"Wonder what's going on?" Paul said. "Do you think there's been a terrorist threat?" Catharina clucked with concern, tightening her lips in serious consideration. Overhead a helicopter flew low, circling the cathedral. Now I was getting nervous.

After the attacks in Paris a few short months ago, the world watched fearfully for the next incident when innocent lives would be taken to make irrational statements. Everything was at risk, from gatherings of heads of states, to national sporting events. I had thought that if anyone wanted to do something that would capture the attention of the whole world, Santiago would be a likely target. At any given service, hundreds of people from all over the world would be inside, oblivious sitting ducks to twisted plots. Should something happen here, every nation would be affected. The world could not help but take notice.

We drained our cups and walked across the square. Police presence had increased. No one looked confrontational, just very alert.

"Should we go in? Do you think it's safe?" I questioned quietly. Catharina eyed the guns on the stairs of the place of worship hesitantly, unable even in her atheist mind, to bring the two into correlation. The flow of pilgrims in through the cathedral doors continued unchecked, so we climbed the stairs and joined the throng. We searched for a good spot where we could be together, and found none.

All of a sudden Paul plucked my sleeve and nodded in the direction of a pillar just behind the first set of pews to the right of the altar. I slipped around the corner and stood on the squared off foot block of the pillar, a great view of the altar, but it meant standing through the whole service I nodded my thanks to Paul as he joined Catharina against the wall across the aisle.

There was a group of well-dressed dignitaries seated in the privileged area adjacent to the altar, their position bestowing an unobstructed view of the service. As the gate surrounding the area was opened, a parade of priests, crowned in a variety of heights and opulence, proceeded, settling into the heavy chairs arranged in accordance with their stature within the church. As had happened the day we arrived, the service proceeded, however a large portion of this service was spoken in English, so easier to follow. It was particularly moving when they read out the names of all the countries whose citizens had reached Santiago the day before. Compostelas in hand, they were likely here, tears in their eyes, celebrating their arrival.

Suddenly the gate opened again and the monks proceeded through with the smoking pan for the *Botafumeiro*. I couldn't believe it! We were two for two! Other pilgrims had come to multiple services and had never seen it swing.

I looked across at Paul who tapped his cellphone. Right! I pulled my phone out and got ready to film the process. This time, I would have an unobstructed view of the incense burner as it swung in wide arcs across the altar. I already envisioned sharing the video with our missing Camino friends. Higher and higher it swung as I tracked the gleaming canister's arc. Just as it looked like it would graze the high plaster ceiling, it started to slow, the arc lessening as the organ music rose. A burly monk stepped up on the dais and, the next time the *Botafumeiro* passed, he reached out and grabbed the chains, wrestling it to a stop. Wild cheering and applause broke out as the congregation expressed their approval at a job well done.

Jubilant chords filled the cathedral as the service came to an end, the church's royalty proceeding out again. Then a phalanx of dark-suited men surrounded the altar area and escorted the privileged guests down a roped off hallway. Only then were the rest of the congregation encouraged to make their way to the heavy, arched doors.

Out on the stairs, I found Catharina and Paul amid the milling crowd. Above us the cathedral bells pealed, and doves flew. It was a surreal environment, and after a few minutes, we sought the peace of the now empty cathedral.

"So obviously some person of importance. Maybe a high-level government official or something," I suggested. Catharina nodded sagely in agreement.

"Did you get the video?" asked Paul. I told him I had and that I would send it to everyone when I got home. He smiled widely, "Zbigniew and Ana will love that!" We wandered the now quiet halls, commenting on the beauty of the statuary and tapestries decorating side chapels. Saints and angels abounded everywhere you looked. No surface seemed bereft of gold and gleam. The opulence was kind of overwhelming, but understandable when you considered the importance so many pilgrims attached to the cathedral.

Out in the plaza, we rested under an umbrella at an outdoor café. Even in the shade, it was hot and cold drinks were in order. A tall, moustachioed Spaniard, crossed the patio to take our order.

I checked my cellphone from time to time, looking for the message from Andi and Esther. We knew they had arrived in the city and were staying in a small apartment near the cathedral. Esther had advised they had made reservations at a special restaurant they always enjoyed, and that she would text us with a meeting place. They had some shopping to do, and they wanted Irma to have a good rest before they joined us.

Meanwhile, the three of us strolled the streets, comparing menus, waving off soliciting waiters trying to lure us inside. We watched as newly-arrived pilgrims found each other, loud celebratory reunions, punctuated by hugs and back-slapping as they met. By now we felt like old hands at this. We were pilgrims no longer. Now we were tourists. I noted that distinction with a small degree of sadness, but reminded myself home was less than forty-eight hours away.

Suddenly my phone pinged and we came to a halt as I checked the message.

"They are over by the main entrance to the cathedral," I advised. "They will wait for us there." Re-energized by anticipation, we trundled around the side of the massive structure, looking everywhere for the happy little family.

"Here we are!" Esther's crisp voice rang out, "Over here!" There stood our friends, tiny Irma, her deep blue eyes sparkling as she held out chubby arms to us. Our Camino bambino, very much the little girl now in a fresh, flowered dress, bare armed, bare footed and bubbly. No longer the leggings, soft moccasins and scarf to protect her from the elements, here in this cosmopolitan world, the sunlight softly caressed pink baby skin as she bounced in her daddy's arms. Esther was also wearing a dress. She had told me that every time she arrives in Santiago, she goes shopping for "girl" things, her reward for the demanding journey. Her lush figure was enhanced by the soft drape of brightly decorated fabric, a significant change from her no-nonsense trekking gear. On her feet she wore strappy, heeled sandals, and yes, there was a splash of pink polish on every toe. Andi enveloped me in a big hug, his long arms holding me tight. As Catharina and Paul got their hugs, I scooped up the baby, delighting in her soft skin and drooly coos.

"You see she has now four new teeth!" exclaimed Andi proudly. So, the tiny pearls had finally worked their way through. A little charmer already, when this little girl was able to flash a full-toothed smile, hearts would break.

"Our reservations are not until 8:00," Esther advised brusquely, "so shall we go have a drink and celebrate together?" We made our way to the outdoor café in the square and pulled white metal chairs around a shaded table.

"Beer all around," Paul announced grandly to the waiter. Catharina tried to decline, but our generous friend was having none of that, and she grinned as the cold, sweating glass was placed before her.

"Cheers!" "Saluti!" "Proost!" We clinked our glasses in multilingual celebration.

"So, tell us all about the rest of your journey; when did you get in, did everything go well?" I asked, taking Irma on my knee.

"Well, first of all, when you sent that warning about the big stairs at Porto Marin, I did not understand what you meant," Esther shared. "I thought you meant the staircase to the city which I knew to not be too bad. Then, when we got there, I realized they had changed the route. The stairs were hard," she looked at

Andi who nodded in agreement, "but we just took it slowly, and so we did fine."

"Yes," Andi nodded again, his curls dancing with the motion. "It was hard to balance. But people behind waited. I do not know why we had to go that way. The road would have been easier with the baby," he suggested, polishing his black-framed glasses with a cloth from his pocket. I filled them in on the story of the accident on the road that the bartender had told me about. "Ohhhh, I see," he intoned.

Irma was using my lap as a trampoline, bouncing up and down, working her legs and chirping happily.

"Here, let's have a go," Paul suggested, scooping up the tiny girl. Holding her in the crook of one arm, he hefted his beer with the other. Suddenly, Irma decided his glass of golden bubbles was very interesting. She dipped her tiny fingers into the foam and waggled them around in the cool beer, before popping them in her mouth. Her face screwed up at the taste and everyone around us was laughing. As usual, the novelty of a baby in this mostly adult world was captivating.

"Here, now! You're a bit young for that aren't you, miss!" Paul protested. But he didn't pull the glass away, the drink becoming a tiny water park for tiny fingers. It was obvious Irma was much more interested in the bubbles than the drink.

"We had only one bad stay for the rest of our journey," Esther shared. "It was an old farmhouse and the people were very nice, but in the night, there were bedbugs!" We cringed in horror. Esther passed Irma to her daddy and pushed up her skirt, displaying a rash-like area of red bite marks on her lower thigh. "Here, and…" she displayed the back of her upper arm, similarly attacked, "here, and also on my stomach and back. Irma did not get bit, and Andi not so much. They liked me," she muttered. "We had to wash everything," The *hospitaleros* were so sorry. The blanket I used had been put away in a trunk since last summer. Obviously, the bugs were there. But I just use cream and the bites do not itch so much." Nonchalantly she shrugged her shoulders, acknowledging bedbugs as one of the risks you take, and then you move on.

"And we have no other problems. We arrived in Santiago and got our Compostelas," Andi announced.

"Did Esther get a Compostela too?" I asked.

"Well," Esther began, "you can get a Compostela only if you walk or ride a bike or a donkey. I told the people in the office Andi was Irma's donkey, but they would not give her a Compostela. They did give her a certificate saying she had completed the journey, so she will have to come again for her own Compostela."

By now Irma was busily trying to remove Paul's watch. Catharina enjoyed watching the little girl, but was in no hurry to take a turn holding her. Catharina's grandsons were older, and I had the feeling it had been a while since she'd handled a toddler.

"And so," Andi suggested seriously, "now it is time we can go to supper as well." He drained his beer. "The restaurant is nearby; only down the next street."

Down the narrow street, we came to *Los Caracoles*, the sign proudly declaring its existence since 1986. We pushed in through the green door surrounded by golden stained-glass windows depicting the namesake snails and were warmly greeted by a robust middle-aged man who seemed to know Andi and Esther. He led us to the back corner of the restaurant, seating us at a table set for six, including a highchair. The proprietors, expecting a toddler had given us a good location that would allow us to enjoy ourselves without disturbing other guests. Funny thing was, all of the guests seated along our path reached out to touch Irma as she passed.

Depositing water, wine, and a basket of bread on the table, our waiter greeted us with a flourish, providing each of us with menus before handing Irma a crusty rusk. Esther smiled her thanks as he returned to the kitchen, and she and Andi busied themselves with securing her in the highchair and fastening her "baby cape" around her neck.

"Right," Paul said, leaning over towards Catharina and me. "I want you to know that supper tonight is my treat. You have what you want, I am paying."

"Oh, nooo," denied Catharina sombrely.

"That is not necessary," I whispered, shaking my head.

"Yes, I am, and there is to be no argument on this!" Paul insisted. I looked at him and he smiled.

"Thank you, Paul. That is very sweet of you." Yup. I think he was blushing! Catharina smiled.

"You must have the scallop!" advised Esther. "It is traditional here, the symbol of the Camino." I looked at the cost for the house specialty, and keeping in mind that Paul was paying, declined.

Hungry by now, I was happy to have a place of fragrant, creamy shrimp risotto placed before me. Savouring every amazing mouthful, I was glad of my choice. Glasses were refilled and another bottle of wine arrived at the table.

"Last night!" Paul winked offering the wine, and I held my glass towards him.

Irma had been enjoying a little bit of her parent's meals as they placed offerings on the highchair tray. Relaxed parents; happy child. It seemed to work. How will things be when Irma has a sibling? I thought.

"Tomorrow we will go by bus to Finisterre. There we will stay at a small hotel and let Irma play on the beach for some time. Then, two days after, we will come here again before flying home. Maybe I will try the risotto then," Esther laughed.

By now Irma was getting ready for bed. I thought this would be the end of our evening together, but again, these young parents had a plan. Andi would return to the hotel with his daughter, and Esther would enjoy the rest of our evening with us. Sad to see them go, I gave Irma one last cuddle, kissing the crown of her soft, silky head. Handing her off to Paul, I disappeared into Andi's long-armed hug, my face pressed against his plaid-shirted chest.

"We will miss you," he said softly. "You are Irma's Camino granny. We will always remember you." In an effort not to cry, I gave my Camino son another hug.

"You take care of these girls, Andi." He took his baby girl back from Paul and carried his tiny treasure from the room, stopping to pay the waiter as he left.

"And now," Esther announced, "we shall walk and find the music!" Paul quickly paid our part of the bill, and we pushed out into the warm Spanish night. As always in Santiago, the evening was alive with people, the sidewalk cafes and bars bustling with pilgrims and tourists alike. Friends called to one another, spontaneously breaking into song as glasses were raised. As much as it seemed one big party, in my three nights here I had never seen things get out of hand. Esther tugged us along, seeming to have a destination in mind.

We rounded the last corner into the Praza de Obradoiro and saw, across the wide, golden square, a large crowd gathered beneath the colonnade of the town hall. Music and laughter filled the night as Esther led us towards the gathering. A traditional Galician folk band invited happy pilgrims to join in the dance and song as their handsome members draped long black and red capes around young women, pulling them into time-honoured steps of courting. There had to be over a hundred of us, laughing and clapping and joining the dance where we could. Even serious Catharina pushed her way forward for a better view. Every nation was represented, as was every age. Everyone happy, everyone celebrating the music, the dance, the city.

Behind us, the cathedral bells rang out midnight, and the doves took to the air once more. Esther took me by the hand and we walked to the centre of the square to watch them fly. Paul and Catharina, making their way out of the crowd, joined our walk as we circled towards the cathedral, now entering the tunnel where we had sought shelter from the rain the day we arrived.

Here music was provided by a young opera singer, in full costume, singing *Figero*. Not wanting to disturb the performance, we paused as the young man's voice rose and fell, the depth enhanced by the tunnel's cool stone walls. Playing to the small crowd gathering, the busker approached one lady after another, eliciting giggles and blushes. As he sang to Esther, she joined in the fun, batting her eyelashes flirtatiously, her hand on her chest. A cascade of coins rained down into the singer's box as the performance ended, and we continued around the cathedral, to the square above our horse fountain.

"Is this your first time in the city?" a tall blonde man questioned. I nodded. "Have you seen the miracle of St. Jacques? There, look!" He gestured to the corner where two cathedral walls met. "The miracle of St. Jacques. The pilgrim's shadow for which there is no explanation." He smiled and was gone.

We gathered around and sure enough, there was a shadow, the height of a man, complete with hat and staff. We could see where light shining from a cathedral floodlight around a post might account for the human shape, but we could find no explanation for the arm and hand holding what looked to be a staff.

"Do you know this Esther?" I questioned our friend.

"No," she denied. "In all the times I have been to Santiago, I have never seen this."

Paul walked around the post to see if he could figure out what was causing the shadow. No movement of his interrupted the cast on the wall. It was amazing. Or maybe it was the wine. Either way, we accepted the gift and carried on down the steps towards the fountain.

Here, we bid Esther a fond farewell with promises of keeping in touch. Swinging her skirt, still hearing music, she sauntered down one road towards her hotel, as Catharina, Paul, and I took another towards mine.

"What time do you catch your bus?" Paul asked. "I am taking Catharina to her bus at 8:30, and then I could come and walk you to yours," he offered.

"You know what," I said, as we passed out of the old city, "I will be okay. I only have my pack and the bus stop is just up the road. You see Catharina on her bus and go enjoy your last day." Paul was flying out late that night. He paused and looked at me, and I think he understood. I would have the hardest time saying goodbye to him, having known him the longest. Despite our occasional bickering, I felt a special closeness with this man, and leaving him tonight would be hard enough. I didn't want to say goodbye again.

At my hotel, the usually reserved Catharina folded me in a tight hug, babbling at me in Dutch. Tears tracked down our faces as I held Netty, and Paul kept clearing his throat, looking around the street distractedly.

"You will always be my friends, and somehow, we will all see each other again," I promised. A tearful Catharina wiped her face on her sleeve and nodded. Paul held me tightly. I clung to him in response.

"You take care now. You come see us in England. And I'll bring Mary to you in Canada," he swore.

Buzzed in by a sleepy Sebastian, I stepped into the dark lobby, leaning back against the cool wall for a moment as I brushed tears from my face.

"It is hard to say good-bye to new friends, yes?" questioned Sebastian from the shadows of his desk. I knew this same scene had played out before him many times. "Tomorrow you go home," he reminded me gently.

I crept into my room, climbed into bed, and slept my last night in Spain.

A nosey pigeon cooed at me from the ledge outside my window, cocking his head in question at this lazy body, still in bed after sunrise. Energized by thoughts of home, I smiled and hit the floor running.

The night before, I had packed everything I owned including my boots, into my backpack. I'd secured my poles to the pack with plastic tie wraps. For my journey, a change of clothes, my Compostela, and all the gifts for my family were crowded into the large, colourful woven bag I'd purchased. My pack would be checked, so I'd pretty much look like any tourist as I flew from Santiago to Madrid, then on to Paris.

After a quick breakfast, I settled my bill, grabbed my bags and set off up the street to the bus circle. I stood among a variety of locals and pilgrims, the latter easily discerned by way of packs and shells. As each bus approached, we leaned towards it, everyone anxious to be going home. Finally seated by a window on the big bus, my pack jammed on the floor between my knees, I enjoyed my last look at Santiago as we travelled to the airport.

Things were looking familiar, and I suddenly realized we were following part of the route I had walked when I arrived. And then I saw them; burdened pilgrims making their own entrance into Santiago. I saw the heat, the exhaustion, and the expectation as they waited to cross an intersection to follow the shells, searching for the cathedral. I placed my open hand against the window, wishing it could open and I could call out to them and cheer them along.

"You are so close!" I wanted to tell them. As the bus slid forward into traffic, I realized tears ran down my cheeks. I turned away from the window and looked forward, words for a farewell poem already forming in my mind.

At the airport I checked my pack and, relieved of its weight, made my way to the waiting room. Around the room I spied other pilgrims returning to their homes. Shy smiles across the open spaces, the boots gave them away. Not sure how they knew me in my travel gear, I remembered my shell, dangling from the side of my bag; my symbol of my journey and my time as a pilgrim.

Flying into Madrid, I was glad the Camino ran through the northern part of Spain. Here the land was all dry and hot and flat, a very different Spain from the lush greenness of my trek. Checking in at the gate, I would see my pack next in Vancouver. A female security guard nudged her male companion, directing his gaze to the shell on my bag. Not understanding all of what she said, I heard the word "pilgrim" as they crossed themselves, reaching out to touch my shoulder as I passed. Wow! Still the power of the Camino held me.

Boarding the plane for Paris, I felt a twinge of concern as to how to get to my hotel since it would be almost midnight by the time I arrived. Before I knew it, we were touching down. I was surprised that we could approach the airport without seeing anything of Paris itself and admitted to a small level of disappointment at being so close and not even seeing the Eiffel Tower. That would have to wait for another time. How could I enjoy the City of Love, without the man I love?

I strode through dimly lit hallways following the signs to hotel shuttles. An information desk was just closing and I asked the clerk the best way to get to my hotel. She told me to take the pink bus, and it would get me there. Well how was I going to know which bus was pink in the dark? I wondered, running up the staircase she had directed me to. At the top, I came to the street and discovered travellers lining up for airport shuttles. Fifteen minutes later, up pulled a shuttle, "Pink Bus" brightly lit in the slot above the windshield.

After a few twists and turns along a complicated roadway, held up often by a surprising amount of traffic at this time of night and stopping frequently to let travellers off at other hotels, we finally pulled up in front of the Hotel Campanile Roissy. Bright light, music, and loud male voices spilled out the door. As I walked up to the registration desk, I realized that a large part of the huge lobby was given over to a sports bar. With the European football championships playing, it was thick with sports fans, boisterously celebrating the latest results.

Clutching my key in my hand, I rode the smooth elevator to my room. Not sure who it was that decided bright lime green was a good choice for room design, but I guessed they were going for the modern look rather than restful décor. Dumping my bag on the bed, I took a quick look out the window to see headlights crawling along a roadway and then checked out the bathroom.

First things first, I headed back down to the lobby and ordered a glass of white wine. I marvelled at the relaxed European attitude towards liquor as I carried my glass back up to my room and settled on the bed to call Al.

I knew morning was breaking back home, and as my husband's voice came on the line, I burst into tears. I could envision his smile as he waited patiently for my sobs to quiet so he could understand my words. The reality of my Camino being over had finally hit. Wiping my tears on my sleeve (where was a tissue when you needed one), I told Al all about my trip and about seeing the incoming pilgrims and how affected by that I had been. I shared my experience with the security staff in Madrid. The words came bubbling out, tumbling one upon the other as I tried to share it all with him.

"Honey, finish your wine," Al counselled, "then get some sleep. You have a long day ahead of you tomorrow. I'll see you at the airport!" Like infatuated teenagers we blew kisses across the miles. "Love you's" said, I went to bed, and slept soundly until my alarm went off.

The desk clerk had told me I could take the shuttle an hour before flying, but nothing could keep me in my room. I hadn't even worried about coffee or breakfast, knowing there would be lots of time for that in the airport. I was going home!

Down in the lobby, I checked out just as a shuttle arrived, and I stepped on board. We were quickly whisked back to the Charles de Gaulle Airport. Still lots of time before my flight, I lingered in the gift shop area, sampling fragrances and selecting a couple of mementos, including a small tin of toffees emblazoned with the Eiffel Tower, the closest I came to seeing that national symbol.

Sauntering down the hallways towards the gates, I came around the corner and all of a sudden, I hit a wall! Customs! So used to travelling from one European country to another without challenge, I forgotten I would have to go through customs to leave France. I looked at the endless serpent of travellers jammed in the cordoned off maze leading to the inspection booths. There were literally hundreds, possibly thousands of people here. I saw the time before my departure evaporating. A mild level of panic rose in my chest.

Then I told myself, "STOP!" I hadn't come all this way only to fail at this point. If God had kept me safe all across Spain, if I'd had His support through all the trials and tribulations, did I think He would fail me now? I took a deep breath and said a small prayer, and waited, allowing my newfound faith to conquer my fear. Around me, stress levels were rising with people becoming more and more agitated. Those successfully through the booths made mad dashes to catch departing planes.

Thanking God that I had arrived early, I continued to breathe, working to maintain faith and calm. It is what it is, I reasoned. If I don't make this plane, somehow, I'll get there. The line inched forward. Patience was exhausted and tempers rose. Airport officials struggled to maintain order in face of growing hysteria. The line inched forward. I kept breathing.

Finally, after an hour and a half, I was through the booth, passport stamped, I rushed down the hallway. I spotted my gate, final passengers disappearing through the doors. I ran up to the desk, flashed my ticket and passport, and I was waived down the ramp. My breathing slowed as the Air France flight attendant welcomed me on board, directing me to my seat by the window.

A large East Indian woman settled in between me and the young blonde girl on the aisle, and even before takeoff, I knew how many children she had, that she was travelling to Vancouver to visit a son in university, and that she had brought enough food in her bag for probably the whole plane. Laughing, I waved off her offer of chocolate.

I popped in my earbuds, selected quiet music, and relaxed back into my seat. As much as my seatmate wanted to talk, I was still savouring my Camino and hugged my experiences closely, not wanting to share and dissect them with a stranger.

A nudge to my elbow wakened me as I was passed a small, hot tray of food. I realized that in another three hours, I would be in Canada. Accepting a sweet glazed cookie from my Indian seatmate, more to appease her than to appease my now satisfied hunger, I selected a movie to get me through the rest of the flight.

Safely down in Vancouver, I echoed the applause of the other passengers. It had been forty-three days since I had touched Canadian ground. In customs I was welcomed home, speeding through the electronic scanners to receive my incoming stamp from the officials. Down at the luggage carousels, I waited patiently for my purple pack to slide down the chute. Slinging it over my shoulder, I took the shuttle to the other terminal. I envied passengers being greeted warmly by those waiting for them. But Vancouver was not my final destination, and my welcome waited on our island.

I chatted with Al by cellphone, our excitement at seeing each other building. He said he had a couple of things to do and that he'd see me at the airport. I sat back and tried to focus on the book I'd purchased in Paris, but my mind was already crossing the strait.

Finally, my flight was called. I boarded the tiny plane, enjoying the vistas of ocean and islands, as we made the crossing. Was it always this beautiful? I questioned. Or was it so wonderful because I was seeing it again for the first time? Blue skies and fluffy clouds mirrored the blue water and sparkling whitecaps. The sun beckoned me on to Vancouver Island.

We flew over our small ocean-side town and circled around to the airport. On the ground, we taxied towards the terminal and I looked to the fence where I had last seen my husband. He was not there! My heart skipped a beat. Scrambling out of the plane, I grabbed my pack and made my way to the building. I pushed through the door and there he was! My Allan!

He sat waiting in his wheelchair, a huge bouquet of flowers clutched in his hands, grinning from ear to ear. I threw my pack down and knelt beside him, tears flowing freely down both our faces. His shoulders shook with quiet sobs, our throats too tight with emotion to speak. We held each other tightly, mindless of the others around us. When I finally stood, I looked around at a circle of smiling faces as complete strangers applauded our reunion. Suddenly shy, I picked up my pack, cocked my head at the door, and we made our way across to the car.

"The kids are coming next weekend," he shared. "They want you to call tonight; they need to know you're safe at home. Kirby's at home. I didn't want to leave her in the car," he advised.

I didn't care! I was home. With Al. Everything and everyone else could wait. Holding hands, we drove home, everything seeming a little foreign after being away so long. Down the last hill, we turned the corner and I saw our little house, a bright yellow banner pinned to the wall. "*La bien venida a casa mi hermosa peregrine!*" My welcome home clear for all to see.

Kirby looked at me, cocked her little head, and bounced off the couch, running for the door. I knelt and she jumped all over me, snuffling and smelling, poking her tiny black nose into my clothes. Once she had assured herself it was me, and that I was truly there, she trotted towards her treat jar and looked up at me expectantly. I laughed. Nothing ever changes.

But I knew deep down inside that everything had changed. At least with me. This had been a once in a lifetime experience, and I knew that I could never be exactly the same. My body was different; leaner and stronger than ever before. I had made special friends, some I was sure, I would see again. I had a new perspective, a new calm, a stronger faith, and a new way of being in the world.

If asked, I still wasn't truly sure why the Camino, and what its lasting effect on me would be. I had all the time in the world to share my journey and answer those questions, both for others and for myself.

Belonging

I saw them on the platform, shells tied to their packs
As the train below the airport, rumbled towards us down the tracks.
We stepped on board, found a seat, and as the train pulled out
I felt a strong belonging; knew them without a doubt.

For these were fellow pilgrims, heading to St. Jean
To stay the night and rest a bit, by the next day moving on.
There was excitement in the air, and a little worry too
As we quietly considered, what we were about to do.

Each of us had our own thoughts, no doubt we shared some fears
Some had just decided, some had planned the trip for years.
And as the rising sun, lit up the morning sky
We laced up boots, shouldered packs, and then began to climb.

For many days we shared the way, and evenings during meals
We spoke of what we'd done so far, not believing it was real.
We'd walked for many miles you see, though sun and wind and rain
We'd conquered hills, strolled through trees, and crossed the grassy plain.

We'd walk with one a day or more, then another would take their place
Yet when we entered Santiago, we welcomed each smiling face.
For every pilgrim on the path, even those we didn't meet
Was part of our pilgrim family, born of our travelling feet.

My heart leapt as I left the city, when from the window of the bus
I saw incoming pilgrims, reach their journey's end like us.
I saw their hopeful, searching eyes, their tired bodies sway
I longed to call out to them, and cheer them on their way.

I knew where they were going, and what they soon would do
They'd arrive at the cathedral, Compostelas now in view.
They'd go to mass and say their prayers, among all their new friends
As we had done, and more will do, all pilgrims to the end.

I saw them in the airport, waiting for the plane
Worn boots tied to their backpacks, and the seashells once again.
Belonging through our journey, and now in travelling home
Even if we walked all by ourselves, we never walked alone.

Roxey Edwards (June 2016)

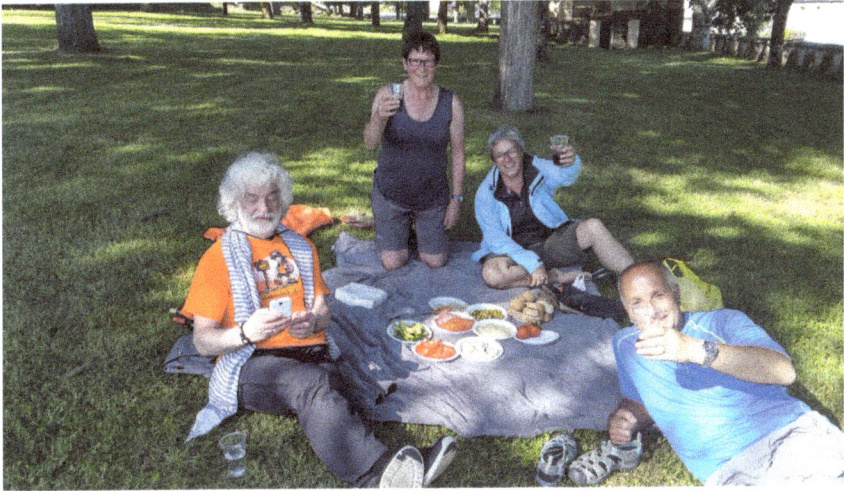

Pilgrim Picnic at Portomarin

Often, we set out on a journey with great expectations, and often we are disappointed. I wasn't really sure what to expect on my Camino pilgrimage, but I certainly wasn't disappointed.

Spain is a breathtakingly beautiful country; its warm, friendly people as diverse as its landscapes. The trail challenged my body, spirit, and soul to the limits, and sometimes beyond. The Camino has left its imprint on me, freeing my inner author, and I haven't stopped writing since my return.

Many of the people I journeyed with disappeared from my life the moment they walked around the corner that separated us. A couple other Camino friends, like Patricia, drop me a line, from time to time. I know Armin had made it home to his wife safely. As to John from Ireland . . . I have been left wondering.

The pilgrims that peopled the last two weeks of my Camino, however, have become a constant part of my life. On any given day, I receive texts and updates from around the world.

In Germany, baby Irma, now a little girl, recently welcomed a baby brother, Jakob, and Andi and Esther are enjoying watching their children grow, planning a future Camino as a family.

The others in our "Final Five" – Ana, Catharina, Paul, and Zbigniew – have become my extended family. We share each other's joys and sorrows, the big events, and the small details that make up our everyday lives in five different countries. We juggle time zones to "meet" for a toast of special events, and we share virtual hugs and words of encouragement when things get tough. We swap recipes and football scores, discuss world events, and share news of our families.

In September 2017, a joke became a plan, as we came together for a reunion at Paul and Mary's home in England. When Al and I stepped (and rolled) off the train from London, there stood Paul and Zbigniew, waiting with open arms. A day later, we returned to the station to welcome Ana with hugs and happy tears. Catharina (aka Netty) had already committed to walking the Portuguese Camino with a friend, so together we followed her progress and cheered her on via *WhatsApp*.

Through the days of our visit, we each confessed we had been worried that our relationship wouldn't be the same "in the real world". To our amazement, we were as close and as natural with each other as if we'd never been apart, and the addition of spouses, families, and friends only added to the party. With everyone jockeying for the honour of pushing Al's wheelchair, we toured the countryside and the impressive Danny's Dream facility, were welcomed at Paul and Mary's church, met their children, grandchildren, and friends, and even attended a football match. *Go Tigers!*

As we each departed for our own countries, the tears flowed freely and the seeds for our next reunion (perhaps in Canada…perhaps with Catharina too!) were planted.

A word of warning: the Camino can be addictive, especially for those living in close proximity. Paul was the first to return, taking his wife, Mary and eldest grandson, Chama, along the Spanish *Primitivo* route from Lugo to Santiago in the spring of 2017. In May, Andi walked alone from Sarria, returning with Holy water from Santiago for Irma's baptism.

After our visit in England, in October, Zbigniew followed in Catharina's footsteps along the inland Portuguese Camino. Paul made his own ocean route Portuguese Camino in the chill of November, and he plans to take his ten-year old grandson, Eugene, the last hundred kilometres of the Camino Frances in February 2018. (Four-year-old Frances waits to grow for his turn to walk with Grandpa.) Esther plans her own Camino *Ingles* in May 2018, with daddy holding the fort at home.

Perhaps Ana and I will overcome the distance and return to the Camino as well one day. And the question has been raised…with Al in mind…*if we all took turns pushing…do you think we could do it with a wheel chair?*

Lightning Source UK Ltd.
Milton Keynes UK
UKHW020458040621
384879UK00008B/135

9 781525 524509